E. P. THOMPSON

E. P. THOMPSON
Critical Perspectives

Edited by
Harvey J. Kaye and
Keith McClelland

Temple

Temple University Press, Philadelphia 19122
Copyright © Introduction, Keith McClelland, 1990; Chapter 1, Geoff Eley, 1990; Chapter 2, William H. Sewell, Jr., 1990; Chapter 3, Catherine Hall, 1990; Chapter 4, Renato Rosaldo, 1990; Chapter 5, Ellen Meiksins Wood, 1990; Chapter 6, Robert Gray, 1990; Chapter 7, John Goode, 1990; Chapter 8, Kate Soper, 1990; Chapter 9, Martin Shaw, 1990; Chapter 10, Harvey J. Kaye, 1990

Published 1990

Printed in Great Britain

Cloth ISBN 0-87722-730-6
Paper ISBN 0-87722-742-X

CIP data available from the Library of Congress

Contents

Preface   vii
Harvey J. Kaye and Keith McClelland

List of contributors   ix

Introduction   1
Keith McClelland

1 Edward Thompson, Social History and Political Culture:
The Making of a Working-class Public, 1780–1850   12
Geoff Eley

2 How Classes are Made: Critical Reflections on
E. P. Thompson's Theory of Working-class Formation   50
William H. Sewell, Jr

3 The Tale of Samuel and Jemima: Gender and
Working-class Culture in Nineteenth-century England   78
Catherine Hall

4 Celebrating Thompson's Heroes: Social Analysis in
History and Anthropology   103
Renato Rosaldo

5 Falling Through the Cracks: E. P. Thompson and the
Debate on Base and Superstructure   125
Ellen Meiksins Wood

6 History, Marxism and Theory   153
Robert Gray

7 E. P. Thompson and 'the Significance of Literature'   183
John Goode

8 Socialist Humanism   204
Kate Soper

9 From Total War to Democratic Peace:
   Exterminism and Historical Pacifism   233
   Martin Shaw

10 E. P. Thompson, the British Marxist Historical Tradition
   and the Contemporary Crisis   252
   Harvey J. Kaye

E. P. Thompson: a Select Bibliography   276

Index   281

Preface

This volume of essays is intended as a critical engagement with E. P. Thompson's work. The range and influence of his writing is such that it was essential to invite contributions from a broad range of perspectives and disciplines in order to indicate the extent of that influence. And in asking the contributors to discuss, sympathetically but critically, some of the historical, theoretical and political problems which have been central to Thompson's work, we intended that these essays should, firstly, assess the limits and achievements of his writings; secondly, extend the discussion in ways that would be neither hagiographical nor unrelentingly critical, for both these tendencies have been present in writing about Thompson; and, thirdly, that they should seek to contribute to the discussion of problems which remain of great importance for both intellectual and political work.

There have been many delays and difficulties in putting together this collection and we must thank the contributors for their patience amid them. In particular, Harvey Kaye wishes to acknowledge the assistance, support and patience of Ellen Wood and Lorna Stewart Kaye, while Keith McClelland is especially indebted to Kate Soper and Catherine Hall.

Harvey J. Kaye
Green Bay, Wisconsin

Keith McClelland
London

January 1989

List of Contributors

Geoff Eley is Professor of History at the University of Michigan, having previously taught at the Universities of Keele and Cambridge in Britain. He is the author of *Reshaping the German Right* (1980) and *From Unification to Nazism: Reinterpreting the German Past* (1986). He is also the co-author with David Blackbourn of *The Peculiarities of German History* (1984) and co-editor with William Hunt of *Reviving the English Revolution* (1988). He is finishing a study of the European Left between the 1860s and the present, and plans a book on nationalism in the nineteenth and twentieth centuries.

John Goode is Professor of English at the University of Keele, and the author of numerous works on nineteenth-century English literature, including *Thomas Hardy* (1988).

Robert Gray, Reader in Social History at Portsmouth Polytechnic, is the author of *The Labour Aristocracy in Victorian Edinburgh* (1976) and *The Aristocracy of Labour in Nineteenth-century Britain, c. 1850–1914* (1981), as well as various articles on aspects of nineteenth-century British social history.

Catherine Hall teaches in Cultural Studies at the Polytechnic of East London. She is the author, with Leonore Davidoff, of *Family Fortunes: Men and Women of the English Middle Class 1780–1850* (1987).

Harvey J. Kaye, Professor of Social Change and Development at the University of Wisconsin-Green Bay, is the author of *The British Marxist Historians* (1984) and editor of *History, Classes and Nation-States* (1988) and *Poets, Politics and the People* (1989), the first two volumes of the Collected Essays of V. G. Kiernan, and *The Face of the Crowd: Selected Essays of George Rudé* (1988). He is presently writing *Breaking the*

Tyranny of the Present: The Necessity of History, an argument on the 'powers of the past'.

Keith McClelland is an historian and teacher who works part-time for the University of Reading, and the Open University. He has written a number of articles on nineteenth-century British working-class history, is a member of the editorial collective of *Gender & History* and is also Treasurer of European Nuclear Disarmament.

Renato Rosaldo teaches at Stanford University, where he is Mellon Professor of Interdisciplinary Studies and Director of the Stanford Center for Chicano Research. His works include *Ilongot Headhunting, 1883–1974: A Study in Society and History* (1980) and *Culture and Truth: The Remaking of Social Analysis* (1989).

William H. Sewell, Jr teaches history and sociology at the University of Michigan. He is the author of *Work and Revolution in France: The Language of Labor from the Old Regime to 1848* (1980) and *Structure and Mobility: The Men and Women of Marseille, 1820–1870* (1985). He is currently working on a book on the Abbé Sieyes and the political culture of the French Revolution.

Kate Soper is a writer, translator and teacher of philosophy at the Polytechnic of North London. She is the author of *On Human Needs* (1981) and *Humanism and Anti-Humanism* (1987). She is an active member of the European Nuclear Disarmament movement.

Martin Shaw is Senior Lecturer in Sociology at the University of Hull. He is the author of *Socialism and Militarism* (1981) and the *Dialectics of War* (1988) and the editor of *War, State and Society* (1984), and, with Colin Creighton, of *The Sociology of War and Peace* (1986). He is currently writing *Post-Militarism: Demilitarized Societies in a Militarized World*.

Ellen Meiksins Wood is Professor of Political Science at York University, Toronto and a member of the editorial board of *New Left Review*. She is the author of *Mind and Politics* (1972); with Neal Wood, of *Class Ideology and Ancient Political Theory* (1978); *The Retreat from Class* (1986), which was awarded the Isaac Deutscher Memorial Prize; and *Peasant-Citizen and Slave* (1988).

Introduction

Keith McClelland

For over thirty years E. P. Thompson has been a major figure of the British and, increasingly, the international left.[1] His first full book, *William Morris* (1955), established its subject as a revolutionary socialist of considerable stature; *The Making of the English Working Class* (1963) – his best-known and most influential book – has had enduring import-ance as an account of the working class and its cultural and political formation in the 'first industrial nation'; and the more recent work on eighteenth-century England has been central to opening up not only the history of the 'popular classes' but also questions about the forms and functions of the state and the law in the period. Thompson has also been one of the most prominent of post-war socialist intellectuals. He played a leading part in the emergence of a New Left after the Soviet invasion of Hungary in 1956. And at various points since the 1960s, he has been heard as a critic of contemporary trends in Marxism, as polemicist against the encroachments of the State upon civil liberties and as an influential writer and campaigner in one of the most important political developments of the 1980s – the internationalization of the peace movement.[2]

In *William Morris* Thompson articulated many of the central concerns of the generation of Marxist historians to which he belongs: the dialectic of desire and necessity, and of determining circumstance and human volition; the place of the moral in socialism; the distinctiveness of an English tradition of socialism; and an ambiguity about the status of the literary.[3] The book also revealed some of the contradictions evident within contemporary Marxist politics. It not only placed Morris within an English socialism but also as part of an international Communist tradition. If it was a book whose concerns broke out of the rigidities of Stalinism, it also affirmed the desirability of Soviet Communism. Yet the effective alternative to adherence to the Soviet Union seemed to be social democracy; and whatever the differences between them, there were crucial respects in which they could be said to inhabit a common political universe. Political choice, in an international context, was posited in terms of the mutually excluding blocs of the Cold War – Stalinism and the Warsaw Pact or Atlanticism and NATO. Both Communism and social democracy were grounded too in a bureaucratic politics which denied the agency of individuals and groups and required their passivity. And both largely expunged morality and a critical consciousness from accountable political life.

It was in this context that oppositional socialists formulated the arguments of 'socialist humanism' when the Soviet invasion of Hungary in 1956 blew apart the political world in which the Communists had operated. 'Humanism' did not have, and does not have, a single meaning within socialism. Moreover, socialist humanism ought to be seen in relation to the wider European tradition of 'humanist' and 'anti-humanist' ideas and politics.[4] However, as Kate Soper argues in her essay, Thompson's socialist humanism was distinguished by its stress on agency, its emphasis upon moral autonomy and the placing of human needs and possibilities at the centre of the socialist project, and its rejection of the forms of politics offered by both Stalinism and social democracy, themes which have been of enduring importance in his work. This outlook was embodied initially not only in Thompson's political writings in the major journals of the New Left, *The Reasoner, The New Reasoner, Universities and Left Review* and early issues of *New Left Review*, but also in *The Making of the English Working Class* (1963).

The Making of the English Working Class was immediately recognized as being of major importance. Its evident moral and political commitment and the depth of its historical research and empathy found high praise in some quarters. For instance, Tom Nairn, who was by no means uncritical of the book, wrote:

> the author's sympathy and passion carry us to a real understanding of happenings; in his company, we penetrate beyond the level of mere chronology, into real history, into an imaginative re-creation of the experience of the past. He is engaged in constant polemic with the academic 'objectivity' which sees history as a relation of the 'facts', and the 'facts' as whatever can be grasped statistically. He tries consistently to grasp for us 'the quality of life' under the Industrial Revolution . . . . Only an imaginative effort of this sort brings us to the reality, the human dimensions of what happened.[5]

There was also some highly critical commentary, concerned with not only particular aspects, like the treatments of Luddism or Methodism, but also with rejecting the notion that a supposedly homogeneous working class and working-class consciousness had been 'made' by 1832.[6] Yet whatever stance is taken on the book, there can be no question that it has become an indispensable point of reference for subsequent generations, particularly in Britain and North America. It is a text that must be engaged with by anyone in the field of late eighteenth- and early nineteenth-century British history. But its impact has been much wider, and not only for those working on other periods. It was a major source of inspiration for the development of feminist history in Britain, as Catherine Hall's essay shows; it was one of the 'founding texts' of cultural studies;[7] its theses and methods have been registered and argued with in anthropology, as Renato Rosaldo discusses, and, to a lesser extent, among sociologists.[8]

The central thesis of *The Making of the English Working Class* is that it is possible for people to make something of themselves other than that which history has made of them. The key issue for historical theory and practice here, and one continually referred to in the essays that follow, is the relationship between determination and agency. Of course, Marxism did not invent the problem; but it did offer a highly original solution to it – that of a determining base and a corresponding superstructure – and it is the problem with which Thompson, like all Marxists, has had to wrestle. As Ellen Meiksins Wood argues in her review of Thompson's thinking on the subject, the problem continues to radiate throughout contemporary debate on the left, whether about relatively abstract theoretical issues or about concrete questions of political strategy.

The 'topographical metaphor' of base and superstructure had been largely understood, within Marxism, as a model of historical explanation in which economic forces were of primary importance and effectively dictated the forms of resulting institutions, activities and consciousness. Thompson, in common with many other 'socialist humanists', used instead Marx's other major formulation, that social being determines social consciousness. In his hands, the notion of social being was stretched to include a wider range of social and political institutions, activities and processes than could be encompassed within the notion of 'the economic': thus it could include, for instance, the determining weight of Methodist work disciplines. At this point entered the category of 'experience' – Thompson's most novel and problematic theoretical notion – which was posited as a mediating term. As Thompson put it in the Preface to *The Making of the English Working Class*: 'The class experience is largely determined by the productive relations into which men are born – or enter involuntarily. Class-consciousness is the way in which these experiences are handled in cultural terms: embodied in traditions, value-systems, ideas, and institutional forms.'[9] At least, this is *one* of Thompson's meanings. As William Sewell argues in his careful and illuminating discussion of historical class formation, 'experience' is a term with an ambiguous and uncertain status within Thompson's work.

What underpins the difficulties is an unresolved tension within Thompson's work between the two terms of determination and agency. For Thompson, determination refers essentially to the exterior and the past, while agency refers to the capacity of people to act in the present and to invent and make choices about the future from a range of possibilities.

The narrative of *The Making of the English Working Class*, which both constructs the history and is posited as the vehicle through which that history becomes transparent, culminates in the forging of the disparate elements of a working class into both a class with a consciousness of common identity and as a class different from and antagonistic to other classes. Among the many problems at issue here three are outstanding.

First, although Thompson is careful not to suppose that every member of the working class somehow developed a uniform class-consciousness, the book is vulnerable to the charge that he has underestimated the disjunctures and unevenness of working-class experience. There are many aspects to this. One is that the movement of the capitalist relations of production is not grasped dialectically so much as a story of the destruction of artisanal forms and of the imposition of new ones. A consequence is that it means that the economic forms cannot really be seen as a structuring moment which enables new possibilities as well as destruction. While the book certainly does stress that capitalist industrialization in Britain was a very partial and uneven process – as much recent historical work has done[10] – it may also be argued, as Eric Hobsbawm has suggested, that in its economic formation as well as in its social and political institutions 'the working class [was] not "made" until long after Thompson's book ends'.[11] Further, what has emerged as a crucial problem is the issue of the structural inequalities of power and position of men and women. The question of gender has been the single most important challenge to existing historiography since the book was written. The work of feminist historians in opening up this field are indicated in Catherine Hall's essay in this volume: whatever the future results of such work, it is clear that, in the long run, the story of *The Making of the English Working Class* will need to be re-written in the light of them.[12]

Second, the transformations of working-class experience into theory and consciousness is seen by Thompson as, arguably, too unproblematic a passage. The most important, and contentious, argument in this regard is Gareth Stedman Jones's critique, which Ellen Meiksins Wood takes issue with in this volume, which suggests a much greater autonomy for the construction of politics and ideology in language and discourse,[13] a position that resonates with the arguments of Sewell in this collection. Like Thompson's work, Stedman Jones' is clearly engaged with contemporary political concerns as well as more strictly historical ones. At the heart of the kinds of problem with which he is contending is not only the issue of how far there is a direct correspondence between 'economics' and 'politics', or between classes as constituted in modes of production and as finding expression in political struggles, but also the extent to which it is possible to create forms of politics and political language that will unify and construct the class(es) and social groups they claim to represent. The problem has moved to the centre of socialist theoretical and strategic debate in the 1980s.[14]

The third issue concerns how and by what the working class was forged. Thompson does not see the making as a uniform process across time but one in which three moments were of critical importance – the 1790s, 1815–19 and 1830–2 – and each of these is one in which the emergent radical political movement was met by resistance and repression from above, and particularly from the State. The question that this raises is how far it was the actions of the State and other forces 'exterior' to the working class which effectively constituted the unity of that class; how far it was the actions of working people themselves who made their own history. It may be argued that it is the political that, in effect, over-determines the formation of the working class. For instance, Thompson's account of Peterloo in 1819[15] stresses that the binding together or fusion of the Radical reformers and the popular classes into a unitary group was largely accomplished by the violence meted out to them by the Manchester Yeomanry acting as the instrument of the State. What the account also does is to suggest a wider process of fusion of the working class which is again dependent upon ulterior forces. Thus the long-term consequences of the defeat of the Radicals were, it is argued, the re-shaping of the terrain upon which social and political relations developed, primarily in that the event shifted the willingness of middle-class reformers and the manufacturing and landed interests to bind together against the working class as a whole and to resist working-class political demands.

In his essay, Geoff Eley proposes that issues about the formation of political culture and the State be moved back to the centre of historical argument, in a manner which would complement and extend the achievements of work in social history like Thompson's. He insists upon the necessity of understanding the transformation of political culture and of 'hegemonic relations' in Britain between 1780 and 1850 in terms not only of their determination from 'above', but also by the formation of a 'working-class public sphere'. Informing Eley's essay is a stress on the importance of the complex relations *between* classes in their full social and political formation rather than merely emphasizing *either* history 'from below' *or* 'from above'.

A further problem with Thompson's notion of determination is that it is one in which the determining stops at a given point and then agency takes over. Yet, of course, whatever the range of meanings that may be attached to the notion of 'agents' and 'agency', agents must always be determined; and the determined is always the result (intended or unintended) of agents' individual and collective volition. As Giddens and others have argued, agency and determination are necessarily logically implicated in each other.[16]

The issues at stake here are manifold, but one dimension of them evident in Thompson's work is a dialectic of hope and pessimism. In his writing, the notion of determination belongs essentially to the exterior and the past of individuals and collectivities. However, at that point where the future becomes past for those living the present, determination reasserts itself. This dialectic haunts not only *The Making of the English Working Class* but also Thompson's other and subsequent work. *The Making* is at once a triumphal assertion of the powers of men and women to invent the future, but is also shadowed by the prospect of possible subsequent defeat and loss. Legal rights fought over and established in the past, a major concern of Thompson's eighteenth-century work as well as his political writings on civil liberties, might yet be lost.[17] An oscillation between the poles of desire and necessity, hope and possible loss, may be registered too in the shifting status of the notion of Utopia in Thompson's work, as is suggested by John Goode's close and critical reading of the two editions of *William Morris* in the course of his assessment of Thompson's relation to literature.

Thompson's writings and work for the peace movement, particularly since the publication of *Protest and Survive* and the formation of European Nuclear Disarmament in 1980, have had a remarkable impact, not only in Britain but in Europe – East and West – and in North America. The movements of international opposition to nuclear weapons and for an end to the divisions of contemporary Europe by the blocs have been seen to hold the potential to unlock a peaceful future for us; but a deep pessimism was also present in Thompson's analysis of what he diagnosed as the 'logic of exterminism'.[18] In his essay, Martin Shaw seeks to move beyond this pessimism, and the debate around Thompson's original essay, by more fully comprehending the historical specificity of 'total war' and other forms of warfare and by arguing that what is now politically and historically appropriate in the epoch of potential nuclear war and global destruction is 'historical pacifism'.

Whether or not optimism or pessimism is appropriate has often been discussed by Thompson in terms of the capacities of the English people.

It is unquestionably the case that there has been a real ambiguity in Thompson's work, inherited from the Marxism of his youth, between the working class and 'the people' as the agent of change and of hope. Yet the issue of the categories deployed is less important than the values and capacities ascribed to them. Thompson has sometimes referred to the English people as if the history of the struggle for democratic rights and the building of popular forms and institutions were indelibly inscribed in the present and that their energies and values endowed by the past need only be summoned up for progressive social and political change in the present to be effected. But at other times, he writes pessimistically of the political indifference or apathy into which the people have sunk.

There are political and historical issues here of real importance. For instance, the question of how far and in what ways the working class has established both a major presence within the social and political life of Britain and set limits on the powers of the State and bourgeoisie to stall or reverse real gains – an issue debated with Anderson and Nairn in the 1960s – remains a crucial one, as Eley's essay indicates. It raises issues about the distinctiveness of political institutions in Britain, the characteristics of its capitalism and the prospects of socialist renewal and advance.[19]

What is also raised here is the question of the role and function of the intellectual. Thompson has often seen himself as a kind of interlocutor of history, one through whose gaze the real meanings of the past will be disclosed and that it is historians in general who are able to do this. The most emphatic and contentious expression of this came in *The Poverty of Theory* in which history is proclaimed as the Queen of Disciplines, its practitioners given a status above all others, not least in their interrogative abilities. This privileging of history and Thompson's account of the relationship between it, historical theory and Marxism carry with them major difficulties. Robert Gray locates the tensions within Thompson's practice as an historian and his writings on the nature of historical enquiry and situates them in relation to the development of post-war Marxism. In his essay, Renato Rosaldo explores the problems which Thompson's method of narrative construction poses for the practice of anthropology. While arguing that Thompson's work exemplifies 'how to write a committed history', he none the less suggests that Thompson's 'compelling moral vision' is limited by too ready a conflation of past and present and is insufficient to the complexities of recognizing radical cultural difference.

As a political intellectual the question is whether or not the intellectual simply reflects what is already in place – the class, the people – and is only in need of articulation; or whether the role is that of *fixing* consciousness, giving it shape and moving it on. Harvey Kaye sees Thompson and other prominent British Marxist historians as articulating a British radical-democratic tradition and argues that what he envisages as the political project at the heart of that articulation – the creation of a critical historical consciousness – is all the more necessary in the face of a culturally and politically dominant conservatism in Britain and the United States. In his life as a socialist intellectual, a distinctive aspect of Thompson's work has been the taking on of others – historians, other socialists or political opponents – in an often abrasive way. It is intrinsic to what Thompson has said of himself in declaring that 'it is only by facing into opposition that I am able to define my thought at all'.[20] This is evident in all the work, but especially in the polemics against Perry Anderson and Tom Nairn in the 1960s or, above all, in *The Poverty of Theory*, in which his wrath was visited upon Althusser, real or supposed Althusserians and the so-called *lumpen-intelligentsia*. Whatever the merits of the book's arguments, the polemical mode demands that readers position themselves simply for or against the stance taken. At its best it can make the blood run and carry the reader in its train; at its worst it can be brutalizing, bludgeoning the reader into submission. This enforced polarization is one that has tended to be mirrored in discussion of Thompson. This has often taken the form of either obsequious piety or simple assault. In inviting the contributors to write for this volume, the editors wished them to avoid either of these positions but, rather, to engage with Thompson's work in the spirit of critique rather than mere criticism, to engage in trying to move on the discussion of issues which are not only central to an understanding of Thompson's work but also the political and historical problems addressed by it.

Notes

1 This Introduction simply flags some of the issues raised by Thompson's work and treated in the following essays: it is not my purpose to discuss them at any length. The single most important assessment of Thompson's work as a whole is Perry Anderson, *Arguments Within English Marxism* (London: Verso, 1980), which contains some biographical information. Other general discussions include Richard Johnson, 'Edward Thompson, Eugene Genovese, and Socialist-Humanist History', *History Workshop Journal*, 6 (1978), an important critique which was responded to in issues 7–9; B. D. Palmer, *The Making of E. P. Thompson* (Toronto: New Hogtown Press, 1981); Harvey J. Kaye, *The British Marxist Historians* (Cambridge: Polity Press, 1984), ch. 6; Gregor McLennan, 'E. P. Thompson and the Discipline of Historical Context', in *Making Histories*, ed. Richard Johnson et al. (London: Hutchinson with the Centre for Contemporary Cultural Studies, 1982); Ellen Kay Trimberger, 'E. P. Thompson: Understanding the process of history', in *Vision and*

Method in Historical Sociology, ed. Theda Skocpol (Cambridge: Cambridge University Press, 1984).

2 For details of Thompson's writings on these issues see the Select Bibliography.

3 In addition to the essays by Robert Gray and John Goode in this volume, see the important article by Bill Schwarz, '"The People" in History: the Communist Party Historians' Group, 1946–56', in Johnson et al., *Making Histories*; see also Kaye, *British Marxist Historians*, esp. pp. 8–22 and, for an assessment by a participant, E. J. Hobsbawm, 'The Historians' Group of the Communist Party', in *Rebels and Their Causes*, ed. M. Cornforth (London: Lawrence & Wishart, 1978). For a general assault upon that generation of Marxist historians and their legacy, see Gertrude Himmelfarb, *The New History and the Old* (Cambridge, Mass.: Harvard University Press, 1987).

4 A very useful introduction is Kate Soper, *Humanism and Anti-Humanism* (London: Hutchinson, 1986).

5 Tom Nairn, 'The English Working Class', in *Ideology in Social Science*, ed. R. Blackburn (London: Fontana, 1972), pp. 195–6. Nairn's essay was first published in *New Left Review*, 24 (1964).

6 A survey of the criticism, which is very sympathetic to Thompson, is F. K. Donnelly, 'Ideology and Early English Working-class History: E. P. Thompson and his critics', *Social History*, 1 (2) (1976), pp. 219–38; Thompson's own reply to critics came in the 'Postscript' to the revised edn of 1968 (Harmondsworth: Penguin). The historiography of class formation in the period 1780–1840 is now very extensive, and a bibliography at this point would be pretentious. But for a judicious survey, which considers both Thompson and major alternatives, see R. J. Morris, *Class and Class Consciousness in the Industrial Revolution 1780–1850* (London: Macmillan, 1979). The essays by Catherine Hall, Geoff Eley and William Sewell in this volume contain extensive references to the recent historical literature.

7 See especially Stuart Hall, 'Cultural Studies: two paradigms', in *Media, Culture and Society. A critical reader*, ed. Richard Collins et al. (London: Sage, 1986).

8 See, e.g., Trimberger, 'E. P. Thompson', although she suggests that while Thompson's work is widely known among historical sociologists, its impact on sociology has generally been 'meagre' (p. 211).

9 *The Making of the English Working Class* (rev. edn London: Gollancz, 1980), p. 11.

10 David Cannadine, 'The Present and the Past in the English Industrial Revolution', *Past & Present*, 103 (1984) surveys the historiography.

11 E. J. Hobsbawm, 'The Making of the Working Class 1870–1914', in *Worlds of Labour* (London: Weidenfeld & Nicolson, 1984), p. 196. Part of the problem here turns upon the issue of how far one should see 'the labour classes of the period before, or even during, Chartism [as] the working class as it was to develop later', as Hobsbawm puts it (p. 195), adding that Thompson does seem to suggest this in *The Making of the English Working Class*. So far as Thompson's views are concerned, he has indicated elsewhere that the working class of post-1850 had a rather different formation. See 'The peculiarities of the English' (1965), in *The Poverty of Theory and Other Essays* (London: Merlin,

1978), pp. 70–1. More generally, the issue of the extent to which there was a 'break' in class formation and relations around mid-century has been the subject of considerable debate. Geoff Eley's essay in this volume discusses aspects of this, as does Robert Gray, *The Aristocracy of Labour in Nineteenth-Century Britain, c. 1850–1914* (London: Macmillan, 1981).

12 An important and controversial contribution to the subject, published since Catherine Hall's essay was written, is Joan Wallach Scott, *Gender and the Politics of History* (New York: Columbia University Press, 1988), which includes discussion of Thompson's work.

13 Gareth Stedman Jones, *Languages of Class. Studies in English working class history 1832–1982* (Cambridge: Cambridge University Press, 1983), esp. the essay 'Rethinking Chartism'. For discussions of Jones's work see among others, John Foster, 'The declassing of language', *New Left Review*, 150 (1985); Robert Gray, 'The deconstruction of the English working class', *Social History*, 11 (1986); Ellen Meiksins Wood, *The Retreat from Class. A New 'True' Socialism* (London: Verso, 1986), ch. 7 and Wood's essay in this volume; Dorothy Thompson, 'The Languages of Class', *Bulletin of the Society for the Study of Labour History*,52 (1) (1987), pp. 54–7; N. Kirk, 'In Defence of Class. A critique of recent revisionist writing upon the nineteenth-century English working class', *International Review of Social History*, 33 (1987); Joan W. Scott, 'On Language, Gender and Working-Class History', *International Labor and Working-class History*, 31 (1987), the responses to Scott in ibid., and her reply in ibid., 32 (1987).

14 See, e.g., Ernesto Laclau and Chantal Mouffe, *Hegemony and Socialist Strategy* (London: Verso, 1985) and the exchanges between Laclau and Mouffe and Norman Geras in *New Left Review*, 163 & 166 (1987) and 169 (1988). For the work of an influential thinker much preoccupied with the problem see Stuart Hall, *The Hard Road to Renewal* (London: Verso, 1988).

15 See *The Making*, esp. pp. 737–68.

16 See among others, Anthony Giddens, *The Constitution of Society* (Cambridge: Polity Press, 1984); and Philip Abrams, *Historical Sociology* (Shepton Mallet: Open Books, 1982).

17 See esp. *Whigs and Hunters* (2nd edn, Harmondsworth: Penguin, 1977); and *Writing by Candlelight* (London: Merlin Press, 1980).

18 See 'Notes on Exterminism, the Last Stage of Civilization', *New Left Review*, 121 (1980); reprinted in *Exterminism and Cold War*, ed. *New Left Review* (London: Verso, 1982). This volume included a wide range of responses to the original article, together with a further piece by Thompson, 'Europe, the Weak Link in the Cold War'. The issues have been re-visited in Simon Bromley and Justin Rosenberg, 'After Exterminism', *New Left Review*, 168 (1988); and are also discussed by Kate Soper in this volume.

19 The key pieces in the original debate were Perry Anderson, 'Origins of the Present Crisis', and Tom Nairn, 'The British Political Elite', both in *New Left Review*, 23 (1964), Nairn, 'The English Working Class', ibid., 24 (1964) and his 'The anatomy of the Labour Party', ibid., 27 and 28 (1964). Thompson's critique, 'The Peculiarities of the English', was originally published in *The Socialist Register 1965*, ed. Ralph Miliband and John Saville

(London: Merlin, 1965) and has been reprinted in *The Poverty of Theory*. Perry Anderson replied in 'The Myths of Edward Thompson, or Socialism and Pseudo-empiricism', *New Left Review*, 35 (1966). The debate – which has wavered between being about England and about Britain as a whole – has recently been revisited by Perry Anderson in 'The Figures of Descent', *New Left Review*, 161 (1987). For a vigorous reply to Anderson, see Michael Barratt Brown, 'Away with all the Great Arches: Anderson's history of British capitalism', ibid., 167 (1988). Other related work includes Philip Corrigan and Derek Sayer, *The Great Arch. English State Formation as Cultural Formation* (Oxford: Basil Blackwell, 1985).

20 'An open letter to Leszek Kolakowski' (1973), in *The Poverty of Theory*, p. 186.

1

Edward Thompson, Social History and Political Culture: The Making of a Working-class Public, 1780–1850

Geoff Eley

I

There is very little tradition of explicit theorizing about state formation and political development among historians. Most political historians seem happy with a narrowly conceived category of the political, a highly institutional notion of the political process and a narrative mode of analysis, concerned mainly with elections, parties and parliaments. Basic theoretical questions receive much shorter shrift. From the character of the State and its relations with economy and civil society, through processes of interest articulation and the formation of social blocs, to the balance of coercion and consent in the governing system, the potentials for conformity and opposition, and the bases of cohesion of the social order, the specific features of national political culture are rarely dealt with as such.

British historians are no better and no worse than others in this respect. The best discussions of British political development in the 1960s – such as the famous exchange between Edward Thompson and Perry Anderson/ Tom Nairn – came from outside the profession, with little impact on the self-enclosed discourse of British political history.[1] Instead, energy has

This is a revised and shortened version of an essay that originally appeared in *Archiv für Sozialgeschichte*, XXI (1981), pp. 427–57, under the title, 'Re-thinking the Political: Social History and Political Culture in Eighteenth- and Nineteenth-century Britain'. The earlier version contained extensive discussions of the eighteenth-century public sphere and of popular Radicalism between the 1790s and 1830s, which are omitted from the present text. Otherwise, I have tried to take some account of intervening literature and debates without altering the basic structure of argument.

been directed to more particularized controversies much less threatening to the conventional boundaries of disciplinary discussion, such as the nature of party in the early eighteenth century, the conflict between *laissez-faire* and State intervention in the mid-nineteenth century or the origins of the welfare state. Here the enormous growth of social history has been of little help, because most social historians have been conspicuously indifferent to the same range of concerns: an interest in the extension of government (as in the Poor Law, education or the criminal law) has rarely graduated into more systematic reflection on the forms of state power. Again, contributions have tended to come from non-historians by immediate professional affiliation.[2]

At the same time, the social history of the late 1960s released an important potential in this respect, notably, an expanded appreciation of the place of 'the political' in social life, which pulled analysis away from the institutional arena of parties and other public organizations towards the realms of 'society' and 'culture'. At the time, this was linked to ideas of alternative life-styles and radical subjectivity, and to the popularity of deviancy theory, the idea of alienation and readings of the young Marx, while over the longer term they gave space for feminist analysis, the flourishing of cultural studies and the appropriation of Gramsci and other cultural theorists. Potentially, this grounded politics more deeply in a social context, investing social relations and everyday life with new political meanings. Politics became inscribed in the texture of the everyday. Our understanding of power, domination and authority – and of the possible sources of resistance thereto – was transformed by this sort of reasoning. Social history was engendering a radically de-institutionalized conception of political process, whose impact on political history was potentially enormous.

So far, such possibilities have had a limited impact on the practice of social and political historians. But one way of making the connection for the eighteenth century is via the concept of the public sphere. As proposed by Jürgen Habermas, this is 'a sphere which mediates between society and state, in which the public organizes itself as the bearer of public opinion'.[3] It originated in the later eighteenth century with the widening of political participation and the crystallizing of citizenship ideals, a consequence of the struggle against absolutism (or, in the British case, for a strengthening of constitutional monarchy) and an attempt to transform arbitrary into rational authority, subject to the scrutiny of a citizenry organized into a public body beneath the protection of the law. It was linked to the demand for representative government and a liberal constitution, together with the basic civil freedoms before the law (speech, press, assembly, association, conscience and religion, no arrest without trial, and so on). Socially, it was borne by the aspirations of a successful and self-conscious bourgeoisie, whose economic functions and social standing implied a cumulative agenda of desirable change.

The public sphere in this sense derived only partly from the conscious demands of reformers and their articulation into government. More fundamentally, it presumed the prior transformation of social relations, their condensation into new institutional arrangements and the generation of new social, cultural and political discourse around this changing environment. In this sense, conscious and programmatic *political* impulses emerged most strongly where underlying processes of social development were reshaping the overall context of social communication. The public sphere presupposed this larger accumulation of socio-cultural change. It was linked to the growth of provincial urban culture as the novel arena for a locally organized public life, to a new infrastructure of social communication (including the press and other literary media, the rise of a reading public, improved transportation and adapted centres of sociability like coffee houses, taverns and clubs) and to a new universe of voluntary association. At the same time, these new conditions were accompanied by a revival of parliamentary politics, dating initially from the 1760s and gathering pace in the next two decades.[4]

The rise of a public sphere in this way required a transformation of authority relations. To put it another way, the reconstitution of authority through the institutional and ideological modalities of the public sphere also implied the supplanting of something else, which in eighteenth-century British terms meant a prior structure of gentry paternalism. Moreover, if one structure of hegemonic relations (gentry paternalism) was in decay, to be gradually and unevenly replaced by another (a parliamentary political culture, organized around a new set of relations between central and local government and the social power of the dominant classes), then how were the masses to be re-integrated on a new basis? What were the consequences for political order? What was the balance of repressive and conciliatory means? How was the labour of ideological renewal conducted? What were the resources of the popular classes and how successfully were they mobilized for resistance?

Keeping these questions in mind, I want to use the work of Edward Thompson to build an argument about some aspects of eighteenth- and nineteenth-century British political culture. First, I shall indicate Thompson's own contribution to this question by combining and juxtaposing his eighteenth-century work with the earlier *Making of the English Working Class*. Then I shall develop an argument about certain features of Chartism as a national popular movement, which reflects critically on the view of working-class formation proposed by Thompson for the pre-Chartist time. In particular, the latter requires a much clearer attention to the forms of national political organization and to the role of

politics in shaping a sense of class collectivity. I shall close with some
general remarks on the problem of working-class consciousness and
formation.[5]

II

Superficially, Thompson's work has been concerned with 'popular
culture' in a generalized and soft, neo-anthropological sense, which
sacrifices discussion of political questions to the sustained pursuit of
'history from below', and this, together with an alleged neglect of
economics, led during the 1970s to the charge of 'culturalism'.[6] However,
in both his earlier and later work, Thompson pays careful attention to
both these dimensions – the political and the economic – and while his
chosen conceptualizations leave plenty of room for debate, it is quite
wrong to accuse him of simple neglect. In particular, his exploration of
eighteenth-century customary practices has become progressively located
in the analysis of a decomposing tenurial economy, constituted by 'a
dense socio-economic nexus' of 'coincident use-rights' – 'the inheritance
customs, the actuality of what was being inherited, the character of the
economy, the manorial bye-laws or field regulations, the poor law'.[7]
Indeed, it is exactly one of Thompson's achievements to have insisted that
in concrete societies the 'cultural' enters directly into economic and
market relations, or rather that productive activity is inserted into a dense
tissue of customary practice. Though his first forays into the eighteenth
century no doubt too easily conflated the particularities of a transformed
agrarian capitalism with an ideal-typical notion of a paternalist traditional
economy, this is no longer a reasonable criticism.[8]

Moreover, on this analysis of the advancing logic of capitalist agrarian
practices is predicated a challenging and innovative argument concerning
the nature of the eighteenth-century state. Proceeding from the partial
and uneven dissolution of a locally specified legitimate authority – 'the
old paternalism at a point of crisis' – and in the absence of a strong
bureaucratic state on the continental model, Thompson suggests that
political domination became 'located primarily in a cultural hegemony
and only secondarily in an expression of economic or physical (military)
power'. Lacking a centralized military or police apparatus, with the
Church badly blunted as an instrument of conformity, the ruling class
had little choice but to tolerate a certain popular ebullience when it came
to crowd actions. In *Whigs and Hunters* and the associated essays
Thompson argues forcefully that the medium of hegemonic domination
was the rule of law, not as a mere instrument of class power but as a
relatively autonomous and complex unity of *contradictory* functions, at

the same time coercive, instrumental and mystificatory, but also constraining, equitable within certain limits and therefore legitimizing:

> The hegemony of the eighteenth-century gentry and aristocracy was expressed, above all, not in military force, not in the mystifications of a priesthood or of the press, not even in economic coercion, but in the rituals of the study of the Justices of the Peace, in the quarter-sessions, in the pomp of the assizes and in the theatre of Tyburn.

This was a specific legacy of the seventeenth century, which simultaneously defended the rights of property against arbitrary royal intrusions, and by that very virtue delivered a means of potential redress for the more humble, i.e. the 'propertyless' who none the less enjoyed 'petty property rights or agrarian use-rights whose definition was inconceivable without the forms of law.'

This has enormous implications for our understanding of the eighteenth-century state, for on this basis the functions of state power had become displaced from a central apparatus on to an unstable reciprocity of half-free labour and part-paternalist gentry, of 'patrician society' and 'plebeian culture'. Such a reciprocity of gentry–crowd relations was permitted – was *determined* in that sense – by the weakness of the state. The latter was expressed in 'an incapacity to use force swiftly, in an ideological tenderness towards the liberties of the subject, and in a sketchy bureaucracy so riddled with sinecurism, parasitism and clientage that it scarcely offered an independent presence'. 'The licence of the crowd' was, in effect, 'the price which aristocracy and gentry paid for a limited monarchy and a weak state'. It provided 'the central structural context of the reciprocity of relations between rulers and ruled'. Thus the nature of the political system cannot be grasped without penetrating beyond the corridors of Westminster to territory normally left happily to a 'depoliticized' social history. The eighteenth-century political historians ignore this context at their peril. As Thompson says: 'To define control in terms of cultural hegemony is not to give up attempts at analysis, but to prepare for analysis at the points at which it should be made: into the images of power and authority, the popular mentalities of subordination.'[9]

The importance of Thompson's work for our current concern may be summarized as follows. First, as already intimated, Thompson is proposing a radical revision in our understanding of the political process. Though his own formal focus may be 'culture', this is expressly motivated by concern for both the social dislocations of capitalist development and the changing forms of State power. Indeed, his work has consistently breached the older disciplinary boundary between 'political' and 'social' history, being mainly concerned with the changing bases of political domination, an interest for which the conceptual vocabulary of a 'Gramscian' analysis ('hegemony') is wholly appropriate. In this sense, neither the practice of government (the growth of political stability, the rise and fall of the Whig oligarchy) nor the growth of provincial political culture can be discussed adequately without exploring wider processes of popular ideological negotiation than are normally encompassed in most political histories.[10]

Second, the emergence of a bourgeois or middle-class public was never defined solely by the struggle against absolutism, but necessarily addressed the problems of popular containment as well. To that extent the 'public sphere' makes less sense as the autonomous and class-specific achievement of the bourgeois citizenry alone than as the structured setting where cultural and ideological contestation takes place – that is, the public domain where authority is constituted as legitimate and exposed to popular review, both inside and outside the accepted terms of the given discourse. In this sense, Thompson's treatment of the crowd bears centrally on the problematic of the public sphere. The three features which distinguish the specificity of eighteenth-century popular action for Thompson – the anonymous tradition, the counter-theatre of threat and sedition, the direct action of the crowd – provide the materials from which Brewer's 'alternative structure of politics' later in the century was built.

Third, the view that a 'plebeian' public flourished in the space vacated by a weak and non-bureaucratic state contains a strong argument concerning the particularity of English history by comparison with, say, Germany or France, which ultimately hinges on an interpretation of the Civil War as the English Revolution. This thesis was forcefully developed in Thompson's earlier writings during the 1960s. In this sense the connection to Habermas's idea of the public sphere is much clearer, for the rule of law in the eighteenth century was a specific legacy of the seventeenth-century struggles against arbitrary kingship, which among other things grounded the legitimate authority of the propertied in the proclaimed majesty and neutrality of the law. The radicalism of the seventeenth century also inaugurated a series of intellectual traditions, which re-emerged with great force in the 1790s. What is less clear is how these formal ideologies (e.g. the dissenting tradition of radical Protestantism, or the idea of the Englishman's 'birthright') bear on Thompson's more recent concept of a generalized plebeian culture.[11]

Fourth, Thompson's sophisticated conception of the political stands in full continuity with his celebrated analysis of the making of the English working class. There is in that earlier work an uncompromising stress on the importance of political determinations that belies the 'culturalist' label of 'history from below' which has been retrospectively attached to it. In Thompson's argument the working class is 'made' not solely from its

experiences in production under the impact of industrialization, but also
from a complex *political* conjuncture, involving old libertarian traditions,
newer ones of egalitarianism and democracy, and most crucial of all, the
repressive action of the state and the forms of popular resistance it
provoked. Indeed, in many ways *The Making of the English Working
Class* is about the final decomposition of the older structure of paternalist
politics discussed above.

Taking Thompson's writings as a whole, there seem to be four major
factors explaining this transition:

1. the rise of a new and independent middle-class political
presence; based partly in
2. the growing penetration of capitalist relations in agriculture and
industry;
3. the global ideological climate, comprising (a) the reaction
against the French Revolution, and (b) the triumph of political
economy; and finally
4. the challenge of a new popular radicalism, which likewise fed
on the first three factors mentioned.

These elements are thought to have combined in a complex process of
change between the 1790s and the 1832 Reform Act, which fundamentally
redrew the lines of social and political conflict and set the scene for
Chartism. This emerges clearly from the intervening local research, where
the magistracy are shown uncomfortably suspended between old and
new: confronting the transformation of the grain trade and the
encroachment of *laissez-faire*, beleaguered by instructions from the
Home Secretary to take a hard line with price controls and grain rioters,
observing the passage of moral economy into political agitation and
nascent trade unionism, yet mitigating the worst excesses of military and
judicial repression.[12] The analysis of popular radicalism has also largely
weathered the polemical hostility of Thompson's early critics, and it is
now fairly clear that the passing of paternalism opened a space where the
transitional ideology of English Jacobinism could flourish. As Thompson
says, during the 1790s, 'the relationship of reciprocity snapped. As it
snapped, so, in the same moment, the gentry lost their self-assured
cultural hegemony. It suddenly appeared that the world was not, after all,
bounded at every point by their rules and overwatched by their power. A
man was a man, "for a' that".'[13]

The greatest difficulty probably arises with the first of Thompson's
four factors, the rise of an independent middle-class politics. On the one
hand, the middle class is given only a subordinate and dependent role of
clientage within the eighteenth-century structure of politics. 'As surveyors,

attorneys, tutors, stewards, tradesmen, etc.', its members 'were contained within the limits of dependency', and 'for at least the first seven decades of the century we can find no industrial or professional middle class which exercises an effective curb upon the operations of predatory oligarchic power.'[14] The commercial bourgeoisie of merchants and bankers had certainly attained a high level of self-consciousness and independence, especially in the aldermanic elite of London, but this only confirmed the same syndrome: the elements of the big bourgeoisie were well integrated within 'the heterogeneous but unified ruling class of the Hanoverian era', and as such offered no challenge to the given paternalist relations.[15] But on the other hand, the middle class is given a key role in stimulating the new artisan radicalism of the 1790s: 'for when the ideological break with paternalism came, in the 1790s, it came in the first place less from the plebeian culture than from the intellectual culture of the dissenting middle class, and from thence it was carried to the urban artisans'.[16] This is currently a point of weakness in Thompson's work. His disclaimers of independent middle-class checks on Old Corruption are well taken, but on this basis the appearance of a dissenting intelligentsia which sponsors or permits the development of a Paineite radicalism seems rather like a *deus ex machina*.

How might this be remedied? Brewer's stress on the 'reconfiguration of politics' in the 1760s offers one solution, because the unlocking of the oligarchy's parliamentary front created a new space for legitimate opposition and gestured towards the two planks of a future reformist programme, bureaucratic rationalization and general constitutional reform. The issues were dramatized in the constitutional crisis of 1782–4, which together with the shock of the American War helped lay the foundations of long-term parliamentary opposition and the ideological basis for party. The provincial counterpart of these departures was the vital Association Movement of the later 1770s. Moreover, there can be little doubt that the process of urban cultural formation will repay more examination in this respect. But in general the nature of the new middle-class presence, its sociology and forms of ideological cohesion require far more elaborate discussion than Thompson has so far provided. The 'making of the English middle class' – despite his stress on class as a relationship – remains the missing dimension in Thompson's work.

Part of the problem is a lack of sociological specificity. In Thompson's usage, for example the term 'plebs' might do equal service with other terms like 'the people', the 'lower classes' and even the 'mob'.[17] In each case the term connotes a heterogeneous social phenomenon whose make-up varied from situation to situation and issue to issue, and whose forms of appearance were defined mainly via ideology or culture. As Thompson says, in 'the issues out of which most riots actually arise: when the

Geoff Eley

"plebs" unite as petty consumers, or as tax-payers or excise-evaders (smugglers), or on other "horizontal" libertarian, economic or patriotic issues.'[18] This amounted to a loose and highly unstable social bloc, which appears partly in a series of precipitating moments (e.g. the great crowd actions of the eighteenth century), partly in the stronger organized context of popular Toryism or Wilkite Radicalism. Thompson expresses this rather aptly through the metaphor of 'a societal "field-of-force" . . . with, for many purposes, the crowd at one pole, the aristocracy and gentry at the other, and until late in the century, the professional and merchant groups bound down by lines of magnetic dependency to the rulers, or on occasion hiding their faces in common action with the crowd.'[19] In this sense, the 'middle strata' (professions, teachers, tradesmen, shopkeepers, small masters, dissenting clergy, petty officials and all kinds of subaltern intellectuals) might be distributed around the two poles in shifting constellations, depending on the circumstances and the issue.

It remains unclear why Thompson resists the logical next step of a more structural analysis. But it seems to follow from his preference for experiential definitions of class ('Class eventuates as men and women *live* their productive relations, and as they *experience* their determinate situations, with "the *ensemble* of the social relations", with their inherited culture and expectations, and as they handle these experiences in cultural ways').[20] However, it is by no means clear that this anti-reductionist position of principle precludes an analysis of social structure *per se*. Thompson naturally provides something of the latter already – the participation of small masters, shopkeepers and parochial intellectuals is a well-observed feature of plebeian manifestations, while some prominence is also accorded the individual casualties of the oligarchy, the *déclassé* and excluded. But arguably, it is only through more systematic and carefully specified studies of regional class formation – in town, country and different localities – that we shall fully understand how the eighteenth-century equilibrium came to be upset.

This becomes especially important once we consider the 1790s. As Thompson says, the new radicalism of that decade originated, at least partly, in the revivified Dissent of a middle-class intelligentsia, for which the agitation against the Test and Corporation Acts was perhaps particularly pertinent. Moreover, for all its democratic magnificence, Paine's *The Rights of Man* centrally privileged an ideal of small property and independence. As Gwyn Williams puts it: 'The target Paine hit every time with unfailing accuracy, even in his subordinate clauses, were the small master, the journeyman, the small manufacturer, the shopkeeper, of questioning and ambitious temper'.[21] This was clearest outside the main centres of population where small groups of radicals took shape, 'reproducing the contours of that social grouping which seems to have responded most warmly to the democratic impulses – journeymen, a liberal Dissenter, a country doctor, small masters, a travelling actor.'[22] But this sociology recurs with unfailing regularity in the early 1790s, varying mainly with the degree of wider support in the general artisanate, from the vanguard of Jacobinism in Sheffield and Norwich to the most unlikely of provincial outposts, where a mere handful of individuals might assemble furtively in a private house or print-shop, or huddle protectively in the warmth of the *Stammtisch*. In other words, the movement was not unlike the Parisian milieu of the *sans-culottes* or the advanced Rhenish radicalism of 1848, and its articulate core largely personified the Paineite ideal of modestly propertied independence and historic liberty: 'traditional' trades, where the lines between journeyman, small employing master, independent artisan and shopkeeper were notoriously fluid, and an emergent petty bourgeoisie 'of printers and apothecaries, teachers and journalists, surgeons and Dissenting clergy'.[23] Of course, the political appeal was both intentionally and actually much wider, extending more deeply into the general populace than ever before. As Thompson says:

> At one end . . . the London Corresponding Society reached out to the coffee-houses, taverns and Dissenting Churches off Piccadilly, Fleet Street and the Strand, where the self-educated journeyman might rub shoulders with the printer, the shopkeeper, the engraver or the young attorney. At the other end, to the east, and south of the river, it touched those older working-class communities – the waterside workers of Wapping, the silk-weavers of Spitalfields, the old Dissenting stronghold of Southwark.[24]

But the mixed sociology of this British Jacobinism, and the Paineite cast of its ideology, imposed a necessary limitation. To be sure, the appeal was militantly democratic, a robust, radicalized libertarianism, which expressly refused the political, as against the economic claims of property. Yet at the same time, the economic individualism exerted a constant pull towards a broadly conceived politics of class alliance, which arraigned all the producers – 'the farmer, the manufacturer, the merchant, the tradesman, and down through all the occupations of life to the common labourer' – against the parasites and drones – the 'Placemen, Pensioners, Lords of the bed-chamber, Lords of the kitchen, Lords of the necessary-house, and the Lord knows what besides', and most of all the rentier aristocracy, fattening off the labour and industry of others.[25] In its pure form this was suppressive of certain kinds of socio-economic contradiction, most clearly articulated through emergent trade union aspirations, for even in the darkest moments of isolation and repression, many Paineite Radicals still strained for good reason towards the beckoning light of the larger liberal alliance; and while this allowed the impressive programme of fiscal, educational and social reform, it equally required the integrity of private property and productive capital, thereby foreclosing on any possibility of consistent trade unionism, let alone full-blooded socialism. This remained a problem well into the 1830s and 1840s, as radicals continued to direct their fire at land-owning aristocrats, bureaucratic corruption and middlemen, as against the legitimate property of manufacturers and merchants. In this sense, the radical democracy of the early 1790s was the originating moment of an enduring anti-aristocratic and anti-clerical critique. It was the authentic opponent of Thompson's gentry paternalism, at the same time profoundly subversive yet subtly confined by the circumstances of its origin.

III

Since *The Making of the English Working Class* was published a flood has passed beneath the bridge. Thompson's general approach, particularly his conceptions of class, culture and experience, together with the nature of his Marxism, has been subjected to exhaustive and searching review.[26] In particular, the structuralist tendency of much Marxist discussion of the 1970s, with its stress on mode of production and an economically-centred conception of class, and simultaneous freeing of politics and ideology for 'relatively autonomous' analysis, anchored to the former via 'structural causality' and 'determination in the last instance', left the under-theorized notion of social totality in *The Making of the English Working Class* extremely exposed. The subsequent anti-reductionist logic of such discussions, which produced increasingly sophisticated readings of culture and ideology via Gramsci, Foucault and the theorists of language and discourse, have left the earlier intellectual moment of the 1960s far behind, to the point of bringing classical materialism radically into question.[27] A key area in this respect has been feminism, and from a vantage-point at the end of the 1980s the neglect of gender questions is one of the clearest limitations of Thompson's earlier work.[28]

One of the most important – and controversial – recent entries of such new perspectives into social history has been Gareth Stedman Jones' rethinking of his own earlier essays on nineteenth-century working-class history, *Languages of Class*. The main vehicle of his new approach, an original essay on Chartism, argues for the constitutive importance of language in ordering perceptions of the social world, exercising political efficacy in its own right rather than being simply the expression of interests and experience formed elsewhere. Chartist ideology was less the reflection of emerging working-class interests, he argues, than an existing body of discourse which itself structured the latter's main direction; and Chartist politics revealed less the maturity of Thompsonian class-consciousness than the inherited baggage of an older eighteenth-century radical tradition. Very much in the Paineite mould (itself shaped by an earlier oppositional discourse), this blamed economic exploitation on political oppression (the parasitic, corrupt and unrepresentative governing system) rather than vice versa, and on this basis raised a general movement of the 'people' against the powerful, as against a class-based or socialist critique of capitalism. The repressive government policies of the 1830s gave this political language its mobilizing power, Stedman Jones argues, just as its declining purchase in the more liberal 1840s spelt the movement's decline. Given social history's stress on the economics and sociology of working-class formation as the main key to Chartism's rise and fall, this account marks a major break with existing work. But more radically, it shifts priorities away from the recognizably materialist problematic of social history altogether towards the very different frame of linguistic analysis: the point is to 'dissociate the ambition of a theoretically informed history from any simple prejudgement about the determining role of the "social" . . . as something outside of, and logically . . . prior to its articulation through language'.[29]

By stressing the primacy of political language in this way, Stedman Jones points us to the problems in Thompson's concept of class-consciousness. While *The Making of the English Working Class* successfully frees the latter from reductionist dependence on the development of productive forces (the factory system and mechanization), highlighting instead the radical movement's experience of repression, it still relies on a culturally mediated relationship between 'social being' and 'social consciousness' whose practical bases and modalities are extremely unspecific. Thus the role of state repression in laying the ground for a broadly-based popular movement between the 1790s and 1830s is clearly shown in Thompson's work: it stifled more moderate opposition, severed the middle-class alliance that seemed to be emerging from the late 1780s and early 1790s, cast the plebeian reformers back on their own resources, and forced the latter into a new radicalization of programme and method. Similarly, the combination of economic deterioration and government intransigence also diminished the fragmenting effects of trades sectionalism and pushed different groups of workers towards cooperation. Iorwerth Prothero for London, and Clive Behagg for Birmingham, have shown a high degree of cross-trade defensive activity among artisans which increasingly moved from the economic to the political plane of agitation – in London, beginning with the watershed of the apprenticeship campaign of 1812–13; in Birmingham, somewhat later in the 1820s. Thus while the State's coercive interventions schooled working-class politicians in the politics of self-reliance and isolated them from potential middle-class allies (and leaders), the pressure of capitalist development engendered new forms of supra-trade solidarity. The result was a potent unity of economic and political demands, concentrated in the panacea of parliamentary reform.[30]

By contrast, the trade societies of London and the West Midlands represented a very particular kind of worker – artisans in the 'old, specialist, unrevolutionized handworking trades', and invariably the better-off 'mechanics', as contemporaries called them – and cannot be made to typify the working class as a whole.[31] Of course, neither Prothero nor Behagg would wish to make that claim, and Edward Thompson (from whom both draw much inspiration) explicitly affirms the diversity of experience from which the working class was composed. But in practice, given his insistence on the determining importance of an achieved, self-made consciousness for the definition of class, Thompson identifies the working class with the skilled and artisanal sections: there is a crucial elision in his argument when the unskilled, the pauper, the casual labourer and the vagrant are being discussed, and in the end the class is defined mainly by a specific configuration of 'strongly-based and self-confident . . . institutions', which may or may not have been generally 'representative'.[32] In this way, an entire complex of relevant questions, concerning the economic formation of the working class and its internal divisions of trade, skill, nationality and gender, is implicitly suppressed.

In other words, Thompson's claim that the working class was already 'made' by the start of the 1830s (which is also taken over by Prothero) deserves some careful reflection, because it assumes a real cultural and political leadership of the artisanal sections over the rest which is never demonstrated in concrete empirical analysis. Thompson certainly considers other groups of non-artisanal workers (e.g. the chapters on agricultural labourers or the Irish immigration), but the crucial final section on 'The Working-Class Presence' (which comprises almost half the entire book) makes central reference overwhelmingly to artisans and specifically to three representative figures – John Gast of the skilled artisanal trades, Gravener Henson of the outworkers and John Doherty of the cotton-spinners as a new type of semi-artisanal skilled proletarian.[33] But if 'class-consciousness' is to be defined in some unitary sense by activity of this kind, then how do we label the consciousness of other groups of workers who are not included in the same solidarities, viz. properly proletarianized factory or detail workers who may certainly have a strong sense of 'us and them', but who also perceive strong contradictions of interest with skilled craft workers of an 'aristocratic' cast of mind? Conversely, how do we deal with artisanal disregard for the interests of unskilled or casual labourers and other groups of proletarians?[34] If, as many admirers of Thompson have done, we take 'artisanal traditions' to be primary in the constitution of European labour movements during the nineteenth and early twentieth centuries, we evade this difficulty and convert a conjunctural moment into a permanent feature of organized working-class culture.[35] Not only was the ideology of the radical artisanate frequently patronizing and intolerant of the class at large and its varying predicament, it was also ill-fitted for the particular needs of an industrial working class, and over the following decades the ideals of producer democracy gradually and unevenly subsided before the different doctrines of trade unionism and early socialism.[36]

In other words, the disunity and sectionalism of the working class – most of all in this early and formative period – should be frankly conceded. We can detect a higher degree of supra-trade solidarity after 1820 without having to claim that this tendential unification somehow extended to the working class as a whole or that significant sectional contradictions were therefore erased. The popular movement's artisanal cast in the 1820s should be accepted for what it was – a passing sectional phenomenon, shortly to be confronted with new contradictions and mobilizations within the class as a whole. So far from artisanal traditions from the late eighteenth/early nineteenth centuries being structurally constitutive of the British labour movement, the latter was actually shaped from the field of contradictions newly created by such traditions in the working class as a whole – e.g. with semi- and unskilled workers, both organized and unorganized, male and female, native and migrant. If this is so, it becomes difficult to accept that there was a *single* working class in 1830, which was 'made' by the preceding experiences in Thompson's strong sense.

Thompson's failing is not to have shown how the lines of representation between the radical culture of the 1820s (which was largely artisanal) and the working class as a whole (a more general category of direct producers working for a wage) were actually and concretely drawn. The basic emphasis on 'strongly-based and self-conscious working-class institutions – trade unions, friendly societies, educational and religious movements, political organizations, periodicals – working-class intellectual traditions, working-class community-patterns, and a working-class structure of feeling', is absolutely correct.[37] But some attention clearly must be paid to the awkward and by no means straightforwardly empirical question of the particular working-class interests such institutions embodied or excluded. If we can hold on to this point, linked to the enduring but continuously reconstituted sectionalism of the working class, then representation becomes the *key* question, in the sense that working-class institutions achieved varying resonance according to the situation. The maximum degree of the latter was articulated through an ideal of community – proud, defensive, impervious to external class intervention, unified on the ground of culture, autonomous within limits – but the forms and extent of that solidarity varied with a range of possible factors: quality of leadership, the internal hierarchies of gender, skill and status, ethnic and religious diversity, the complexity or homogeneity of the area's industrial structure, the effectiveness of repression, and so on.

Then, as now, the crucial strategic problem confronting labour movements (or, for that matter, any political movement) was how to mobilize the maximum solidarity from a socially defined constituency which has no *essential unity* in the sphere of consciousness, but on the contrary a series of particularistic loyalties and preferences and a widely differing experience of everyday life, a mosaic of individual histories. The analysis of working-class politics begins with this dialectic – the contradictory and dynamic intersection of unifying and fragmenting tendencies within the class as a whole (quite apart from the larger field of relationships with other classes and the state). The 'unity' of the working class, though postulated through the analysis of production and its social relations, remains a contingency of political agitation. This is what is meant by the adage that the history of the class is inseparable from its struggles. It allows us to retain Thompson's stress on achieved conscious-ness without suppressing the 'objective' dimension of class and its economic formation.

IV

In practice, therefore, there remains a lacuna in Thompson's account. It moves by grand inference from the actions and beliefs of an articulate radical minority to the implied solidarity of the skilled trades and beyond to the ascribed consciousness of the working class at large. The process is driven by the experiential motor of exploitation and state repression, but the key connections are still made at a level of general assertion – an unwarranted abstraction of unified consciousness, assumed to be both politically operative and rooted in a generalized culture of common values. But if, on the other hand, we problematize working-class consciousness by exchanging notions of expressive causality for linguistic analysis of working-class political discourse, as Stedman Jones suggests, what place remains for a materialist social history? In fact, Stedman Jones by no means exhausts the case for Chartism's social causes. His account comes surprisingly close to a conventional – if sophisticated and acute – intellectual history. As Gray says: 'In a curious way [it] is not really about language at all, but about the filiation of ideas.' It concentrates on specifying the underlying coherence – the origins, contents, and appeal – of 'public political language', without looking further at the institutional, social and cultural settings in which meanings were actually produced.[38] Once language is concretely located in that way, Stedman Jones arguably will look less disconcertingly 'idealist' (the common criticism at present) from the social historian's point of view.[39] That is, we can acknowledge the constitutive importance of language, and still keep a place for social history of the recognized kind. We can admit that language enters into all social practices *without* having to remove language itself from all social determination.[40]

If we follow this logic, there may be some value in the idea of a distinctively working-class or proletarian public. This would retain Thompson's salutary stress on culture and experience, modulated through specific institutions and processes of struggle, without recourse to a poorly specified notion of 'class-consciousness', with its Lukácsian connotations of necessary and progressive working-class unification. The outlines of such an analysis were developed programmatically by Michael Vester in an interesting work which has passed completely unnoticed by British historians:

Given the heterogeneity of situations, the unity of the working class could only be achieved indirectly in a coalition . . . . Only a broad and intense communicative system, continuously recharged via its own press, educational, protective, and fighting organizations, created a sufficient basis for the articulation, exchange, examination, and further development of ideas. The right to communication was a central issue in the conflict between establishment and working-class movement. The flipside of *laissez-faire* was a strict regulation of the freedoms of correspondence, speech, press, assembly, and association, which was exercised at first by force and then by manipulation. But it was precisely the repression, above all the exceptional laws of 1792–1818, that taught the movement the necessity of greater cohesion. As a result of the repression, and of the discontinuous advance of the industrial revolution, the working-class movement lacked continuity. Instead, it developed through cycles of defeat, re-evaluation, and renewal, each at a qualitatively higher level. Analyzing the failures was essentially the role of the movement's leading theoreticians, journalists, and organizers . . . . The most significant source of theory in the early working-class movement was the 'worker-intelligentsia' ['*Arbeiterintelligenz*'], a group of urban and to some extent rural artisans and skilled industrial workers, on the basis partly of their own ideas, partly of ideas originating elsewhere.[41]

On this basis it is possible to abstract a number of features of the 'working-class presence' in the earlier nineteenth century, maturing under Chartism but arising in the experiences presented by Thompson, which collectively composed what might be called a working-class public sphere.

1   A first characteristic of the new working-class presence was its consciously political and oppositional stance. This already distinguished it from the popular rebelliousness of the eighteenth century, which remained largely 'primitive' or 'pre-political' in Hobsbawm's sense: e.g.

> resistance to work disciplines, the defence of customary rights of relief, the practices of customary sports and pastimes, the equally traditional use of alcohol in sociability or need, the spending of hard-won wages on petty luxuries, the theft of property or the street life of children and adolescents . . . a range of cultural responses that were resistant to capitalist imperatives and their corresponding values.[42]

Of course, this distinction might easily break down in practice, and the very attack on custom might be enough to turn its defence into a self-consciously political enterprise.[43] But whatever the complexities in practice, the idea of a proletarian public sphere clearly requires some developed conception of political order and of power in the state, i.e. a coherent orientation towards the system as a whole, whether within the given institutions or as a challenge to them. Between the 1790s and 1830s such a conception clearly took shape, and for the Chartists it was axiomatic.

2   Second, we may observe a growing unity of political and economic discontents. The tendency of artisanal spokesmen to predicate their demand for protection on a political strategy of parliamentary lobbying was a key point of Thompson's for the years 1810–32, and any attempt to distinguish rigidly between 'industrial' and 'political' activity in these years is surely misguided. It has recently been said of Luddism – the classic site of the 'compartmentalist' argument – that it represented one 'stage in the process whereby working men came to regard democratic control of the state as an essential means to the improvement of their condition.'[44] The years 1833–4 were a crucial moment in this respect, when democratic, trade union, social reform and cooperative agitations conjoined in a broad correspondence of aspirations.[45] Chartism embodied this unity.

3   The emergence of an independent working-class public presupposed the new urban provincial cultures of the eighteenth century – 'an emanation from the rising public opinion of the provinces which, fostered by the growth of industry and the improvement of communications, began to snatch the leadership of English radicalism from London in the closing years of the eighteenth century.'[46] The relations here are extremely complex. It seems that the working-class public achieved its maximum independence in manufacturing communities beyond the effective control of the authorities. Conversely, it was weakest where a reconstituted paternalism had managed to re-incorporate the subordinate classes within a new structure of authority relations radiating from church and chapel, often in smaller or newer industrial towns. At all events this can only be settled through meticulous local study.[47]

4   The degree of independence naturally depended on far more than structural factors alone. More than anything else it hinged on the attitude of the progressive bourgeoisie. Attention has already been drawn to the effects of the repression, which ruptured the potential of a larger social bloc in the 1790s, and for the duration of the wars a combination of patriotism and counter-revolutionary panic was enough to keep the middle class in line. The post-war conjuncture of 1816–20 was a further moment of fission in this respect, by which the 'legitimate' parliamentary opposition was driven still further from the unconstitutional' popular movement. There were efforts to rebuild a populist alliance in the later 1820s (e.g. through Brougham's educational politics, and the re-emerging pressure for parliamentary reform), but the great betrayal of the Reform Bill in 1831–2 produced a cleaner break than ever before. As Stedman Jones says:

> The Reform Bill was regarded as the great betrayal of what had been thought of as a common struggle. The measures of the Whig government which followed it – the Irish Coercion Bill, the rejection of the Ten Hours Bill, the attack on Trade Unions, the Municipalities Act and the New Poor Law – were seen as confirmation of the treachery of the middle class. The practical consequence to be drawn was that the working class must fight for its own emancipation.[48]

5   Among the institutions of the working-class public the press was paramount. Between 1830 and 1836 – i.e. at the height of government attempts to suppress the 'unstamped' press – at least 562 newspapers and journals, 'containing every sort of prose and poetry, were written, printed, published, sold and bought by working men'.[49] The importance of the press had many sides. Most obviously it functioned as an independent organ of working-class opinion, and the first priority of a

local movement cast back on its own resources by the withdrawal of middle-class patronage was the creation of a local newspaper. Equally clearly it was a source of news and information from other regions and helped bind a supra-regional movement together. The most impressive service of this kind was provided by Feargus O'Connor's *Northern Star*, founded in 1837–8, which probably contributed more than any other single factor to the coherence of a national movement in the early years of the Charter: with some 50,000 sales at its peak and an effective readership infinitely larger, it was a genuinely national organ of opinion and provided an unprecedented means of articulating local grievances into a national arena. The press was also a crucial focus for local agitation. As David Jones says, 'the newspapers did the work of a weak organization; imposing a unity on the movement, publicizing leaders, nationalizing problems and keeping a few issues constantly in front of the popular mind.'[50]

6   Similar in kind were other forms of literary production. The best-known pamphlet, *What is a Chartist? – Answered*, achieved enormous circulation and was translated into both Welsh and Gaelic. Certain individuals specialized in servicing the movement with statistical compilations and handbooks of opinion: e.g. 'R. J. Richardson, who had his own Popular Library, Joshua Hobson and Joseph Barker wrote and edited cheap political almanacs and the famous Red, Blue and Black Books which provided the vital statistics for Chartist lecturers.' Much of this activity took place on a local level, and there were considerable efforts to centralize and coordinate the flow of published literature – e.g. by exchanges between local associations and by the so-called Tract Loan Societies established in Edinburgh, London and parts of Yorkshire.[51] As David Vincent points out, this was facilitated by a favourable moment in the conditions of literary production: 'For a while technical advance brought the availability and cost of literature, and access to the means of publication, increasingly within the grasp of working men, and it was not until after the turn of the half-century that all forms of publication began to become capital intensive and both access and control began to move out of their reach.'[52]

7   Furthermore, the movement managed to generate its own agitations and organizational forms. Some years ago, Hobsbawm pointed to an important bifurcation of the radical–democratic tradition into two wings: a radical-secularist one based in the artisanal culture of London and flowing from Paine, through Owen, Carlile, Holyoake and Bradlaugh, to the Marxist departures of the 1880s, and a nonconformist one based in the new mining and factory centres of the North. Where one delivered the organizational devices of the 'Corresponding Society', the pamphlet, the working-class newspaper, the petition and the public debate, the

other provided the organizational schooling of chapel and circuit and the agitational vehicles of camp meeting, class meeting and Sunday school.[53] This is an important distinction, with vital bearing on the emergence of new proletarian forms as opposed to the transmuted culture of 'the small-producer-becoming-proletarian', which was rooted in a much older tradition of corporate solidarity.[54] Hobsbawm suggests that it was in the school of nonconformity 'that the new factory proletarians, rural labourers, miners and others of the sort learned how to run a trade union, modelling themselves on chapel and circuit': in this sense Primitive Methodism 'was to the Durham miners of the 1840s or the Lincolnshire labourers of the 1870s, what the Communist Party is to the French workers today, the cadre of leadership'.[55]

But it is equally important not to see these different influences as antagonists or rival movements, at least in the first half of the nineteenth century. The vigorously secularist Owenites consciously adopted the ritual forms of religious practice for their social and educational activities, whereas after 1839 the Chartists adapted the Primitive Methodist camp meeting to overcome the banning and harassment of mass demonstrations, infusing the agenda of hymns and sermons with a democratic and frequently anti-clerical content. Both cases were as much an act of subversive mimicry as a positive appropriation from a cognate culture.[56] The Chartists were particularly inventive in this respect, combining the petition, the lecture circuit, the public meeting, the popular political festival, and a panoply of educational and recreational activity into a varied repertoire of popular agitation.[57]

8   The strength of Chartism was revealed most impressively in the cultural sphere. Here the crucial form was the local association. Meeting in homes, schoolrooms, church halls, coffee-houses, inns or specially erected 'Chartist Halls', on a monthly, weekly or even daily basis, the Chartist club was 'the basic machinery of the movement'.[58] As well as the more obviously political cycle of public meetings, lectures, sermons, festivals and commemorations, 'a plethora of subcommittees organized a full range of family activities, from public breakfasts, tea-parties and dinners to dramatic productions, poetry-readings, oratorios and balls'. Public manifestations were accompanied by an imaginative profusion of banners, portraits, tableaux, radical iconography and other emblematic devices. This was perhaps the true radicalism of the Chartist movement, which was not replicated in the experience of European labour movements until the much later achievements of the German Social-Democratic subculture and Mediterranean syndicalism: occupying the 'private' terrain of everyday life and the family, fashioning new forms of collective sociability, newly integrating the personal and the political, and creating by these virtues a distinct *public* space of independent working-

class activity, at the same time defensively closed against the culture of the dominant classes and affirmatively committed to a new way of life. It is here, where a wider sphere of social intervention became consciously articulated into a radical political vision, that the ideas of subculture, hegemony and proletarian public sphere acquire their potential significance.

Eileen Yeo is one of the few people to have explored these possibilities. As she says, 'It seems a striking fact that some working-class movements between 1830 and 1850 and especially protest movements, aggregated to themselves leisure activities along with the ritual of religion and the life-cycle, even if these did not seem directly relevant to their professed aims and objects.' In so doing they repudiated both the imposed culture of the middle class and the inchoate roughness of the unorganized proletariat. Several features are worth noting. First, because 'total group solidarity and harmony was the aim, the culture was family–oriented and placed great emphasis on the equality and participation of women.' Secondly, this entailed a practical critique of rival institutions, whether the church, the pub, the apparatus of middle-class philanthropy, or the varied system of 'provided' education. Thirdly, the radical culture developed an alternative calendar of festivity and ceremonial, based both on 'the inverted Christian year' and on a range of specifically radical festivals. Finally, there was a deliberate attempt to capture the life-cycle, 'taking out of the hands of the church the crucial rites of passage: baptism, marriage and death.' This could embrace everything from the formation of a Chartist church to the aggressive secularization of religious ritual and the naming of children (in one extreme case a child was baptised 'Feargus O'Connor Frost O'Brien McDouall Hunt Taylor').[59] In a different but related setting this has been called 'battling through ritual' – a struggle for 'ritual supremacy', centred on 'the private rites of passage' and 'the public rites of community'.[60]

9   One particular aspect of this self-conscious independent culture was a highly developed sense of the past – not just as an assemblage of myths and ideas *about* the past (e.g. as in the idea of the 'Norman Yoke' or the mythology of the 'freeborn Englishman'), though these are clearly important, but as a continuous and developing *radical tradition*. A sense of belonging to such a living tradition was vital for the maintenance of solidarity and for socializing new recruits into the movement. In the early years of the nineteenth century the 'Village Politician' described by Thompson was doubtless the main guardian of this tradition, but by the start of the 1820s it was being transmitted by an active process or reproduction in all the ways alluded to above. The celebration of heroic moments, the commemoration of martyrs and the glorification of leaders were all part of this radical iconography and the remembered experience of 'Peterloo' particularly important to the symbolism.[61]

10   The Radical culture found its most effective political expression in an ideal of community. This was true in two ways. The first, as Vincent says, concerns 'the extent to which politics involved an entire community'. Thomas Dunning's autobiography 'emphasizes at every turn the extent to which the entire working class community was involved in the conflict (over the trial of the Nantwich shoemakers), turning out *en masse*, for instance, to welcome the prisoners back from Chester'. Another good example from the same autobiography concerns the mobilization of the local community (conducted at a neighbourhood and street level) for a reforming assault on the entrenched oligarchic corruption of the Nantwich vestry, achieving an impressive degree of discipline: on one occasion a disciplined queue of some 70–80 people, strategically monopolizing the voting booth in the last hour of polling, managed to prevent 'the well-to-do' from voting and successfully carried a lower rather than a much higher church rate.[62] This already introduces the second point, because an ideal of community was most effectively realized by the wielding of local political power, either through parliamentary elections or the control of police, vestry and Poor Law. The handicap of the restricted parliamentary franchise was partially compensated by the broader popular base of local government and in favourable circumstances the working class might secure its own representation by exerting pressure on the system from the outside – e.g. by an elaborate system of exclusive dealing, as in John Foster's Oldham.[63]

11   It is also worth making specific mention of education. It is possible, without subsuming the larger complexity, to discuss the structure of practice presented above as a concerted attempt by the radical movement to contest the *specific* terrain of educational policy. Richard Johnson has argued this convincingly in a number of major essays.[64] In a discontinuous and extremely uneven process between the 1780s and 1846 the foundations were laid for a state-regulated system of mass schooling, and it was against this process of aggressive cultural intervention, Johnson argues, that the radical culture described above was a response. The enterprise of mass schooling was as much a matter of public order as one of philanthropy or the needs of the new economy for basic skills, and by the same virtue radicals developed through the medium of educational practice a searching critique of the existing political system. In other words, education provided the ground on which fundamental questions of legitimacy and consent were posed – what Johnson calls 'an extended war over the winning of consent, a prolonged crisis in hegemony, marked by partial stabilizations but also, in default of this, the repeated use of the rather underdeveloped coercive apparatuses of the state to reinforce the economic power of the gentry and industrial bourgeoisie.'[65]

Moreover the very resistance of the working class to an increase in provided schooling (e.g. through the unstamped press, or the Owenite and Chartist schools and halls of science) provoked an intensification of efforts. In course of the struggle, the popular movement quickly elaborated a remarkably ambitious strategy of *substitution*, whereby government and philanthropic intervention would be defeated and eventually replaced altogether by the collective self-education of the people themselves. In its refusal of provided education on principle this arguably went far beyond most later left-wing movements and came fairly close to Gramsci's ideal of the revolutionary party and its cultural goals. It relied on both the informal resources of the working-class community and the organizational inventions of the new radical culture.[66] Finally, in these respects it exactly mirrored the structural contradiction hinted at earlier in this essay – namely, that of a radical–democratic movement claiming leadership of the people in general, which was strongly dominated by artisanal or semi-artisanal workers, was heavily indebted to an ideal of producer democracy in its ideology, and originated to a great extent in a series of transformed artisanal traditions.

Johnson suggests that radical hostility to institutionalized educational provision by the state and the preference for informal learning in home, work-place and neighbourhood (e.g. Cobbett's ideal of practical 'competences' learned within the patriarchal small-producer household) both corresponded to the artisan's experience of incipient proletarianization: 'The main mechanism here seems to have been the curtailment or interruption of the educative or reproductive autonomies of family and community through, primarily, the more complete subordination of labour (male, female and juvenile) in production.'[67] Continuing the argument, Johnson characterizes radical education 'as an attempt to expand and develop those areas of autonomy and control over reproduction which remained'. If this were so, the possible material bases of the substitutionist strategy were rapidly shrinking, whereas the acquisition of a 'more fully proletarian base' – 'the spread of the factories, the deepening subordination of the outworkers, the growth of sweated trades, together with the geographic shift northwards in Chartism' – made radicalism more receptive to the notion of state provision. In both respects, of course, the implicitly patriarchal-artisanal and the prospectively state-welfarist, radical strategy took women's subordination within households for granted.

12   But the artisanal backbone of early nineteenth-century radicalism, which clearly persisted to some extent into Chartism, was not the whole of the story. The transformed conditions of existence of artisanal labour – for which incipient proletarianization is probably the best description –

should, in any case, caution against a simple reading of continuity. But more importantly, by the 1830s the radical Movement was providing a series of institutional foci around which the working class as a whole (and the subordinate classes more widely) could begin to rally. Chartism was evidently not an exclusively or even predominantly artisanal movement, though the artisanal presence (however we choose to define it) retained its influence in several key respects (e.g. the 'producer' ideology or the recruitment of the activist leaders). In the end the *most* significant feature of the mature radicalism of the Charter was precisely its appeal to the *whole* class through an inclusive ideal of community. In conclusion, therefore, two further aspects are worth mentioning. First, the radical working-class politicians who shouldered the daily labours of Chartist agitation corresponded closely to Gramsci's challenging concept of the organic intellectual.[68] In this case the latter arose *from* and were sustained *within* the working-class movement itself, most obviously as journalists, lecturers, booksellers, newsagents, shopkeepers, functionaries, and so on. The Owenite movement in the 1830s was especially important in pioneering the kind of organized 'subcultural' milieu which could nurture and support such a stratum of working-class intellectuals. But secondly, Chartism was above all a *national* political movement, and as such arguably the first of its kind in British history. Dorothy Thompson has summed this up well:

> [Recent scholarship has shown] that important shifts in attitudes and behaviour that undoubtedly occurred in the first half of the century cannot simply be attributed to the filtering downwards of rather vaguely defined 'middle-class attitudes', but can be seen to have occurred within the working communities themselves. One of the manifestations of a change from an episodic, picaresque way of living to a more planned and apparently rational way was the development of national organizations with a permanent institutional structure. Among the working classes trade unions, friendly societies and political organizations took on this more formal shape in the middle decades of the nineteenth century. It should be noted, however, that in political terms at any rate, a formal national structure occurred earlier among working-class radicals than among the traditional political parties, and that such organization owed nothing to middle-class encouragement or example. So far from national education preceding the growth of a working-class press and the spread of working-class literacy, it could be argued that the support which the movement for a national system achieved in the 1830s and 1840s was largely a response to working-class radicalism rather than to working-class illiteracy.[69]

V

In conclusion three general points might be made: one concerning the cohesion of the working-class movement; one concerning the cohesion of society; and one concerning the role of the state.

Together, they rejoin the general issue raised at the beginning of this essay, namely the limitations of much British political history and the need to re-think the latter's problems in terms of recent social-historical discussion. Though the latter is not without its own rather glaring problems – after all, social historians should be far more willing than they are to initiate such a re-thinking themselves – hopefully, I have been able to indicate how the re-integration of social and political history might begin to take place.

The first point is mainly a recapitulation of the immediately preceding discussion. Between roughly 1816 and 1848, therefore (the dates are necessarily rather arbitrary), we may diagnose the construction of a consciously independent and distinctively working-class public sphere, from materials which originated in the experiences of the 1790s. This implies a qualified criticism of Edward Thompson's pioneering analysis of the English working class, for this attributes a resolution and determinacy to the period 1790–1832 that the transitory and partial character of the dominant artisanal radicalism of that time cannot really sustain. Though Thompson's great work retains its uncontestable value in delineating some important continuities, in another way it tends to elide an area of difficulty by identifying the 'making' of the working class with a transitional radicalism of the artisanate which bore a somewhat uncertain relationship to the working class as a whole. In this respect the question of *representation* becomes the key one, because although Thompson shows the existence of a rich and developing radical culture, the unifying power of that radical culture (its impact on the consciousness of the class as a whole) awaits proper demonstration.

This is not necessarily to imply that the class-consciousness of the following period or any other succeeding one is more 'authentically' working class because of its greater revealed or essential unity. Within the basic context of capitalist productive relations an immense variety of proletarian interests and experience may be imagined, and as Alastair Reid has recently argued, the forces making for greater unity and homogeneity of the working class are also accompanied by tendencies in an opposing direction, towards greater fragmentation and sectionalism in the division of labour. On this basis the economic disunity and fragmentation of the working class, 'frequently compounded by sexual and cultural divisions', is a permanent and structural feature of capitalist relations, though the specific forms of that fragmentation are continually reconstituted and divisions between artisans, outworkers and factory proletarians are consequently just as 'working-class' as those between skilled machinists and casual labourers. If this is so, the element of political determination becomes all the more crucial, and the 'active unity' of the working class will depend on an 'area of conscious manoeuvre, choice, negotiation and compromise between working-class sections, whether in the arenas of local and national politics, in the building of united industrial movements or in the development of cultural and social institutions'.[70]

Chartism, I have suggested, embodied an impressive degree of this 'active unity', and one which has seldom been matched since.[71] Artisans may have retained their leading role in the political culture of the working class, but the latter's institutions now achieved a much wider resonance than before. The outstanding problem is to establish the *bases of popularity*, or the ability of a movement, a type of practice or an ensemble of institutions to articulate different aspirations into a coherent and unified strategy, coordinated through stable national organizations, and aimed at redefining power in the state. This is a question of more than historical relevance.

Of course, another of Chartism's striking features was its political failure. If the first of our three points concerns the varying cohesion of the working-class movement, the second concerns its location in the larger field of social relations and the overall cohesion of society. If the period 1816–48 saw the growth of an independent working-class public within the public sphere as a whole – a counter-hegemonic potential against the imperfectly consolidated hegemony of the bourgeoisie – then that period still ended with the *suppression* of radical possibilities. The Chartist challenge was contained and the subordination of the working class confirmed by a highly exclusive political system. The point of principle is well stated by Eric Hobsbawm, though part of his emphasis is certainly open to debate:

Class is not merely a relationship between groups, it is also their coexistence within a social, cultural, and institutional framework set by those above. The world of the poor, however elaborate, self-contained, and separate, is a subaltern and therefore in some senses incomplete world, for it normally takes for granted the existence of the general framework of those who have hegemony, or at any rate its inability for most of the time to do much about it. It accepts their hegemony, even when it challenges some of its implications because, largely, it has to. Ideas, models, and situations in which action becomes possible tend to reach it from outside, if only because the initiative that changes conditions on a national scale comes from above or because the mechanisms for diffusing ideas are generated outside. Only in the nineteenth century did the working class itself generate, or become identified with, a potentially hegemonic force – the organized labour and socialist movement – with the potential, for instance, to transform itself into a system of national rule, as in the case of communist parties after revolutions.[72]

The main effect of Chartism was to complicate the process already interrupted by the agitations of 1790–1832, namely the re-integration of the popular classes in a new structure of authority to replace the vanishing one of gentry paternalism. It could challenge the hegemonic capability of the dominant classes, but not destroy it. A number of explanations have been advanced for the re-stabilization that occurred in the 1850s and 1860s and for the increasing accommodation of politically conscious workers to a measure of liberal reform. A full discussion of these lies beyond the scope of this essay, but most of them rely on some model of incorporation (Reid distinguishes between 'normative consensus', 'pragmatic acceptance' and 'social control' versions) or of the labour aristocracy.[73] Without entering the detail of these debates, it is notable that authors have taken increasing recourse to the sociological analysis of culture, with special stress on status patterns and associational life, and it may be useful to follow a similar logic by examining the processes making for working-class participation within liberalism. While recently the tendency has been to stress the relative independence of the labour aristocracy and its ideals of self-help and respectability, thereby drawing attention to the limits of simple domination or imposed control, it may now be time to re-examine the forms of labour's positive subordination.

The most fundamental of the latter was clearly economic – viz. the restabilization of the labour process on the basis of labour's real subordination to capital, the newly consolidated *permanence* of capitalist relations in British industry.[74] But the construction of a new popular liberalism was also vital, and though John Vincent provided an agenda for tackling this problem some years ago, we are still surprisingly ignorant of how it took place.[75] By directing us back to the field of relations between dominant and subordinate classes, the stress on working-class containment – the painful reconstitution and re-legitimizing of authority relations during the decay of gentry paternalism and the Chartist interruption – also returns us to that most extraordinary of absences in British historiography, the making of the middle class. In effect the middle class leaves the stage of social-historical analysis somewhere between the 1790s and 1832, and does not really re-enter it until the defeat of Chartism, and then more as a socio-cultural abstraction represented in certain administrative, religious and philanthropic practices than as a carefully specified social phenomenon.[76]

Moreover, by raising the problem of containment we also raise the last of our three questions, that concerning the state. One of the main points made in this essay has been that questions of public order and political stability, of political culture and political development, cannot be grasped by examining the formal political process alone, but require attention for the larger processes by which popular consent is negotiated, reproduced, modified and occasionally withdrawn. This is perhaps most evident in the sphere of local government, where the very creation and continued existence of a local state derived from the voluntary labours of an emergent citizenry. Moreover, as suggested above (but not demonstrated in detail through lack of space), both the idea of the public sphere and the Gramscian triplet of State, hegemony and civil society are potentially valuable for making sense of such a phenomenon, providing we hold firm to a notion of contestation and of the unstable constitution of public life from conflicting interests and pressures. The most important field of contradiction in that respect is provided by the interactions between dominant and subordinate classes, and the striking feature of the period 1790–1850 is the ability of the British working class to raise an overt challenge to the emergent hegemony of the bourgeoisie, by elaborating an independent public sphere of its own. The containment of this radical challenge required not only repression, but a more constructive effort to neutralize popular antagonisms by transforming them into objects of compromise. This ability 'to articulate different visions of the world in such a way that their potential antagonism is neutralized', rather than merely *suppressing* them beneath 'a uniform conception of the world', is precisely an index of the hegemony of a ruling class.[77] After the panics of the 1830s and 1840s had passed, it was on this terrain of constructive social intervention that the work of stabilization mainly took place, embracing 'poor law reform, the beginnings of elementary education, religious evangelism, propaganda against dangerous "economic heresies" the fostering of more acceptable expressions of working-class self-help (friendly societies, co-ops etc.) and of safe forms of "rational recreation"'.[78]

To itemize these areas is not to adopt an over-totalized conception of the State or a neo-functionalist notion of 'ideological state apparatuses', but simply to indicate the site of hegemonic construction – i.e. the complex field of official and voluntary interventions from which the Victorian State gradually and unevenly emerged. Such an approach might easily contribute to a number of pressing tasks. It might re-open the discussion of popular liberalism. It might lift the discussion of the state above the pedantries of administrative history. It might hopefully re-unite the fractured labours of political and social historians.

Notes

1 For the exchange in question, conducted via a series of essays in *New Left Review* and *The Socialist Register* during 1964–6, see Richard Johnson, 'Barrington Moore, Perry Anderson, and English Social Development', in Stuart Hall et al. (eds), *Culture, Media, Language* (London: Hutchinson, 1980), pp. 48–70; Keith Nield, 'A Symptomatic Dispute? Notes on the relation between Marxian theory and historical practice in Britain', in *Social Research*, 47 (1980), pp. 479–595; Perry Anderson, *Arguments Within English Marxism* (London: NLB, 1980). Recently, Anderson has returned to the original theses in 'The Figures of Descent', in *New Left Review*, 161 (Jan.–Feb. 1987), pp. 20–77, with a subsequent critique by Michael Barratt Brown, 'Away with All the Great Arches: Anderson's history of British capitalism', ibid., 167 (Jan.–Feb. 1988), pp. 22–51. See also Philip Corrigan and Derek Sayer, *The Great Arch. English State Formation as Cultural Revolution* (Oxford: Basil Blackwell, 1985); and Geoffrey Ingham, *Capitalism Divided: The City and Industry in British Social Development* (London: Macmillan, 1984); and David Sugarman, 'Law, Economy and the State in England, 1750–1914: some major issues', in David Sugarman (ed.), *Legality, Ideology and the State* (London and New York: Academic Press, 1983), pp. 214–66. Again, these more recent contributors are sociologists rather than historians by disciplinary background. Similarly, there has been almost no discussion of Barrington Moore Jr's *Social Origins of Dictatorship and Democracy* (Harmondsworth: Penguin, 1966) among British historians – by contrast with, say, German historiography, where Moore's influence has been central during the last twenty years.

2 See the work produced under the auspices of the Birmingham Centre for Contemporary Cultural Studies and the Open University course 'State and Society': Mary Langan and Bill Schwarz (eds), *Crises in the British State 1880–1930* (London: Hutchinson, 1985); Gregor McLennan, David Held and Stuart Hall (eds), *State and Society in Contemporary Britain* (Cambridge: Polity Press, 1984). See also David Nicholls, 'Fractions of Capital: the Aristocracy, the City and Industry in the Development of Modern British Capitalism', in *Social History*, 13 (1988), pp. 71–83, which is also a further contribution to the discussions mentioned in note 1 above.

3 Jürgen Habermas, 'The Public Sphere', in *New German Critique*, 3 (Fall 1974), p. 49. Habermas originally presented his thesis in *Strukturwandel der Öffentlichkeit* (Neuwied: H. Luchterhand, 1962), his earliest and least-known work in the English-speaking world. For a survey of its reception, see Peter Hohendahl, 'Critical Theory, Public Sphere, and Culture: Jürgen Habermas and his Critics', in *New German Critique*, 16 (Winter 1979), pp. 89–118. The ideas have been further explored in a series of books by John Keane, though with surprisingly little direct discussion of *Strukturwandel* itself: *Public Life and Late Capitalism* (Cambridge: Cambridge University Press, 1984); *Democracy and Civil Society* (London: Verso, 1988); and idem. (ed.), *Civil*

Society and the State. New European Perspectives (London: Verso, 1988). A translation of *Strukturwandel* has been promised by MIT Press for 1989.

4 This argument is developed more extensively in Eley, 'Rethinking the Political', pp. 428ff. It is based on a wide reading of secondary literature, of which the most important are as follows: John Brewer, 'Commercialization and Politics', and J. H. Plumb, 'Commercialization and Society', in Neil McKendrick, John Brewer and J. H. Plumb, *The Birth of a Consumer Society* (London: Hutchinson 1982), pp. 197–262, 265–334; Peter Borsay, 'The English Urban Renaissance: The Development of Provincial Urban Culture *c.* 1680–*c.* 1760', in *Social History*, 2 (1977), pp. 581–604; P. J. Corfield, *The Impact of English Towns 1700–1800* (Oxford: Oxford University Press, 1982); John Brewer, *Party Ideology and Popular Politics at the Accession of George III* (Cambridge: Cambridge University Press, 1976); John Brewer, 'English Radicalism in the Age of George III', in J. G. A. Pocock (ed.), *Three British Revolutions: 1641, 1688, 1776* (Princeton, Princeton University Press, 1980), pp. 265–88; Linda Colley, *In Defiance of Oligarchy: The Tory Party, 1714–1760* (Cambridge: Cambridge University Press, 1982); John Money, *Experience and Identity. Birmingham and the West Midlands 1760–1800* (Manchester: Manchester University Press, 1977); Nicholas Rogers, 'The Urban Opposition to Whig Oligarchy, 1720–60', in Margaret Jacob and James Jacob (eds), *The Origins of Anglo-American Radicalism* (London: Allen & Unwin, 1984), pp. 132–48; Linda Colley, 'Whose Nation? Class and National Consciousness in Britain 1750–1830', in *Past & Present*, 113 (Nov. 1986), pp. 97–117.

5 Aside from *The Making of the English Working Class* (London: Gollancz, 1963), the relevant works by Thompson are as follows: 'Time, Work-discipline and Industrial Capitalism', in *Past & Present*, 38 (Dec. 1967), pp. 59–97; 'The Moral Economy of the English Crowd in the Eighteenth Century', ibid., 50 (Feb. 1971), pp. 76–131; 'Rough Music: *le charivari anglais*', in *Annales E.S.C*, 27 (1972), pp. 285–312; 'Patrician Society, Plebeian Culture', in *Journal of Social History*, 7 (1973–4), pp. 382–405; 'Anthropology and the Discipline of Historical Context', in *Midland History*, 1 (1972), pp. 41–55; *Whigs and Hunters: The Origin of the Black Act* (Harmondsworth: Penguin, 1975); 'The Crime of Anonymity', in Douglas Hay et al. (eds), *Albion's Fatal Tree. Crime and Society in Eighteenth-Century England* (Harmondsworth: Penguin, 1975), pp. 255–344; 'The Grid of Inheritance: A Comment', in Jack Goody, Joan Thirsk and Edward Thompson (eds), *Family and Inheritance. Rural Society in Western Europe 1200–1800* (Cambridge: Cambridge University Press, 1976), pp. 328–60; 'Eighteenth-century English Society: Class Struggle without Class?', in *Social History*, 3 (1978), pp. 133–66; *Folklore, Anthropology, and Social History* (Brighton: John L. Noyce, 1979).

6 See Richard Johnson, 'Edward Thompson, Eugene Genovese, and Socialist–Humanist History', in *History Workshop Journal*, 6 (Autumn 1978), esp. pp. 90ff., and two additional essays by the same author: 'Culture and the Historians', and 'Three Problematics: Elements of a Theory of Working-class Culture', in John Clarke, Chas Critcher and Richard Johnson (eds), *Working-*

class Culture. Studies in History and Theory (London: Hutchinson, 1979), pp. 41–76, 201–307. For the subsequent debate, see the contributions by Stuart Hall, Richard Johnson and Thompson himself to 'Culturalism: Debates around *The Poverty of Theory*', in Raphael Samuel (ed.), *People's History and Socialist Theory* (London: Routledge & Kegan Paul, 1981), pp. 375–408; and Susan Magarey, 'That Hoary Old Chestnut, Free Will and Determinism: Culture *vs*. Structure, or History *vs*. Theory in Britain', in *Comparative Studies in Society and History*, 29 (1987), pp. 626–39. See also Gregor McLennan, 'E. P. Thompson and the Discipline of Historical Context', in Richard Johnson et al. (eds), *Making Histories. Studies in History-writing and Politics* (London: Hutchinson, 1982), pp. 96–130.

7 Thompson, 'Grid of Inheritance', pp. 347, 328, 342.

8 See Thompson, 'Moral Economy', and the comment by Elizabeth Fox Genovese, 'The Many Faces of Moral Economy', in *Past & Present*, 58 (Feb. 1973), pp. 161–8. By 'Patrician Society, Plebeian Culture' (1973–4), this was no longer such an issue.

9 Quotations as follows: Thompson, 'Patrician Society', pp. 387, 403; and *Whigs and Hunters*, pp. 262, 264.

10 Both Brewer, *Party Ideology and Popular Politics*, and Money, *Experience and Identity*, come close to meeting this need. See also Nicholas Rogers, 'Aristocratic Clientage, Trade and Independency: Popular Politics in pre-Radical Westminster', in *Past & Present*, 61 (Nov. 1973), pp. 70–106; Rogers, 'Popular Protest in Early-Hanoverian London', ibid., 79 (May 1978), pp. 70–100; John Brewer and John Styles (eds), *An Ungovernable People: The English and their Law in the Seventeenth and Eighteenth Centuries* (London: Hutchinson, 1980).

11 See esp. Thompson, *Making of the English Working Class*, pp. 17–101, and the statement on p. 830f.: 'It was perhaps a unique formation, this British working class of 1832. The slow, piecemeal accretions of capital accumulation had meant that the preliminaries to the Industrial Revolution stretched backwards for hundreds of years. From Tudor times onwards this artisan culture had grown more complex with each phase of technical and social change. Delaney, Dekker, and Nashe: Winstanley and Lilburne: Bunyan and Defoe – all had at times addressed themselves to it. Enriched by the experiences of the seventeenth century, carrying through the eighteenth century the intellectual and libertarian traditions which we have described, forming their own traditions of mutuality in the friendly society and trades club, these men did not pass, in one generation, from the peasantry to the new industrial town. They suffered the experience of the Industrial Revolution as articulate, free-born Englishmen.' The statements concerning popular ideology are more specific in the earlier than in the more recent work.

12 See esp. the two excellent case studies: Roger Wells, 'The Revolt of the South-West, 1800–1801: A Study in English Popular Protest', in *Social History*, 2 (1977), pp. 713–44; Alan Booth, 'Food Riots in the North-West of England 1790–1801', in *Past & Present*, 77 (Nov. 1977), pp. 84–107.

13 Thompson, 'Eighteenth-century English Society', p. 165.

14 Ibid., p. 143.

15 Nicholas Rogers, 'Money, Land and Lineage: The Big Bourgeoisie of Hanoverian London', in *Social History*, 4 (1979), pp. 437–54.

16 Thompson, 'Eighteenth-century English Society', p. 163f.

17 For Thompson's own explanation, ibid., p. 145, n. 25; and for a useful discussion of contemporary connotations, Brewer, *Party Ideology*, p. 235f.

18 Thompson, 'Eighteenth-century English Society', p. 145.

19 Ibid., p. 151.

20 Ibid., p. 150.

21 Gwyn A. Williams, *Artisans and Sans-Culottes. Popular Movements in France and Britain during the French Revolution* (London: Edward Arnold, 1968), p. 18.

22 Ibid., p. 66.

23 Thompson, *Making of the English Working Class*, p. 20.

24 Ibid., p. 20f.

25 Thomas Paine, *Rights of Man*, ed. Henry Collins (Harmondsworth: Penguin, 1969), p. 148.

26 See above all Anderson, *Arguments*, together with the works cited in note 6 above. See also Harvey J. Kaye, *The British Marxist Historians* (Cambridge: Polity, 1984), esp. pp. 167–220; and Ellen Meiksins Wood, 'The Politics of Theory and the Concept of Class: E. P. Thompson and His Critics', *Studies in Political Economy*, 9 (1982), pp. 45–75.

27 For an introduction to these processes, see Perry Anderson, *In the Tracks of Historical Materialism* (London: Verso, 1983); and Stuart Hall, 'Cultural Studies and the Centre: Some Problematics and Problems', in Hall et al. (eds), *Culture, Media, Language* (London: Hutchinson, 1980), pp. 15–48.

28 At the same time, *The Making of the English Working Class* was a strong influence on early feminist history of the late 1960s/early 1970s, notably the pioneering work of Sheila Rowbotham. On Thompson, see Catherine Hall's essay in this volume. More generally, see Sally Alexander, 'Women, Class and Sexual Differences in the 1830s and 1840s: Some Reflections on the Writing of a Feminist History' in *History Workshop Journal*, 17 (Spring 1984), pp. 125–49; and Sonya A. Rose, 'Gender at Work: Sex, Class and Industrial Capitalism', ibid., 21 (Spring 1986), pp. 113–31.

29 Gareth Stedman Jones, *Languages of Class. Studies in English Working-Class History 1832–1982* (Cambridge: Cambridge University Press, 1983), p. 7.

30 See in general, Iorwerth Prothero, *Artisans and Politics in Early Nineteenth-century London. John Gast and his Times* (Folkestone: Dawson, 1979); Clive Behagg, 'Custom, Class and Change: the Trade Societies of Birmingham', in *Social History*, 4 (1979), pp. 455–80.

31 Prothero, *Artisans*, p. 5.

32 Thompson, *Making of the English Working Class*, pp. 193ff., 264.

33 This is especially true of the generalizing final chapter on 'class-consciousness': ibid., esp. p. 774.

34 Like Francis Place, John Gast could be scathing in his denunciations of the ignorance, brutality and fecklessness of the labouring poor: see especially Prothero, *Artisans*, pp. 298, 331.

35 For references to this general literature, see ibid., pp. 1–8, 332–40. For

representative examples: Robert J. Bezucha, 'The "Pre-Industrial" Worker Movement: the *Canuts* of Lyons', in Bezucha (ed.), *Modern European Social History* (Lexington, Mass.: D. C. Heath, 1972), pp. 93–123; Joan Wallach Scott, *The Glassworkers of Carmaux. French Craftsmen and Political Action in a Nineteenth-century City* (Cambridge, Mass.: Harvard University Press, 1974); William H. Sewell, 'Social Change and the Rise of Working-class Politics in Nineteenth-century Marseilles', in *Past and Present*, 65 (Nov. 1974), pp. 75–109; Donald H. Bell, 'Worker Culture and Worker Politics: The Experience of an Italian Town, 1880–1915', in *Social History*, 3 (1978), pp. 1–22.

36 See especially Gareth Stedman Jones, 'Class Struggle and the Industrial Revolution', in *Languages of Class*, pp. 50ff.

37 Thompson, *Making of the English Working Class*, p. 194.

38 Robert Gray, 'The Deconstruction of the English Working Class', in *Social History*, 11 (1986), p. 369; Stedman Jones, 'Rethinking Chartism', in *Languages of Class*, p. 95, n. 10.

39 The main critiques from this point of view (as opposed to a more sympathetic one, such as Gray's) have been: John Foster, 'The Declassing of Language', in *New Left Review*, 150 (March–April 1985), pp. 29–45; Dorothy Thompson, 'The Languages of Class', in *Bulletin of the Society for the Study of Labour History*, 52, Part 1 (1987), pp. 54–7; Neville Kirk, 'In Defence of Class. A Critique of Recent Revisionist Writing upon the Nineteenth-Century English Working Class', in *International Review of Social History*, 32 (1987), pp. 2–47; Ellen Meiksins Wood, *The Retreat from Class. A New 'True' Socialism* (London: Verso, 1986), pp. 102–15.

40 In fact, Stedman Jones is ambiguous on this score. He disclaims any desire to 'obliterate the significance of the social historian', wishing only to 'locate[s] its significance in a different perspective' (*Languages of Class*, p. 24). But on the other hand, his detailed account removes Chartist political language rather completely from material context, and it is unclear how he now sees the place of social history.

41 Michael Vester, *Die Entstehung des Proletariats als Lernprozess* (Frankfurt: Europäische Verlagsanstalt, 1970), p. 21f. The key theoretical text, which sought to extend and recast Habermas's framework to the problem of working-class emancipation, is Oskar Negt and Alexander Kluge, *Öffentlichkeit und Erfahrung: Zur Organisationsanalyse von bürgerlicher und proletarischer Öffentlichkeit* (Frankfurt: Suhrkamp, 1972). Though emblematic for a major current of West German social history, it has had absolutely no impact in the English-speaking world, including (rather surprisingly) the various Habermas discussions in *New German Critique*. More generally, the public sphere discussion has attracted no attention among historians of the British working class, with the exception of Francis Hearn, *Domination, Legitimation, and Resistance. The Incorporation of the Nineteenth-Century English Working Class* (Westport, Conn.: Greenwood Press, 1978), an unfortunate exercise in sociological schematism.

42 Richard Johnson, 'Notes on the Schooling of the English Working Class 1780–1850', in Roger Dale et al. (eds), *Schooling and Capitalism. A*

Sociological Reader (London: Edward Arnold, 1967), p. 49.

43 On the other hand, working-class politicians could be equally hostile to the brutality and waste of many 'traditional' recreations and activities. The social history of leisure has not been unmarked by a misplaced romance of suppressed popular vitality. For some acute observations on this theme, see Gareth Stedman Jones, 'Class Expression versus Social Control? A Critique of Recent Trends in the Social History of "Leisure"', in *Languages of Class*, pp. 76–89.

44 John Dinwiddy, 'Luddism and Politics in the Northern Counties', in *Social History*, 4 (1979), p. 63.

45 See esp. Iorwerth Prothero, 'William Benbow and the Concept of the "General Strike"', in *Past & Present*, 63 (May 1974), pp. 132–71; and Stedman Jones, 'Class Struggle and the Industrial Revolution', pp. 57–62.

46 F. C. Mather, *Chartism* (London: Historical Association, 1965), p. 8.

47 This distinction was drawn by Dorothy Thompson in a paper given in Cambridge to the Social History Seminar in March 1978, entitled 'The geography of Chartism', but does not emerge with striking clarity from her synthetic account in *The Chartists. Popular Politics in the Industrial Revolution* (London: Temple Smith, 1984). But see esp. pp. 106–19, 173–233, 237–70, and for a tabulation of the 'Location and timing of Chartist activity', the Appendix, pp. 341–68. Also see the companion volume of essays, James Epstein and Dorothy Thompson (eds), *The Chartist Experience. Studies in Working-Class Radicalism and Culture, 1830–1860* (London: Macmillan, 1982), which is the best guide to current research.

48 Stedman Jones, 'Class Struggle and the Industrial Revolution', p. 57.

49 David Vincent (ed.), *Testaments of Radicalism. Memoirs of Working-Class Politicians 1790–1885* (London: Europa Publications, 1977), p. 11. For full sources, see Joel H. Wiener, *A Descriptive Finding List of Unstamped British Periodicals, 1830–1836* (London: The Bibliographical Society, 1970); Patricia Hollis, *The Pauper Press: A Study in Working-class Radicalism of the 1830s* (Oxford: Oxford University Press, 1970); Wiener, *The War of the Unstamped* (Ithaca, NY: Cornell University Press, 1969).

50 David Jones, *Chartism and the Chartists* (London: Allen Lane, 1975), p. 97.

51 The preceding is based on the excellent summary, ibid., pp. 94ff.

52 Vincent (ed.), *Testaments*, p. 11. For the full context of Chartist and working-class literacy, see the other works of David Vincent: *Bread, Knowledge and Freedom. A Study of Nineteenth-Century Working-Class Autobiography* (London: Europa, 1981), pp. 109–95; 'The Decline of the Oral Tradition in Popular Culture', in Robert D. Storch (ed.), *Popular Culture and Custom in Nineteenth-century England* (London: Croom Helm, 1982), pp. 20–47; 'Communication, Community and the State', in Clive Emsley and James Walvin (eds), *Artisans, Peasants and Proletarians 1760–1860. Essays Presented to Gwyn A. Williams* (London: Croom Helm, 1985), pp. 166–86.

53 Eric J. Hobsbawm, 'Labour Traditions', in *Labouring Men. Studies in the History of Labour* (London: Weidenfeld & Nicolson, 1968), p. 372f.

54 For this distinction, see Richard Johnson, '"Really Useful Knowledge":

Radical Education and Working-Class Culture, 1790–1848', in Clarke, Critcher and Johnson (eds), *Working-Class Culture*, pp. 75–102.

55 Hobsbawm, 'Labour Traditions', p. 373f. Of course, since the late 1970s Hobsbawm's comparison with the PCF has become much less persuasive, though without diminishing its pertinence for the earlier post-war period. For an excellent further discussion of nonconformity, see Robert Moore, *Pit-Men, Preachers and Politics. The Effects of Methodism in a Durham Mining Community* (Cambridge: Cambridge University Press, 1974); and for an important qualification, Edward Thompson, 'On History, Sociology and Historical Relevance', in *British Journal of Sociology*, 27 (1976), pp. 387–402.

56 See especially Eileen Yeo, 'Robert Owen and Radical Culture', in Sidney Pollard and John Salt (eds), *Robert Owen. Prophet of the Poor* (London: Macmillan, 1971), pp. 104ff.

57 Jones, *Chartism and the Chartists*, pp. 77–113.

58 Ibid., p. 77, also for the following.

59 Yeo, 'Robert Owen', pp. 103, 96, 99, 101, 105. See the same author's 'Christianity in Chartist Struggle 1838–1842', in *Past & Present*, 91 (May 1981), pp. 99–139; and 'Some Practices and Problems of Chartist Democracy', in Epstein and Thompson (eds), *Chartist Experience*, pp. 345–80. Aspects of the 'movement culture' are also dealt with in James Epstein, 'Some Organisational and Cultural Aspects of the Chartist Movement in Nottingham', ibid., pp. 221–68; and Paul A. Pickering, 'Class without Words: Symbolic Communication in the Chartist Movement', in *Past & Present*, 112 (Aug. 1986), pp. 144–62. The role of women in the movement is a major question, which is not dealt with explicitly in the current essay. Dorothy Thompson and others have argued that working-class women were actively displaced and marginalized from the politics and institutional culture of Chartism – partly as the communally-based protests of the eighteenth century gave way to the organized movements of the nineteenth, partly via the social and ideological construction of a female domestic sphere in contradistinction to the male world of aspiring citizenship and public agency, and partly through the emergent masculinist ideology of the family wage. Thus, just as working-class men were declaring themselves responsible political subjects in the 1830s and 1840s, as Sally Alexander has argued, working-class women became condemned to public silence. However impressive the Chartists' oppositional public sphere and accompanying sense of counter-community, therefore, they none the less engendered a working-class political tradition predicated on the subordination of women. As Barbara Taylor has shown, this contrasted with the culture of Owenism, which was more radical in its approach to relations between the sexes and the conduct of personal life. See especially Hall, 'Tale of Samuel and Jemima'; Dorothy Thompson, 'Women in Nineteenth-century Radical Politics', in Juliet Mitchell and Anne Oakley (eds), *The Rights and Wrongs of Women* (Harmondsworth: Penguin, 1976), pp. 112–38, and *The Chartists*, pp. 120–51; Vincent, *Bread, Knowledge and Freedom*, pp. 39–107; Alexander, 'Women, Class and Sexual Differences'; Rose, 'Sex, Class and Industrial Capitalism'; Barbara Taylor, *Eve and the New Jerusalem. Socialism and Feminism in the Nineteenth Century* (New York: Pantheon, 1983). For a

major study of the relationship between gender and culture in the formation of the middle class in this period, see now Leonore Davidoff and Catherine Hall, *Family Fortunes. Men and Women of the English Middle Class 1780–1850* (London: Hutchinson, 1987).

60 David I. Kertzer, *Comrades and Christians. Religion and Political Struggle in Communist Italy* (Cambridge: Cambridge University Press, 1980), pp. 131–68. See also the reflections scattered through Maria Antonietta Macciocchi, *Letters from Inside the Italian Communist Party to Louis Althusser* (London: NLB, 1973).

61 See especially the account of a Chartist celebration cited by Jones, *Chartism and the Chartists*, p. 78f. For Thompson's description of the 'Village Politician', taken from a satirical sketch of 1849, see *Making of the English Working Class*, pp. 183–5. In general, see Vincent, *Bread, Knowledge and Freedom*, pp. 14–38.

62 Vincent (ed.), *Testaments*, pp. 17, 144.

63 John Foster, *Class Struggle and the Industrial Revolution. Early Industrial Capitalism in three English Towns* (London: Weidenfeld & Nicolson, 1974), pp. 47–72.

64 'Educational Policy and Social Control in Early Victorian England', in *Past & Present*, 49 (Nov. 1970), pp. 96–119; '"Really Useful Knowledge"'; 'Notes on the Schooling of the English Working Class'.

65 Johnson, '"Really Useful Knowledge"', p. 50.

66 As Johnson says: 'Struggle of some kind was possible, of course, in every type of school or institute, but there were also whole areas that were relatively immune from direct intervention or compulsion by capital or capital's agencies. We include, then, the educational resources of family, neighbourhood, and even place of work, whether within the household or outside it, the acquisition of literacy from mothers or fathers, the use of the knowledgeable friend or neighbour, or the "scholar" in neighbouring town or village, the workplace discussion and formal and informal apprenticeships, the extensive networks of private schools and, in many cases, the local Sunday schools, most un-school-like of the new devices, excellently adapted to working-class needs.' At the same time, 'Radicals made their own cultural inventions. These included the various kinds of communal reading and discussion groups, the facilities for newspapers in pub, coffee house or reading room, the broader cultural politics of Chartist or Owenite branch-life, the institution of the travelling lecturer who, often indistinguishable from "missionary" or demagogue, toured the radical centres, and, above all, the radical press, the most successful radical invention and an extremely flexible (and therefore ubiquitous) educational form.' See '"Really Useful Knowledge"', p. 80. For a wonderful evocation of this milieu, see Gwyn A. Williams, *Rowland Detrosier, A Working-Class Infidel, 1800–1834* (York: St Anthony's Press, 1965).

67 Johnson, '"Really Useful Knowledge"', p. 101, also for the following.

68 See Quintin Hoare and Geoffrey Nowell Smith (eds), *Selections from the Prison Notebooks of Antonio Gramsci* (London: Lawrence & Wishart, 1971), esp. pp. 3–43. Of course, in some places Chartism could also build on the prior formation of a radical popular intelligentsia going back to the late

eighteenth century, notably London and the provincial centres of English Jacobinism. We now have a sequence of major books on London's radical culture between the 1780s and 1840s, which collectively allow us to pose the question in 'Gramscian' terms. Aside from Prothero, *Artisans*, see the following: Günther Lottes, *Politische Aufklärung und plebejisches Publikum. Zur Theorie und Praxis des englischen Radikalismus im späten 18. Jahrhundert* (Munich and Vienna: Oldenbourg, 1979); J. Ann Hone, *For the Cause of Truth: Radicalism in London, 1796–1821* (Oxford: Oxford University Press, 1982); David Goodway, *London Chartism 1838–1848* (Cambridge: Cambridge University Press, 1982); Ian McCalman, *Radical Underworld. Prophets, Revolutionaries and Pornographers in London, 1795–1840* (Cambridge: Cambridge University Press, 1988). Of these, the most explicitly conceptual is Lottes (whose book badly needs a translator), the most imaginative McCalman. See in addition the latter's 'Unrespectable Radicalism: Infidels and Pornography in Early Nineteenth-century London', in *Past & Present*, 104 (Aug. 1984), pp. 74–110. See also Noel W. Thompson, *The People's Science. The Popular Political Economy of Exploitation and Crisis 1816–34* (Cambridge: Cambridge University Press, 1984).

69 Dorothy Thompson, 'Friendliness and Formalization', in *Times Literary Supplement*, 18 September 1977.

70 Alastair Reid, 'Politics and Economics in the Formation of the British Working Class: A Response to H. F. Moorhouse', in *Social History* 3 (1978), pp. 359–61. This is not incompatible with Thompson's own approach, it should be said.

71 For comparisons we must go forward to the less substantial and finely textured radicalisms of 1917–26 and 1939–45, or abroad to German Social Democracy before 1914 and Italian Communism after 1943. Other examples can obviously be found.

72 Eric Hobsbawm, 'Religion and the Rise of Socialism', in *Workers. Worlds & Labor* (New York: Pantheon, 1984), p. 39f. The stress on external intervention is reminiscent of Perry Anderson's powerful indictment of the 'corporateness' of the English working class – seeking 'to defend and improve its own positions within a social order accepted as given', pursuing 'its own ends within a social totality whose global determination lies outside it', and 'essentially characterized by an extreme disjunction between an intense consciousness of separate identity and a permanent failure to set and impose goals for society as a whole'. See Perry Anderson, 'Origins of the Present Crisis', in Perry Anderson and Robin Blackburn (eds), *Towards Socialism* (London: Collins, 1966), p. 33. Where this leaves the putative ability of the working class to generate its own culture is unclear, for Anderson's analysis leaves it structurally imprisoned in an iron cage of hegemonic domination, vulnerable only to the corrosion of an oppositionist intelligentsia. See Edward Thompson, 'The Peculiarities of the English', in *The Poverty of Theory* (London: Merlin, 1978), pp. 35–91. However, while Thompson exposed weaknesses in Anderson's argument, the fundamental point about working-class subordination remains largely intact as a commentary on post-Chartist history. For a similar analysis which appears to owe much to Anderson's

approach, see John Saville, 'The Ideology of Labourism', in Robert Benewick et al. (eds), *Knowledge and Belief in Politics. The Problem of Ideology* (London: Allen & Unwin, 1973), pp. 213–36. For the fuller context of such discussion, see the citations in note 1 above.

73 For the problem of the labour aristocracy and possible alternative processes, see the exchange between Reid and Moorhouse: H. F. Moorhouse, 'The Marxist Theory of the Labour Aristocracy', in *Social History*, 3 (1978), pp. 61–82; Reid, 'Politics and Economics'; with subsequent contributions by Moorhouse (4, 1979, pp. 481–90), Reid (ibid., pp. 491–3), Gregor McLennan (6, 1981, pp. 71–81), and Moorhouse again (6, 1981, pp. 229–33). There are fine critical surveys of the debate in Robert Gray, *The Aristocracy of Labour in Nineteenth-century Britain c. 1850–1914* (London: Macmillan, 1981), and Gregor McLennan, *Marxism and the Methodologies of History* (London: NLB, 1981), pp. 206–32. Hobsbawm, who originally pioneered the analytical use of the idea in an essay of 1954, has returned to it in three essays in *Workers*, pp. 214–72. See also the related exchange between Moorhouse and Gray on 'The Political Incorporation of the Working Class', in *Sociology*, 7 (1973), pp. 341–59, and 10 (1975), pp. 101–10; and the one between Richard Price and Patrick Joyce on the relative value of an approach based on the labour process, *Social History*, 8 (1983), pp. 57–75, and 9 (1984), pp. 67–76, 217–31. See also Derek Gregory, 'Contours of Crisis? Sketches for a Geography of Class Struggle in the Early Industrial Revolution in England', in Alan R. H. Baker and Derek Gregory (eds), *Explorations in Historical Geography. Interpretative Essays* (Cambridge: Cambridge University Press, 1984), pp. 68–117.

74 Stedman Jones, 'Class Struggle and the Industrial Revolution', pp. 47ff.

75 John Vincent, *The Formation of the Liberal Party, 1857–1868* (London: Constable, 1966).

76 There are naturally some key exceptions. By far the most important work to appear on the subject is Davidoff and Hall, *Family Fortunes*. See also Mark Billinge, 'Hegemony, Class and Power in Late Georgian and Early Victorian England: Towards a Cultural Geography', in Baker and Gregory (eds), *Explorations*, pp. 28–67; Janet Wolff and John Seed (eds), *The Culture of Capital: Art, Power and the Nineteenth-Century Middle Class* (Manchester: Manchester University Press, 1988); John Seed, 'Unitarianism, Political Economy and the Antinomies of Liberal Culture in Manchester, 1830–1850', in *Social History*, 7 (1982), pp. 1–25; Ian Inkster and Jack Morrell (eds), *Metropolis and Province. Science in British Culture 1780–1850* (Philadelphia: University of Pennsylvania Press, 1983); Foster, *Class Struggle*, esp. pp. 161ff. See also Robert Gray, 'Bourgeois Hegemony in Victorian Britain', in John Bloomfield (ed.), *Class, Hegemony and Party* (London: Lawrence & Wishart, 1977), pp. 73–94.

77 Ernesto Laclau, 'Towards a Theory of Populism', in *Politics and Ideology in Marxist Theory* (London: NLB, 1977), p. 161.

78 Gray, 'Bourgeois Hegemony', p. 85.

2

How Classes are Made: Critical Reflections on E. P. Thompson's Theory of Working-class Formation

William H. Sewell, Jr

E. P. Thompson's *The Making of the English Working Class* is the obligatory starting point for any contemporary discussion of the history of working-class formation. The general transformation and revitalization of labour history over the past two decades can be read as a dialogue with Thompson; *The Making of the English Working Class* effectively set the agenda for an entire generation of labour historians.[1]

It is worth recalling how much this book enriched and enlarged our conception of working-class history. In the two or three decades prior to its publication in 1963, studies of the working class had been confined primarily to four established genres: histories of labour unions and labour parties, biographies of labour leaders, histories of socialist doctrines and investigations of 'the condition of the workers', conceived almost exclusively as a question of the rise or fall in workers' material standards of living. My first reading of *The Making of the English Working Class*, when I was a graduate student at Berkeley in 1964, produced a kind of revelation. I was already dissatisfied with the narrow focus of most existing labour history and determined to find some way to get at a broader range of workers' experiences. Yet I was astounded by the sheer mass of 'ethnographic' detail about workers that Thompson had collected. Thompson's version of working-class history included not only trade unions, socialist doctrines and real wages, but popular political and religious traditions, workshop rituals, back-room insurrectionary conspiracies, popular ballads, millenarian preaching, anonymous threatening letters, Methodist hymns, dog fights, trade festivals, country dances, strike fund subscription lists, beggars' tricks, artisans' houses of call, the iconography of trade banners, farmers' account books, weavers' gardens, and so on in endless profusion. For me, and for a whole generation of young historians, the horizons of working-class history – and of history in general – were suddenly and enormously expanded. We were launched by Thompson into the major historiographical project of the past twenty years – 'history from below'. This revolutionary enlargement of the scope of working-class history has been Thompson's greatest achievement.[2]

In *The Making of the English Working Class*, Thompson avoids an explicit statement of his theoretical argument about class formation – except, in somewhat cryptic form, in his preface. At the time, he was in full flight from Stalinist formalism and did not want his readers to be able to reduce his book to a set of abstract propositions.[3] His crucial contention was that the emergence of the working class was a product of the complex and contradictory *experience* of workers in the turbulent years from 1790 to 1832, and that it could not be understood apart from that experience. The genius of his long, sprawling, picaresque, Dickensian narrative was to give his readers some semblance of the workers' experience – to make them participate vicariously in the suffering, the heroism, the tedium, the outrage, the sense of loss and the sense of discovery that constituted the formation of the working class. The result is the greatest literary *tour de force* in recent historiography.

The narrative is, to be sure, informed by theoretical notions about class formation, but theory is usually present by implication, woven into and only occasionally emerging out of Thompson's rich tapestry of working-class experience. Thompson's one explicit theoretical statement in the book – his preface – has been enormously influential; it may be the most frequently cited preface since Marx's preface to *A Contribution to the Critique of Political Economy*. It has been a potent resource for validating historical approaches to class and a ready argument against any simple-minded economic determinism. It has also formed a handy authorized interpretation of the theoretical implications of a book whose scale, complexity, denseness and resolute concreteness makes the drawing of such implications difficult. But in spite of the preface's importance, much of what Thompson says there is either unclear or theoretically problematic. Moreover, the preface is by no means a sufficient theoretical account of his historical practice. Some of the most important implicit theoretical innovations of *The Making of the English Working Class* remain completely unvoiced in its preface.

The object of this chapter is to state and evaluate Thompson's theory of class formation. I shall subject Thompson's explicit theory, mainly as set forth in his preface, to a close reading and critical analysis, attempting to demonstrate its inadequacy both as a theory and as an account of what he has achieved in his book. I shall also attempt to tease at least some implicit theoretical notions out of his narrative of class formation, and to suggest my own amendments, critiques and reformulations. This entire exercise should perhaps be seen as an effort to explain to myself how and why I have always found this extraordinary book at once deeply inspiring and deeply mystifying.

The Theory of Class Formation in Thompson's Preface

I shall try to set forth the major theoretical propositions contained in the preface of *The Making* briefly and somewhat formally.

Class is an historical phenomenon

In opposition to the deductive formalism of Stalinists and the static definitions of structural-functional sociologists, Thompson insists that class is essentially historical.

> I do not see class as a 'structure', nor even as a 'category', but as something which in fact happens (and can be shown to have happened) in human relationships.[4]
>
> If we stop history at a given point, then there are no classes but simply a multitude of individuals with a multitude of experiences. But if we watch these men over an adequate period of social change, we observe patterns in their relationships, their ideas, and their institutions. Class is defined by men as they live their own history, and, in the end, this is its only definition.[5]
>
> ... The notion of class entails the notion of historical relationship. Like any other relationship, it has a fluency which evades analysis if we attempt to stop it dead at any given moment and anatomize its structure.[6]

These passages enunciate a vigorous conception of the essential historicity of class. For Thompson class exists *only* in time, and consequently can only be known historically. Non-historical approaches to class necessarily distort, perhaps even obliterate, their object.

Class is an outcome of experience

Thompson's insistence on the primacy of experience in class formation was a reaction against Stalinist formulations, which tended to be highly abstract and deductive. Thompson characterized Stalinist practice as follows:

'It', the working class, is assumed to have a real existence, which can be defined almost mathematically – so many men who stand in a certain relation to the means of production. Once this is assumed it becomes possible to deduce the class-consciousness which 'it' ought to have (but seldom does have) if 'it' was properly aware of its own position and real interests.[7]

Thompson took the opposite tack, insisting, as we have seen, that 'class is defined by men as they live their own history, and, in the end, this is its only definition'. 'Experience', I would argue, is the central – and the most problematic – theoretical concept in *The Making of the English Working Class*, as well as the key to its narrative strategy. Thompson's discovery and adumbration of working-class experience, his ability to ferret out, interpret and convey the textures and meanings of working-class lives, is the greatest triumph of his book.

Workers are active and conscious participants in class formation

The Making of the English Working Class, as Thompson puts it, 'is a study of an active process, which owes as much to agency as to conditioning. The working class did not rise like the sun at an appointed time. It was present at its own making.'[8] That this now seems self-evident is an indication of *The Making*'s influence. At the time Thompson wrote, most Marxist argumentation about class formation was highly determinist: factories produced a proletariat almost as mechanically as they produced cloth or rails. Even non-Stalinist labour historians showed little curiosity about what workers actually felt, said, wrote and did. The conventional forms of historiography enabled them to write biographies of Fergus O'Connor or Jean Jaurès, or to write institutional histories of trade unions or the Independent Labour Party, but before Thompson, no one knew how to write the history of a *class*. One of Thompson's lasting contributions to historiography was to show how workers could be given voices and wills and could be constituted as a collective agent in an historical narrative.[9]

Class is defined by consciousness

'Class', Thompson writes,

> happens when some men, as a result of common experiences (inherited or shared), *feel* and *articulate* the identity of their interests

as between themselves, and as against other men whose interests are different from (and usually opposed to) theirs.[10]

It is not the 'objective' identity of interests that makes a class, but rather the feeling and articulating of an identity. No consciousness, no class. Once again, this point is part of Thompson's polemic against Stalinism, which, he claims, defined class 'mathematically' as 'so many men who stand in a certain relation to the means of production', and then *deduced* class-consciousness from this definition.[11] Thompson, by denying that class exists apart from real people's consciousness, the awareness of their common interests, radically shifted the problematic of class-formation by pushing to the fore the question of how this awareness came about historically. Class-consciousness became not a corollary deducible from the real (economic) existence of class, but rather an historical achievement of workers who pondered their experiences and who constructed (with the collaboration of sympathetic intellectuals) a vocabulary and conceptual framework through which their identity as a class could be thought and actualized.

A Critique of Thompson's Theory

These four propositions form the core of Thompson's theory. Taken together, they mark a significant re-working of the problematic of class formation – one whose overall value as a stimulus to research and as a corrective to pre-existing approaches can hardly be disputed. Yet what Thompson's preface provides is less a systematic alternative theory of class formation than a set of admonitions whose value is largely determined by their place in a specific polemic. Thompson admonishes us to avoid sterile formalisms and to be ever aware that the 'making' of the working class was a temporal human process, lived out in the experiences of real men and women. But he tells us very little about how we might structure an account of class formation theoretically – or, indeed, about how he has structured his own account. In fact, as I shall argue below, Thompson implicitly assumes the essential correctness of precisely the theory of class formation that he seems to be denying. Thompson's explicit theoretical reflections are so fixed upon his polemical opponent that he fails to articulate his own transcendence of classical Marxism.

Determination

Thompson's entanglement with his polemical opponent is nowhere clearer than in his statements about determination. His championing of working-class agency and his rejection of the classical Marxist metaphor of the determining economic base and the determined cultural and political superstructure has done much to free labour history from the bonds of a rigid economic determinism. Yet Thompson's own theory of how class formation is determined remains highly ambiguous. His most general statement is in the preface of *The Making of the English Working Class*.

> Class happens when some men, as a result of common experiences (inherited or shared), feel and articulate the identity of their interests as between themselves, and as against other men whose interests are different from (and usually opposed to) theirs. The class experience is largely determined by the productive relations into which men are born – or enter involuntarily. Class-consciousness is the way in which these experiences are handled in cultural terms: embodied in traditions, value-systems, ideas and institutional forms. If the experience appears as determined, class-consciousness does not. We can see a *logic* in the responses of similar occupational groups undergoing similar experiences, but we cannot predicate any *law*. Consciousness of class arises in the same way in different times and places, but never in *just* the same way.[12]

For all its particular accents, this passage appears to be stating a theory of determination of a recognizably Marxist type. Economic relations (or class-in-itself) generate a set of class experiences, and these experiences give rise to class-consciousness (class-for-itself). In its general form, this is very close to the classical Marxist formulation – say, in the *Communist Manifesto* – where exploitative capitalist economic relations give rise to class struggles through which the proletariat becomes conscious of itself as a class with the historical destiny of abolishing the exploitation of man by man. But there are important differences.

First, for Thompson it is class *experience* that provides the historical mediation between productive relations and class-consciousness, whereas for classical Marxism it is class *struggle*. Class struggle – political movements, union organizing, workshop conflicts, strikes and boycotts – is a crucially important form of class experience for Thompson. But his notion of class experience is vastly broader. It includes the whole range of workers' subjective responses to their exploitation – not only in movements of struggle, but in their families and communities, in their leisure-time activities, in their religious practices and beliefs, in their workshops and weaving-sheds, and so on. Between the hard facts of productive relations and the discovery of class-consciousness lies the vast, multiple, contradictory realm of experience, not the neat and unidirectional process of learning-the-truth-through-struggle posited by classical Marxism.

Thompson's second difference from classical Marxism, not surprising given the amorphousness of his mediating term, is a much looser theory of determination. The process of class formation is not driven by inexorable laws of history. Class experience, he affirms, *is* determined by the productive relations into which men are born or enter involuntarily – although he qualifies this determination with the modifiers 'largely' or 'appears as'. The way these experiences are 'handled in cultural terms' is determined far more loosely. It is, apparently, in the cultural handling of class experience that human agency enters the picture decisively – with the consequence that we can predicate no 'law' of the development of class-consciousness. A weaker form of determination is retained, however; there is some sort of parallel 'logic' at work in the development of class consciousness even if there is no 'law'. Thompson keeps the directionality of the classical Marxist account – the causation moves from economic relations, to social experience, and thence to consciousness. But the determination is much weaker – productive relations determine experience largely, but presumably not fully, and class experience determines consciousness yet more loosely. Thompson's account leaves plenty of room, within broadly determined limits, for the exercise of human agency and the vagaries of human experience.

But in spite of his denial of a base–superstructure model of society, Thompson really offers no alternative to an economic determinist theory of class formation. He assigns a significant role to human agency and experience, but this simply loosens the causal linkages to the form of probabilistic laws rather than absolute 'iron laws'; no non-economic cause of the rise of class-consciousness is introduced into the account, simply a variation in how consciousness will arise in different times and places. Moreover, in this sketch of the class-formation process, Thompson implicitly affirms what he elsewhere denies: that class is, in fact, present in the economic structure independently of the workers' consciousness or lack of consciousness of class. If workers' experiences produce class-consciousness, rather than some other sort of consciousness, this is because their experiences are *class* experiences. And if these class experiences are determined, as Thompson asserts, by productive relations, then these productive relations must be *class* productive relations, prior, in a logical sense, to the class experiences which they generate. And if the class-consciousness that arises the same way in different times and places follows a single logic, this implies that the class experiences, and hence the class productive relations that determine them, must have an even more unified single logic. In short, we are led to capitalism as conceived by Marx – a system of productive relations with a unitary logic wherever it appears. Now this ought to be perfectly acceptable in a Marxist work, but it in fact puts Thompson in a very tight conceptual spot. If he intends this sort of account of class formation, how can he deny that class exists *in the productive relations themselves*? It seems utterly metaphysical and arbitrary to deny the presence of class in the productive relations yet affirm its presence in the experiences and the consciousness that those productive relations generate.

Thompson's explanatory account of class formation, thus, turns out to contradict implicitly certain of his major theoretical propositions. In his preface Thompson attempts to outline a novel approach that assigns a much greater than usual role to experience, agency and consciousness, and that abandons the deductive base–superstructure model of his Stalinist–Marxist predecessors. But he also, in the passage I have been analysing here, embraces the old determinist model even while he is attempting to surpass it. The classical Marxist schemata of base–superstructure and the movement from class-in-itself to class-for-itself thus implicitly underlie and structure his account of working-class experience, agency and consciousness, but do so in unacknowledged and unexamined fashion.

This problem appears in *The Making of the English Working Class* on a narrative and empirical as well as a theoretical level. Although Thompson explicitly disavows economic determinism, he also assumes it as a kind of unconscious rhetorical backdrop against which specific empirical accounts of working-class experience, agency and consciousness are placed and assigned their significance. Or, to change the metaphor, economic determinism acts in *The Making* as a kind of hidden dynamo that, unknown to the actors and felt rather than seen by the author and reader, propels the narrative in a certain direction. By suppressing but unconsciously retaining economic determinism, Thompson cleared a vast narrative space that could be filled almost exclusively by specific accounts of working-class experience, agency and consciousness, untroubled, yet globally shaped by the underlying rhythm of a classical Marxist movement from class-in-itself to class-for-itself. The result is an account of class formation that, for all its empirical richness and persuasive power, remains elusive and mystifying.

Diachrony and synchrony

Thompson's statements about the historicity of class are in many ways parallel to his statements about determination; once again, his polemical zeal leads him to deny in his theory what he is unable to deny in his practice. Thompson's assertion of the essential historicity of class implies an extremely radical – in my opinion quite untenable – ontological and epistemological position. He appears to be saying not only that class comes into being through an historical process, but that it only *exists* over time. ('If we stop history at a given point *there are no classes* . . .') As an ontological commitment this is perhaps acceptable – in some sense nothing exists except in time. But Thompson appears to draw from this the dubious epistemological conclusion that no synchronic *analysis* of class can be valid. (Class 'evades analysis if we attempt to stop it dead at any given moment and anatomise its structure'.)

This, I think, is mistaken. While class exists in time, it is also necessary as a moment in any adequate historical analysis of class to stop or bracket time, to look at class as a set of synchronic relations – between individuals, between various groups of workers, between workers and their employers, between workers and the means of production, between workers and available ideologies, etc. In contrast to Thompson, I would argue that the notion of *relationship*, which he takes as implying fluency, is in fact profoundly synchronic. To call class a relationship is to imply that we cannot capture it through a purely diachronic narration of events, but that we must pause now and again to describe it as a structure – one that, to be sure, crystallizes out of events and will be transformed by subsequent events. In his polemic against the ahistorical conceptions of Stalinism and structural-functionalism, Thompson appears to have gone beyond the sound position of insisting that an account of class must maintain a dialectic between synchronic and diachronic approaches to embrace pure diachrony.

A moment's thought about the text of *The Making* makes it evident that Thompson's own historical practice is very far from pure diachrony. To begin with, Thompson's Dickensian narrative style, with its omniscient narrator commenting self-consciously on events, is hardly well adapted to pure diachrony. Thompson's theoretical position, if taken seriously, would imply a style of narration more akin to Virginia Woolf's or Robbe-Grille's.[13] Moreover, Thompson's text is, in fact, densely inter-woven with synchronic analyses. This is not to say that Thompson 'stops time' in some literal sense in his text. What we mean when we say that an historian 'stops time' is that she momentarily suspends time by abstracting some pattern, structure or relationship out of the flow of events in order to contemplate, categorize, anatomize or construct it in her mind and in her text. The pattern, structure or relationship will normally be constructed from bits of evidence whose creation was not literally simultaneous but which in some sense fit together, constitute a whole. Certainly, Thompson does this in his brilliant analysis of London artisans when he uses Mayhew's observations from 1849 and 1850 as evidence about the distinction between honourable and dishonourable trades in London in the teens and the twenties.[14] This move is legitimate only because he is building up a synchronic picture of a structure that he regards as having endured in at least important essentials for several decades. In short, Thompson's text, more than many historical texts, is punctuated by synchronic analyses, in spite of his theoretical advocacy of pure diachrony.

One might well object that Thompson is no philosopher, and that he surely does not intend to rule out the kind of practical dialectic between synchrony and diachrony that characterizes his own text. Why should we hold Thompson to the literal meaning of the statements he makes in his preface? But the preface is only one instance of a pervasive theme in Thompson's writings – an adamant refusal of deductive theory that is stated most eloquently (and most brutally) in his attack on Althusser in *The Poverty of Theory*.[15] Whatever one thinks about the relative merits of Althusser and Thompson (if forced to choose I would unhesitatingly take Thompson) it should be noted that Thompson's position tends consistently to stigmatize *explicit* synchronic theorization as illegitimate and unhistorical while refusing to recognize the no less synchronic character of the implicit theorizations in his own narratives. Thompson therefore refuses the possibility of a rational confrontation between his own theories and those of his opponents, in effect ruling them out of court on procedural grounds. In this sense, Thompson's passionate embrace of radical diachrony is as mystifying as his unfulfilled renunciation of a base–superstructure model of determination.

Experience

If the rich narrative portrayal of working-class experience is the great triumph of *The Making of the English Working Class*, the heavy explanatory load placed on the concept of experience is, in my opinion, *The Making*'s cardinal weakness.[16] The meaning of the term 'experience' is so intrinsically amorphous that it is difficult to assign it any delimitable role in a theory of class formation, and Thompson makes matters worse by using it in inconsistent and confusing ways. Quite explicitly in his essay 'Folklore, Anthropology, and Social History', and at least implicity in the preface to *The Making*, Thompson presents experience as *mediating* between productive relations and class-consciousness, or between 'social being' and 'social consciousness'.[17] The problem with such a formulation is that experience appears to encompass both the terms between which it is supposed to mediate. Do 'productive relations' or 'social being' or 'consciousness' exist outside of experience? Any 'social being' that exists outside of experience would have to be a synchronic structure of the kind whose existence Thompson explicitly denies. And consciousness that exists outside of experience would be the kind of deduced consciousness that Stalinists had attributed to the working class. One major triumph of Thompson's narrative of English working-class formation is to portray productive relations not as an abstraction but as the experiences of real men and women. This, it seems to me, is the principal achievement of Part Two of *The Making* ('The Curse of Adam'). Likewise, the 'class-consciousness' described in the final chapter is not a set of abstract and logical doctrines that workers ought to have held, but the concrete experience of Radicals, journalists, autodidact workers and Owenites who wrote and read tracts, handbills and newspaper articles or made speeches in the context of their own political and social struggles and who practised class-consciousness in their own lives. In short, in spite of Thompson's explicit claims to the contrary, experience cannot play a *mediating* role in his account of English working-class formation because, for him, working-class formation is *nothing but* experience.

If experience is a medium in *The Making*, it is a medium not in the sense of 'a substance through which a force acts or an effect is transmitted' (this, Webster's second meaning, would cover mediation between being and consciousness) but 'that through which or by which anything is accomplished' (Webster's third meaning).[18] Rather than mediating *between* social being and consciousness, experience appears in Thompson's account as the medium *in which* theoretical structures are realized (even though Thompson officially denies that these structures exist). The class relations tacitly posited as present in the material base are realized in the medium of human experience – experience of productive relations, of struggles and of consciousness. A tacitly posited synchronic structure works itself out in the real, historical, experienced lives of human actors.

This interpretation of experience as medium seems authorized by a passage in *The Poverty of Theory* where Thompson reflects on the accomplishments of the English Marxist historians (and pre-eminently, it seems clear, of *The Making*). 'We explored', he says, 'those junction concepts (such as "need", "class", and "determine") by which, through the missing term, "experience", *structure is transmuted into process, and the subject re-enters into history*.'[19] Here, quite unambiguously, experience appears as the medium through which structure is realized in actual historical human subjects.

The precise nature of the 'structure' and the way it is realized in experience is not clear in this sentence. But these questions are elaborated on thereafter in a complex and murky passage, which must be quoted at some length.

And at 'experience' we [that is, the English Marxist historians] were led on to re-examine all those dense, complex and elaborated systems by which familial and social life is structured and social consciousness finds realization and expression (systems which the very rigour of the discipline in Ricardo or in the Marx of *Capital* is designed to exclude): kinship, custom, the invisible and visible rules of social regulation, hegemony and deference, symbolic forms of domination and of resistance, religious faith and millenarial impulses, manners, law, institutions and ideologies – all of which, in their sum, comprise the 'genetics' of the whole historical process, all of them joined, at a certain point, in common human experience, which itself (as distinctive *class* experiences) exerts pressure on the sum.[20]

The very opacity and contradictions of this passage are revealing. At first, Thompson seems to be saying that those 'dense, complex and elaborated systems' which could not be understood within the traditional Marxist framework were themselves structures, more or less parallel to the structures (that is, modes of production) which could be grasped in Marxist terms. They are, at least, presented as having the power to structure social life and as being realized in social consciousness. Then he seems to say that these structures must all be understood purely under the category of experience. They are, at least, all 'joined . . . in common human experience'. Thompson then equates this common human experience (made up, remember, of that long string of 'systems' beginning with 'kinship' and ending with 'ideology') with 'distinctive *class* experiences'. In other words, Marxist historians, pursuing an analysis centred on the mode of production, encounter in their research a series of systems that are not reducible to modes of production. But these systems, which together constitute a realm of 'experience', turn out to have in common the fact that they are all class experiences. And since class is itself ultimately determined by the mode of production, this implies that systems not reducible to the mode of production are, nevertheless, in some sense attributable precisely to the mode of production. The passage, in short, seems utterly contradictory.

A clearer but no less distressing picture begins to emerge in the very next paragraph.

But, in my view, we did not discover other, and coexistent, *systems*, of equal status and coherence to the system of (anti-) Political Economy, exerting co-equal pressures: a Kinship Mode, a Symbolic Mode, an Ideological Mode, etc. 'Experience' (we have found) has, in the last instance, been generated in 'material life', has been structured in class ways, and hence 'social being' has determined 'social

consciousness'. *La Structure* still dominates experience but from that
point of view her determinate influence is weak. For any living
generation, in any 'now', the ways in which they 'handle' experience
defies prediction and escapes from any narrow definition of
determination.[21]

Here Thompson seems to be saying that the systems which constitute the
realm of 'experience' (that is, kinship, custom, etc.) are not really systems
after all, at least not of a type parallel to modes of production. These
various crypto-systems are now portrayed as lacking the 'coherence' and
the 'determining pressures' that Thompson attributes to 'the system of
(anti-) Political Economy' – that is Marx's materialist science of the mode
of production. He asserts that the English Marxist historians have 'found'
in their research that experience (including, remember, kinship, custom,
etc.) has in the last instance been 'generated in "material life"' and
'structured in class ways'. These crypto-systems apparently have been
found to have no independent causal dynamics; hence they can be said to
be, ultimately, experienced through class, whence all causal pressure
flows. The crypto-systems that make up 'experience' are themselves an
inert medium; their life is derived entirely from the dynamic of the mode
of production.

    But in what sense have the English Marxist historians 'found' this to be
true? Not in the usual empirical sense that the science of the mode of
production has accounted for most of the observed historical behaviour.
In fact, the empirical finding Thompson trumpets is just the opposite:
that the determinate influence of '*La Structure*' is *weak*. The way in
which any living generation handles experience 'defies prediction and
escapes from any narrow definition of determination'. This is an odd
argument from a fervent advocate of empirical investigation and sworn
enemy of dogmatic *a priori* theorizing. The weakness of the posited
explanation should have driven Thompson to consider that the assortment
of crypto-structures – kinship, law, ideology, and so on – might, as he
initially suggested, have some *independent* explanatory power. But
Thompson has ruled this out, on grounds that obviously are not
empirical, and therefore must be *a priori* theoretical. Faced with only
weak determination by his chosen explanation, he concludes not that
other systems of determination are also operative, but, since only
the mode of production can be regarded as determining, that anything
it cannot explain must be assigned to the vagaries of experience – to
the deep complexities of human existence and the unpredictable operation
of human agency. Ironically, Althusser, with his insistence on the
'relative autonomy' of different levels in a social formation and his notion
of 'overdetermination', here turns out to be more flexible and less

dogmatic than Thompson the anti-dogmatist defender of empirical knowledge.

Once again we arrive at a mystification, at bottom the same mystification that ruled out yet assumed the determination of the superstructure by the base and that suppressed in principle but could not suppress in fact the importance of synchrony in historical analysis. In attempting to specify the nature and role of experience, Thompson returns straight to the theoretically excluded but in fact unexcludable *a priori* Marxist synchronic structure *par excellence*: the mode of production. The vast realms of history not explainable in terms of the dynamic of the mode of production are then relegated to a residual category of 'experience', which is not capable of explanation at all, or at least not in determinate terms. All sorts of systems apparently discoverable in human societies are in fact not systems, but part of the murky and complex medium of 'experience' – the balky, effervescent, cranky, resistant and independent-minded human stuff in which the mode of production very incompletely determines history.

Once again, Thompson's theory obviously does not square with his practice, either in *The Making of the English Working Class* or elsewhere. In his narratives, the various crypto-structures appear as anything but inert, as having their own definable dynamics and their distinct determinate pressures. This is perhaps clearest in *Whigs and Hunters*, where Thompson's eloquent celebration of the 'rule of law' argues precisely that law has its own causal force in history.[22] But the same observation also holds for *The Making*. Such 'systems' as the Paineite tradition, Methodism or institutions of trade solidarity are not merely media for dynamics originating in the mode of production, but palpable causal forces in their own right. By casting all these systems as 'experience', Thompson hides from himself the extent to which his narrative tacitly assumes not only a determination in the last instance by the base of productive relations, but also an overdetermination by a whole series of relatively autonomous cultural, institutional and political systems. In this respect, his tacit model of the architectonics of society is actually very close to Althusser's.

Experience Demystified

Thompson's claims about experience as a theoretical category are so incoherent that one is tempted to discard the term entirely. Yet experience seems an appropriate label for what Thompson has captured so brilliantly in his narrative in *The Making*. It therefore seems worthwhile instead to deflate the concept, to clarify it and extract it from the untenable philosophical claims Thompson makes for it. Restored to something like its usage in ordinary language, experience has a place in the theory of class formation – and in the theory of historical change more generally.

The first step is to disengage the notion of experience from the quite distinct problem of multiple causation. Deviations of historical events from a strict economic determinist model should not automatically be assigned to 'experience', and thereby tacitly explained as consequences of an essentially mysterious human 'agency'. Much of such deviation can be accounted for relatively straightforwardly as the outcome of causal interactions between a diversity of more or less autonomous structures or systems. Experience should be conceptualized much more narrowly, in line with *Webster's*, as 'the actual living through an event or events . . .; actual enjoyment or suffering; hence, the effect upon the judgement or feelings produced by personal and direct impressions . . .; as to know by *experience*.'[23] Although experience may refer merely to the actual 'living through of events', it ordinarily implies an 'effect upon the judgement or feelings', with knowledge as a result. When we call an event an experience, we usually mean that the person who has enjoyed or suffered the event has reflected upon it. Experience, as Clifford Geertz puts it, is something 'construed'.[24] Thompson himself, in *The Poverty of Theory*, at one point gives a definition of experience very similar to that in *Webster's* – before going on to inflate and confuse the concept by arguing that it mediates between social being and consciousness. '*Experience*', he says, 'comprises the mental and emotional response, whether of an individual or of a social group, to many interrelated events or to many repetitions of the same kind of events.'[25] This definition is reasonably clear and specific. It indicates something important but not very mysterious – that people respond mentally and emotionally, both individually and in groups, to what happens to them.

This also seems consistent with Thompson's practice in *The Making of the English Working Class*. His narrative reconstructs not so much the actual events people lived through as the way people construed events as they were living through them. By patiently assembling the surviving documents and carefully attending to judgements and feelings expressed in them, he has rendered the familiar events of early nineteenth-century English history – Peterloo, the Industrial Revolution, the suspension of habeas corpus, Luddism – as *experiences* of ordinary people. What makes Thompson's account different from those of earlier labour historians is that he enables us to see events – or perhaps we should say, creates the narrative illusion that we can see events – from the standpoint of those who lived through them. Thompson's narrative tells us where people are coming from; he invariably presents their experience (that is, their emotional and mental response to events) as *structured* – by productive relations, political institutions, habits, traditions and values. What gives Thompson's portrayal of experience such persuasive force is that it is based on a structured and explicable, rather than a purely voluntarist and mysterious, concept of agency.

Thompson is right to insist that his difference with Althusser is profound, but the difference is obscured rather than clarified by the long discussion of experience in *The Poverty of Theory*. The essential contrast is in their theories of the subject. In Althusser's theory, subjects are deprived of agency; they are reproduced in a rigidly determined fashion by the operation of education, the family, religion and other so-called ideological state apparatuses.[26] Althusser's theory, as Goran Therborn points out, constitutes subjects so hegemonized by the ideology of the ruling class that they would be incapable of resistance or struggle.[27] Thompson develops no elaborate theory of the subject, but he spends a lot of time constructing subjects in his narrative, and these subjects are utterly different from Althusser's. They are endowed with agency – not with a naive individualist's 'freedom of the will', but with a structured agency. His subjects are formed by the various systems or structures that constitute their historical life space; what they can think, feel and do is determined by the fact that they are Methodists, 'free-born Englishmen', journeymen in a craft undergoing degradation, Londoners, and so on. But the determination is not mechanical, for Thompson's subjects are what Anthony Giddens calls 'knowledgeable'. They are intelligent and wilful human beings, who reflect on the events they live through (that is, have *experiences*) and are capable of acting purposefully and rationally on the basis of their experiences, within the constraints imposed and the possibilities opened up by the structures that constitute their subjectivity and their environment.[28]

I have cast this statement of Thompson's implicit theory of the subject in Giddens' theoretical terms because I believe that Giddens' notions of agency and structure provide a better theoretical pivot for Thompson's account of class formation than Thompson's own amorphous concept of experience. Giddens incorporates what is useful about Thompson's 'experience': he insists that human beings are constantly engaged in 'reflexive monitoring' of both their own and others' action, and that their conduct of and understanding of social life grow out of this reflexive monitoring.[29] But his theory incorporates experience without mystifying the relationship between agency and structure.

In large part, this is because Giddens develops an alternative to the reified Stalinist or Althusserian (or structural-functionalist) concept of structure, whereas Thompson rails against it but proposes no alternative. Because he continues to conceive of structure in reified supra-human terms, Thompson casts experience and structure as antagonistic principles. The role of experience in his theory is to frustrate and blunt structural determination. Giddens, by contrast, de-reifies structure, making it no less human than agency. He sees structure and agency not as antagonistic but as indissolubly linked: agency and structure *'presuppose one another'*.[30] Structures for him are at once the medium and the outcome of human interactions. They are transformed by agents, but they are also reproduced by agents. Structures are not only determining or constraining, but enabling as well: agents could not exist without the structures that provide their constraints and possibilities, and structures could not exist without the agents who enact and/or transform them. This concept of structure and of its relationship to agency requires no mystification to account for the transformative effects of experience. If structures are seen as the continuing product of reflexive monitoring in the first place, then it stands to reason that changes in structures arise out of the same reflexive monitoring process.

Simply invoking Giddens' theory does not solve all the theoretical problems posed by Thompson's account of English working-class formation. It does not tell us when to be abstract and when concrete, how to recognize or describe structures, or how to constitute appropriately knowledgeable agents in our narratives. But I think it provides a theoretical vocabulary capable of accounting for what Thompson actually achieves in the text of *The Making* – a portrayal of English workers as structurally constrained and endowed agents whose experience and knowledgeable action produced, in interaction with other agents operating under different structural constraints and endowments, a self-conscious working class.[31]

One advantage of this theorization of Thompson's history – as an account of structurally-formed agents enacting and/or transforming structures – is that it offers a solution to a widely recognized weakness in *The Making*: Thompson's unwillingness to address explicitly the role of structures in class formation. Thompson avoids structures because he does not wish to introduce any extra-human forces into his account; his critics counter that by concentrating on 'subjective' forces, he leaves out the 'objective' forces which in fact play the dominant role in class formation. But both Thompson and his critics share the misconception that structures are 'objective' and therefore exist at a different ontological level than agents. If we accept Giddens' position on structures, then any contrast between 'objective' and 'subjective' becomes purely *methodological*. Abstraction becomes only a moment in the analysis: a necessary strategic move in any complex historical argument. We can introduce structures without ceasing to be ontological humanists, and can recognize the efficacy of 'experience' without ruling out a structural argument.

Culturalism or Experientialism?

When Thompson's Marxist critics have accused him of insufficient attention to structural determinants, they have virtually always had in mind *economic* determinants. Most Marxists implicitly equate structure with economic explanations and agency with ideological or cultural explanations. Hence it is easy for Richard Johnson to leap from a cogent critique of Thompson's 'overbearing stress on "experience"', to a mistaken indictment of Thompson as a 'culturalist'.[32] While it is true, as Johnson, Perry Anderson and others argue, that Thompson sacrifices analytical bite by refusing to include a more structural approach to the history of capitalist productive relations, it is not true, as the term 'culturalism' would indicate, that Thompson has relegated economics or productive relations to a secondary or derivative role. We have seen that Thompson's theoretical statements imply, in spite of occasional explicit disavowals of economic determinism, that development of the capitalist mode of production is the fundamental underlying cause of the formation of the working class. Nor has Thompson neglected productive relations empirically in *The Making*. Chapters 6 to 10 ('Exploitation', 'The Field Labourers', 'Artisans and Others', 'The Weavers' and 'Standards and Experiences') and significant portions of his account of Luddism in chapter 14 are crammed with brilliant analyses of the economic life and productive relations of English workers. What distinguishes these analyses is not so much their emphasis on culture – although Thompson quite rightly insists on the inextricable interpenetration of culture and productive relations – as their insistence on depicting productive relations as lived human experiences rather than as abstract structures. Here, and throughout the book, Thompson resists abstraction and insists on recounting of all aspects of the 'making' of the English working class – whether economic, or cultural, or political, or religious, or social – exclusively from the perspective of concrete historical experiences. Thompson is not really a 'culturalist' – which implies someone who privileges cultural over other types of explanations. He is, rather, an 'experientialist', whose narrative perspective privileges the point of view of concrete historical agents over that of the theoretically self-conscious analyst.

One indication that 'experientialism' rather than 'culturalism' is the appropriate label for Thompson's perspective is that his account of the emergence of class consciousness – a cultural change, after all – suffers from the same lack of theoretical specification as his account of changes in productive relations. At the end of *The Making* we feel that class-conscious conceptualizations of society and class-conscious protest movements have somehow arisen out of the history Thompson has recounted, but it is not easy to specify precisely how and why. Class-conscious ideologies obviously included a reflection on the experience of exploitation so powerfully narrated in Part Two of *The Making*, but they were certainly not mere 'reflections' of that experience. They were also, it is clear, strongly influenced by the political traditions described in Part One ('The Liberty Tree') and by the political struggles recounted in Part Three ('The Working-class Presence'). But how these influences and forces resulted in a particular cultural transformation – the emergence of class consciousness – remains unclear. Instead, class-consciousness appears in the early 1830s as the result of a tumultuous and inspiring but conceptually murky 'experience'.

Reconstructing the Argument

In reconstructing Thompson's argument, I shall make no attempt to indicate how *The Making* could be improved by a more structural approach to the dynamics of capitalism; others have done that before.[33] Instead, I shall attempt to supply what previous critiques have left out: a structural argument about the emergence of working-class consciousness – one that is compatible with Thompson's narrative but that clarifies its conceptual foundations and theoretical significance. What I say will also draw on my own study of France, where I see the emergence of class-consciousness as having taken place in the same years as in England and by a remarkably similar process.[34]

This reconstruction of Thompson's argument can usefully be focused on a much-disputed claim of his book: that the working class had really been 'made' by the early 1830s. This supposition is made plausible both by the feverish working-class activity of the immediate post-Reform Bill years, and by Chartist domination of English popular politics from the mid-1830s to the late 1840s. But doubts remain as to how definitive this 'making' was. Although Chartism was a mass movement of workers, its programme and language were only very incompletely class-conscious. Chartism concentrated on electoral reform, and its critique of monopoly and corruption were more trenchant than its critique of property relations. After the final collapse of Chartism in 1848, English workers lapsed into a long period of conservatism, apathy or narrow 'trade union consciousness'. Rather than a definitive 'making' of the working class in the early 1830s, it can be argued that the history of English workers is one of successive makings, unmakings and remakings.[35] From this perspective, the achievements of 1790 to 1832 were not so impressive after all; they were not definitive, but reversible. Yet I think there was something special about the first making that renders it more fundamental than any of the subsequent makings, unmakings and remakings. To see why, however, will require some theoretical distinctions that take us beyond the purely experiential level of Thompson's own narrative.

What does Thompson mean when he claims the English working class was 'made' by the early 1830s? In the first place, the working class had defined itself as a class and had divided itself conceptually from the middle class. In doing so, it had developed a particular critique of capitalist society and property relations. It had, in short, developed a class *discourse*. At the same time, it had developed a working-class *movement*. This movement had its distinct institutions (trade unions and con-federations of trade unions, newspapers, clubs and embryonic political parties such as the National Union of the Working Class). In and around these working-class institutions, hundreds of thousands of workers were mobilized to struggle self-consciously for working-class goals. The discourse and the movement were intimately linked: it was within the institutions of the working-class movement that militants developed and disseminated working-class discourse; and it was the notions contained in working-class discourse that shaped and motivated the working-class movement. Scattered through Thompson's intensely experiential narrative of the emerging working-class movement is a parallel account of the emergence of class discourse, an account that, in my opinion, needs more explicit theoretical formulation.

What is Thompson's implicit theory of the emergence of working-class discourse? First, working-class discourse is a transformation of pre-existing discourses. This is implied by the very organization of his book. Class-conscious discourse does not arise, as one might have gathered from Thompson's preface, purely as a reflection of and reflection on the exploitation of workers in capitalist productive relations. If this were the case there would be little point in the long and impassioned discussion of pre-nineteenth-century popular political traditions, which occupies Thompson's first five chapters. These traditions were important because they contained notions that were transformed into a new working-class discourse around 1830. In other words, the political and religious traditions described in Part One, when subjected to the experience of exploitation described in Part Two, were transformed via the political agitations described in most of Part Three into the 'class-consciousness' described in the final chapter. The fact that class discourse is a trans-formation of previously existing discourse has an important theoretical implication: it means that to explain the emergence of class discourse, we must understand the nature, the structure and the potential contradictions of the previously existing discourses of which it is a transformation.

Although understanding the genesis of class discourse requires a long chronological sweep, the actual emergence of class-consciousness took place by a relatively sudden conceptual breakthrough during a period of intense political struggle. The suddenness of the breakthrough is in large part a consequence of the formal structure of the conceptual transformation itself: the emergence of working-class consciousness required a *simultaneous* transformation of two quite different previously existing discourses.

In both England and France, working-class consciousness first emerged in almost precisely the same period (the early 1830s), out of analogous political agitations (the Reform Bill crisis and the July Revolution), and from strictly parallel conceptual transformations.[36] In both countries, the emergence of working-class discourse was a consequence of the breakdown of political alliances between workers and bourgeois following successful struggles against regimes dominated by landed aristocracies. In both cases, workers had every reason to feel that having carried the major burden of the battle against what they saw as a common aristocratic enemy, they were abandoned by the bourgeoisie (or the middle class, to use English terminology), who took all the spoils of victory for themselves. In both cases, workers were shut out of the State by steep property requirements for the franchise, and saw their collectivist or mutualist goals pulverized by the patronizing and uncompromising individualism of the now dominant bourgeoisie. The shock of this betrayal led to a deep disillusionment with the bourgeoisie and an attempt to rethink and restate the workers' grievances.

What resulted was a dual transformation of existing discourses. First, the workers' collectivism, which arose out of the traditional discourse of trade and community solidarity, was universalized so as to encompass all workers. Because workers' traditional solidarities had been constituted in exclusivist trade and community terms, this meant developing a new vocabulary that instead emphasized the brotherhood of all workers. The obvious source of such a vocabulary was the discourse of individual rights and democratic participation in whose terms the joint struggle against the landed aristocracy had so recently been waged. But here a serious problem presented itself: in both its English and French variants, this discourse was so deeply individualist that it would not authorize the kinds of collective claims that workers were attempting to make.

The universalization of traditional trade and community solidarities was based on a second transformation: the radical or republican tradition was made compatible with collective claims. The centrality of private property in the Radical tradition was challenged and replaced with some notion of collective control. In both England and France, this was accomplished from two different angles simultaneously. First, the right of individuals to associate freely in pursuit of common goals was invoked as a justification for collective organization to limit the destructive effects of competitive individualism. In England this was accomplished under the banner of 'cooperation', in France under the banner of 'association'. Second, the Lockean theory of property was reinterpreted so as to invest political rights not in property, which the Lockean tradition regarded as a product of labour, but directly in labour itself. From this perspective, property became an abusive privilege that simultaneously exempted its idle owners from labour and (under existing suffrage laws) gave them a monopoly of political power as well. This logically interlocking complex of structural transformations created a working-class discourse that established a solidarity between workers of all trades, empowered workers to make collective claims about the character and products of productive activities, gave them a moral claim to political power, and stigmatized wealthy property owners as privileged and greedy monopolists.

Once it had been achieved by both English and French workers in the early 1830s, this discursive transformation was remarkably durable. Class institutions could disintegrate or atrophy, and class-conscious mass movements could be crushed or could lapse into apathy. But conceptual or discursive transformations are not so easily reversed. They are far less vulnerable to repression than are class institutions, because they can be preserved intact by a tiny cadre of militants, or in print, or in the memories of vast masses of workers. Thus preserved, they are immediately available when a more favourable conjuncture returns. Institutions must be painfully rebuilt, masses must be remobilized, but ideas do not have to be re-invented. Thus, the genie of class discourse, once created, proved very difficult to get back into the bottle. In this sense, Thompson was right to claim the English working class was in some important sense 'made' by the early 1830s, even though it was subsequently 'unmade' and 'remade' at the institutional level. But to see that this is true requires a theorization of Thompson's narrative of working-class formation in such a way that these different levels of 'making' can be distinguished.

Conclusions

These few words can hardly pretend to a complete theorization of *The Making of the English Working Class*. But I think they indicate the direction which an adequate theory of working-class formation will have to take.

Theoretical discussion of working-class formation cannot remain on a purely diachronic and experiential level. Numerous critics have pointed out that a clear understanding of the making of the English working class requires an account of the structural dynamics of early industrial capitalism. Similarly, understanding the emergence of class discourse in England and France in the early 1830s requires abstracting both the structure of class discourse and the structures of pre-existing discourses out of the experiences and the temporal sequences in which they exist. It also requires the elaboration of a synchronic transformational model of the logic posited to underlie the emergence of class discourse. Only by such a process of synchronic and structural abstraction, I would argue, can the true nature and consequences of the experienced history be understood. In particular, the sudden and simultaneous rather than gradual and piecemeal emergence of class-consciousness is a consequence of the logically interlocking character of the conceptual transformations. An adequate theory of class formation must include a dialectic between structural and experiential and between synchronic and diachronic moments.

Theorizing the emergence of working-class discourse explicitly helps us to determine *why* 'consciousness of class arises in the same way in different times and places, but never in *just* the same way'.[37] If class discourse is a transformation of pre-existing discourses, then national differences in forms and content of class-consciousness need not be attributed purely to the vagaries of agency, nor purely to different patterns of capital accumulation, but also to differences in the nature of the discourses that were transformed into class-consciousness. Thus, the much more pronounced socialism of French than of British working-class consciousness is probably in large part a consequence of the difference between French and British Radical traditions. The centrality of private property as the touchstone of individual liberty in the ideology of the French Revolution made a critique of property absolutely central in French workers' discourse, and the revolution's equation of productive work with the 'sovereignty of the people' and of idleness with the counter-revolutionary 'aristocracy' almost invited workers to define property-owners as aristocrats and enemies of the people.[38] British Radicalism, with its 'country party' heritage and its powerful moral animus against corruption and monopoly gave rise, as Gareth Stedman Jones has demonstrated, to a quite different constellation of working-class political consciousness.[39]

It is also very important to recognize that class discourse is only one of several discourses available to workers to conceptualize and act out their place in society and the State. Even workers involved in class institutions are interpellated (to use the Althusserian term) by various other discourses: unreconstructed Radical democracy, reformist meliorism, self-help, Toryism, nationalism, various religious ideologies, consumerism, and so on. These rival discourses may coexist not only in the same class, but in the same mind; class discourse, once invented, does not necessarily remain the privileged discourse of workers. Which discourse prevails depends on changing political, economic and social conjunctures. And while the invention of a given political discourse cannot be reversed, all such discourses are transformed in the course of historical experience. In extreme cases, such as the United States after World War II, class discourse can be so marginalized as to be virtually effaced. While class discourse may commonly have been more durable than class institutions in the nineteenth century, class movements have sometimes outlasted class discourse in the twentieth.

A final conclusion: the process of class formation, or any other historical process, must be conceptualized as an outcome of temporal conjunctures between multiple causal structures. Thompson's implicit notion that only productive relations have genuine causal power, while other apparent systems must be assimilated to the category of experience, leads only to mystification and confusion. Whether one accepts the Althusserian formulation of a multitude of relatively autonomous levels or systems determined in the last instance by the economic base, or a more agnostic formulation that eschews any notion of final cause, is not important – a question of metaphysics rather than of method. What matters is that one recognize the internal structure and dynamic, and hence the autonomous causal force, of each of the systems in question, as well as, of course, their mutual influence and systematic interrelations. Until some systematic and autonomous determinants beyond the mode of production are recognized and theorized, any attempt to transcend a base–superstructure model is illusory.

In the case of English and French working-class formation, the emergence of class-consciousness must be seen as resulting from a temporal conjunction of at least two systems: a system of capitalist productive relations in which labour in the handicraft trades undergoes a relentless formal subsumption to capital; and an ideological system in which trade solidarity and Radical notions of individual rights undergo a mutual transformation into a new discourse of class-consciousness. Each system has independent causal power, and their conjunction is necessary to explain the historical emergence of class-consciousness. In fact, to represent the emergence of class-consciousness as resulting from the conjunction of only two systems – economic and ideological – would itself be a gross over-simplification. My own abbreviated account of developments in England and France actually signals the importance of another system: that of political alliances between classes. The emergence of class-consciousness in both countries followed a joint working-class and bourgeois political struggle against a landed aristocracy, in the course of which workers participated in institutions and ideologies of struggle that could be transformed into resources for a struggle of the working class against the bourgeoisie when the original class alliance broke down. Once again, the structure and dynamic of class alliance had an independent causal force that cannot be reduced to the reflection of ideology or economics. The importance of a broken inter-class political alliance for the development of working-class consciousness also emerges from Sean Wilentz's study of New York City in the same era, where the parallels with England and France were remarkable.[40]

The American case also suggests yet other systems with an important bearing on working-class formation. The nature of class-consciousness was different in New York, where workers had long since gained the franchise, from France and England where they were denied the vote; and whereas the development of working-class discourse and a working-class movement in London or Paris more or less guaranteed the national significance of the working-class political presence, this was by no means true in the United States, where the highly regionalized federal political system meant that developments in the premier city did not necessarily spread to the rest of the country. In short, a glance at the American case suggests the importance of State structure as an autonomous determinant of working-class formation. And the subsequent history of the American working class also suggests the importance of demographic structures: in a country where the labour force was growing far more rapidly than the natural increase of the population, the working class was continually fed by a flood of European immigrants. Attempting to maintain a class-conscious workers movement in these circumstances was an altogether different matter than doing so in England, where the population grew more quickly than the labour force, or in France, where the industrial labour force itself grew only relatively slowly. Explaining the patterns of working-class formation in the various countries that underwent capitalist development in the nineteenth century will require a theoretical framework that can manipulate several different relatively autonomous causal systems simultaneously.

But the point of all this theorizing is not to list the various causal systems that conspire in the process of class formation or to show how different permutations of their formal features will give us the different types of working-class movements and ideologies found in different European and North American countries. That would be a retreat into precisely the kind of dessicated formalism that Thompson drove from the field when he published *The Making of the English Working Class*. The point is to make possible the writing of more complex and satisfying histories of working classes, histories that embrace Thompson's vision of experience, diachrony and agency in the historical process, but that elaborate the diachronic experience of agency in a continuing and acknowledged dialectic with synchronic structures of determination. For we cannot claim to know such synchronic structures of determination until we can show in circumstantial narratives how they shape and are shaped by real actions in experienced historical time. To believe that abstract theoretical generalizations are the end-point of our enterprise would cast our lot with the ghost of the same sclerotic Stalinism that Thompson routed two decades ago – when *The Making of the English Working Class* awoke labour history from its long dogmatic slumbers.

Notes

1 I would like to thank Benjy Ben-Baruch, Belinda Davis, Geoff Eley, Michael Kennedy, Howard Kimeldorf, Max Potter, Bill Reddy, Joan Scott and Mark Steinberg for reading and commenting on earlier versions of this paper.

2 It should be noted that Thompson was by no means the only inspiration for my generation's embracing of 'history from below'. Such historians as Albert Soboul, George Rudé, Richard Cobb, Eric Hobsbawm, Charles Tilly and Stephen Thernstrom also had an important impact. But Thompson's influence seems to me to have been the widest, deepest and most lasting.

3 On Thompson's split from the British Communist Party, see B. Palmer *The Making of E. P. Thompson*, (Toronto: New Hogtown Press, 1981).

4 E. P. Thompson, *The Making of the English Working Class* (London: Victor Gollancz, 1963), p. 9.

5 Ibid., p. 11.

6 Ibid., p. 9.

7 Ibid., p. 10.

8 Ibid., p. 9.

9 Again, it must be noted that Thompson was not alone in this historiographical achievement. Other historians who were simultaneously finding means to restore wills and speech to the common people include Eric Hobsbawm, *Primitive Rebels: Studies in Archaic Forms of Social Movement in the Nineteenth and Twentieth Centuries* (New York: W. W. Norton, 1959): George Rudé, *The Crowd in the French Revolution* (London: Oxford University Press, 1959); Richard Cobb, *Les Armées revolutionnaires: instrument de la Terreur dans les departements, avril 1793–floréal an II*, 2 vols (Paris: Mouton, 1961–3); and Albert Soboul, *Les Sans-culottes parisiens en l'an II: mouvement populaire et gouvernement revolutionnaire, 2 juin 1793–9 thermidor an II* (Paris: Librairie Clavreuil, 1962).

10 Thompson, *The Making*, p. 9 emphasis mine.

11 Ibid., p. 10.

12 Thompson, *The Making*, pp. 9–10.

13 Anyone who thinks that this sort of 'modernist' writing style is incompatible with social historical narrative should look closely at Carlo Ginsburg's *The Night Battles: Witchcraft and Agrarian Cults in the Sixteenth and Seventeenth Centuries*, trans. by John and Anne Tedeschi (New York: Penguin Books, 1983). Although this book is hardly an example of pure diachrony, its narrative passages are written, with a certain self-conscious modernist

austerity, from the perspective of a historian 'overhearing' inquisitorial interviews. Ginsburg's own interventions are marked off quite sharply from the narration – much more sharply than is the case in *The Making*, where the abstracting, moralizing, generalizing, and (let us not forget) *synchronizing* voice of the narrator is present even in the apparently barest recitations of events.

14 Thompson, *The Making*, pp. 249–60.
15 E. P. Thompson, 'The Poverty of Theory or an Orrery of Errors', in *The Poverty of Theory and Other Essays* (New York: Monthly Review Press, 1978), pp. 1–210.
16 Thompson's concept of experience is the subject of some controversy. Critics of Thompson include Perry Anderson, *Arguments Within English Marxism* (London: Verso, 1980), pp. 25–9; Richard Johnson, 'Edward Thompson, Eugene Genovese, and Socialist-Humanist History', *History Workshop* 6 (Autumn 1978), pp. 79–100; and Sande Cohen, *Historical Culture: On the Recoding of an Academic Discipline* (Berkeley and Los Angeles: University of California Press, 1986), pp. 199–204. Thompson's defenders include Harvey J. Kaye, *The British Marxist Historians* (Cambridge: Polity Press, 1984); and Ellen Meiksins Wood, 'The Politics of Theory and the Concept of Class: E. P. Thompson and His Critics', *Studies in Political Economy*, 9 (Fall 1982).
17 E. P. Thompson, 'Folklore, Anthropology, and Social History', *Indian Historical Review*, 3 (January 1977), pp. 247–66; *The Making*, pp. 9–10.
18 *Webster's New International Dictionary of the English Language*, 2nd edn, unabridged (Springfield, Mass., C. C. Merriam, 1959), p. 1528.
19 *Poverty of Theory*, 170, emphasis mine.
20 Ibid., pp. 171–2, emphasis in original.
21 Ibid., p. 172, emphasis in original.
22 E. P. Thompson, *Whigs and Hunters: The Origin of the Black Act* (New York: Pantheon Books, 1975), pp. 258–69.
23 *Webster's New International Dictionary*, p. 896.
24 Clifford Geertz, *The Interpretation of Cultures* (New York: Basic Books, 1973), p. 405.
25 Thompson, *Poverty of Theory*, p. 7. Emphasis in original.
26 Louis Althusser, 'Ideology and Ideological State Apparatuses (Notes towards an Investigation)', in *Lenin and Philosophy* (New York: Monthly Review Press, 1971), pp. 127–86.
27 Goran Therborn, *The Ideology of Power and the Power of Ideology* (London: Verso Editions, 1980), pp. 8–10.
28 Anthony Giddens, *Central Problems in Social Theory: Action, Structure and Contradiction in Social Analysis* (University of California Press, Berkeley and Los Angeles, 1979); *A Contemporary Critique of Historical Materialism* (London: Macmillan, 1981); and *The Constitution of Society: Outline of the Theory of Structuration* (University of California Press: Berkeley and Los Angeles, 1984).
29 Giddens, *Central Problems*, pp. 53–9; and *The Constitution of Society*, pp. 5–14.
30 Giddens, *Central Problems*, p. 53. Emphasis in original.

31 Marx himself provides a warrant for such a view. Remember his aphorism: 'Men make their own history, but they do not make it just as they please; they do not make it under circumstances chosen by themselves, but under circumstances directly found, given and transmitted from the past'. Karl Marx, *The Eighteenth Brumaire of Louis Bonaparte* (New York: International Publishers, n.d.), p. 13.

32 Johnson, 'Socialist-Humanist History', p. 97.

33 See, e.g., Johnson, 'Socialist-Humanist History'; and Anderson, *Arguments Within English Marxism*.

34 William H. Sewell Jr, *Work and Revolution in France: The Language of Labor from the Old Regime to the French Revolution* (Cambridge: Cambridge University Press, 1980).

35 Cogent critiques of Thompson on this point have been mounted by Tom Nairn, 'The English working class', *New Left Review* (March–April 1964); Anderson, *Arguments Within English Marxism*, pp. 43–9; Gareth Stedman Jones, 'Rethinking Chartism', in *Languages of Class: Studies in English Working Class History, 1832–1982* (Cambridge: Cambridge University Press, 1983), pp. 90–178; and, more gently, by Eric Hobsbawm, *Workers: Worlds of Labor* (New York: Pantheon Books, 1984), pp. 194–213.

36 The assertions about France are argued and documented more fully in my *Work and Revolution in France*, especially chapter 10.

37 Thompson, *The Making*, p. 10.

38 On the property question and French socialism, see William H. Sewell Jr, 'Property, Labor, and the Emergence of Socialism in France, 1789–1848', in *Consciousness and Class Experience in Nineteenth-Century Europe*, John M. Merriman (ed.) (New York: Holmes & Meier, 1979), pp. 45–63. On the people–producer/aristocrat–idler idea, see William H. Sewell Jr, 'The Abbé Sieyes and the Rhetoric of Revolution', *Consortium on Revolutionary Europe Proceedings*, ed. by Harold T. Parker, Louise Salley Parker and William M. Reddy (Durham, N.C.: Duke University Press, 1986), pp. 1–14.

39 'Rethinking Chartism'.

40 Sean Wilentz, *Chants Democratic: New York City and the Rise of the American Working Class* (New York: Oxford University Press, 1984).

3

The Tale of Samuel and Jemima: Gender and Working-class Culture in Nineteenth-century England

Catherine Hall

Samuel Bamford, the Radical weaver, described in his famous auto-biography *Passages in the Life of a Radical* his experience of the Peterloo massacre of 1819.[1] The account has rightly become a classic. Bamford first recounted how the restoration of habeus corpus in 1818 made it possible to campaign again openly for reform. The decision was taken in the North to hold a reform meeting in St Peter's Field, Manchester. Committees were set up to organize the event and issued their first injunctions, CLEANLINESS, SOBRIETY and ORDER to which was added PEACE on the suggestion of Orator Henry Hunt. Then came the weeks of drilling by 'the lads' on the moors, after work and on Sunday mornings, learning 'to march with a steadiness and regularity which would not have disgraced a regiment on parade'. As a reward maidens with milkcans, 'nymphs blushing and laughing' would sometimes refresh the men with 'delicious draughts, new from the churn'.[2] Then came the day of the gathering of the procession in Bamford's native town of Middleton. At the front were

> twelve of the most comely and decent-looking youths, who were placed in two rows of six each, with each a branch of laurel held presented in his hand, as a token of amity and peace, – then followed the men of several districts in fives, – then the band of music, an excellent one, – then the colours; a blue one of silk with inscriptions

This paper is a revised version of the paper first published in T. Bennett, C. Mercer and J. Woollacott (eds), *Popular Culture and Social Relations* (Milton Keynes: Open University Press, 1986). Thanks to the Open University Press for permission to re-publish and to Keith McClelland for help with the revisions.

in golden letters, 'UNITY AND STRENGTH'. 'LIBERTY AND FRATERNITY'.
A green one of silk, with golden letters, 'PARLIAMENTS ANNUAL'.
'SUFFRAGE UNIVERSAL'; and betwixt them on a staff, a handsome cap
of crimson velvet, with a tuft of laurel, and the cap tastefully braided
with the word, LIBERTAS in front.

Next came the men of Middleton and its surroundings, every hundred
with its leader who had a sprig of laurel in his hat, the 3000 men all ready
to obey the commands of a 'principal conductor', 'who took his place at
the head of the column with a bugleman to sound his orders'. Bamford
addressed the men before they set off, reminding them that it was
essential that they should behave with dignity and with discipline and so
confound their enemies who represented them as a 'mob-like rabble'.
Bamford recalled the procession as 'a most respectable assemblage of
labouring men', all decently if humbly attired and wearing their Sunday
white shirts and neck-cloths.[3]
     The Middleton column soon met with the Rochdale column and
between them, Bamford estimates, there were probably 6000 men. At
their head were now about 200 of their most handsome young women
supporters, including Bamford's wife, some of whom were singing and
dancing to the music. The reformers arrived in Manchester, having
changed their route following the personal request of Hunt that they
would lead his group in. This did not particularly please Bamford, who
had elevated views of his own dignity as leader and was not especially
sympathetic to Hunt, but he agreed and then, while the speeches were
going on, he and a friend, not expecting to hear anything new, went to
look for some refreshment. It was at this point that the cavalry attacked
and that the great demonstration was broken up with terrible brutality.
Hundreds were wounded, eleven killed. Bamford managed to get away
and after much anxiety met up with his wife, from whom he had been
separated for some hours.
     The human horror of Peterloo was differently experienced by Jemima
Bamford, for from the moment of realizing that something had gone
badly wrong her anxieties and fears were focused on her husband's safety.
As a leader of the reformers he would be particularly subject to
persecution and, indeed, was arrested and charged with high treason soon
afterwards. Reform demonstrations were predominantly male occasions,
as we can see from the description of the Middleton procession. There
was usually a good sprinkling of women present and 'a neatly dressed
female, supporting a small flag' was sitting on the driving seat of Hunt's
carriage.[4] Mary Fildes, President of the Female Reform Society of
Manchester, was on the platform, dressed all in white. Over 100 women
were wounded in St Peter's Field and two were killed, but nevertheless

the majority of participants, of speakers and of recognized leaders, were men.[5]

When Bamford first began to worry as to where his wife was he blamed himself that he had allowed her to come at all. In her account she says that she was determined to go to the meeting and would have followed it even if her husband had not consented to her going with the procession. She was worried before the event that something would go wrong and preferred to be near Samuel. He finally agreed and she arranged to leave their little girl, Ann, with a 'careful neighbour' and joined some other 'married females' at the head of the procession. She was dressed simply, as a countrywoman, in her 'second best attire'. Separated from her husband and the majority of the Middleton men by the crowd, she was terrified when the soldiers started the attack and managed to escape into a cellar. There she hid until the carnage was over when she crept out, helped by the kindly people in the house, and went in search of Samuel, who was first reported as dead, next said to be in the infirmary, then in the prison, but with whom she eventually managed to meet up safely. At the end of the tragic day, Bamford tells us,

> Her anxiety being now removed by the assurance of my safety, she hastened forward to console our child. I rejoined my comrades, and forming about a thousand of them into file, we set off to the sound of fife and drum, with our only banner waving, and in that form we re-entered the town of Middleton.[6]

Peterloo was a formative experience in the development of popular consciousness in the early nineteenth century and Bamford's account takes us into the question of the meanings of sexual difference within working-class culture. In E. P. Thompson's classic account of the making of the English working class, that process whereby groups of stockingers and weavers, factory workers and agricultural labourers, those in the old centres of commerce and the new industrial towns came to see themselves as having interests in common as against those of other classes, Peterloo is seen as one of the decisive moments, significantly shifting disparate individuals and groups towards a defined political consciousness.[7] By 1832, Thompson argues, working people had built up a sense of collective identity and shared struggle, had come to see themselves as belonging to a class. Placing the emphasis on class as process and as relationship rather than 'thing' or fixed structure, Thompson argued that 'class happens when some men, as a result of common experiences (inherited or shared), feel and articulate the identity of their interests as between themselves, and as against other men whose interests are different from (and usually opposed to) theirs.'[8] Shifting away from the classical Marxist emphasis on relationships of production, he focused on the experience of new forms of exploitation and the meanings given to that experience through the construction of a class-consciousness. *The Making of the English Working Class* documented and celebrated the emergence of that working-class consciousness between the 1790s, when a distinctively English artisanal Radicalism came to threaten the established social and political order, and the early 1830s, which saw the beginnings of Chartism, a national political movement dominated by working-class people. Working people's consciousness, Thompson argued, was embedded in their cultural institutions, their traditions and their ideas. *The Making* thus departed radically from the established routes of Marxists and of labour historians in its stress on the cultural and ideological aspects of class politics.

The book constituted a major political and intellectual intervention and has remained at the centre of debates on history, class and culture ever since. As a history undergraduate in 1963 when it was published, I devoured it and tried slowly to come to terms with its theoretical implications. More than twenty years later and now teaching it myself to students I still feel excited by its story, its rich material, the power of its political vision. In 1963 the re-emergence of feminism was still to come but from the beginning of that new dawn, the first national event of which took place under the aegis of the History Workshop (itself deeply indebted to Thompson's work), feminist history has been powerfully influenced by Thompsonian social history. His insistence on the rescue of 'the poor stockinger, the Luddite cropper, the "obsolete" hand-loom weaver, the "utopian" artisan, and even the deluded follower of Joanna Southcott, from the enormous condescension of posterity' and his triumphant demonstration of the possibility of such a rescue was echoed in the feminist commitment to recover the forgotten sex, captured in Sheila Rowbotham's title *Hidden From History*.[9]

The Making of the English Working Class featured women political activists – members of reform societies and trade unionists – as well as the occasional female prophet or seer. In the context of the early 1960s, Thompson was certainly attentive to those women who appeared in the historical records which he examined. But feminism was to re-cast ways of thinking about women's political and cultural space. In 1983, Barbara Taylor published *Eve and the New Jerusalem* which both built upon Thompson's achievement and extended his analysis. In her account of the place of the skilled workers in the Owenite movement, for example, she used the framework established by Thompson in his seminal chapters on artisans and weavers but looked beyond the threat posed to those workers by the forces of new methods and relations of production to the tensions and antagonisms which this fostered between male and female workers. The fragile unity of the English working class in the 1830s, she argued, was constructed within a sexually divided world, when on occasion, as one Owenite woman put it, 'the men are as bad as their masters'.[10]

This recognition that class identity, once theorized as essentially male or gender-neutral, is always articulated with a masculine or feminine subject, has been a central feminist insight and the story of Samuel and Jemima helps us to pursue the implications of this insight for the radical working-class culture of the early nineteenth century. The culture to which Bamford belonged was a culture that originated with artisans but extended to factory operatives, a culture that stressed moral sobriety and the search for useful knowledge, that valued intellectual enquiry, that saw mutual study and disputation as methods of learning and self-improvement. Such a culture placed men and women differently and the highlighting of these forms of sexual division can give us some access to the gendered nature of popular culture in the early nineteenth century.

Men and women experienced that culture very differently as we can see from Bamford's story. He had been involved with the organization of the day, with the training of the men so that they would march in disciplined procession, with the arrangements as to the route, with the ceremonial and ritual which would help to give the reformers a sense of strength and power. He belonged unambiguously to the struggle; as a leader he was concerned to articulate the demands of honest weavers, to help to develop strategies which would make possible the winning of reform. For his wife it was a very different matter. She too had a commitment to the cause but it was her husband who wrote down her tale, hoping that it would not be 'devoid of interest to the reader'.[11] Her arrangements were to do with their child, her first concern, once she knew that he was safe, was to get back to her. Like the majority of female reformers at the time she positioned herself, and was positioned by others, as a wife and mother supporting the cause of working men. The men, on the other hand, like her husband, entered the political fray as independent subjects, fighting for their own right to vote, their own capacity to play a part in determining forms of government. It is this distinction, between men as independent political beings and women as dependants, that the tale of Samuel and Jemima vividly illustrates.

The emergence of the working man as a political subject in his own right was part of the process of the development of male working-class consciousness. As E. P. Thompson has demonstrated, eighteenth-century society had not primarily been dominated by class issues and class struggles. It was King Property who ruled and the hegemony established by the landowning classes and the gentry rested on an acceptance of a patriarchal and hierarchical society. Consent had been won to the exercise of power by the propertied in part through the shared acceptance of a set of beliefs and customs, the 'moral economy' of the society, which unlike the new political economy of the nineteenth century, recognized communal norms and obligations and judged that the rich would respect the rights of the poor, particularly when it came to the issue of a 'just price' for bread. When that moral economy was transgressed, eighteenth-century crowds believed they had the right to defend their traditional customs. Bread riots, focused on soaring prices, malpractices among dealers, or just plain hunger, were one of the most popular forms of protest. Women were often the initiators of riots for they were the most involved in buying and inevitably the more sensitive to evidence of short weight or adulteration. Their concern was the subsistence of their families.[12]

But traditional ideas of family and household were shifting at the end of the eighteenth and beginning of the nineteenth centuries. In some regions the traditional family economy was breaking up as new productive processes required different forms of labour and proletarianization gathered pace.[13] Such changes played a part in structuring and organizing the family and shaping ideas about marriage and parenthood. Among the rural poor of the South and East, for example, as John Gillis has argued, typical labouring families, which no longer owned their means of production, were driven to push their children into the labour market in order to survive. Couples could scarcely support their little ones, never mind their kin. At the same time, the decline of living-in meant more sexual and marital freedom than had previously been hoped for from servants in husbandry. From the late eighteenth century, employers and overseers in this area were likely to favour marriage as a source of cheap and docile labour whereas previously they had favoured celibacy among living-in servants. Labouring couples developed what might be described as a 'narrow conjugality' in these circumstances. In the North and West, however, particularly in the areas of proto-industrialization, the family remained the economic unit and kinship continued to be a powerful bond while master artisans in the old urban centres clung to their tradition of late marriage. But this richness or variety in familial and marital patterns, which even extended to sexual radicalism among some pockets of Owenites, freethinkers and radical Christians, gave way by the 1850s to what Gillis sees as an era of 'mandatory marriage'.[14] There was no longer a viable alternative to the nuclear family and heterosexual monogamy for working people and the undermining of the independence of the family economy went together with the recognition of the man as the breadwinner, the woman as dependant. As yet, historians have not charted in any detail the interconnections and dissonances between the narratives of family and sexuality and the narrative of politics, more narrowly defined. The separation between marketplace and home, between production and consumption, so powerfully inscribed in our culture has been difficult enough to begin to repair.[15] Next must come the insistence that the politics of gender does not rest with issues around State regulation of the family and sexuality but affects such apparently gender-neutral arenas as foreign affairs and diplomatic relations, commercial and financial policy, as well as ideas of nation and nationality.

English politics took a sharp turn in the turbulent decade of the 1790s when the established hierarchy was challenged and the movement began towards a new sense of distinctive interests, of class interests, not only for working people but for aristocrats and entrepreneurs as well.[16] The degree of sympathy which food rioters had been able to expect from some magistrates disappeared and more punitive strategies began to be adopted by the authorities after the start of Jacobin activities in England. The repudiation of customary rights by those in power meant that such expectations had to be re-thought and re-interpreted. It was the writings of Tom Paine and the revolutionary ideals of liberty, equality and fraternity that inspired the 1790s version of the 'freeborn Englishman' and the creation of new traditions of Radicalism and protest. In the clubs and the meeting places of the 1790s serious reformers gathered to discuss the vital subject of the day – PARLIAMENTARY REFORM. As Thomas Hardy, the first secretary of the London Corresponding Society, wrote in his autobiography, describing their first meeting,

> After having had their bread and cheese and porter for supper, as usual, and their pipes afterwards, with some conversation on the hardness of the times and the dearness of all the necessaries of life ... the business for which they had met was brought forward – *Parliamentary Reform* – an important subject to be deliberated upon and dealt with by such a class of men.[17]

The artisans and small tradesmen of the reforming societies had come to the conclusion that their demand must be for political representation. It was Parliament that carried the key to a better future. With the moral consensus eroded and the refusal of the rich to take their responsibilities seriously, whether in the field of wages, the customary control of labour, or poverty and hunger, the only solution could be to change the government for the better. It was men who were in the forefront of formulating such demands. Drawing on and re-working the established traditions of English liberalism and dissent, they defined themselves as political agents while their wives, mothers and daughters were primarily defined as supporters and dependants. As bread riots gave way to new forms of political protest, whether constitutional societies, demonstrations for reform or machine-smashing, it was men who led the way organizationally, who dominated the meetings and defined the agendas for reform. This is not to say women were not represented. Indeed Samuel Bamford regarded himself as the initiator of female voting and even of female philanthropic societies, an idea that could have astonished the many women who had been active in such organizations since the 1790s. When speaking at Saddleworth he recounts,

> I, in the course of an address, insisted on the right, and the propriety also, of females who were present at such assemblages, voting by show of hand, for, or against the resolutions. This was a new idea; and the women who attended numerously on that bleak ridge, were mightily pleased with it, – and the men being nothing dissentient, – when the resolution was put, the women held up their hands, amid much laughter; and ever from that time, females voted with the men at the radical meetings.[18]

Females may have voted with the men at many of the Radical meetings but females certainly did not carry the same weight in the overall political process. The later decision by the Chartists to abandon universal suffrage in favour of universal male suffrage depended on the notion of men representing women.

Jemima 'never deemed any trouble too great' if bestowed for the cause according to Samuel, but the troubles that visited her were different from those of her husband.[19] Samuel was arrested and tried for high treason, found guilty and imprisoned. In the course of all this he had to get himself to London twice, mostly by walking, be interviewed by Lord Sidmouth, have a defence committee set up in his name, meet many of the prominent reformers of the period and have his trial reported in the national press. Jemima, on the other hand, stayed at home working on the loom to support herself and her child while Samuel was away, sending him clean linen when she could, venturing out for two visits to Lincoln gaol to stay with him while their daughter was cared for by an aunt and uncle. Home was for Samuel, as he tells us, his 'dove-nest' to which he could return after the storm. His first description of it comes when he had risked a trip home while lying low in fear of arrest, coming in from the 'frozen rain' and the night wind. He emphasizes the good fire, the clean, swept hearth and his wife darning, while their child read to her from the Bible, 'Blessed are the meek for they shall inherit the earth.' 'Such were the treasures', he tells us, 'I had hoarded in that lowly cell.'[20]

As working men defined themselves as political subjects of a new kind, 'craving for something for "the nation"' beyond the contentment of domestic blessings, as they learnt organizational skills, made contacts across the country, opened up new avenues for themselves as radical journalists or political activists, so they increasingly saw themselves as representatives of their families in the new public world.[21] Radical working-class culture came to rest on a set of commonsense assumptions about the relative places of men and women which were not subjected to the same critical scrutiny as were the monarchy, the aristocracy, representative forms of government and the other institutions of Old Corruption.

What were the beliefs, practices and institutions of this working-class culture that emerged in the early nineteenth century and in what ways did they legitimate men and women differently? It was the reform movement that lay at the heart of that culture. This does not, of course, mean that there were not other extremely significant elements within popular culture. Methodism, for example, provided one such alternative discourse, intersecting at some points with the beliefs of serious and improving artisans, as in their shared concern to challenge the evils of alcohol, but at other points having sharply different concerns. Meanwhile heavy drinking and gambling remained very popular pastimes for sections of the working class, however much the sober and respectable disapproved of them. But in Thompson's powerful narrative it was the characteristic beliefs and institutions of the Radicals that emerged as the leading element within working-class culture in the early nineteenth century, carrying more resonance and with a stronger institutional base, than any other.[22] The main thrust behind the reform movement came from the 'industrious classes' – stockingers, handloom weavers, cotton-spinners, artisans and, in association with these, a widespread scattering of small masters, tradesmen, publicans, booksellers and professional men.[23] These different groups were able to come together and on the basis of their shared political and industrial organization, through the Hampden Clubs, the constitutional societies, the trade unions, the friendly societies, the educational groups and the self-improvement societies they were able to come to feel an identity of interest. Such clubs and societies were, therefore, central to the task of building a common culture but such locations offered a much easier space for men to operate in than for women.

Bamford tells us of the Hampden Clubs and their importance:

Instead of riots and destruction of property, Hampden clubs were now established in many of our large towns, and the villages and districts around them; Cobbett's books were printed in a cheap form; the labourers read them, and thenceforward became deliberate and systematic in their proceedings. Nor were there wanting men of their own class, to encourage and direct the new converts; the Sunday Schools of the preceding thirty years, had produced many working men of sufficient talent to become readers, writers, and speakers in the village meetings for parliamentary reform; some also were found to possess a rude poetic talent, which rendered their effusions popular, and bestowed an additional charm on their assemblages, and by such various means, anxious listeners at first, and then zealous proselytes, were drawn from the cottages of quiet nooks and dingles, to the weekly readings and discussions of the Hampden clubs.[24]

Bamford is describing male gatherings; the men who had learnt to read and write in the Sunday schools of the late eighteenth century made use of their new talents, spoke to others, sometimes even in popular poetic form, and built up weekly reading and discussion meetings. Work on literacy rates suggests that working-class women lagged significantly behind men.[25] Teachers were less likely to give them time and energy. They were less likely to have time or space or freedom to pursue study and discussion. As David Vincent has shown, the difficulties associated with women writing are reflected in the autobiographical material which has survived. Of the 142 autobiographies which he has analysed, only six were by women. He attributes this silence in part to the lack of self-confidence among women, for who could possibly be interested in their lives? We remember Jemima Bamford, writing her few notes to be included in her husband's story. Vincent also points to women's subordinate position within the family. Men could demand that their wives and children would recognize their need for quiet and privacy in circumstances where such conditions were almost impossible to obtain. The wife would hush the children and quell the storms while her husband struggled with his exercises in reading and writing. Such efforts were rarely forthcoming for women. Furthermore, self-improvement societies were normally for men only. It was hard for women in these circumstances to have the same kind of commitment to intellectual inquiry and the search for useful knowledge, values which were central to Radical culture.[26]

But the characteristics of the subordinate position of women within the family were not fixed and unchanging. Customary assumptions about 'a woman's place' were re-thought and re-worked in this period. There was nothing new in the assumption that men and women were different and that women were inferior in some respects. There was a great deal that was new in the political, economic and cultural relations within which traditional notions of sexual difference were being articulated. Take the new political culture of the reform movement. As Dorothy Thompson has argued, the replacements of the more informal and communal protests of the eighteenth century with the more organized movements of the nineteenth century resulted in the increasing marginalization of women.[27] As formal societies with constitutions and officers replaced customary patterns of crowd mobilization, women withdrew. Many meetings were seen as occasions for male conviviality and women were excluded informally if not formally. Meetings might be held at times when they could not go, for once they were removed from the street the automatic participation of men, women and children was broken. They were often held in places to which it was difficult for them to go, for pubs were coming to be seen as unsuitable places for respectable women. If they did manage to get there, they might well feel alienated by the official jargon and constitutional procedures so beloved by some Radical men.[28]

Radical men were certainly sometimes happy to welcome women as supporters of their demands. In the Birmingham Political Union, for example, resuscitated in 1839 after its triumphs in the lead-up to the Reform Act 1832, a Female Political Union was established through the efforts of Titus Salt, a leading Radical, who argued that the support that women could provide would be invaluable. At a giant tea party held by the Female Political Union in the grand, new town hall in the city, the male leaders of the BPU demonstrated the ambiguous and contradictory nature of their feelings about women's engagement in politics. Tea and plum cake were served to the assembled thousand and then the men on the platform delivered their addresses. Thomas Attwood, the hero of 1832, spoke first. 'My kind and fair and most dear countrywomen', he began,

> I most solemnly declare my affection for the women of England has been mainly instrumental in causing all my exertions in the public cause, not that I do not feel for the men, but I have a stronger desire to promote the comforts of the women.

The women, according to the report of the *Birmingham Journal*, the mouth-piece of the Radicals, were suitably grateful for his efforts on their behalf. After Attwood came Scholefield, the first MP for the city, elected after the triumph of Reform. Scholefield proceeded to enunciate his contradictory impulses to his audience. 'It was gratifying to him to meet so many excellent and intelligent women', he began, 'who, by their presence, showed very plainly that they took a lively interest in all that concerned the welfare of their husbands, fathers, brothers and sons, and which also', he added, 'deeply affected their own welfare.' Scholefield went on to argue for women's politics, citing the importance of the women's storming of the Bastille. He concluded, however, that, 'He was far from wishing that politics should ever supersede the important duties of social and domestic life, which constituted the chief business of the female; but he also hoped the women of Birmingham would never become indifferent to politics.'

Titus Salt followed Scholefield, arguing that by their good conduct the women had won over everybody to the cause of female unions and that, 'by a continuance of the same conduct, and the force of moral power, they would gain all they required'. All these Radical men wanted support from women. Their capacity for fund-raising was particularly welcomed. But in seeking this support they were breaking in part with traditional assumptions about politics being a male sphere, traditional assumptions which had been rudely challenged by the female revolutionaries in France who were constantly invoked in the debate over women's political activity. Not surprisingly, many men had mixed feelings about this potential field of action for 'the fair sex'. So, indeed, did many women. Attwood's patronage of his female audience, Scholefield's insistence that they were involved primarily for their menfolk, Salt's emphasis on good conduct and moral force as the ways in which women could be politically effective, all point to the difficulties arising from the mobilization of women, the tensions generated by the spectacle of 1000 women in the Birmingham Town Hall and what they might do. Would they properly recognize that Attwood had achieved reform for them? Would they be content with acting for their fathers, husbands and sons? Would they continue to behave well and conduct themselves according to female proprieties? Could the men control them? Would Mrs Bamford have gone to Manchester without her husband's permission? What was a woman's place? They were certainly not willing to be rendered silent. At a subsequent Female Political Union meeting with a Mrs Spinks in the chair, Mr Collins, a prominent BPU member, spoke. Birmingham had at last achieved incorporation and the right to representative local government. Mr Collins said, 'He could not but congratulate them on the glorious victory that had been that day achieved in the Town Hall by the men of Birmingham.' A woman in the meeting, resenting this slur on her sex, piped up, 'And by the women, Mr Collins, for we were there.' Mr Collins had to admit 'the assistance the women had rendered'.[29]

Given the institutional framework of Radical working-class culture, it was difficult for women to engage straightforwardly in it as political agents in their own right. Nevertheless, they were there in considerable numbers and with considerable strength, in Female Reform Associations, in the Owenite communities and among the Chartists.[30] For the most part it seems that they sought primarily to advance the cause of their menfolk, and, in the case of Chartism, to assure that the male voice could be properly represented in Parliament. But there were sounds of discord.

Discussion as to the nature of womanhood was an ever-present feature of both working-class and middle-class society in this period. Debates over the character of woman's moral influence, over her potential for moral inspiration, over the tension between spiritual equality and social subordination, over the proper nature of woman's work, permeated political, religious and scientific discourses as well as the fields of literary and visual representation.

Radical circles provided no exception to this. Attempts by feminists such as Mary Wollstonecraft to open up questions of sexual difference and sexual equality in the 1790s had met with a barrage of hostility. But those women who wanted to question the primacy of women's status as wives and mothers, who wanted to argue for women to have rights for themselves not only the right to improve men through their spiritual inspiration, but to be independent workers in the vineyards of Radical and socialist culture, were able to use and subvert the language of moral influence to make new claims for themselves as women. As Barbara Taylor has shown, the most sustained attempts to interpret political Radicalism as centrally to do with not only class politics but also gender politics, came from the Owenite feminists.[31] Owenism provided less stony ground than other varieties of Radicalism and socialism for the developments of new forms of socialist feminism. Its commitment to love and cooperation as against competition and its critique of the relations of domination and subordination, whether between masters and men or men and women, meant that Owenite analysis potentially focused on all the social relations of capitalism, including the institutions of marriage and the family.

But the Owenite moment was a transitional political moment. Owenite men were not immune to the sexual antagonism fostered by new methods of production which aimed to marginalize skilled men and make use of the cheap labour of women and children. Even within the movement, Owenite feminists had to struggle to be heard and as Owenism declined in strength and Chartism increasingly occupied centre-stage within Radical culture, feminist voices were quietened. The institutions of Radical working-class culture, as we have seen, tended to centre on men and legitimate male belonging. The self-improvement clubs, the debating societies, the Hampden clubs and the mutual education evenings were more accessible to men than to women. If the institutional framework positioned men as agents and women as supporters, what of the belief system?

Paineite Radicalism was central to the political discourses of working people at this time. With its stress on Radical egalitarianism, its rejection of the traditions of the past, its conviction that the future could be different, its belief in natural rights and the power of reason, its questioning of established institutions and its firm commitment to the view that government must represent the people it gave a cutting thrust to radical demands.[32] Mary Wollstonecraft was to build on that Radical egalitarianism and extend the demand for individual rights to women. In her new moral world women would be full subjects able to participate as rational beings, no longer tied into the constraining bonds of a frivolous femininity. But her cause won few adherents, the countervailing forces were too strong and her ideal of woman's citizenship while it survived in feminist thinking and debate was lost in the more public discourses of Radicalism in the next fifty years.[33]

Paine's stress on individual rights and on the centrality of consent to representative forms of government drew on the classical tradition of Locke, which was itself built on the inalienable Puritan right to individual spiritual life. This tradition had attained considerable power in eighteenth-century England. But Locke's concept of the individual agent never extended beyond men. For him the origins of government lay in the consent of the propertied. The only people who were qualified to give consent were those propertied men who would take responsibility for their dependants, whether wives, children or servants. Political authority for Locke rested with men. Locke then further reinforced the differences between men and women by arguing that within the family men would inevitably carry greater authority than women. In line with the political break he represented with Filmer and conservative ideas of the divine and patriarchal nature of kingly authority, he insisted that marriage was a contractual relation to which both partners had to consent. To this extent Locke was arguing *for* individual rights for women. The husband was not seen as having any absolute sovereignty within the family. But Locke saw it as only to be expected that in every household someone would take command. Both parents had obligations to their children but the superior ability of the husband would give him the right to act as head and arbiter. This was a *natural* outcome. Locke thus distinguished between the 'natural' world of the family in which men would emerge as more powerful than women, and the political world of civil society in which men consented to forms of government.[34] This distinction between the two spheres, the family and civil society, with their different forms and rules, was played upon and developed by Enlightenment thinkers in the eighteenth century. As Jane Rendall has argued, writers across England, France and Scotland elaborated theories of sexual difference which built upon this primary distinction. They stressed that woman's nature was governed more by feeling than by reason, it was imaginative rather than analytic, and that women possessed distinctive moral characteristics which, in the right setting, could be fulfilled. Thus Rousseau combined his critique of the moral and sexual weakness of women with a belief that women could act as sources of moral inspiration and guidance, if they were allowed to blossom in their domestic worlds. The domestic sphere, Enlightenment thinkers argued, could provide a positive role for women but a role that was premised on an assertion of difference from rather than similarity to men.[35]

Radical thinking was embedded in these assumptions about sexual difference. Mary Wollstonecraft herself argued for the rights of women as wives and mothers and thought that most women in the new world would put those duties first. For her such a view was balanced with her belief that women should have the right to fulfilment for themselves. For others it was only too possible to combine a clear commitment to political Radicalism with a deep and entrenched social conservatism. William Cobbett, the writer and journalist whom Thompson sees as the most important intellectual influence on post-war Radicalism, was in the forefront of such tendencies. It was Cobbett who created the Radical culture of the 1820s, Thompson argues,

> not because he offered its most original ideas, but in the sense that he found the tone, the style, and the arguments which could bring the weaver, the schoolmaster, and the shipwright, into a common discourse. Out of the diversity of grievances and interests he brought a Radical consensus.[36]

But Cobbett's Radical consensus was one which placed women firmly in the domestic sphere. He came to be categorically in favour of home life and what he saw as established and well-tried household patterns. Wives should be chaste, sober, industrious, frugal, clean, good-tempered and beautiful with a knowledge of domestic affairs and able to cook. The nation was made up of families, argued Cobbett, and it was essential that families should be happy and well managed, with enough food and decent wages. This was the proper basis of a good society. In writing *Cottage Economy*, Cobbett hoped to contribute to the revival of homely and domestic skills, which he saw as seriously threatened by the development of a wage economy. He offered precise instructions on the brewing of beer, not only because it could be made more cheaply at home, but also because a good home brew would encourage men to spend their evenings with their families rather than at the tavern. A woman who could not bake, Cobbett thought, was 'unworthy of trust and confidence . . . a mere burden upon the community'. He assured fathers that the way to construct a happy marriage for their daughters was to 'make them skilful, able and active in the most necessary concerns of a family'. Dimples and cherry cheeks were not enough; it was knowing how to brew, to bake, to make milk and butter' that made a woman into 'a person worthy of respect'. What could please God more, asked Cobbett, than a picture of 'the labourer, after his return from the toils of a cold winter day, sitting with his wife and children round a cheerful fire, while the wind whistles in the chimney and the rain pelts the roof?'[37] Given that so much depended on it, men should take care to exercise their reason as well as their passion in their choice of a wife. Wives should run the household and forget the new-fangled 'accomplishments' of femininity with which he had no patience. Men should honour and respect their wives and spend their time at home when not occupied away. Cobbett shared the commonly-held view that women were more feeling than men and he saw that women had more to lose in marriage, for they gave up their property and their person to their husband. Husbands should consequently be kind to their wives, but there was no question that wives were subject to the authority of their husbands, that they must obey and must not presume to make decisions. Reason and God, thundered Cobbett, both decreed that wives should obey their husbands, there must be a head of every house he said, echoing Locke, and he must have undivided authority. As the head of the household men must represent their dependants and themselves enjoy the most salient right of all. There could be no rights, Cobbett believed, without that most central right 'the right of taking a part in the making of the laws by which we are governed'. Without that, the right to enjoy life and property or to exert physical or mental powers meant nothing. Following directly in the tradition of Locke, Cobbett argued that the right to take part in the making of laws was founded in the state of nature. 'It springs', he argued,

> out of the very principle of civil society; for what compact, what agreement, what common assent, can possibly be imagined by which men would give up all the rights of nature, all the free enjoyment of their bodies and their minds, in order to subject themselves to rules and laws, in the making of which they should have nothing to say, and which should be enforced upon them without their assent? The great right, therefore, of every man, the right of rights, is the right of having a share in the making of the laws, to which the good of the whole makes it his duty to submit.

Cobbett argued strongly, breaking entirely with Locke at this point, that *no* man should be excluded from this 'right of rights' unless he was insane or had committed an 'indelible crime'. He would have no truck with the view that it was property in the sense of landownership that conferred the right.

For Cobbett it was those properties associated with 'honourable' labour and property in skill which gave men the right to vote. Minors he

saw as automatically excluded from such privileges since the law classified
them as infants. But the rights of women to share in the making of the
laws, to give their assent to the abandonment of the right of nature and
the free enjoyment of their bodies and their minds, he disposed of in one
sentence. 'Women are excluded', he wrote, from the right of rights
because, 'husbands are answerable in law for their wives, as to their civil
damages, and because the very nature of their sex makes the exercise of
this right incompatible with the harmony and happiness of society'.
There was no escape from this. Single women who wanted to argue that
they were legal individuals with civil rights were caught, when it came to
political rights, by their *nature*. Women could only become persons
'worthy of respect' through their household skills. Society could only be
harmonious and happy if they behaved as wives and daughters, subject to
the better judgements of their fathers. By nature the female sex were
unsuited to the public sphere.[38]

The positioning of women as wives, mothers and daughters within
Radical culture at the same time that men were positioned as active
and independent agents was in part connected to similar processes within
middle-class culture. The period from the 1790s to the 1830s also saw the
emergence of the English middle class, with its own beliefs and practices,
its own sense of itself as a class, with interests different from those of
other classes. The middle class defined itself in part through certain
critical public moments; the affair of Queen Caroline, the events of 1832
and the repeal of the Corn Laws in 1846, but it also defined itself through
the establishment of new cultural patterns and new institutional forms.
Central to its culture was a marked emphasis on the separation between
male and female spheres. Men were to be active in the public world of
business and politics. Women were to be gentle and dependent in the
private world of the home and family. The two most powerful cultural
and intellectual influences on middle-class formation were serious
Christianity and political economy. Both, in their own ways, emphasized
the different interests of men and women and articulated the discourses of
separate spheres.[39]

Middle-class men from the late eighteenth century were striving to
establish their power and influence in the provinces, long before they
achieved full national recognition. They sought to make their voices
heard in both town and countryside, to influence Parliament on matters
that concerned them, to intervene in different forms of local government,
to establish and maintain religious and cultural institutions, to exercise
their charity and to build new mercantile, financial and commercial
associations. In every field of interest they were active and energetic,
fulfilling the precept that 'a man must act'. Their initiatives were multiple,

their fields of enterprise boundless. Assumptions about sexual difference permeated all their schemes. Their political committees excluded women, their churches demarcated male and female spheres, their botanical gardens assumed that men would join on behalf of their families, their philanthropic societies treated men and women differently, their business associations were for men only. In defining their own cultural patterns and practices the men and women of the middle class had a significant impact on working-class culture. The middle class was fighting for political and cultural pre-eminence. In rejecting aristocratic values and the old forms of patronage and influence they sought to define new values, to establish new modes of power. In the process they were both defining themselves as a class and asserting dominance. In many areas, particularly new industrial towns where aristocratic interest was not well entrenched, they were able to occupy the field, to be the providers of education and philanthropy, to establish whole new ranges of institutions which bore their imprint.

In Birmingham, for example, large numbers of schools, Sunday schools and charitable ventures were established in the late eighteenth and early nineteenth centuries, which all operated with middle-class notions of what were properly male and female. In recommending domestic values to Sunday school pupils, charity school girls or aged and infirm women, middle-class women at one and the same time defined their own 'relative sphere' and their sense of the proper place of working-class women. That proper place was either as servants in the homes of their betters, or as respectable and modest wives and mothers in their own homes. The Birmingham Society for Aged and Infirm Women sought money on behalf of 'those who have discharged the relative duties of a wife and mother' and were left, perhaps deserted, in their old age.

The organizers paid the strictest attention to establishing whether the women really deserved such assistance, whether their lives had been humble and respectable.[40] Schools taught boys and girls separately, often in different buildings and with emphasis on different achievements.[41] Self-improvement societies and debating societies, such as the Birmingham Brotherly Society, were for men only.[42] The new Mechanics' Institute was exclusively male and aimed to train men to become better husbands, servants and fathers. As the first report of the Birmingham Institute stressed, a man's whole family would benefit from his involvement with such an establishment. He himself would become more 'sober, intelligent and tranquil' they claimed,

> his presence at home will diffuse pleasure and tranquillity throughout his household. His own improvement will be reflected in the improved condition of his family. Perceiving the benefit of a

judicious economy, he will still be able to command a larger expenditure in the education of his children, and in the accessories of rational enjoyment. Cheerfulness, cleanliness, and the smile of welcome will constantly await his approach to his domestic fireside. Beloved at home and respected abroad, it will not be too much to assert, that he will become a better servant, husband and father; a higher moral character; and consequently a happier man, from his connection with the MECHANICS INSTITUTE.[43]

These were grandiose claims indeed! Not surprisingly, working-class men and women were not miraculously transformed into respectable and sober men, domestic and home-loving women, by the action of institutions inspired by the middle class. But as many historians have demonstrated, nor did they simply refuse the values of this dominant culture. As R. Q. Gray has shown in his perceptive study of the aristocracy of labour in Edinburgh, a process of negotiating took place between dominant and subordinate, negotiation that resulted in the emergence of distinctive concepts of dignity and respectability, influenced by middle-class values yet holding to a belief in trade union action, for example, and a strong sense of class pride.[44] Similarly, David Vincent in his study of the meaning of 'useful knowledge' to working-class autobiographers has demonstrated the independence from middle-class meanings of the term and the creation of a separate and class-specific concept.[45] The same story could be told in relation to male and female spheres. Working-class men and women did not adopt wholesale the middle-class view of a proper way of life. But aspects of both religious and secular discourses on masculinity, femininity and domestic life did have resonance in some sections of the working class, did make sense of some experience and appeal to some needs.

Take the case of temperance. Temperance, it has been argued, provides a prime example of the successful assertion of middle-class hegemony.[46] Working men became volunteers in the cause of middle-class respectability. They aimed to improve themselves, to educate themselves, to raise themselves to their betters. The initiative for the total abstinence movement had come from class-conscious working men and there were many connections between them and the Chartist Movement but the Radical belief in individual improvement was extremely vulnerable to assimilation to the cultural patterns of the middle class. Arguments against drink made heavy use of an appeal to home and family, for one of the major evils associated with alcohol was its propensity to ruin working-class families and reduce them to depravity. In the famous series of Cruikshank plates entitled *The Bottle*, for example, the first image was of a respectable and modest working-class family enjoying a meal in their simple but clean and comfortable home. They represented the model happy family with clothes carefully mended, a family portrait, the young children playing, a fire burning cosily in the grate and a lock on the door ensuring that the home would remain a place of refuge and security. Then the man offered his wife a drink and in scene after scene Cruickshank documented the horrifying destruction of the home and family ending up with the husband insane, having murdered his wife with a bottle, the youngest child dead and the other two a pimp and a prostitute.[47] It was a cliché of temperance lecturers to rely on the comparison between the unhappy home of the drunkard and the contented domestic idyll of the temperate worker. As a reformed drinker poetically declared.

> I protest that no more I'll get drunk –
> For I find it the bane of my life!
> Henceforth I'll be watchful that nought shall destroy
> That comfort and peace that I ought to enjoy
> In my children, my home and my wife.[48]

Such protestations did not simply imply the acceptance of middle-class ideals of domesticity for working men and women developed their own notions of manliness and femininity which, while affected by dominant conceptions, nevertheless had inflections of their own. As John Smith, a Birmingham temperance enthusiast argued,

> The happiness of the fireside is involved in the question of temperance, and we know that the chief ornament of that abode of happiness is woman. Most of the comforts of life depend upon our female relatives and friends, whether in infancy, in mature years, or old age . . .[49]

Here he touched on a vital nerve, for the comforts of life for the working man did indeed depend on female relatives. But those female relatives needed different skills from their middle-class sisters. While middle-class ideologues stressed the moral and managerial aspects of womanhood, for wives were to provide moral inspiration and manage the running of their households, working-class blueprints for the good wife and mother emphasized the practical skills associated with household management, cooking, cleaning and bringing up children. For the wife to manage the family finances seems to have been a very widespread pattern in both town and countryside, a distinctive difference from their middle-class counterparts with their exclusion from money matters. The working man was to earn, the working woman to spend, using her hard-won knowledge of domestic needs and the relative merits of available goods, to eke out what money was coming in.[50]

This evaluation of woman's domestic role coincided with the emergence of working women as a publicly defined 'social problem'. As Sally Alexander has argued, the period of the 1830s and 1840s saw the confirmation of men as responsible political subjects while women were largely condemned to public silence.[51] An important aspect of this was the emergence of the idea of the 'family wage', a wage which a male breadwinner would earn, sufficient to support his wife and children.[52] Such an ideal of male support and female dependence was already firmly established within middle-class culture but was to become embedded in working-class practice as well through, for example, the bargaining procedures of skilled trade unions.[53] Again, this did not involve the straightforward acceptance of middle-class standards but rather an adaptation and re-shaping of class-specific notions.

In the early 1840s, to take one case, middle-class fears and anxieties about the employment of women in unsuitable work reached a pitch over the issue of women's work in the mines. The commissioners appointed to enquire into the incidence of child labour underground were shocked and horrified at the evidence that emerged of female conditions of work. Bourgeois views of femininity were violently assaulted by the spectacle of women in various stages of undress working alongside men. The affront to public morality and the fears generated as to the imminent collapse of the working-class family and consequently working-class morality, led to the campaign spearheaded by the Evangelicals, for the exclusion of women from underground work. The Mines and Collieries Act 1842, which excluded women from underground work, marked one attempt by the State, together with other interventions such as the bastardy clause of the New Poor Law, to regulate the form of the working-class family and to legislate a moral code. Many working miners supported the ban on women's work but their reasons were different from those of the middle-class campaigners. As Angela John has shown, they did not accept the judgement of commissioners such as Tremenheere that female exclusion was, 'the first step towards raising the standard of domestic habits and the securing of a respectable home'. They resented middle-class interlopers who told them how to live their lives and organize their families. They emphasized working-class control over their own culture. They argued for better lives for their wives and daughters and insisted that if the wives of the owners could stay at home, then so should theirs. They stressed that their wives were entitled to a decent life above ground and attacked those coal-owners, such as the Duke of Hamilton, who continued to employ women illegally.

But the miners had another powerful motive for supporting exclusion. The Miners Association of Great Britain and Ireland was formed in 1842, three days before the date designated for the exclusion of females under eighteen. As clearly stated in the *Miners Advocate*, the union was firmly against female employment from the start. They sought to control the hours of labour and obtain the highest possible wages. For women to work was seen as a direct threat to this enterprise, for women's work kept down wages. For their own reasons men in the mines preferred, as an ideal, to be able to support their women at home.[54] The women, unable to speak publicly for themselves, were lost. They hated the conditions of work but they needed the money, but their voices were not heard and in one of the major public debates of the 1840s, blazoned across the press, men were legitimated as workers, women as wives and mothers, by the State, by middle-class philanthropists and by working men.

Samuel and Jemima went together to Peterloo. They shared the excitement, they shared the horror and the fear. But they experienced it differently on account of their sex. Men and women did not occupy the culture of their class in the same way. Ideologically their differences were emphasized, institutionally they were often segregated. The complexities of the relation between class and culture have received much attention. It is time for gender and culture to be subjected to more critical scrutiny.

Notes

1 S. Bamford, *Passages in the Life of a Radical* (Oxford: Oxford University Press, 1984). The account of Peterloo is on pp. 141–56. Subsequently only direct quotes are footnoted.

2 Ibid., pp. 132–3.

3 Ibid., pp. 146–7.

4 Ibid., p. 151.

5 Ibid., pp. 161, 150.

6 Ibid., p. 156.

7 E. P. Thompson, *The Making of the English Working Class* (London: Victor Gollancz, 1963).

8 Ibid., p. 9.

9 Ibid., p. 12. For Sheila Rowbotham's own account of the development of her fascination with history, see 'Search and Subject, Threading Circumstance', in S. Rowbotham, *Dreams and Dilemmas* (London: Virago, 1983).

10 Barbara Taylor, *Eve and the New Jerusalem. Socialism and Feminism in the Nineteenth Century* (London: Virago, 1983), chapter 4.

11 Bamford, *Passages in the Life of a Radical*, p. 161.

12 On the eighteenth-century crowd, see E. P. Thompson, 'The Moral Economy of the English Crowd in the Eighteenth Century', *Past & Present*, no. 50 (1971). See also, E. P. Thompson, 'Patrician Society, Plebeian Culture', *Journal of Social History*, vol. 7, no. 4 (1974).

13 For discussions of the family economy, see, for example, M. Berg, *The Age of Manufactures 1700–1820* (Oxford: Basil Blackwell, 1985); L. Tilly and

J. Scott, *Women, Work and Family* (New York: Holt, Rinehart & Winston, 1978).

14 J. Gillis, *For Better For Worse. British Marriages 1600 to the present* (Oxford: Oxford University Press, 1985), p. 229.

15 For an attempt to do this in relation to the middle class in the early nineteenth century, see L. Davidoff and C. Hall, *Family Fortunes: Men and Women of the English Middle Class 1780–1850* (Chicago: University of Chicago Press, 1987).

16 The literature on class in the early nineteenth century is extensive. See, for example, H. Perkin, *The Origins of Modern English Society 1780–1880* (London: Routledge, 1969); R. J. Morris, *Class and Class Consciousness in the Industrial Revolution* (London: Macmillan, 1979); A. Briggs, 'The language of "class" in early nineteenth-century England', in A. Briggs and J. Saville (eds), *Essays in Labour History* (London: Macmillan, 1960); J. Foster, *Class Struggle and the Industrial Revolution: Early Capitalism in Three English Towns* (London: Methuen, 1974); G. Stedman Jones, *Languages of Class. Studies in English working class history 1832–1982* (Cambridge: Cambridge University Press, 1983).

17 T. Hardy, *Memoir of Thomas Hardy . . . Written by Himself* (1832), p. 16.

18 Bamford, *Passages in the Life of a Radical*, p. 123.

19 Ibid., p. 121.

20 Ibid., pp. 110, 61.

21 Ibid., p. 115.

22 Thompson, *The Making of the English Working Class*, particularly chapter 16, 'Class Consciousness'.

23 Ibid., p. 610.

24 Bamford, *Passages in the Life of a Radical*, p. 14.

25 T. W. Laqueur, 'Literacy and Social Mobility in the Industrial Revolution in England', *Past & Present*, no. 64 (1974).

26 D. Vincent, *Bread, Knowledge and Freedom: A Study of Nineteenth-Century Working-Class Autobiography* (London: Methuen, 1981).

27 D. Thompson, 'Women and Nineteenth-century Radical Politics: a lost dimension', in J. Mitchell and A. Oakley (eds), *The Rights and Wrongs of Women* (Harmondsworth: Penguin, 1976).

28 For a delightful example of such constitutional practice, see Thompson, *The Making of the English Working Class*, pp. 738–9.

29 *Birmingham Journal*, 5 January 1839, 12 January 1839 and 2 February 1839.

30 On women's militancy and engagement with radical politics, see I. B. O'Malley, *Women in Subjection: a study of the lives of English-women before 1832* (1933); Taylor, *Eve and the New Jerusalem*; M. I. Thomis and J. Grimmett, *Women in Protest, 1800–1850* (London: Macmillan, 1982); D. Jones, 'Women and Chartism', *History*, no. 68 (February 1983). There is an excellent introduction to the literature in J. Rendall, *The Origins of Modern Feminism: Women in Britain, France and the United States 1780–1860* (London: Macmillan, 1985).

31 Taylor, *Eve and the New Jerusalem*.

32 T. Paine, *The Rights of Man* (Harmondsworth: Penguin, 1963). The best

discussion of Paine in the context of English Radicalism is in Thompson, *The Making of the English Working Class.*

33 M. Wollstonecraft, *Vindication of the Rights of Woman* (Harmondsworth: Penguin, 1982). There is a voluminous literature on Mary Wollstonecraft. For an excellent recent analysis, see M. Poovey, *The Proper Lady and the Woman Writer. Ideology as style in the works of Mary Wollstonecraft, Mary Shelley and Jane Austen* (Chicago: University of Chicago Press, 1984).

34 J. Locke, *Two Treatises of Government* ed. P. Laslett (1965); G. Schochet, *Patriarchalism in Political Thought. The Authoritarian Family and Political Speculation and Attitudes, especially in Seventeenth Century England* (Oxford: Oxford University Press, 1975); S. Moller Okin, *Women in Western Political Thought* (London: Virago, 1980); R. W. Krouse, 'Patriarchal Liberalism and Beyond: from John Stuart Mill to Harriet Taylor', in J. B. Elshtain (ed.), *The Family in Political Thought* (Brighton: Harvester Press, 1984); E. Fox-Genovese, 'Property and Patriarchy in Classical Bourgeois Political Theory', *Radical History Review*, vol. 4, nos 2–3 (1977).

35 J. Rendall, *The Origins of Modern Feminism*, chapter 2.

36 Thompson, *The Making of the English Working Class*, p. 746.

37 W. Cobbett, *Cottage Economy* (1822), pp. 60, 62, 63, 199.

38 W. Cobbett, *Advice to Young Men, and Incidentally to Young Women in the Middle and Higher Ranks of Life* (Oxford: Oxford University Press, 1980). See particularly chapters 4 and 6. For a discussion of the importance of 'honourable' labour and property in skill to working men's claims for manhood, see S. Alexander, 'Women, Class and Sexual Differences in the 1830s and 1840s: some reflections on the writing of a feminist history', *History Workshop Journal*, no. 17 (1984). On independence and self-respect, see T. Tholfsen, *Working-class Radicalism in mid-Victorian England* (New York: Columbia University Press, 1976).

39 Davidoff and Hall, *Family Fortunes.*

40 *Aris's Birmingham Gazette*, 17 January 1831 and 21 January 1833.

41 For example, the Sunday schools of the Anglican Christ Church in Birmingham. J. G. Breay, *The Faithful Pastor Delineated* (Birmingham, 1839).

42 Birmingham Brotherly Society, Minutes of the Meetings, Birmingham Reference Library, Mss. no. 391175.

43 Birmingham Mechanics Institute, *Address of the Provisional Committee* (Birmingham, 1825).

44 R. Q. Gray, *The Labour Aristocracy in Victorian Edinburgh* (Oxford: Oxford University Press, 1976). Gray's study deals with the later nineteenth century. See also, T. Tholfsen's discussion of middle-class hegemony in *Working Class Radicalism in Mid-Victorian England*; T. W. Laqueur's argument in *Religion and Respectability; Sunday Schools and Working Class Culture 1780–1850* (New Haven: Yale University Press, 1976) that working-class people subverted middle-class intentions and made Sunday schools into institutions of their own culture. For two sensitive accounts of the class-specific mediations which occur in cultural practice, see R. Colls, *The Collier's Rant. Song and Culture in the Industrial Village* (London: Croom Helm, 1977); and

M. Vitale 'The Domesticated Heroine in Byron's Corsair and William Hone's Prose Adaptation', *Literature and History*, vol. 10, no. 1 (1984).

45 Vincent, *Bread, Knowledge and Freedom*, especially chapter 7.

46 Tholfsen, *Working-Class Radicalism in Mid-Victorian England*, especially chapter 7.

47 There is a fascinating discussion of Cruikshank in L. James, 'Cruikshank and Early Victorian Caricature', *History Workshop Journal*, no. 6 (1978).

48 A selection of tracts and handbills published in aid of the Temperance Reformation, Birmingham, 1839.

49 J. Smith, *Speech at the Birmingham Temperance Meeting*, Birmingham, 1835.

50 K. D. M. Snell, *Annals of the Labouring Poor. Social Change and Agrarian England* (Cambridge: Cambridge University Press, 1985), especially chapter 7; D. Vincent, 'Love and Death and the Nineteenth-century Working Class', *Social History*, no. 5 (1980).

51 S. Alexander, 'Women, Class and Sexual Differences in the 1830s and 1840s'.

52 For the best introduction to the literature on the family wage, see H. Land, 'The Family Wage', *Feminist Review*, no. 6 (1980).

53 For a discussion of sex and its relation to skill, see A. Phillips and B. Taylor, 'Sex and Skill: Notes towards a Feminist Economics', *Feminist Review*, no. 6 (1980). For the development of a particular union and its restrictive practices, see J. Liddington and J. Norris, 'One hand tied behind us'. The rise of the Women's Suffrage Movement (London: Virago 1978).

54 A. John, *By the Sweat of their Brow. Women Workers at Victorian coal mines* (London: Croom Helm, 1980); and 'Colliery Legislation and its Consequences: 1842 and the Women Miners of Lancashire', *Bulletin of the John Rylands University Library of Manchester*, vol. 61, no. 1 (1978). Tremenheere, quoted p. 90.

4

Celebrating Thompson's Heroes: Social Analysis in History and Anthropology

Renato Rosaldo

I often wish that E. P. Thompson were an anthropologist. His work is admirable and it has served as an inspiration for my own. It embodies an anthropologically sophisticated conception of culture. For him, cultural traditions are selected, recombined and invented as an active part of class formation.[1] Cultural traditions, understood as actively selected versions of the past, constitute and reconstitute themselves through social conflicts that project themselves from the past into an imagined future. The analysis of traditions so conceived becomes the historical narrative of their struggles, not the synchronic analysis of static cultural forms. From this perspective ideology, not social analysis, has created the dichotomy between vital culture (the active creation of new cultural forms) and inert tradition (the passive reception of an unchallenged frozen heritage handed down from the past).

Doing history (or, for that matter, anthropology) involves finding modes of composition adequate for the analysis of ongoing struggle. The conflictual movements of cultural traditions are both invented in narrative forms *and* discovered in the historical past itself. Historians listen to voices from the past as part of the creative process of developing their analytical narratives. In the movement between historical narrative and 'what really happened', neither should be reduced to the other. The historical past always constrains its narratives, and a narrative always selects from and organizes more complex historical pasts. A historical narrative can neither be reduced to brute facts (because they do not articulate it), nor can it be treated as mere fiction (because, once invented, it must 'fit' the facts). Indeed, historians constantly tack back and forth, from their narratives to the facts, and from the facts to their narratives. Although they may appear to be so, such narratives are never innocent. Critical assessments of historical accounts raise questions of how carefully the evidence has been weighed, and the other possible narratives that could have been written about the same events.

In what follows, my admiration for Thompson's work will be tempered by an anthropological critique of *The Making of the English Working Class*. After reviewing Thompson's explicit polemical views of anthropology, I shall suggest that critical anthropology shares much with the project of writing a committed history. This overlap, however, is less evident in explicit polemics than in the practices of the historian's craft. The paper thus turns to Thompson's classic work, particularly its illuminating analysis of human agency, with a view to showing how it can instruct and be instructed by critical anthropology. Thompson's work is especially instructive as an exemplary instance of the practical study of the interplay of conditioning and making.[2] My main critique, from an anthropologist's perspective, will be that Thompson's compelling narrative often glosses over the problem of whether central concepts belong to the author or to the agents of historical change.

In recent years a number of anthropologists have cited Thompson as if he were an ancestral figure.[3] However, as so often happens in human worship, these ritual offerings have not moved their beneficiary. Rather than recognize his reverential would-be descendents from a neighbouring discipline, Thompson objects to what he sees as anthropology's excessive reliance on the method of 'stopping the process of history' in order to engage in 'static, synchronic structural analysis'.[4] In a debate about European witchcraft, for example, Thompson sided with historian Keith Thomas against anthropologist Hildred Geertz in the following terms:

> The eighteenth-century evidence appears to me to gesture towards a rather more coherent mental universe of symbolism informing practice than Thomas allows for the seventeenth. But the coherence (and here I would expect some anthropologists to lay this paper down in disgust) arises less from any inherent cognitive structure than from the particular field of force and sociological oppositions peculiar to eighteenth-century society; to be blunt, the discrete and fragmented elements of older patterns of thought become integrated by *class*.[5]

In violation of Thompson's expectations, I avidly read on and found myself agreeing with his argument, rather than laying down his paper in disgust. His rejection of a concept of culture whose coherence derives from harmonic cognitive structures rather than conflicting social forces coincides with current critical perspectives being developed by a number of anthropologists.

Indeed, the objects of criticism for Thompson and critical anthropologists are much the same. Anthropologists themselves have more than matched Thompson by mounting a critique against ethnographic writings that objectify in the name of objectivity.[6] Such writing relies too much on disciplinary norms of writing that prescribe a detached third-person point of view from which social activity is described in the present tense as if it were always repeated in the same manner. The notion of culture which Thompson and critical anthropologists find objectionable can be illustrated, among other places, by the following passage from E. E. Evans-Pritchard's deservedly classic ethnography, *The Nuer*:

> Seasonal and lunar changes repeat themselves year after year, so that a Nuer standing at any point of time has conceptual knowledge of what lies before him and can predict and organize his life accordingly. A man's structural future is likewise already fixed and ordered into different periods, so that the total changes in status a boy will undergo in his ordained passage through the social system, if he lives long enough, can be foreseen.[7]

The ethnographer speaks interchangeably of the Nuer or of a Nuer man because, differences of age aside (questions of gender barely enter Evans-Pritchard's androcentric work), the culture is conceived as uniform and static. Yet at the very time the ethnographer was conducting his research, the Nuer were being subjected to enforced changes by the British colonial regime's efforts at so-called pacification. Uncomfortably like Edward Said's version of 'orientalism', Evans-Pritchard's Nuer have been represented ethnographically as internally homogeneous and unchanging through time.

The terms of Thompson's intellectual battle over the concept of culture are probably familiar to most readers. His disagreements with anthropology resemble his attacks on Louis Althusser's structuralism and his critique of Raymond Williams' notion of culture as consensus.[8] Among key words informing the version of culture under attack are static, synchronic structure and consensus. Thompson conceives of culture as a field of contention, not as a uniformly shared static world. Among his key words are change, experience, conflict and struggle.

In Thompson's cosmology, anthropology often represents the benign Other (as contrasted with the malignant Other, the Althusserians).[9] On one occasion, for example, he distances anthropology from history by saying, 'It is generally true that anthropology, sociology, and criminology, have evolved either as unhistorical disciplines, or with an inadequate historical component, or with an actively anti-historical bias.'[10] On another occasion, the distance looms so large that merely contemplating a convergence between history and anthropology makes Thompson's prose turn purple as he mockingly (but uncritically) uses sexist stereotypes to depict a perverse erotics: 'In some eyes, the "systematic indoctrination" of historians "in the social sciences" conjures up a scene of insemination, in which Clio lies inert and passionless (perhaps with rolling eyes) while anthropology or sociology thrust their seed into her womb.'[11] Thompson forcefully argues that the two disciplines should continue their abstinence and not engage in sexual or any other kind of union.

Although he rejects a dated version of the concept of culture, Thompson proposes that historians use anthropological questions to open new areas of research, modify or demolish received concepts, and test propositions through the 'discipline of historical context'. In this vein, for example, he says, 'for us, the anthropological impulse is chiefly felt, not in model-building, but in locating new problems, in seeing old problems in new ways, in an emphasis on norms or value-systems and upon rituals, in attention to expressive functions of forms of riot and disturbance, and upon symbolic expressions of authority, control and hegemony.'[12]

Far from disagreeing, however, most anthropologists of any stripe would applaud Thompson's remarks. Indeed, we have said much the same thing about applying concepts and methods useful for understanding one culture to the study of another.[13] Nor do many anthropologists imagine that the discipline has produced laws, findings or methods that can be transported from one historical or cultural context to another without serious modification. Perhaps Thompson would be disappointed to learn that anthropologists find his polemics, not wrong-headed and controversial, but articulate and sensible. For ethnographers, Thompson's most original contributions cannot readily be deduced from his polemical writings.

Arguably, Thompson's polemic refers more to the concept of culture appropriated by his fellow historians than to the state of the art in anthropology. Not unlike Thompson's notion of cultural traditions, anthropology itself has developed through a process of ongoing struggle and change. Neither consensus nor stasis characterizes most of its central issues. In fact, as I have said, Thompson's criticisms have been more than met by an onslaught from within the discipline against a view of culture based on cognitive coherence. As in so many instances of cultural borrowing, the notion of culture subjected to critique by Thompson is already more residual than dominant in its homeland.[14]

Critical Anthropology

Since the late 1960s a number of anthropologists have embarked on the project of making history, politics and conflict central to the study of culture and society.[15] Where structure and system once reigned as central concepts, process and practice now stand in their stead. Local ethnographic research has found it increasingly difficult to ignore historical studies and more global contexts for analysis.

Although related changes occurred during the late 1960s in other fields and in other countries, the initial impetus for this disciplinary shift in the United States was the civil rights movement, followed by the mobilization against the war in Vietnam. Teach-ins, sit-ins, demonstrations and strikes set the political tone for this period on American college and university campuses. The annual business meetings of the American Anthropological Association became a verbal battleground where resolutions on certain major issues of the day were fiercely debated. Anthropological research in Chile and Thailand was attacked from within the discipline because of its potential uses in counter-insurgency efforts. A number of 'natives' answered back and charged anthropologists with perpetuating stereotypes and failing to resist the domination and oppression of their subjects of research. Received ideas that Thompson, in passages cited above, called 'static, synchronic structural analysis' and cultural coherence based on an 'inherent cognitive structure' simply seemed irrelevant (to use a term from the time) to those of us who were involved in struggles aimed at social transformation.

In part as an accidental consequence of its own blind-spots, the New Left in the United States helped produce a spectrum of political movements responsive to forms of oppression based on gender, sexual preference, and race. Women, for example, began to organize, among other reasons, because the New Left more often placed them in secretarial than leadership roles. As emergent feminists immediately realized, sexism permeated the entire society, not simply the New Left in its beginning phases. Racism and homophobia led to similar realizations in other sectors of society. Feminism, gay and lesbian movements, the Native American movement, the struggles of Blacks, Chicanos and Puerto Ricans, all called for global social analyses that made central the aspirations and demands of groups all too often overlooked by standard progressive politics, not to mention the dominant national ideology. Although many anthropologists who came of age in the late 1960s have been involved in one or another of these struggles, my own political vision has been most directly shaped through involvement in the campus Chicano movement. This experience has provided, as can be seen below, a sense of the centrality of political struggle, and of the urgency of attending with care to the perceptions and aspirations of subordinate groups.

The political ferment of the late 1960s and early 1970s transformed American anthropology through the work of such figures as David

Aberle, Gerald Berreman, Kathleen Gough, Joseph Jorgenson, Dell Hymes, Louise Lamphere, Sidney Mintz, Laura Nader, Rayna Rapp, Michelle Rosaldo, Sydel Silverman and Eric Wolf.[16] French and British anthropology of the time also shaped American research agendas. Pierre Bourdieu and Talal Asad, for example, through their respective writings on a theory of practice and colonial domination, sharpened the political edge on Clifford Geertz's seminal formulations on cultural systems.[17] The re-invention of anthropology was also influenced by broader trends in social thought, ranging from such writers as Antonio Gramsci and Michel Foucault through Anthony Giddens and Richard Bernstein to Raymond Williams and E. P. Thompson.

Most anthropological students of Thompson have been schooled in symbolic analysis, historical materialism, or both. They share broad concerns with questions of political consciousness, ideology, class struggle, domination and the interplay of power and knowledge. For them, cultures are understood, not as unanchored cognitive systems, but as negotiated processes; they are both received and made. In a dialectical process, cultures shape, and are shaped by, politics, society and economics; they can neither be reduced to nor divorced from the hard surfaces of everyday life. Their histories result from the interplay of structure and human agency. This strand of anthropology clearly overlaps with Thompson's analytical project. In this vein, *The Making of the English Working Class* is often cited as 'a study in an active process, which owes as much to agency as to conditioning'.[18]

My own discovery of Thompson's work came in classic anthropological fashion, by listening to natives rather than by reading. In this case the natives were members of a discipline, social history, not a tribe. It all began during 1975–6 when I spent a year at Princeton's Institute for Advanced Study as a member of an interdisciplinary group, comprised primarily of social historians and cultural anthropologists. My project was to write an ethnography about the Ilongots, a hill tribe of Luzon, Philippines. The data for this ethnography-to-be included extensive oral testimonies that extended back almost a century in time. The idea was to write a history about the sort of people (so-called primitives) who supposedly have none.[19]

The politics of the late 1960s and early 1970s had by then made the severe limits of restricting temporal variation to the annual cycle apparent to most practitioners of the discipline. The received notion of culture, defined as a cognitive system, failed to account for the political processes that produce historical change in societies. The received concept of social structure, defined as the enduring forms of human relations, had been more assumed than investigated. Social structure usually was inferred from short-term inquiry, rather than studied over the long term. In studying the life-cycle, for example, analysts would assume a homogeneous unchanging culture and deduce their models by observing infants, children, teenagers, adults and the aged during a single year. It was as if an anthropologist happened to observe me and my children in the mid-1980s, and then explained adult character (mine) in relation to daycare centres (my children's, but neither thinkable nor institutionally available in my childhood). The shortcomings of exclusive reliance on synchronic analysis were by then overwhelmingly evident. Alternative modes of analysis were rather less clear.

The immediate problem was how, in practice, to write a social description of change, conflict and political processes. Slogans and abstract concepts did not get one very far. Shifting the object of analysis from structure to process required major changes, not only in analytical concepts, but also in modes of composition.[20] Yet conventional ethnographic writing provided precious little exemplary prose for exploring cultural traditions as conflictual processes. Inscribed in a distanced normalizing present, norms of writing had been designed for the study of timeless social structures and static cultural configurations. Violating such compositional norms as the timeless ethnographic present or the anonymous group noun (the Nuer, for example, rather than personal names) left one without alternative models for composition. Decisions about composition in turn often contained (implicit) issues for conceptual analysis. Thus matters of craft and composition began to loom as large as those of theory and method, with which they were inextricably intertwined.

In the following my project is to analyse Thompson's practice in conceiving and writing social descriptions attuned to politics, history, and conflict. Hence I shall turn to his early work, rather than his more recent polemical writings. Studying *The Making of the English Working Class* has been both illuminating, because Thompson's narrative is so artful and convincing, and vexing, because his theory of analysis and composition is not fully explicit. The gap between an abstract model of political processes in their historical unfolding and actually doing an ethnographic history is enormous. In this respect, Thompson's most significant contributions to anthropology arguably reside less in his explicit comments on the discipline than in the modes of composition through which he develops supple empirical social analyses of conflictual cultural traditions and human agency. The following sections on *The Making of the English Working Class* attempt to explore, in a manner at once critical and appreciative, a number of conceptual issues pertinent to developing social analyses informed by the interplay of history and anthropology.

Cultural Traditions as Conflictual Movements

The Making of the English Working Class raises a number of central
questions for social thought. If irreducible conflicts constitute certain
cultural traditions, then their analyses must account for divergent
perceptions of the stakes and tactics in political struggle. Within the
singularity of their historical moments, political conflicts are so
incommensurable as to remain beyond synthesis. From this perspective,
social analysis can no longer rob its subjects of their politics by simply
seeking cultural patterns or structural determinants. Instead, one should
grant centre-stage to the shifting divergent positions and contending
relations through which political processes unfold.

The conflicting traditions in *The Making of the English Working Class*
become articulated, not only among working people and Romantic artists
of the historical past, but also among the historians who have written
about the period. It is above all in Part Two that Thompson pits his
professional historian colleagues against one another. Thompson begins
his narrative by lining up two sides to do battle in this manner:

> [T]he territory of the Industrial Revolution, which was first staked
> out and surveyed by Marx, Arnold Toynbee, the Webbs, and the
> Hammonds, now resembles an academic battlefield. At point after
> point, the familiar 'catastrophic' view of the period has been
> disputed. Where it was customary to see the period as one of
> economic disequilibrium, intense misery and exploitation, political
> repression and heroic popular agitation, attention is now directed to
> the rate of economic growth (and the difficulties of 'take-off' into
> self-sustaining technological reproduction). The enclosure movement is
> now noted, less for its harshness in displacing the village poor, than
> for its success in feeding a rapidly growing population. (p. 195)

Facing off in this field of argument, two untitled married couples, the
Hammonds and the Webbs, stand on one side against their titled
opponents, Sir John Clapham and Professor Ashton, on the other side.
This bout pits what Thompson calls an old 'catastrophic orthodoxy'
against a new 'anti-catastrophic orthodoxy'.

Shortly after the battle-lines have been drawn, both Professor Ashton
and Sir John Clapham are defeated by the Hammonds. Perhaps Sir John
Clapham suffers the graver humiliation when Thompson mocks his
discussion of the national average in this manner: 'Throughout this
painstaking investigation, the great empiricist eschews all generalisations
except for one – the pursuit of the mythical "average". In his discussion of

agriculture we encounter the "average farm", the "average small-holding", the "average" ratio of labourers to employers' (p. 213). After his flamboyant taunting, Thompson assumes the voice of reason. He persuasively argues for not confusing the real issue – appraising well-being and immiseration among working people – with its proxy, the pursuit of a statistical average.

After winning the initial battle, however, the Hammonds and Webbs go on to lose the war. They begin well, as participants in a Radical tradition, but then they follow the flight pattern of Icarus and fall. Thompson condemns them because of their Fabian, utilitarian or generally ameliorist views. Aside from being more reformist than Radical, they provoke the historian's ire by discounting all spontaneous working class movements, particularly the Luddites, as being 'either highly improbable or, alternatively, wrong' (p. 591). The dissenting tradition itself is constituted by dissent.

Making a Radical Tradition

In developing his narrative, Thompson constructs a social network through which he textually creates a Radical tradition at once grounded in and transcending the working class. When people from the Radical tradition enter into conflicts, Thompson subjects their conduct to complex judgements in which political virtue and vice always are at issue, but often coexist, at times as tensions, within a single protagonist. In making such judgements Thompson usually considers self-assessments and evaluations from the person's contemporaries. Incorporating the judgements of historical figures and their peers implicitly underscores the analytical import of consciousness in understanding human agency. Thompson takes perceptions into account because they shape the conduct of his subjects of study. This web of interconnected persons makes up the Radical tradition, and bears a problematic relation, as shall be seen, to the formation of the working class.

Thomas Hardy and Francis Place, for example, are colleagues in the London Corresponding Society. Thompson initially unites them further by saying that: 'Place himself, with his sober manner, his great capacity for organisation, his intellectual application and his experience of trade union organisation was in the tradition of Hardy' (p. 139). Early in the narrative, however, Thompson foreshadows Place's later fate by remarking that: 'The self-respecting virtues often carried with them corresponding narrowing attitudes – in Place's case leading him to the acceptance of Utilitarian and Malthusian doctrines' (p. 58). Virtue and vice thus intersect within a single figure, not unlike the manner in which Henry

James (with his very different personal and political agenda) assesses the characters in his novels.

Place's reformist politics can never receive the full approval of Thompson's more radical vision. The historian assesses Place as a writer in the following manner:

> But Place was far from being that mythical creative, the 'objective observer'. He also was highly partisan, deeply involved in the Radical quarrels which disfigure the entire period, 1806–1832, and impatient of opponents – Cobbett he saw only as 'an unprincipled cowardly bully', Orator Hunt as 'impudent, active, vulgar'. The official fact-finder on working-class problems for the Utilitarians, when he came to write his reminiscences he was anxious to emphasize the contribution of the moderates, and to belittle the importance of the 'mob agitators'. Moreover, he was profoundly suspect among advanced reformers. (p. 486)

The historian deals his victim (along with certain of his historian colleagues) the crowning blow by revealing that Place has been portrayed as a hero by Fabian historiography (p. 592). In its pattern of initial ascent followed by rapid fall, Place's trajectory in Thompson's judgement parallels the assessment of the Webbs and the Hammonds.

Hardy's network links yet other historical protagonists in the work. He and John Thelwall, for instance, are fellow prisoners. Thompson maintains a complex judgement of Thelwall who combines a (positive) gift for words with a (debilitating) flair for self-dramatization. In characterizing his protagonist as a leading theorist of the London Corresponding Society, Thompson says: 'John Thelwall, the son of a silk mercer, was the most important – he straddled the world of Wordsworth and of Coleridge, and the world of the Spitalfields weavers' (p. 157). The capacity to straddle two worlds, that of working people and Romantic artists, constitutes high praise for Thompson (as will be seen below, in the discussion of Blake). Yet Thelwall's visits and hikes in the countryside with William Wordsworth were an ambiguous virtue.

In Thompson's judgement, Wordsworth follows the now familiar pattern of initial rise, then fall. The poet enters Part One by being praised for verse that captures the optimism of late eighteenth-century revolutionary spirit. The reader is warned that this was an 'optimism (which Wordsworth was soon to lose) but to which Radicalism clung tenaciously' (p. 95). Later, the historian remarks: 'There commenced, for an intellectual generation, that pattern of revolutionary disenchantment which fore-shadows the shoddier patterns of our own century' (p. 176). Thompson's appraisal of Wordsworth encompasses, through a process of exclusion and inclusion, workers and artists within a Radical tradition that stretches from past to present.

Thompson's conception of traditions making themselves through struggles still vital for people living today has been written as a series of running conflicts that pervade the work as a whole. There are clashes between the working class and the middle class, between opposed groups within the working class, between pamphleteers and their audiences, between Thompson and other historians, and between Thompson and his readers. The narrative of these conflicts unfolds in such distinct, yet arguably interconnected social realms as those of the working class and Romantic art. In all these cases, parallel battles often appear, pointing to the existence of a larger Radical tradition that permeates and shapes experience through quite distinct social sectors as it extends from the past into the present.

Who Made the Network?

An anthropologist studying cultural traditions extending beyond face-to-face groups has to consider fictions of collective identity. How do people who do not know one another develop a conviction of mutual allegiance? How, for example, do people construct nationality or other such invisible communities?[21] This is the kind of problem that Thompson faces as he delineates the making of the English working class. To what extent has working-class consciousness been inferred by the historian, and to what extent (and in what vocabulary) was it available to historical actors?

One of Thompson's techniques for constructing the working class involves making connections along a network of alliance and enmity that emanates from Thomas Hardy. In a virtuoso instance of network construction, Thompson links Hardy and William Blake through an imaginative excursion that reminds one of the Great Chain of Being and literary devices for connecting characters in novels of the time. Thompson begins this excursion by saying 'Hardy was certainly an artisan' (p. 20). He then explains that, one link away: 'The line between the journeymen and the small masters was often crossed' (p. 20). He describes the movement two, and then three links away, as follows:

And the line between the aristan of independent status (whose workroom was also his 'shop') and the small shopkeeper or tradesman was even fainter. From here it was another step to the world of self-employed engravers, like William Sharp and William Blake, of printers and apothecaries, teachers and journalists, surgeons and Dissenting clergy. (p. 20)

Although Hardy and Blake inhabited different worlds and never knew one another, the historian has connected them, moving one step at a time, through a series of intervening links uniting the tradition of Dissent. Thompson's breathtaking rhetorical fiction discloses a theory of society as an organic unity, which includes yet transcends the working class, much in the manner envisaged by John Ruskin and William Morris.

The anthropological question remains: did Thompson or the people of the time construct the network? Have the people been united because of similarity of idiom and perception (as is apparent in the text), or because they conceived their unity as a dissenting tradition in web-like fashion (as is much less clear)? It is critical for readers to be able to distinguish the ways in which Thompson as opposed to his subjects have contributed to the making of the Radical tradition. Furthermore, the web-like version of the Radical tradition appears overly coherent, and it sits rather uneasily with the notion of traditions as conflictual processes.

Narrative and Agency

One prominent critique of Thompson asserts that he over-emphasizes agency at the expense of structure. Foremost among others, Perry Anderson has attacked Thompson for his use of such vague concepts as culture and experience, and for failing to delineate the structural determinants of working class formation. In opposition to Anderson, I find that *The Making of the English Working Class* nicely sketches structural determinants and integrates them into a study of human agency. Indeed, Thompson persuades me when he asserts that social class should be regarded as an on-going process that cannot even be discussed in the slice in time to which most structuralists restrict their analyses. Instead, I disagree with Thompson's use of culture and experience, not because such concepts should be discarded, but because the historian's notions have been conflated with those of his subjects.

My point of departure is that human agency always transcends conditioning. It can neither be reduced to, nor simply derived from, the structural factors by which it is, in part, determined. Action should be understood with reference to agents' goals, purposes and signifying practices. In this project historians (and anthropologists) maintain a double vision, informed by their synoptic knowledge of the long-term consequences of conduct and by their grasp of how historical agents (who cannot know the eventual consequences of their actions) conceive the purposes and stake of their struggles.

Put differently, the issue involves what Anthony Giddens has called the 'double hermeneutic'.[22] The analyst should understand both the course of human events *and* agents' subjective understandings of their own conduct. In the latter case, whether a movement of the eyelids (to borrow an example Clifford Geertz borrowed from Gilbert Ryle) is a nervous tick or a wink, and whether the wink is joking or conspiratorial can be discerned only with reference to intersubjective understandings, not with an objectivist's camera eye.[23] The understandings of actors cannot be omitted from explanations because human intentions, among other factors, determine human conduct. This issue is particularly salient for studies that focus on agency. Lest there be any confusion, one should probably add that human actors cannot fully know their motives, the conditions under which they act, or the consequences of their acts. In other words, to say that subjective understandings cannot be omitted from explanations is not to say that they provide complete accounts.

My concern, as an anthopologist, focuses on Thompson's failure to separate his own understandings from those of his subjects. In failing to make this crucial distinction, Thompson treats his own narrative as if it were a neutral medium, rather than a culturally constructed form selected from a range of possible modes, such as tragic, comic, ironic, pastoral and melodramatic. The choice of a narrative mode in turn conditions the selection, organization and explanation of historical facts.

Whose Melodrama is it?

In narrating the history of class formation, Thompson has implicitly adopted an aesthetic, which moves readers more by the sentimental heroics of victimization than by the heroics of superhuman feats. This aesthetic of the period under analysis can be found, for instance, in the novels of Charles Dickens or in popular theatre.

Indeed, the literary scholar Peter Brooks argues that a particular narrative mode has shaped the work of Dickens, and of such authors as Victor Hugo, Balzac, James, Dostoevsky, Conrad, Lawrence and Faulkner (as opposed, for example, to Flaubert, Maupassant, Beckett, Robbe-Grillet and possibly Joyce and Kafka). In his words:

> In teaching and writing about a number of authors, particularly Balzac and Henry James, I found myself using the adjective *melodramatic*. It seemed to describe, as no other word quite did, the mode of their dramatizations, especially the extravegence of certain representations, and the intensity of moral claim impinging on their characters' consciousness. Within an apparent context of 'realism' and the ordinary, they seemed in fact to be staging a heightened and hyperbolic drama, making reference to pure and polar concepts of

darkness and light, salvation and damnation. They seemed to place
their characters at the point of intersection of primal ethical forces
and to confer on the characters' enactments a charge of meaning
referred to the clash of these forces.[24]

Rather like Dickens, among others, Thompson has drawn on a popular
idiom of the period, the melodramatic, to convey his sense of historical
process.[25] The melodramatic imagination, with its 'polar concepts' and
'primal ethical forces', informed (as we have seen, without yet naming as
such) Thompson's complex assessments of such figures as the Webbs, the
Hammonds, Place, Thelwall and Wordsworth.

Thompson's use of the melodramatic literary mode, however, is never
made explicit in his work. Hence a definition of the melodramatic is
probably in order. As a literary form, melodrama follows the logic of the
excluded middle by portraying conflicts between good and evil. Such
tales are narrated with a quality of earnest exaggeration that heightens
partisanship among readers or listeners. They can be characterized by the
participants' heightened sense of persecution, the audience's feelings of
horror, panic or sympathetic pity, and the narrator's moral stance
regarding the course of events. The dramas that ensue move readers to
take sides in Manichaean battles between virtue and vice. The melodramatic
imagination compels its audience to enter a field of combat where the
middle ground has been eroded.

Doubtless, melodrama was the cultural form through which artisans
and other working people often experienced the events of their lives.
Thompson's astute choice of melodrama, however, begs a central
question. Does he depict working-class suffering as melodrama because
this is an appropriate way to tell the story, or because particular
individuals or groups experienced certain episodes through this idiom?
Was the narrative mode selected because of its broad appropriateness to
the subject matter, or because the working class actually acted in relation
to a melodramatic understanding of its own history?

Consider, for example, the way Thompson constructs his narrative so
that his readers side firmly with Thomas Hardy. On the first page of the
book Hardy enters as the 'founder and first secretary' of the London
Corresponding Society. One page and two years later his epithet becomes
more modest: simply 'shoemaker'. Having established Hardy's humble
position as a commoner, Thompson engages our sympathy by saying:

Mrs Hardy died in childbirth as a result of shock sustained when her
home was beseiged by a 'Church and King' mob. The Privy Council
determined to press through with the charge of high treason: and the
fully penalty for a traitor was that he should be hanged by the neck,

cut down while still alive, disembowelled (and his entrails burned before his face) and then beheaded and quartered. A Grand Jury of respectable London citizens had no stomach for this. (p. 19)

Thompson describes the popular image current during Hardy's trial in these terms: 'The public found in Hardy once again one of those images of independence in which the "free-born Englishman" delighted: a firm and dignified commoner, defying the power of the State. The circumstances of Mrs Hardy's death attracted further sympathy' (p. 135). The perceptions of Hardy's contemporaries articulate the sympathy Thompson's readers feel for a common man who in their imaginations has assumed mythic proportions.

In the final chapter of Part One, Thompson reviews the previous incidents, but with a difference. In his words: 'It was in celebration of the naval victory of the "Glorious First of June" that a mob attacked Mrs Hardy's house; and one London newspaper jeered that "the woman died in consequence of being haunted by visions of her dear Tommy's being hanged, drawn, and quartered"' (p. 132). The brutal treatment given the poor shoemaker and his wife becomes even more vivid in the repetition than in the original description.

Thompson's melodramatic imagination has served well as a vehicle for his political vision. His readers are clearly meant to side with Hardy and his wife because their sympathies have been aroused by (evil) persecutors inflicting suffering upon (good) victims. Yet the jeering newspapers appear mockingly anti-melodramatic. Once again, is it Thompson or Hardy and his contemporaries who experience their trials as melodrama? The sentimental heroics of victimization are mediated by particular cultural forms and not given in universal human nature. Hardy's trials could potentially have been interpreted as the wrath of God, the result of moral flaws, a quirk of destiny or a consequence of unjust human conduct. His suffering could have been experienced as cleansing, humiliating, pathetic or heroic. For an anthropologist, it is crucial to be explicit about the idiom through which people experience their histories.

Doing Committed History

When Thompson discerns opposing political forces and encapsulates them in opposing texts, he often locates himself among the contending protagonists because their issues are also his. The past and the present become contemporaneous within a single field of conflict. These conflicts and their contending parties have been selected out of a denser past for their vitality in the historian's own period. Among its other accomplishments, the work actively constructs a Radical tradition for those of us living in the present.

Like his characters, Thompson takes sides. He refuses to stand outside his history because its anatagonisms live on into the present. Often writing in the first person, Thompson positions himself more as a partisan than as an omniscient narrator. His position as narrator cannot be omniscient because the still vital conflicts have not yet reached their resolution.[26] There simply is no place to stand above or outside the conflict. Hence the logic of the excluded middle and the call for readers to take sides.

In this committed history William Cobbett emerges as the most insightful commentator on the formation of the working class in whose making he was an active participant. Thompson characterizes this influential figure as follows:

> Cobbett throws his influence across the years from the end of the Wars until the passing of the Reform Bill. To say that he was in no sense a systematic thinker is not to say that his was not a serious intellectual influence. It was Cobbett who *created* this Radical intellectual culture, not because he offered its most original ideas, but in the sense that he found the tone, the style, and the arguments which could bring the weaver, the schoolmaster, and the shipwright, into a common discourse. (p. 746)

Cobbett appears as the maker of and the one made by working-class awareness. Thompson describes this dialectical process in the following uncharacteristically cumbersome metaphor: 'Cobbett's ideas can be seen less as a one-way propagandist flow than as the incandescence of an alternating current, between his readers and himself' (p. 758). Drawing on vigorous oral speech and everyday experience, Cobbett's writings embody a relationship, create a tradition and mobilize a movement more than they articulate a cogent doctrine.

In Thompson's powerful concluding vision the reader encounters partisanship *par excellence* in the apotheosis of William Blake. Thompson extends his earlier position within the radical versus ameliorist argument by saying that the best people among what he calls the two cultures or traditions, the working class and Romantic art, battled Utilitarianism 'with intelligence and moral passion' (p. 832). In the final paragraph of his work Thompson says:

> After William Blake, no mind was at home in both cultures, nor had the genius to interpret the two traditions to each other. It was a muddled Mr Owen who offered to disclose the 'new moral world',

while Wordsworth and Coleridge had withdrawn behind their own ramparts of disenchantment. Hence these years appear at times to display, not a revolutionary challenge, but a resistance movement, in which both the Romantics and the Radical craftsmen opposed the annunication of Acquisitive Man. In the failure of the two traditions to come to a point of juncture, something was lost. How much we cannot be sure, for we are among the losers. (p. 832)

Thompson speaks to the present as he writes about the past. The failure of English society to transcend capitalism and achieve its organic unity, in the manner William Morris conceived, by pulling together the working class and Romantic art, becomes a failure of consciousness and imagination.

Thompson himself appears as a major protagonist in his own history. He is the inheritor of Cobbett's persuasive prose and the articulator of Blake's complex vision. Far from being a detached observer, Thompson takes sides as he enters the fray through which the working class was made. At times, he speaks in the voice of reason about the central concerns of the labour historian in a manner apparently incontrovertible. On other occasions, he indulges invective and attacks his fellow historians, working-class people and Romantic artists alike. Elsewhere, he preaches, exhorting his readers and his major protagonists with his incisive moral judgement. His masterful committed history is passionate and convincing.

The Making of the English Working Class stands as an exemplar of how to write a committed history. Among critical anthropologists it provides a model of reflexivity in which the analysis explicitly takes the position of the analyst into account. This notion resembles the scientist's practice of studying both the data and the instruments through which they have been gathered. It also calls to mind the artist's notion that the medium can inspire as much creativity as (or even become) the object represented. What in the analyst's moral vision, political commitments, or life could be a source of insight or blindness? Not unlike human agents who act relative to their own goals, analysts understand the world through their institutional position, political commitments, moral stances and personal histories.

Yet Thompson's compelling moral vision cannot readily be exported to anthropology because the people we write about have cultural traditions whose antagonisms differ from our own. Perhaps we and members of other cultures share certain problems in relation to the world system of capitalism, but only the most presumptuous anthropologist could claim to hold a legitimate position on other people's internal debates. Indeed, this problem applies to Thompson as well. Much as the historian

too readily conflates his vision with that of his subjects, he also too
quickly affirms a continuity of past and present encompassed within the
Radical tradition. Surely he is somewhat at odds with himself because this
tradition, like all other cultural traditions, embodies discontinuity,
heterogeneity and conflict more than continuity, coherence and consensus.

Imagine, for example, how a decidedly anti-melodramatic writer like
Michel Foucault might make the Radical tradition strange rather than
familiar. He could make the class struggles without class of the eighteenth
century appear more intelligible than those of the nineteenth and
twentieth centuries. In the play of distance and closeness, Thompson
creates a Radical tradition within which an identification of past and
present occupies the foreground, and strangeness remains hidden in an
obscure background. The very identification which enables other voices
to be heard in their full persuasive force as they speak to the present can at
the same time muffle the distinctive tones of the past. When voices
become particularly muffled as their issues diverge from our own, the
problem of accurately perceiving the role of agency in historical struggles
only increases. Hence the sense in which Thompson's history can be at
odds with itself.

Notes

The following people have provided comments on this paper: Amy Burce, Natalie
Davis, Donald Donham, Hugh Gusterson, Keith McClelland, Mary Louise Pratt
and William Reddy. I am grateful for their suggestions.

1 This view of tradition has been articulated, among other places, in Raymond
   Williams, *Marxism and Literature* (Oxford: Oxford University Press, 1977),
   pp. 115–20.
2 In speaking of an 'exemplary instance', I have in mind the term 'exemplar' as
   used in Thomas Kuhn, *The Structure of Scientific Revolutions*, (Chicago:
   University of Chicago Press, 1970 second edition, enlarged). His notion is
   that in learning how to do science one learns how to recognize a piece of good
   work and hopefully to produce one. Because the making of a good work
   (exemplary) cannot be reduced to rules or recipes only a close study of the
   work itself allows practitioners to achieve mastery in the discipline. Such a line
   of reasoning can justify the study of 'classic' texts in history and anthropology.
3 Thompson was prominently cited, for example, by nearly all the papers at a
   symposium on 'Culture and Historical Materialism' during the 1984 meetings
   of the American Anthropological Association.
4 E. P. Thompson, 'Folklore, Anthropology, and Social History', *The Indian
   Historical Review* 3 (2) (1978), p. 260.
5 E. P. Thompson, 'Eighteenth-century English Society: Class Struggle without
   Class?', *Social History* 3 (2) (1978), p. 156.

6 Renato Rosaldo, 'Grief and a Headhunter's Rage', in *Text, Play, and Story*, ed. Edward Bruner (Washington, D.C.: American Ethnological Society, 1984), pp. 178–85, and 'Where Objectivity Lies', in *The Rhetoric of the Human Sciences* ed. John Nelson, Donald McCloskey and Alan Megill (Madison: University of Wisconsin Press, 1986).

7 E. E. Evans-Pritchard, *The Nuer* (Oxford: Oxford University Press, 1940), pp. 94–5.

8 These debates have been long and heated, but a few works can provide a basic orientation. E. P. Thompson's critique of Raymond Williams appears in, 'The Long Revolution I', *New Left Review*, 9 (1961), pp. 24–33, and 'The Long Revolution II', *New Left Review*, 10 (1961), pp. 34–9. Raymond Williams judiciously clarified his position in *Politics and Letters* (London: New Left Books, 1979), pp. 135–6. E. P. Thompson's assault on Louis Althusser appears in *The Poverty of Theory and Other Essays* (New York: Monthly Review Press, 1978). Perry Anderson's vigorous response to Thompson appears in *Arguments Within English Marxism* (London: New Left Books, 1980).

9 E. P. Thompson's criticisms of anthropology, of course, pale beside his treatment of Althusser in *The Poverty of Theory and Other Essays*.

10 E. P. Thompson, 'Anthropology and the Discipline of Historical Context', *Midland History*, 1 (3) (1972), p. 45.

11 Ibid., p. 46.

12 E. P. Thompson, 'Folklore, Anthropology, and Social History', p. 248.

13 Clifford Geertz, for example, has said, 'The famous studies purporting to show that the Oedipus complex was backwards in the Trobriands, sex roles were upside down in Tchambuli, and the Pueblo Indians lacked aggression (it is characteristic that they were all negative – "but not in the South"), are, whatever their empirical validity may or may not be, not "scientifically tested and approved" hypotheses. They are interpretations, or misinterpretations, like any others, arrived at in the same way as any others, and as inherently inconclusive as any others, and the attempt to invest them with the authority of physical experimentation is but methodological slight of hand.' 'Thick Description: Toward an Interpretive Theory of Culture', *The Interpretation of Cultures* (New York: Basic Books, 1973), p. 23.

14 Emmanuel Le Roy Ladurie's *Montaillou: The Promised Land of Error* (New York: George Brazilier, 1978) can be subjected to a similar critique, as seen in Renato Rosaldo, 'From the Door of His Tent: the Fieldworker and the Inquisitor', in *Writing Culture: The Poetics and Politics of Ethnography* (Berkeley: University of California Press, 1986), pp. 77–97.

15 A seminal source for making political processes central in anthropology has been Pierre Bourdieu, *Outline of a Theory of Practice* (Cambridge: Cambridge University Press, 1977). Max Gluckman and his followers, collectively known as the Manchester School, did much to lay the groundwork for this theoretical concern (see, for example, A. L. Epstein (ed.), *The Craft of Social Anthropology* (London: Tavistock, 1967) and Max Gluckman, *Custom and Conflict in Africa* (London: Basil Blackwell, 1956). Edmund Leach, who also developed this view, asserted the following: 'I hold that social structure in practical situations (as contrasted with the sociologist's abstract model)

consists of a set of ideas about the distribution of power between persons and groups of persons' *Political Systems of Highland Burma* (Boston: Beacon, 1965), p. 4. The central concern of my own ethnography [*Ilongot Headhunting, 1883–1974: A Study in Society and History* (Stanford: Stanford University Press, 1980)] grew out of these strands of anthropological thought, as has a more recent paper of mine ['While Making Other Plans', *Southern California Law Review* 58 (1) (1985), pp. 19–28]. Sherry Ortner has reviewed these developments in 'Theory in Anthropology Since the Sixties', *Comparative Studies in Society and History* 26 (1) (1984), pp. 126–66. This conceptual preoccupation is of a family with E. P. Thompson's desire to make politics central to his analysis by attending as much to making as to conditioning.

16 Although numerous works could be cited here, the tenor of the times can be discerned from Dell Hymes (ed.), *Reinventing Anthropology* (New York: Random House, 1969), Rayna Rapp Reiter (ed.), *Toward an Anthropology of Women* (New York: Monthly Review Press, 1975); and Michelle Zimbalist Rosaldo and Louise Lamphere (eds), *Woman, Culture, and Society* (Stanford: Stanford University Press, 1974). Unfortunately, minority voices have had less of an impact on mainstream anthropology (for a recent review of Chicano writings, see Renato Rosaldo, 'Chicano Studies, 1970–1984', in *Annual Review of Anthropology*, Bernard Siegel, Alan Beals and Stephen Tyler (eds), 14: 405–27).

17 Among influential works by the three writers are: Pierre Bourdieu, *Outline of a Theory of Practice*, Talal Asad (ed.), *Anthropology and the Colonial Encounter* (London: Ithaca Press, 1973), Clifford Geertz, *The Interpretation of Cultures*.

18 E. P. Thompson, *The Making of the English Working Class* (New York: Vintage, 1966), p. 9. (Hereafter Thompson's classic work will be cited in the text simply by page number.) In social thought this issue appears under the guise of the interplay of human agency and structure. In this context writers frequently cite Marx's dictum that people make their own history but not under conditions of their own choosing. Representative works in this vein include Richard Bernstein, *The Restructuring of Social and Political Theory* (Philadelphia: University of Pennsylvania Press, 1978) and *Beyond Objectivism and Relativism* (Philadelphia: University of Pennsylvania Press, 1983); Anthony Giddens, *New Rules of Sociological Method* (New York: Basic Books, 1976); and *Central Problems in Social Theory* (Berkeley: University of California Press, 1979), and Raymond Williams, *Marxism and Literature*. For a more strictly sociological perspective, see Alan Dawe, 'The Two Sociologies', *The British Journal of Sociology* 21 (1970), pp. 207–18; and 'Theories of Social Action', in *A History of Sociological Analysis* ed. Tom Bottomore and Robert Nisbet (New York: Basic Books, 1978), pp. 362–417.

19 This project became *Ilongot Headhunting, 1883–1974: A Study in Society and History*.

20 Much thought has been given by philosophers and others to rhetorical forms in history, but these reflections appear to have had little influence on practicing historians. This tradition of thought can be found in the journal

History and Theory. Other sources include W. B. Gallie, *Philosophy and the Historical Understanding* (New York: Schocken Books, 1968), J. H. Hexter, 'The rhetoric of history', in *The International Encyclopedia of the Social Sciences*, ed. David L. Sills (New York: Crowell Collier and Macmillan, 1968), vol. 6, pp. 368–94; Paul Ricoeur, *Time and Narrative* (Chicago: University of Chicago Press, 1984), vol. 1; and Hayden White, *Metahistory* (Baltimore: The Johns Hopkins University Press, 1973). Within this tradition of thought one can distinguish those who attempt to read histories 'in their own terms' (as a form of aesthetic appreciation) from those who read them in relation to particular analytical projects, as I have attempted to do here.

Rhetorical analysis has entered anthropology rather more recently but much more centrally than in history. Among relevant works in anthropology see James Boon, *Other Tribes, Other Scribes* (Cambridge: Cambridge University Press, 1982), James Clifford, 'On Ethnographic Authority', *Representations* 1 (2) (1983), pp. 118–46; James Clifford and George Marcus (eds), *Writing Culture: The Poetics and Politics of Ethnography*; Vincent Crapanzano, *Tuhami* (Chicago: University of Chicago Press, 1980); Kevin Dwyer, *Moroccan Dialogues* (Baltimore: The Johns Hopkins University Press, 1982); Clifford Geertz, 'Slide Shows: Evans-Pritchard's African Transparencies', *Raritan* (Autumn, 1983), pp. 62–80; George Marcus and Dick Cushman, 'Ethnographies as Texts', in *Annual Review of Anthropology*, ed. Bernard Siegel, Alan Beals and Stephen A. Tyler (Palo Alto: Annual Reviews, Inc., 1982), vol. 11, pp. 25–69; George Marcus and Michael Fischer, *Anthropology as Cultural Critique: An Experimental Moment in the Human Sciences* (Chicago: University of Chicago Press, 1986); and Renato Rosaldo, 'Doing Oral History', *Social Analysis*, 4 (1980), pp. 89–99; 'Ilongot Hunting as Story and Experience', in *The Anthropology of Experience*, ed. Victor Turner and Edward Bruner (Urbana: University of Illinois Press, 1986), pp. 97–138; and 'Where Objectivity Lies'. The general project has gone under the name of studying ethnographies as texts. The idea in brief is that anthropologists have devoted much methodological discussion to the collection and manipulation of data, but remarkably less to conceptual issues involved in writing.

21 For a fine study conducted from this perspective, see Benedict Anderson, *Imagined Communities: Reflections on the Origin and Spread of Nationalism* (London: Verso, 1983).

22 *New Rules of Sociological Method*, p. 162.

23 'Thick Description: Toward an Interpretive Theory of Culture', pp. 6–7.

24 *The Melodramatic Imagination: Balzac, Henry James, Melodrama, and the Mode of Excess* (New Haven: Yale University Press, 1976), p. ix.

25 Needless to say, anthropology has its own melodramas. One of the most recent has revolved around Derek Freeman's vituperative attack on Margaret Mead. For an analysis of this debate in melodramatic terms see Martin Silverman, 'Our Great Deception, or, Anthropology Defiled!', *American Anthropologist* 85 (1983), pp. 944–7.

26 For pertinent writings on narrative, see Alisdair MacIntyre, 'Epistemological

Crises, Dramatic Narrative and the Philosophy of Science', *The Monist*, 60 (1977), pp. 453–72, on traditions as arguments, and Louis Mink, 'Narrative as a cognitive instrument', in *The Writing of History*, ed. Robert H. Canary and Henry Kozicki (Madison: University of Wisconsin Press, 1978), pp. 129–49, on the incommensurability of different narratives 'about the same thing'.

5

Falling Through the Cracks: E. P. Thompson and the Debate on Base and Superstructure

Ellen Meiksins Wood

There have always been divisions among Marxists, but fashions have been no less changeable in Marxist controversy than in any other domain. Lines have been variably drawn not only in accordance with changing intellectual trends but, more particularly, in response to political exigencies. A few years ago, one of the principal divisions among Marxist theorists in Britain was between 'Althusserians' and a loose collection of people variously described as 'culturalists', 'humanists' or even 'Thompsonians'. Today, new divisions have emerged which in many ways have grown out of the earlier controversies but which also have a more immediate political charge. A theoretical-political current has developed whose principal characteristic is a denial of class politics supported by theoretical innovations whose first premise is that there is no privileged connection between the working class and socialist politics, because there is in any case no necessary correspondence between the 'economic' and the 'political'. Any connection between these two spheres must, according to this argument, be 'discursively constructed'.[1] On the other side, there remain those Marxists who are dismissed by their 'post-Marxist' opponents as 'orthodox', 'hard-line' or 'vulgar', to the extent that they still insist on the material foundations of politics and the centrality of class struggle in the transition to socialism. Perhaps contrary to the expectations of some observers, the denial of class politics, the ultimate assault on Marxist 'orthodoxy', has tended to come not so much from the 'soft-headed' culturalists or humanists, but rather from theorists nurtured in the 'rigorous' Althusserian tradition, though there have been some convergences between erstwhile adversaries in a common distaste for Marxist 'economism'. In their various ways, these evolving debates have all had to do with one underlying theoretical problem, the relation between 'base' and 'superstructure'.

The base/superstructure metaphor has always been more trouble than it is worth. Although Marx himself used it very rarely and only in the most aphoristic and allusive formulations, it has been made to bear a theoretical weight far beyond its limited capacities. To some extent, the problems already inherent in its original short-hand usage were aggravated by Engels' tendency to use language suggesting the compartmentalization of self-enclosed spheres or 'levels' – economic, political, ideological – whose relations with one another were external. But the real problems began with the establishment of Stalinist orthodoxies which elevated – or reduced – the metaphor to the first principle of Marxist-Leninist dogma, asserting the supremacy of a self-contained economic sphere over other passively reflexive subordinate spheres. More particularly, the economic sphere tended to be conceived as more or less synonymous with the technical forces of production, operating according to intrinsic natural laws of technological progress, so that history became a more or less mechanical process of technological development. These deformations of Marx's original historical-materialist insights have fixed the terms of Marxist debate ever since. Both sides of the various disputes that have raged among Marxists in the past several decades have been effectively locked into this theoretical grid. Sometimes there has been a tendency to treat the deformations as the Marxist gospel, and to accept or reject Marxism accordingly. Anyone, like E. P. Thompson, working somewhere in the fissures between the alternatives presented by this theoretical framework is likely to be badly misunderstood by supporters and critics alike, or to be dismissed as an anomaly, a theoretical impossibility.

Objections to the base/superstructure metaphor have generally concerned its 'reductionism', both its denial of human agency and its failure to accord a proper place to 'superstructural' factors, to consciousness as embodied in ideology, culture or politics. Corrections to this reductionism have most commonly taken the form of a so-called Marxist 'humanism', or else an emphasis on the 'relative autonomy' of the 'levels' of society, their mutual interaction, and a deferral of determination by the 'economic' to 'the last instance'. The most important development in contemporary western Marxist theory, the structuralist Marxism of Althusser, rejected the humanist option and elaborated the other in a number of peculiar and theoretically sophisticated ways. Faced with a choice between a simplistic and mechanical base/superstructure model on the one hand, and apparently unstructured 'human agency' on the other, Althusser and his adherents found an ingenious solution. They redefined the relations between base and superstructure in such a way that the vagaries of human agency could be 'rigorously' excluded from the science of society, insisting on completely 'structural' determinations, while at the same time allowing for the unpredictable specificity of historical reality. This they achieved by a certain amount of conceptual trickery; for while a rigid determinism prevailed in the realm of social structure, it turned out that this realm belonged for all practical purposes to the sphere of pure theory, while the real, empirical world – albeit of little interest to most Althusserian theoreticists – remained (all explicit denunciations of contingency notwithstanding) effectively contingent and irreducibly particular.

The critical Althusserian distinction between 'mode of production' and 'social formation' illustrates the point. The structurally determined mode of production simply does not exist empirically, while the actually existing social formation is particular, 'conjunctural', and capable of combining the various modes of production, and even various 'relatively (absolutely?) autonomous' structural levels, in an infinite number of indeterminate ways. The consequences of this simple dualism between the determinism of structuralist theory and the contingency to which it relegated history were disguised by the fact that Althusserians wrote very little history, but also by the deceptive rigour of their ventures into the empirical world, where simple *description* was dressed up as theoretically rigorous causal explanation through the medium of infinitely expandable taxonomic categories derived from the theory of structure.

Althusserian Marxism, then, did little to shift the terms of Marxist theoretical debate decisively away from the terrain established by Stalinist orthodoxy. The base/superstructure model retained its mechanical character and its conceptualization of social structure in terms of discrete, discontinuous, externally related 'factors', 'levels' or 'instances', even if the mechanically deterministic relation between the base and its super-structural reflections was rendered effectively inoperative in the real world by the rigid separation between structure and history and by the indefinite postponement of economic determination to an unforeseeable 'last instance'. Furthermore, the structuralist conceptual apparatus tended to encourage the kind of separation of the 'economic' from the 'social' and 'historical' which often entails the identification of the 'economic' with technology; and it is not surprising to find Marxists of structuralist persuasion looking to technological determinism to supply the historical dynamism missing from their view of the world as a series of discontinuous, self-enclosed and static structures.

For the time being, then, without abandoning the false alternatives of the debates surrounding Stalinism, Marxists could have their cake and eat it too. They could eschew 'crude economism' or 'vulgar reductionism' without abandoning the crudely mechanical model of base and superstructure. All that was required was that they adopt the sharp Althusserian dualism between structure and history, absolute determinism and irreducible contingency. And despite the Althusserian contempt for 'empiricism' – or precisely because of it (at least, precisely because of the conceptual dualism on which it was based) – it was in principle even possible to engage in the purest theory and the most unalloyed empiricism at once.

It was, however, only a matter of time before this uneasy synthesis fell apart. It soon turned out that Althusserianism had simply replaced – or supplemented – the old false alternatives with new ones. Marxists had in effect been offered a choice between structure and history, absolute determinism and irreducible contingency, pure theory and unalloyed empiricism. It is not surprising, therefore, that the purest theoreticists of the Althusserian school became the most unalloyed empiricists of the post-Althusserian generation, at least in theory. In the work of writers like Hindess and Hirst, formerly the most rabid of anti-'historicists' and anti-'empiricists', the absolute and unconditional determinations of structure have now given way to the absolute and irreducible contingency of the particular 'conjuncture'.[2] The 'post-Marxist' assertion of the 'non-correspondence' between the 'economic' and the 'political' – as well as the abandonment of class politics which this implies – the rejection not only of the crude base/superstructure model but also of the complex historical materialist insights for which that unfortunate metaphor was intended to stand are thus simply the other side of the Althusserian coin.

The result has been a completely distorted framework of debate which threatens to exclude Marx himself from the range of theoretical possibility. According to the 'post-Marxist' frame of reference, which seems now to be setting the terms of Marxist theoretical controversy, it is simply not possible, for example, to reject 'crude economism' – generally conceived as technological determinism – and still to believe in class politics, the centrality of class conflict in history or the primacy of the working class in the struggle for socialism. If a united, revolutionary working class does not emerge full-grown from the 'natural' development of productive forces in capitalism, there is no organic or privileged connection between the working class and socialism, or indeed between economic conditions and political forces. In other words, again, where there is no simple, absolute and mechanical determination, there is absolute contingency. So much for Marx and historical materialism.

And so much, too, for Edward Thompson; for it can be argued that he numbers among those who have fallen through the cracks of Marxist debate in recent years because he fails to match any of the recognized alternatives. This is, of course, not to say that he has been ignored, discounted or undervalued, but rather that both his critics and his admirers have often misrepresented him by forcing him into one of the available categories. In the opposition between 'crude economism' and 'Marxist humanism', he must be a humanist for whom economic laws give way to an arbitrary human will and agency. In the debate between Althusserians and culturalists, he is a – even *the original* – culturalist, for whom structural determinations are dissolved in 'experience'. And in the current configuration whose terms are being established by 'post-Marxist' post-Althusserians, he is perhaps equally likely to be mis-appropriated by the philosophers of 'discourse', relegated to the camp of 'class-reductionists', or else dismissed as a theoretical anomaly who, while showing a healthy disdain for 'crude economism' and an appreciation of ideology and culture, still retains an irrational belief in the centrality of class. To some extent he has invited these distorting classifications by allowing himself to be trapped in the prevailing terms of debate; but in his explicit pronouncements on theoretical matters, and even more in his historiographical practice, can be found the lost threads of a Marxist tradition which these false choices have systematically hidden from view.

II

Let us approach the question as it were from behind, with Thompson's controversial criticisms of Althusser and in particular his remarks on the Althusserian conceptions of mode of production and social formation. In *The Poverty of Theory*, Thompson accused Althusser of identifying the mode of production with the social formation – for example, the capitalist mode of production with capital*ism* – so that an abstract, though not crudely economistic, account of the laws of capital comes to stand for 'a social formation in the totality of its relations'.[3] In other words, Althusser, like Marx in his '*Grundrisse* face', was accused by Thompson of treating capital virtually as a Hegelian Idea unfolding itself in history and embodying within itself the whole of capitalist society, 'capital in the totality of its relations'.

This criticism, as it stands, was rather ill-judged; for as Perry Anderson pointed out, Althusser and Balibar took up the concept of social formation, deliberately distinguishing it from 'mode of production', precisely in order to correct the '. . . constant confusion in Marxist literature between the *social formation* and its economic infrastructure'.[4] The concept 'social formation' was adopted by the Althusserians in preference to 'society' – a concept that 'suggested a deceptive simplicity and unity . . . the Hegelian notion of a circular, expressive totality' –

as a forcible reminder that the diversity of human practices in any society is irreducible to economic practice alone. The issue it

addressed was precisely that which gives rise to Thompson's
anxieties about base and superstructure: the difference between the
bare economic structures of 'capital' and the intricate fabric of social,
political, cultural and moral life of (French or English or American)
capitalism.[5]

In other words, argued Anderson, Thompson had 'contrived to convict
his opponents of an error which they were the first to name'.

And yet, there remains an important sense in which Thompson was
right, because the very form in which the distinction between mode of
production and social formation was drawn by Althusser and Balibar
reinforced rather than corrected the confusion. In part, their correction
simply reproduced the very mistakes in the base/superstructure metaphor
which it was intended to correct; in part, they deprived the metaphor of
precisely those valuable insights which it was intended to convey.

The 'mode of production' as conceived by Althusserians has theoretically
inscribed within it an entire social structure, containing various 'levels',
economic, political, ideological. In the case of Althusser and Balibar
themselves, it is perhaps not so clear that the concept 'mode of
production' is actually *synonymous* with that totality, but it certainly
constitutes the basis from which a social totality – 'capitalism' in the
totality of its economic, political and ideological relations – can be
theoretically generated. In other prominent theorists of Althusserian
provenance – notably Nicos Poulantzas – the 'mode of production' itself
explicitly stands for the totality:

> By *mode of production* we shall designate not what is generally
> marked out as the economic (i.e. relations of production in the strict
> sense), but a specific combination of various structures and practices
> which, in combination, appear as so many instances or levels, i.e. as
> so many regional structures of this mode. A mode of production, as
> Engels stated schematically, is composed of different levels or
> instances, the economic, political, ideological and theoretical.[6]

The concept of 'social formation' as used by these theoreticians is not
intended to deny this relation between the mode of production and the
social totality embodied in it – it is not, for example, intended to deny
that the capitalist mode of production (CMP) = capitalism in the totality
of its relations. Instead, the concept of social formation simply implies
that no historically existing individual social entity is 'pure'; for example,
no existing society represents the CMP pure and simple. Or, to put it
another way, 'The mode of production constitutes an abstract-formal
object which does not exist in the strong sense in reality.'[7] Only impure

'social formations' actually exist, and these will contain several coexisting modes of production with all their constituent 'levels', or even several 'relatively autonomous' fragments of modes of production. The various elements comprising a social formation may even be out of phase with one another. Thus, rigidly determined and monolithic structural relations between self-enclosed economic and superstructural levels continue to exist in the theoretically constructed mode of production; but in the historical world, this structural bloc can be fragmented and recombined in an infinite number of ways. It is as if 'real, concrete' historical social formations are composed of elements whose inner structural logic is theoretically determined, while historical processes simply break up and recombine these elements in various (arbitrary and contingent?) ways. Historical analysis can, then, do little more than describe and classify the combinations of modes of production and fragments of modes of production that constitute any given social formation.

The practical consequences of this theoretical framework are vividly illustrated by Poulantzas' approach to the problem of politics in capitalist society. Having established the principle that an entire social structure – with economic, political, ideological and theoretical levels – is embodied in the 'abstract-formal' mode of production, he proceeds theoretically to construct the 'political instance' of the CMP and to produce a 'type' of State structurally befitting this mode of production. This involves the theoretical construction of connections between the State and different levels of the mode of production, as well as an elaboration of characteristics specific to the capitalist 'type' of state.

The effect of this argument is rather paradoxical. The implication seems to be that the connection among 'levels' of a mode of production, and specifically the correspondence between the CMP and the capitalist 'type' of State, is 'abstract-formal' rather than 'real-concrete', that the components of a mode of production may be related 'structurally' but not necessarily historically. On the one hand, then, structural logic overwhelms historical fact. On the other hand, it appears that the relations which actually do prevail between the State and the mode of production in historically existing social formations may have little to do with this structural logic and appear almost accidental. The parts of a mode of production, which may be related by an ineluctable structural logic in the 'abstract-formal' realm, can be easily detached from one another in historical reality.

A state is capitalist, then, not by virtue of its relation to capitalist relations of production but by virtue of certain structural characteristics derived by autonomous theoretical construction from an abstract formal CMP. Thus, it is possible to say that a social formation in which capitalist relations of production do not yet prevail may nevertheless be characterized by a 'capitalist' state. This is, in fact, how Poulantzas describes European absolutism.[8] The absolutist state is designated as a capitalist type of state not because of any actual relation it bears to underlying capitalist relations of production (Poulantzas is at pains to stress that capitalist relations are very rudimentary at this stage) but because it displays certain formal structural characteristics which he has, more or less arbitrarily, established as corresponding in theory to the CMP. There is no place in this conception for the kind of analysis undertaken by Perry Anderson, or in a different mode, Robert Brenner, of the ways in which the absolutist state emerged out of the dynamic of feudal relations.[9]

There is in these theoretical principles both too much rigid determinism and too much arbitrariness and contingency – that is, too much abstract, almost idealist, theoretical determination and not enough historical causality. On the one hand, the mechanical simplifications of the base/ superstructure model have been left intact; on the other hand, the critical questions indicated by that metaphor about the effects of material conditions and production relations on historical processes have simply been begged. In fact, *a priori* theoretical correspondences have been allowed to conceal real historical relations.

All this is in sharp contrast to Marx's own account of the connection between production relations and political forms:

> The specific economic form, in which unpaid surplus labour is pumped out of direct producers, determines the relationship between rulers and ruled, as it grows directly out of production itself and, in turn, reacts upon it as a determined element . . . . It is always the direct relationship of the owners of the conditions of production to the direct producers . . . which reveals the innermost secret, the hidden basis of the entire social structure, and with it the political form of the relations of sovereignty and dependence, the corresponding specific form of the state. This does not prevent the same economic base – the same from the standpoint of its main conditions – due to innumerable different empirical conditions . . . from showing infinite variations and gradations in appearance, which can be ascertained only by analysis of the empirically given circumstances.[10]

Although parts of this passage are much quoted by Poulantzas et al., it reveals a conceptual framework rather different from the Althusserian distinction between 'mode of production' and 'social formation'. It conveys neither the mechanical determinism of the Althusserian 'mode of production' nor the arbitrary contingency of the 'social formation'. Instead, it suggests both the complex variability of empirical reality *and* the operation within it of a logic derived from production relations.

The difference is further illustrated by Marx's own use of the concept rendered by the Althusserians as 'social formation', a usage that differs substantially from that of Althusser, Balibar or Poulantzas (quite apart from whether the concept was ever intended to carry the theoretical burden it has recently acquired). In a passage that figures centrally in Althusserian theory, Marx writes:

> In all forms of society [which is in the context a less misleading translation of *Gesellschaftsformen* than is 'social formation'] there is a specific kind of production which predominates over the rest, whose relations thus assign rank and influence to the others. It is a general illumination which bathes all the other colours and modifies their particularity. It is a particular ether which determines the specific gravity of every being which has materialized within it.[11]

It is instructive to note precisely what he means by 'forms of society'. They include 'pastoral peoples', 'antiquity', 'the feudal order', 'modern bourgeois society'. Whatever else this passage may mean – and whatever problems may arise from Marx's formulations – it implies that:

1.   'form of society' refers to something like feudal*ism* (the feudal order) or capital*ism* (bourgeois society), not simply an individual and unique 'concrete' phenomenon like 'England during the Industrial Revolution' (one of Poulantzas' examples of a 'social formation'), but a *class* of concrete phenomena which have some kind of common socio-historical logic; and
2.   the point of the passage is, if anything, to stress the *unity*, not the 'heterogeneity', of a 'social formation'.

It is not a question of several modes of production dominated by one, but, for example, different branches of production assimilated to the specific character of the branch that predominates in that social form: the particular nature of agriculture in feudal society – characterized by peasant production and feudal appropriation – affects the nature of industry; the particular nature of industry in 'bourgeois society' – industry dominated by capital – affects the nature of agriculture. Marx's use of the concept here has a rather limited and narrow application, but one which is not inconsistent with his later, more developed insights as stated in Volume III of *Capital*.

Taken together, then, these passages from *Capital* and the *Grundrisse* convey that there is a unifying logic in the relations of production which imposes itself throughout a society, in the complex variety of its empirical reality, in a way that entitles us to speak of a 'feudal order' or 'capitalist society' but without depriving individual feudal or capitalist societies of their 'intricate fabric of social, political, cultural, and moral life'.

Thompson himself, despite his reservations about Marx's '*Grundrisse* face', makes a distinction that nicely sums up Marx's approach. The 'profound intuition' of historical materialism as conceived by Marx, argues Thompson, is not that capitalist societies are simply 'capital in the totality of its relations', but rather 'that the logic of capitalist process has found expression within all the activities of a society, and exerted a determining pressure upon its development and form: hence entitling us to speak of capitalism, or of capitalist societies.'[12] There is a critical difference, he continues, between a structuralism which suggests an 'Idea of capital unfolding itself', and historical materialism, which has to do with 'a real historical process'.

Thompson was, then, at least half-right in his criticism of Althusser, not because Althusser dissolved history into structure, but, on the contrary, because, while indeed adhering to a kind of structuralism, which identified the CMP with capital*ism*, he reserved its operations for the sphere of pure theory while leaving history more or less to itself. In fact, Thompson himself formulated his criticism of Althusser in almost exactly these terms in an essay far less well known than *The Poverty of Theory*, but dating from about the same time: in Althusserian theory, he writes, 'with its emphasis upon "relative autonomy" and "in the last instance determination", the problems of historical and cultural materialism are not so much solved as shuffled away or evaded; since the lonely hour of the last instance never strikes, we may at one and the same time pay pious lip-service to the theory and take out a licence to ignore it in our practice.'[13] If there is some truth in the suggestion that the Althusserian distinction between mode of production and social formation was intended to make Marxists, brought up in the shadow of a crudely economistic and reductionist base/superstructure model, more sensitive to historical specificity and the complexity of social life, this too is only a half-truth; for the distinction achieved its end simply by driving a wedge between structure and history and creating a rigid dualism between determination and contingency which left structural determinations more or less impotent in the sphere of historical explanation and in effect disabled historical materialism as a way of explaining historical processes. This was simply an evasion of the challenge posed by Marx himself: how to encompass historical specificity, as well as human agency, while recognizing within it the logic of modes of production.

III

It is precisely this challenge that Edward Thompson has tried to meet in his historical writings. His theoretical pronouncements have not always been helpful in illuminating his historical practice – partly because he has occasionally allowed himself to be trapped in the false alternatives offered by the prevailing terms of Marxist debate.[14] Even here, however, there is much wealth that could be mined to emancipate Marxist theory from these Hobson's choices and put it back on the fruitful track marked out by Marx himself. One or two things are particularly worth noting in Thompson's explicit remarks on the base/superstructure metaphor over the years. It is well known that he has always been concerned to rescue human agency and consciousness from the dead hand of crudely reductionist economisms, and there is no need to rehearse that point here. His preoccupation with 'experience' has received more than enough attention, even if the effects of that attention have often been misleading.[15] What has tended to get lost in this emphasis on Thompson's 'humanism' is that its corollary has often been an appreciation of structural determinations in historical processes which arguably exceeds that of his structuralist critics.

The mechanical base/superstructure model, with its 'levels' conceived as self-enclosed, spatially separate and discontinuous boxes, allows only two unacceptable choices: either we adhere to the 'orthodox' simplistic reductionism according to which the basic 'economic' box is simply 'reflected' in superstructural boxes; or – as in Althusser et al. – we can avoid 'crude economism' only by postponing determination by the 'economic' to some infinitely distant 'last instance', an effect achieved by rendering the rigid determinations of structure inoperative in history. It is significant that, although the 'last instance' in its original meaning is not intended to convey a *temporal* distancing as much as an analytic one, and although Althusser maintained that determination by the economic was somehow always present, he nevertheless chose to stress the infinite temporal and causal distance of the 'last instance' by insisting that its 'lonely hour . . . never comes'. But even if this now famous formula is dismissed as poetic licence, the indefinite deferral of economic determination that it implies is reproduced in the Althusserian separation of structure and history embodied in the distinction between mode of production and social formation. There is little room in this conceptual framework for 'economic' determinations which, while allowing the full range of historical complexity and specificity, are nevertheless (to quote Thompson) 'there all the time' – not just 'in the last instance', not 'thrust back to an area of ultimate causation . . . [which] can be forgotten in its empyrean', not 'operative only in an epochal sense', but *all the time*.[16]

This is the difficult dialectic between historical specificity and the always present logic of historical process that historical materialism asks us to comprehend. And it requires, as Thompson has always understood, a conception of the 'economic', not as a 'regionally' separate sphere which is somehow 'material' *as opposed to* 'social', but rather as itself irreducibly *social* – indeed, a conception of the 'material' as constituted by social relations and practices. Furthermore, the 'base' – the process and relations of production – is not just 'economic' but also entails, and is embodied in, juridical-political and ideological forms and relations that cannot be relegated to a spatially separate superstructure. If the base/superstructure metaphor can be made to encompass these insights, all well and good; but it is, according to Thompson, a bad metaphor because it obscures the nature of the very relations which it is meant to indicate. 'We must say', Thompson suggests about this unfortunate metaphor, 'that the sign-post was pointing in the wrong direction, while, at the same time, we must accept the existence of the place towards which it was mispointing . . .'[17] That place is the 'kernel of human relationships' embodied in the mode of production, a kernel of relationships which imposes its logic at every 'level' of society. In a comment on Raymond Williams' *The Long Revolution*, Thompson writes:

> when we speak of the capitalist mode of production for profit we are indicating at the same time a 'kernel' of characteristic human relationships – of exploitation, domination, and acquisitiveness – which are inseparable from this mode, and which find simultaneous expression in all of Mr Williams' 'systems'. Within the limits of the epoch there are characteristic tensions and contradictions, which cannot be transcended unless we transcend the epoch itself: there is an economic logic *and* a moral logic and it is futile to argue as to which we give priority since they are different expressions of the same 'kernel of human relationship'. We may then rehabilitate the notion of capitalist or bourgeois culture . . .[18]

There are perhaps dangers in this formulation too. An unwary application of Thompson's insights – which is perhaps encouraged by his often ambiguous language and by his apparent lack of interest in the 'economic' workings of capitalism – may lead to an indiscriminate conflation of all social relations and practices which, like the Althusserian approach but from the opposite direction, again incapacitates historical materialism, this time by depriving the relations of production of any effective meaning. The 'unitary' conception of social experience courts this danger by threatening to deny any integrity and specificity to production and production relations, expanding their conceptual reach beyond all meaning.[19]

If relations of production are redefined to *include* all social – or at least all class – experiences, there is no sense in which the relations of production can be said to shape or exert pressure on other aspects of social life. *Relations* presuppose *difference*, some separation between the factors in the relationship. And this also implies the possibility of imperfect relationship, tension and contradiction, which a 'unitarian' approach cannot accommodate. The question of historical causality is, again, effectively begged.

But if there are pitfalls in the formula that production relations 'find simultaneous expression' at all 'levels' of society, not in an ascending sequence proceeding from a determinative economic 'base' to an epiphenomenal superstructure, and if Thompson himself occasionally slides into these pitfalls, his own explicit account of this 'simultaneous' determination has a very different effect from the sloppy 'unitarianism' which throws all social forces into an indeterminate stew.[20] Thompson's argument, very simply, is that the process and relations of production which constitute a mode of production are expressed in a 'moral' as well as an 'economic' logic, in characteristic values and modes of thought as well as in characteristic patterns of accumulation and exchange. It is only in the capitalist mode of production that it is even possible to distinguish institutions and practices which are purely and distinctly 'economic' (in the narrow sense of the word, which is itself derived from the experience of capitalism); and even here, the mode of production is expressed simultaneously in those 'economic' institutions and practices and in certain attendant norms and values that sustain the processes and relations of production and the system of power and domination around which they are organized. These values, norms and cultural forms, argues Thompson, are no less 'real' than the specifically 'economic' forms in which the mode of production is expressed.

There are two inseparable and equally important sides to Thompson's argument about the simultaneity of 'economic' and 'cultural' expressions in any mode of production. The first, which is the one most commonly stressed by his critics and admirers alike, insists that ideology and culture have a 'logic' of their own which constitutes an 'authentic' element in social and historical processes. 'We may legitimately analyse ideology not only as product but also as process,' he observes in his critical appreciation of Christopher Caudwell, in which he both approves Caudwell's understanding of the 'authenticity' of culture and castigates him for attributing to the logic of ideology an autonomy that suggests 'an idea imposing itself on history'.[21] He continues:

> it has its own logic which is, in part, self-determined, in that given categories tend to reproduce themselves in consecutive ways. While we cannot substitute the ideological logic for the real history – capitalist evolution is not the acting out of a basic bourgeois idea – nevertheless this logic is an authentic component of that history, a history inconceivable and indescribable independent of the 'idea'.

The other side of the argument is that, if the determinative effects of the mode of production are simultaneously operative in both the 'economy' and in 'non-economic' spheres, they are also *ubiquitous*. The intent of the argument is not to deny or play down the determinative effects of the mode of production, but on the contrary, to reinforce the proposition that they are 'operative *all the time*' and everywhere. In other words, Thompson is perhaps at his most materialist at the very moment when he refuses to privilege the 'economy' over 'culture'. Indeed, the insistence on 'simultaneity' appears not as a departure from, or correction of, classical Marxist materialism but as a gloss on Marx's own words. Commenting on the above-cited 'general illumination' passage of the *Grundrisse*, for example, Thompson writes:

> What this emphasizes is the simultaneity of expression of characteristic productive relations in *all* systems and areas of social life rather than any notion of primacy (more 'real') of the 'economic', with the norms and culture seen as some secondary 'reflection' of the primary. What I am calling in question is not the centrality of the mode of production (and attendant relations of power and ownership) to any materialist understanding of history. I am calling in question . . . the notion that it is possible to describe a mode of production in 'economic' terms, leaving aside as secondary (less 'real') the norms, the culture, the critical concepts around which this mode of production is organized.[22]

We might wish for more precise indications of the boundaries between the 'mode of production' and that which is determined by it, and perhaps something less of a tendency to slide from the proposition that the mode of production is 'expressed' simultaneously in both economic and non-economic spheres, into the rather different suggestion that the mode of production *is* every social thing at once. But there can be little doubt that the intention of this argument is not only to stress the 'authenticity' of culture but also to rescue a materialist understanding of history from formulations which separate out the social 'levels' in a way which effectively detaches the 'superstructure' from the effects of the material 'base'. It is also an effort to rescue the original Marxist conception of the 'mode of production' from its identification with the capitalist 'economy', as embodied in market relations and/or some abstractly autonomous 'technology'. This is an identification which Stalinist orthodoxy shared with bourgeois ideology; which Althusserian theory perpetuated in its delineation of 'levels' or 'instances', in the very process of seeking to detach itself from 'vulgar economism'; and which today's 'post-Marxist' critics of Marxism – so many of whom were formed in the Althusserian school – have repeated, somewhat irrelevantly repudiating their own straw Marxism while reproducing its distortions in their own conceptions of the 'economic' sphere.

It may be true that Thompson does not always sustain the clarity of his 'unitary' conception and sometimes appears to allow the 'mode of production' to expand into an indeterminate totality of human relations. Nevertheless, there is a significant difference between his approach and the indiscriminate 'unitarian' view. A distinction must be drawn between the principle that relations of production are all the relations between people in a class society, that 'base' is also and at the same time 'superstructure', and Thompson's own very different proposition that

> Production, distribution and consumption are not only digging, carrying and eating, but are also planning, organizing and enjoying. Imaginative and intellectual faculties are not confined to a 'super-structure' and erected on a 'base' of things (including men-things); they are implicit in the creative act of labour which makes man man.[23]

Another illustration might be his argument that the law (for example) does not 'keep politely' to a superstructural 'level' but appears 'at *every* bloody level' and is 'imbricated within the mode of production and productive relations themselves (as property-rights, definitions of agrarian practice . . .)', and so on.[24] These propositions do not mean that the base includes all superstructure, or that production relations are synonymous with all social relations structured by class antagonisms. (Isn't this just another way of saying that mode of production = social formation, a conception to which Thompson strongly objects?) They mean that some so-called 'superstructure' belongs to the productive 'base' and is the form in which production relations themselves are organized, lived and contested. In this formulation the specificity, integrity and determinative force of production relations are preserved; and, in a sense, the requisite distance, which makes causality possible, between the sphere of production and other social 'levels' is established, while at the same time the principle of connection and continuity between these separate spheres is indicated by treating the 'economy' itself as a *social* phenomenon.

This brings us to another, especially subtle, reason for Thompson's rejection of the conventional base/superstructure metaphor; and here again the object is arguably not to weaken but to reinforce the materialism in the Marxist theory of history. Thompson has suggested that the metaphor fails to take account of the different ways in which different classes are related to the mode of production, the different ways in which their respective institutions, ideologies and cultures 'express' the mode of production.[25] While the base/superstructure model may have a certain value as an account of partisan ruling-class institutions and ideologies, the supportive structures of domination and the 'common sense of power', it is ill-suited to describe the culture of the ruled. The customs, rituals and values of subordinate classes can, as Thompson puts it, 'often be seen to be intrinsic to the mode of production' in a way that the dominant culture is not, because they are integral to the very processes of reproducing life and its material conditions. They are, in short, often the very practices which constitute productive activity itself. At the same time, although the culture of the ruled often remains 'congruent' with the prevailing system of production and power, it is because production relations are experienced by subordinate classes in their own particular ways that they can come into contradiction with the 'common sense of power'; and it is such contradictions that produce the struggles which determine the reorganization and transformation of modes of production. Historical transformations of this kind, argues Thompson, do not occur simply and spontaneously because (autonomous) changes in the base produce changes in the superstructure (as, for example, in technological determinism). They occur because changes in material life become the terrain of struggle. If anything, it could be said – although Thompson does not say it in so many words, preferring to avoid the language of base and superstructure – that if historical transformations are produced by contradictions between base and superstructure, it is in the sense that these contradictions represent oppositions between, on the one hand, the experience of production relations as they are lived by subordinate classes, and on the other, the institutions and 'common sense' of power. But to put it this way is already to acknowledge that the single model of the relations between material 'base' and ideological 'super-structure' suggested by the conventional metaphor is not enough. That model misleads because it universalizes the ruling culture, or, more precisely, the relation between the ruling culture and the mode of production, and conceptualizes away precisely that different kind of relation which generates historical movement.

Perhaps Thompson's view can best be summed up as an attempt to reassert Marx's own account of historical materialism as against the mechanical materialism of bourgeois philosophy. His emphasis, like that of Marx, is on 'human sensuous activity, practice' (as Marx formulates his materialism in the famous attack on previous materialisms in the 'Theses on Feuerbach'), instead of on some abstract 'matter' or 'matter in motion'. And like Marx, Thompson recognizes that mechanical materialism is nothing more than another idealism, or the other side of the idealist coin. He recognizes, too, that the framework of contemporary Marxist debate has in many ways reproduced the same false dichotomies of bourgeois thought from which historical materialism was intended to liberate us (even if he sometimes allows himself to be trapped in that constricting framework of debate):

> we may have been witnessing within the heart of the Marxist tradition itself a reproduction of that phenomenon which Caudwell diagnosed within bourgeois culture: the generation of those pseudo-antagonists, mechanical materialism and idealism. The same subject/object dualism, entering into Marxism, has left us with the twins of economic determinism and Althusserian idealism, each regenerating the other: the material basis determines the superstructure, independent of ideality, while the superstructure of ideality retires into the autonomy of a self-determining theoretical practice.[26]

This is not, it must be stressed, simply a demand for a question-begging 'interactionism', or what Thompson himself calls a 'barren oscillation' between determinants in a process of 'mutual determination'. As Thompson understands very well, 'mutual interaction is scarcely determination';[27] and it is no more his intention than it was Marx's to evade the issue of determination in this way. His formulation is simply a way of taking seriously the Marxist understanding of the 'material base' as embodied in human practical activity, which, however much it may violate the sensibilities of 'scientific' Marxists, requires us to come to grips with the fact that the activity of material production is *conscious* activity.

IV

The meaning of all this becomes fully apparent only in Thompson's historical practice, and the value of his disagreements with the language of base and superstructure can be tested only by examining what he can perceive through his conceptual prism which others cannot see as clearly through their own. Two aspects of his historical work in particular stand out: a profound sense of *process*, expressed in an unequalled capacity for tracing the intricate interplay between continuity and change; and an ability to reveal the logic of production relations not as an abstraction but as an operative historical principle visible in the daily transactions of social life, in concrete institutions and practices outside the sphere of production itself. Both these skills are at work, for example, in his characteristic 'decoding' of evidence indicating the presence of class forces and modes of consciousness structured by class in historical situations where no clear and explicit class-consciousness is available as unambiguous proof of the presence of class.

The theme running through *The Making of the English Working Class*, for example, is how a continuous tradition of popular culture was transformed into a *working-class* culture as people resisted the logic of capitalist relations and the intensification of exploitation associated with capitalist modes of expropriation. Thompson's critics have tended to focus on the *continuities* in this process, suggesting that his insistence on the continuity of popular traditions betokens a preoccupation with cultural, 'superstructural' factors at the expense of objective determinations, movements in the 'base' where capitalist accumulation takes place. The point of Thompson's argument, however, is to demonstrate the *changes* within the continuities precisely in order to show the logic of capitalist production relations at work in the 'superstructure'.[28] Where a structuralist Marxist, who tends to view history as a series of discontinuous chunks, might see nothing but an ideological 'level' out of phase with the economic, a superstructural fragment left over from another mode of production, a juxtaposition of structural boxes, Thompson sees – and can give an account of – an historical dynamic of change within continuity (which is, after all, the way history generally proceeds) structured by the logic of capitalist relations. The structuralist, for whom *a priori* theoretical correspondences would render the actual historical connections invisible (as in the case of Poulantzas and the absolutist state), would be disarmed in the face of non-Marxist historians who dismiss the concept of class as nothing but an abstract theoretical category imposed on the evidence from without, or those who would deny the existence of a working class in this 'pre-industrial' or 'one-class' society, citing as evidence the continuity of 'pre-industrial' patterns of thought. Thompson, in contrast, is able to trace the changing social meanings of popular traditions, tracking the operations of class in these changes within continuity. He can account for the emerging working-class formations, institutions and intellectual traditions which, despite their visible presence in the history of the period, are conceptualized out of existence by his adversaries. It is worth adding that, for those who regard the 'base' as something 'material' *as opposed to* 'social' – which generally means that the base consists of the technical forces of production and history is a technological determinism – the existence of working-class formations joining together 'industrial' and 'pre-industrial' workers must remain inexplicable. The conceptual framework of technological determinism compels us to place a premium on the technical process of work as a determinant of class, rather than on the relations of production and exploitation which for Thompson (as for Marx) are the critical factor and which alone can explain the common experience imposed by the logic of capitalist accumulation upon workers engaged in different labour processes.[29]

The principles underlying Thompson's 'decoding' procedures are made more explicit in 'Eighteenth-century English Society: Class Struggle without Class?'. Here his object is, among other things, to demonstrate that class struggle can operate as an historical force even when fully developed notions of class and class consciousness do not yet exist, that '[b]ecause in other places and periods we can observe "mature" (i.e. self-conscious and historically developed) class formations, with ideological and institutional expression, this does not mean that whatever happens less decisively is not class.[30] This project requires a 'decoding' of evidence which to other historians bespeaks a 'traditional', 'paternalistic' or 'one-class' society, in which the labouring classes lack any class-consciousness and social divisions are vertical rather than horizontal.

Significantly, here Thompson again invokes the 'general illumination' passage from the *Grundrisse*, which the Althusserians cite in support of their views on modes of production and social formations. And significantly, too, like Marx but unlike the Althusserians, he stresses the *unity*, not the heterogeneity, of social forms as they come within the 'field of force' of a particular mode of production:

it seems to me that the metaphor of a field-of-force can co-exist fruitfully with Marx's comment in the *Grundrisse*, that: 'In all forms of society . . .'

What Marx describes in metaphors of 'rank and influence', 'general illumination' and 'tonalities' would today be offered in more systematic structuralist language: terms sometimes so hard and

objective-seeming . . . that they disguise the fact that they are
still metaphors which offer to congeal a fluent social process. I
prefer Marx's metaphor; and I prefer it, for many purposes, to
his subsequent metaphors of 'base' and 'superstructure'. But
my argument in this paper is (to the same degree as Marx's) a
structural argument. I have been forced to see this when considering
the force of the obvious objections to it. For every feature of
eighteenth century society to which attention has been directed may
be found, in more or less developed form, in other centuries . . . .
What then is specific to the eighteenth century? What is the 'general
illumination' which modifies the 'specific tonalities' of its social and
cultural life?[31]

Thompson then sets out to answer these questions by examining '(1)
the dialectic between what is and is *not* culture – the formative
experiences in social being, and how these were handled in cultural ways,
and (2) the dialectical polarities – antagonisms and reconciliations –
between the polite and plebeian cultures of the time.'[32] Though it would
be helpful to have a clearer account of what is 'not culture', the result is an
intricate and subtle argument which reveals how 'traditional' patterns of
culture, which on the surface remain apparently unchanged, acquire a
new social meaning as they come within the 'field of force' of 'capitalist
process' and capitalist modes of exploitation. Thompson demonstrates
how customary behaviour and plebeian culture are shaped by new class
experiences, citing as a particularly evocative example the riots for the
possession of the bodies of the hanged at Tyburn, 'decoded' by Peter
Linebaugh in *Albion's Fatal Tree*:

we cannot present the rioter as an archaic figure, motivated by the
'debris' of older patterns of thought, and then pass the matter off
with a reference to death-superstitions and *les rois thaumaturges* . . . .
The code which informs these riots, whether at Tyburn in 1731 or
Manchester in 1832, cannot be understood only in terms of beliefs
about death and its proper treatment. It involves also class
solidarities, and the hostility of the plebs to the psychic cruelty of the
law and to the marketing of primary values. Nor is it, in the
eighteenth century, just that a taboo is being threatened: in the case
of the dissection of corpses or the hanging of corpses in chains, one
class was deliberately and as an act of terror breaking or exploiting
the taboos of another.
It is, then, within this class field-of-force that the fragmented
debris of older patterns are revivified and reintegrated.[33]

What makes the eighteenth century an especially complicated case is that customary behaviour and ritual acquire a particular significance because the logic of capitalism was experienced by the plebs so often as an attack on customary use-rights and traditional patterns of work and leisure – a process vividly described by Thompson in several of his works. Rebellion against the processes of capitalist accumulation, therefore, often took the form of a 'rebellion in defence of custom', creating that characteristic paradox of the eighteenth century, 'a *rebellious* traditional culture'.[34] Class conflict, then, tended to take the form of 'confrontations between an innovative market economy and the customary moral economy of the plebs'.[35]

If there is a danger in Thompson's formulations, it is perhaps that, as some critics have suggested, he is *too* ready to see opposition and rebellion in popular traditions and customs, and that there is too little room in his account for regressive impulses in popular consciousness or for its frequent penetration by ruling-class ideas. But excessive optimism is not required by his conceptual framework, and it has distinct advantages over theoretical systems which can recognize only 'backwardness' in popular traditions. The argument, of course, belongs to his larger project of rescuing the agency of subordinate classes from analyses which effectively relegate them to permanent subordination, bondage to ruling-class hegemony, ancient superstition and irrationality. But there is also a sense in which his emphasis on the creative transformation of old traditions to meet new circumstances and resist new oppressions represents a reaffirmation of materialist principles against theories of history which deny their efficacy in the explanation of historical process. His subtle analysis, for example, makes nonsense of historical treatments which see in these traditions and customs nothing but cultural remnants or 'debris', or regard their persistence as proof that class has no relevance for these 'traditional' 'pre-industrial' societies or even that culture is completely autonomous from material conditions. It should be said, too, that in this respect Thompson accomplishes what the structuralists cannot with their version of the base/superstructure metaphor. The latter can have little to say in response to the advocates of the 'debris' theory – which seems remarkably congruent with the Althusserian conception of 'social formation' – or, indeed, to those who deny the efficacy of class (or material conditions in general) in societies where ideological 'superstructures' apparently fail to correspond to the economic 'base'. Such arguments can be met only by acknowledging that history does not consist of discrete and discontinuous structural chunks, with separate and distinct superstructures to match every base; instead, it moves in continuous processes, in which relations of production exert their pressures by transforming inherited realities.

It has long been one of Thompson's central projects to respond to historians who deny the existence, or at least the historical importance, of class in cases where clearly defined class institutions or self-conscious languages of class, on the model of industrial capitalism, are not immediately present in the evidence. One cannot, then, help wondering why he has burdened himself with formulations – however poetically evocative (including 'class struggle without class?') – which have led his critics, and indeed often his admirers, to maintain that he identifies class with class-consciousness, thereby effectively denying the very existence of class where such consciousness does not exist. This is directly contrary to his intention of demonstrating the determinative effects of class '*situations*' even where 'mature' classes do not yet exist. Perhaps he has adopted these ambiguous formulas because he has always seen himself as fighting on two fronts at once: against the anti-Marxist denial of class, and against those Marxisms which deny the working class its proper self-activity by postulating for it a predetermined ideal consciousness. Nevertheless, his historiographical actions speak – or ought to speak – louder than his theoretical words; and it must be said that, in place of Thompson's very effective demonstrations of class forces operating in the absence of 'mature' class-consciousness, his structuralist critics can offer little more than theoretical assertions according to which class may exist by definition but without implications for historical processes.

It is instructive to contrast Thompson's approach to that of Gareth Stedman Jones in his most recent study of Chartism.[36] Explicitly disavowing his earlier Marxist belief in the connection between politics and material conditions, Stedman Jones argues here that the politics of Chartism were 'autonomous' from the class situation of the Chartists. His principal evidence for this autonomy is the fact that there was a fundamental continuity between their ideology and an older radical tradition born in very different social conditions. He seems, among other things, to attach little significance to the changes which that radical tradition underwent as it came within the 'field of force' of capitalist relations, changes which he himself notes without allowing them to affect his argument about the autonomy of Chartist politics and his general conclusions about the non-correspondence of politics and class. In other words, Stedman Jones' reading of evidence is exactly opposed to that of Thompson in similar circumstances: where one sees the autonomy of ideology from class in the continuity of popular traditions, the other sees the magnetic force of class in the transformation of a continuous popular culture. It is as if Stedman Jones has given up historical materialism because he has discovered that history moves in continuous processes, disappointing his expectation that every new base at least in principle must have a pristinely new superstructure to match. This may have something to do with the fact that, by his own testimony, he was in his earlier (Marxist) days strongly influenced by Althusserian theory. Another flip of the Althusserian coin?

Thompson's attempts to refine the base/superstructure metaphor are not simply a matter of supplementing the old mechanical model with an acknowledgement that, even though superstructures are erected upon bases, 'bases need superstructures'.[37] This proposition does not adequately convey, for example, the insights which inform his study of *law*. Thompson contrasts his own 'older Marxist position' to a 'highly sophisticated, but (ultimately) highly schematic Marxism' for which the law is quintessentially and simply 'superstructural', 'adapting itself to the necessities of an infrastructure of productive forces and productive relations' and serving unambiguously as an instrument of the ruling class.[38] His answer to this 'schematic' Marxism, however, is not simply to assert that the law, like other superstructures, is 'relatively autonomous', that it 'interacts' with the base, or even that it acts as an indispensable condition of the base. His argument is more complex, both more historical and more materialist.

Accepting at the outset the 'class-bound and mystifying functions of the law', he continues:

First, analysis of the eighteenth century (and perhaps of other centuries) calls in question the validity of separating off the law as a whole and placing it in some typological superstructure. The law, when considered as institution (the courts, with their class theatre and class procedures) or as personnel (the judges, the lawyers, the Justices of the Peace) may very easily be assimilated to those of the ruling class. But all that is entailed in 'the law' is not subsumed in these institutions . . . .

Moreover, if we look closely into such an agrarian context, the distinction between law, on the one hand, conceived of as an element of 'superstructure', and the actualities of productive forces and relations, on the other hand, becomes more and more untenable. For law was often a definition of actual agrarian *practice*, as it had been pursued 'time out of mind' . . .

Hence 'law' was deeply imbricated within the very basis of productive relations, which would have been inoperable without this law. And, in the second place, this law, as definition or as rules (imperfectly enforceable through institutional legal forms), was endorsed by norms, tenaciously transmitted through the community. There were alternative norms; that is a matter of course; this was a place, not of consensus, but of conflict.[39]

The notion of the 'imbrication' of the law 'within the very basis of productive relations' (which, incidentally, illustrates Thompson's point about the difference between those ideas, values and norms which are 'intrinsic' to the mode of production, and those that constitute the ruling apparatus and the 'common sense of power'), while not denying the 'superstructural' character of some parts of the law and its institutions, is something different from, and more than, the idea that 'bases need superstructures'. It is a different way of understanding the base itself, as it is embodied in actual social practices and relations. Nor is it simply a matter of analytically distinguishing the material base from the social forms in which it is inevitably embodied in the real world. Thompson's conception is, first, a refusal of any analytic distinction which conceals the social character of the 'material' itself (which is constituted not simply by a 'natural' substratum but by the social relations and practices entailed by human productive activity) – a refusal that is indispensable to historical materialism; but, beyond that, it is a way of discouraging analytic procedures which tend to obscure historical relations.

As Perry Anderson has pointed out, the principal objection levelled against the base/superstructure metaphor by Thompson and others is that the analytic distinction between various 'levels' or 'instances' may encourage the view that they 'exist substantively as separate objects, physically divisible from each other in the real world', creating a confusion between 'epistemological procedures' and 'ontological categories'.[40] He suggests that Althusser sought to avoid such confusions by insisting on a distinction between the 'object of knowledge and the real object'. And yet, there is a sense in which the Althusserians have had the worst of both worlds; for while their 'instances' and 'levels' tend consistently to slip into 'ontological categories' physically separated from one another in the real world, the *relations* between these 'levels' has tended to remain in the realm of pure theory, as 'objects of knowledge' that have little connection with 'ontological categories'. For Thompson, it is the relations that count; and if he occasionally errs on the side of allowing 'ontological' relations to become analytic conflations, this mistake is far less disastrous than the other for an understanding of history.

Notes

My thanks to Neal Wood, Peter Meiksins, Harvey Kaye and Nicholas Rogers for their comments and suggestions, and especially to Perry Anderson, who with his usual generosity helped me to strengthen my argument even on points with which he strongly disagrees.

I am very conscious that the following interpretation may have to be substantially qualified when Thompson returns to writing history after several years of thorough and passionate commitment to the peace movement. If during these years he has moved very far away from class politics, it would without doubt mean a profound change in what I take to be the theoretical underpinnings of his major historical work up to now.

1 This current is discussed in detail in my book, *The Retreat from Class: A New 'True' Socialism* (London: Verso, 1986).

2 These bald assertions about Hindess, Hirst et al. are developed at greater length in the *The Retreat from Class*.

3 E. P. Thompson, *The Poverty of Theory* (London: Merlin, 1978), p. 346.

4 Perry Anderson, *Arguments Within English Marxism* (London: Verso, 1980), p. 67.

5 Ibid., p. 68.

6 Nicos Poulantzas, *Political Power and Social Classes* (London: New Left Books and Sheed and Ward, 1973), p. 15. There is, incidentally, little justification for Poulantzas' appeal to Engels' authority for this conception of the mode of production. Engels' reference to 'factors' or 'elements' – however much it may have contributed to the treatment of the 'economic', the 'political', etc., as spatially separate and self-enclosed spheres or 'levels' – applies to the various forces which together determine the history of any social whole; but it does not appear as a gloss on the meaning of the 'mode of production' itself.

7 Ibid.

8 Ibid., pp. 157–67.

9 Despite Anderson's favourable references elsewhere to Poulantzas' conception of mode of production and social formation, the conclusions which he draws from his historical investigation of absolutism in *Lineages of the Absolutist State* (London: New Left Books, 1974) are exactly contrary to Poulantzas' and reflect an underlying theoretical framework quite different from the latter's. There are substantial differences between Anderson's analysis and that of Robert Brenner in his two important articles, 'Agrarian Class Structure and Economic Development in pre-Industrial Europe', and 'The Agrarian Roots of European Capitalism', republished in *The Brenner Debate: Agrarian Class Structure and Economic Development in Pre-Industrial Europe* (Cambridge: Cambridge University Press, 1985), pp. 10–63 and 213–327; but both Anderson and Brenner trace the development of absolutism to the actually existing social relations of feudalism instead of treating it as somehow a foretaste of capitalism, or as a reflection of a temporary balance between a declining feudal class and a rising bourgeoisie. The latter interpretations have been common among Marxists and reflect a tendency to beg the question of the transition from feudalism to capitalism by assuming the existence of capitalism somewhere in the interstices of feudalism, just waiting to be released. This procedure of assuming precisely what needs to be explained has arguably reached its apotheosis in structuralist Marxism, where bits of any or all modes of production can, as required, be assumed to be present, without explanation and without *process*, in any social formation, simply waiting to

become 'dominant'. The rise of capitalism can be 'explained' simply by asserting, tautologically, that the CMP, or some significant piece of it (like a capitalist 'type' of state?) was already present in the combination of modes of production that constituted the relevant social formations. For a forceful criticism of this aspect of Althusserianism, and of the Marxist tradition from which it arises, together with a powerful argument demonstrating the origins of this view of history in 'bourgeois' historiography and ideology, see George Comninel's *Rethinking the French Revolution*, (London: Verso, 1987).

10 Karl Marx, *Capital* (Moscow: Progress Publishers, 1971), vol. III, pp. 791–3.

11 Karl Marx, *Grundrisse*, tr. M. Nicolaus (Harmondsworth: Penguin, 1973), pp. 106–7.

12 *Poverty of Theory*, p. 254.

13 'Folklore, Anthropology, and Social History', *Studies in Labour History Pamphlet* (1979), p. 19 (originally published in *Indian Historical Review*, III (2) (1978), pp. 247–66).

14 Nowhere is this more vividly illustrated than in Thompson's distaste for Marx's '*Grundrisse* face' and his analysis of Marx's political economy. It is difficult to explain Thompson's failure to see that it is precisely in Marx's critique of political economy that he spells out the fully developed principles of historical materialism (as Perry Anderson has cogently argued in *Arguments Within English Marxism*, especially pp. 61–4). Indeed, it can be argued that this is where Marx laid down the very principles that Thompson has found most valuable in his own historical work. In contrast, the *German Ideology*, which falls within the corpus that for Thompson apparently constitutes the real foundations of historical materialism, still bears the traces of a relatively uncritical adherence to bourgeois historiography. (This argument concerning the difference between Marx's uncritical historiography, and the critique of political economy in which his own distinctive views receive their fullest elaboration, appears in Comninel, *Rethinking the French Revolution*). One possible explanation of Thompson's blind spot is that he has been too ready to accept the dichotomies arising from Stalinist theory, which seem to compel us to choose between a crudely reductionist economism and a complete abandonment of Marx's political economy 'face'.

15 This point, for which there is no room here, is discussed in my article, 'The Politics of Theory and the Concept of Class: E. P. Thompson and His Critics', *Studies in Political Economy*, 9 (1982), pp. 45–75. Also see Harvey J. Kaye, *The British Marxist Historians* (Cambridge: Polity, 1984) on Thompson's relationship to the Anglo-Marxist historiographical tradition of Dobb, Hilton, Hill et al.

16 'The Peculiarities of the English', in *The Poverty of Theory*, pp. 81–2.

17 'An Open Letter to Leszek Kolakowski', in *The Poverty of Theory*, p. 120.

18 'The Long Revolution, II', *New Left Review*, 10 (1961), pp. 28–9.

19 This 'unitarian' approach is discussed at somewhat greater length in my article, 'The Separation of the Economic and the Political in Capitalism', *New Left Review*, 127 (1981), pp. 74–5. See also Kaye, *The British Marxist Historians*, pp. 19–22 and 232–41.

20 The notion of 'simultaneity' is also discussed in 'Folklore, Anthropology, and Social History', pp. 17–18.

21 'Caudwell', *Socialist Register* (1977), pp. 265–6.

22 'Folklore, Anthropology, and Social History', pp. 17–18.

23 'Socialist Humanism', *New Reasoner*, 1 (1957), pp. 130–1.

24 *Poverty of Theory*, p. 288.

25 See especially 'Folklore, Anthropology, and Social History', pp. 20–2.

26 'Caudwell', p. 244.

27 Ibid., pp. 246–7.

28 *The Making of the English Working Class* is discussed in greater detail in Wood, 'The Politics of Theory and the Concept of Class', pp. 52–9.

29 For an example of a criticism of Thompson which castigates him for uniting 'different kinds of workers' in a single working class, a criticism based on a conceptual framework that makes it impossible to understand how class formations can and do arise which combine such 'different' workers, see Ernesto Laclau and Chantal Mouffe, *Hegemony and Socialist Strategy: Towards a Radical Democratic Politics* (London: Verso, 1985), pp. 156–7. Their conceptual framework is discussed in detail in Wood, *The Retreat from Class*, chapters 4 and 5.

30 'Eighteenth-century English Society: Class Struggle without Class?', *Social History* 3 (2) (1978), p. 150.

31 Ibid., pp. 151–2. Thompson is using a different translation from the one cited above. Thus, the word he renders as 'tonalities' appears as 'colours' in the translation cited earlier.

32 Ibid., p. 152.

33 Ibid., p. 157.

34 Ibid., p. 154.

35 Ibid., p. 155.

36 'Rethinking Chartism', in *Languages of Class: Studies in English Working Class History, 1832–1982* (Cambridge: Cambridge University Press, 1983). This argument is examined at length in Wood, *The Retreat From Class*. Stedman Jones distances himself from the tradition of historical materialism much more explicitly and emphatically in the introduction to *Languages of Class* than in the articles compiled in that volume. In the brief survey of his own development which he sketches in the introduction, he identifies 'Rethinking Chartism' as a turning-point marking a 'shift in [his] thinking', not only on the subject of Chartism 'but also about the social historical approach as such' (pp. 16–17). It is possible that when he wrote the article in 1981 and published it in a shorter version as 'The Language of Chartism', in J. Epstein and D. Thompson (eds), *The Chartist Experience* (London: Macmillan, 1982), he did not intend to go quite as far in renouncing Marxism as he was later to claim, and a reading of 'Rethinking Chartism' without the benefit of his own later gloss on it might not be enough to reveal the full extent of his movement away from historical materialism; but in *Languages of Class*, he has certainly chosen to interpret his own intentions in that way.

37 G. A. Cohen, *Karl Marx's Theory of History: A Defense* (Oxford: Oxford University Press, 1978). It is worth adding, incidentally, that if Cohen's

technological determinism really did represent an accurate account of Marx's views on base and superstructure, then Thompson might not be so far wrong in his account of Marx's '*Grundrisse* face'.

38 *Whigs and Hunters* (London: Allen Lane, 1975), p. 259.
39 Ibid., pp. 260–1.
40 Perry Anderson, *Arguments Within English Marxism*, p. 72.

6

History, Marxism and Theory

Robert Gray

The 'historical school' of British Marxism is recognized as a distinctive voice in the international dialogue of history, Marxism and the 'social sciences'.[1] Yet Marxist historians – or, if one prefers, historians in the tradition of Marx – have tended, for good reasons, to wear their theory lightly. The main emphasis in their theoretical pronouncements has been on a flexible and open-ended reading of Marx's work, a necessary dialogue with other traditions and practices, and the historian's vocation to 'find out' what actually happened.[2] How particular modes of production are linked to political and cultural forms; how boundaries between classes are drawn in practice and in lived experience; how far conscious human agency can push back the determining limits of the historically possible. These and similar issues have usually been posed by historians in specific contexts, while a more self-consciously 'theoretical' strand in Marxist work has engaged in a separate exercise of conceptual clarification.

This separation has been damaging and distorting, and there are some welcome signs that it is becoming less marked. Thompson's *Poverty of Theory* and the discussion it provoked seem, in retrospect, to occupy a symbolic but paradoxical place in this wider development.[3] Thompson's work has always been distinguished by its theoretical engagement. Yet he employs a rhetoric that can obscure this and send up noise warning others off from the theoretical region. If Thompson and other historians have managed without the theoretical heavy breathing characteristic of some modes of Marxist writing, this is partly because a certain understanding of Marx's ideas has been implicit in their work. 'The talismanic concepts are "relative autonomy" and "in the last instance determination". We were given these by Engels, and we learned them in our theoretical cradle.'[4] That 'cradle' was presumably the Communist movement of the 1940s, and Marxism is none the worse for having been acquired outside, or even against, the academy. In more recent years, however, Marxism has had more influence inside the academy – not least by virtue of the intellectual distinction of Marxist historiography – while the political culture of the labour movement has fragmented. Some of the tensions of this development are registered in the *Poverty of Theory*, as well as in the essays of the preceding twenty years collected in the same volume. Thompson – oddly, in view of the widespread interest in his work among younger generations – seems to view the Marxism of the academy as a largely negative phenomenon, and himself as the isolated representative of a critical and empirical Marxist tradition, linked to political practice. The explosion of 'academic Marxism' has, however, been registered differently, for example by Raymond Williams, who sees it as ending a period of relative personal isolation: 'my own long and often internal and solitary debate with what I had known as Marxism now took its place in a serious and extending international inquiry.'[5]

Thompson's relationship to 'post-1960s Marxism' is thus a paradoxical one. He was himself a major influence, both through his work as historian and his more directly political interventions, in stimulating renewed interest in Marxism. Moreover, his work suggested a necessary engagement with Marxist *theory*, as well as a critical awareness of its possible limitations; he was, for example, among the first to suggest that the experience of Stalinism might raise questions about received Marxist categories, and not just about Russian history or bureaucratic 'distortions' of Marxism.[6] *The Making of the English Working Class* is prefaced by some now classic remarks about mechanistic Marxism, mainstream economic history and functionalist sociologies of development. The subsequent debate centred on the reality of 'class' and 'consciousness' as objects of historical study.[7] For many readers, including the present writer, this was a first introduction, not only to Marxist debate, but also to social theory of any kind. The theoretical issues are further developed in 'The Peculiarities of the English' and 'Eighteenth-century English Society'.[8] Thompson is quite wrong to suppose – if he really does suppose this – that 'the young' have failed to attend to his arguments.

I

Thompson's voice has been an important one in the opening of debate and the transformation of Marxism since the 1950s. Yet he has himself taken some distance from aspects of recent Marxisms, notably in the *Poverty of Theory*. He thus stands in a complex double relation to what may be loosely termed 'pre-' and 'post-1960s' Marxisms. On the one hand, there has been a diversification of debate, a refusal of centres of 'orthodoxy' (whether in Moscow or anywhere else) and, finally, a hesitant move towards a critical engagement with the limitations of Marx himself.[9] These features of Marxism since the 1960s seem to continue the project initiated by Thompson and others during the crisis of the Communist Party (CP) and in the early New Left. The space won in the CP itself, as well as elsewhere on the left, for a critical Marxism marked the intellectual horizons of the 'Althusserian' generation, despite periodic resurgences of dogmatist mania. On the other hand, Thompson has rightly been irritated by an over-facile dismissal of earlier Marxist traditions and the political struggles associated with them. This irritation has found increasingly sharp expression, and it is certainly true that the intellectual revival of Marxism has at times adopted a 'young Turk' tone, which marked it as a movement of intellectuals without much firm political anchorage outside the intellectual world.

Thompson has thus been concerned to vindicate what he sees as a distinctively 'English' empirical and historical Marxism. He emphasizes a privileged relation between Marxism and history, and the value of certain distinctive English traditions, especially a literary 'moral realism'. As Bill Schwarz has argued, this relationship can be traced from aspects of cultural politics within and around the Community Party in the 1930s and 1940s, under the aegis of the popular front and democratic struggles against fascism.[10] A characteristic theme was the recovery of revolutionary and progressive popular traditions, and the attempt to present the modern working class, with the Communists as its conscious vanguard, as the inheritor of such traditions. This could be seen as a response to the minority, at times even marginal, position of Marxism within British politics and culture; against the weight of popularized Conservative or Whig histories, revolutionary politics could be argued to draw from authentically English sources. The work of A. L. Morton and Dona Torr – both very much 'party' figures rather than professional academics, but also scholars of major significance in fields which the academy studiously neglected – was central in this respect. Whatever the wider political fortunes of the CP in more recent years, the formation of a substantial British Marxist tradition was one achievement of the 1940s. The more recent flowering of Marxist historiography, and its contribution to the development of a distinctive social history, would be unthinkable without this work, undertaken at a time when academic life was much less hospitable to Marxist perspectives than it has since become.

History was thus central to the formation of a British Marxist tradition, and the subsequent development of Marxist historiography has been marked, both in its strengths and its weaknesses, by that formative moment. The strengths included a sharp sense of political relevance, an understanding of the past as actively shaping responses to present problems. It was, moreover, a mode of history writing informed by an engagement with English literary traditions. This involved some difficult problems of Marxist cultural theory – and at times some original and 'heterodox' solutions.[11] The relationship to literary currents had to be worked for, rather than simply assumed. The importance of literature can probably be related to the way in which literary humanisms have carried, in Britain, much of the weight of critical social thought, in some ways paralleling the work of the so-called 'founding fathers' (*sic*) of sociology.[12] Whatever one thinks of the label 'culturalism', it seems indisputable that a focus on cultural change in its broadest sense is a distinctive feature of British Marxist historiography; and this owes much to the protracted engagement of Marxist intellectuals with literary problems.

These appropriations of Marxism as it was understood in the 1930s and 1940s shaped a distinctive British Marxism. Certain unresolved but fruitful tensions were among the determining conditions of this creativity. The tradition was marked by an encounter between a determinist understanding of Marxism and a pressing need to assert the moment of struggle and human agency – in political practice as well as historical interpretation. There were also ambiguities of interpretation surrounding the 'popular front' line. It could be read to indicate a new strategic path for socialist transformation in advanced capitalist countries (and can, indeed, be seen as the beginning of the shift towards what is somewhat unsatisfactorily labelled 'Eurocommunism'); but it could also be read as a defensive response to fascism, conceived in rather narrowly 'tactical' terms (with the implication that 'liberal-bourgeois' allies in the struggle against fascism might be dumped at some later stage, rather than drawn into a more permanent system of social and political alliances).[13] The dissolution of the Comintern in 1943 and the subsequent adumbration of national roads to socialism certainly did not end fidelity to the Soviet model; national roads, passing through parliamentary forms and traditions or the construction of 'new democracies', could still be understood as tactically contingent routes to a common Soviet-style destination. The work of the Communist historians can be seen as a creative response to some of the tensions and contradictions of this situation. In circumstances of growing political isolation after the war, accompanied by deeper social and cultural changes which both the social democratic and Marxist lefts had difficulty in confronting, the fruitful tensions could collapse into a sentimental populism, a recourse to radical popular and class traditions as a symbol of hope.

To suggest that there were problems of this kind is not at all to belittle the fundamental achievements of the period, in some futile quest for the holy grail of a 'pure' and fully rigorous and coherent Marxist history. But any body of work has its own political and theoretical conditions, and to attempt critically to locate these is simply to apply the canons of historical materialism to specific Marxisms.[14] Thompson is undoubtedly right to suggest that the political and intellectual activity of Communists in these years can at no time be reduced to Stalinist dogmatism.[15] There is, however, a sense in which the construction of a critical Marxism was necessarily at one or two removes from the central political and theoretical questions confronting Communists in the late 1940s and 1950s, not least, for historians, the history of their own party. The baneful effects of dogmatism and of a centralist style of leadership did not extend to less immediate areas of history, and 'the living line of Marx's analysis of British history' gave impeccable authority for serious historical work.[16] At the theoretical level, mechanical readings of Marxism may have been prevalent (though it is possible to exaggerate the degree to which 'official' readings of Marx, even in the Soviet Union, even in Stalin's own writings, *were* uniformly based on a simple version of determinism); but these interpretations could still leave wider or narrower spaces for 'superstructural' mediations and the 'subjective' element in historical change. There was then some licence for the practice of a serious Marxist scholarship, including, it should be noted, in the Soviet Union. The main direction of British Marxist historiography was the exploration of cultural mediations and the moment of struggle and human agency, inscribed within a Marxist theory and a Communist politics whose wider premises were, of necessity, more obliquely addressed. Nor was such work necessarily antithetical to official orthodoxy, which could itself recognize 'subjective' consciousness and cultural transformation as political problems, however crudely conceived.

The crisis of 1956 was, for Thompson, the point at which a critical Marxism and a popular democratic Communist politics had to be definitively severed from the Communist Party. The validity or otherwise of Thompson's stance in 1956 is not here at issue; quite apart from this, it is necessary to place the moment of 1956 in a wider context. The problems of a critical Marxism and a democratic Communist politics did not begin or end at that moment. Thompson has argued that 'the Communists of the 1930s and 1940s were not altogether wrong, intellectually or politically',[17] and sought to identify these choices with an authentically democratic politics and a critical tradition in theory. But it is doubtful how helpful this construct is in understanding the inner-party history of these years – which undoubtedly requires further study.[18] In particular, the characteristic Thompsonian themes of popular agency and voluntarism, with a consequent Romantic voluntarist 'infiltration' of the vocabulary of Marxism,[19] are not necessarily antithetical to Stalinism. This is obvious enough when efforts to elicit popular activity fall on deaf ears, become dislocated from any real base and reduced to empty bureaucratic routines. The heroic popular will of Stalingrad, the London blitz and the resistance movements, which the Communists were able effectively to address, was of a different quality; but the conditions of its effectivity have to be analysed. Voluntarism did not disappear from the vocabulary of Marxism with the onset of the Cold War, but it came to function increasingly as empty rhetoric. The origins of this stasis have to be sought in the difficulties the Communist movement faced in coming to terms with the political situation of the later 1940s – difficulties to which certain Stalinist practices and reflexes certainly made a contribution – and not simply in the presence or absence of voluntarist themes. Stalinism itself contained important elements of utopian voluntarism.[20]

It is not my intention in raising these questions to blame Thompson, or for that matter the party to which he belonged, for failing to see things clearly enough. It is merely to draw attention to areas of ambiguity, which make it hard simply to disentangle a 'good' side of the Communist movement at this period from its Stalinist deformations. Stalinism itself was a complex phenomenon, with popular as well as bureaucratic elements.

After 1956, some of these ambiguities and problems became more prominent and openly expressed. The identification of Marxism with the party (and of both with the working class), and of the Soviet Union with socialism and the cause of peace could no longer hold in any simple way. Changes in capitalist societies, the decomposition and recomposition of classes, and new forms of protest altered the social and political landscape. Marxists, including those critical Marxists associated with the dissension in the Communist Party, were probably led to underestimate the weight of these changes, in a concern to refute crudely ideological accounts of the 'withering away of class', the 'end of ideology', and so on. The changes, and the consequent need to re-think Marxism, have become inescapable in the 1970s and 1980s. Ironically, predictions of the break-up of 'class politics' as traditionally understood seem to have been partly fulfilled – but in conditions of chronic recession rather than the celebrated 'affluence' of the 1960s. The new political agendas of women and black peoples have perhaps posed the biggest challenge to Marxists. There are thus important elements of crisis and (possible) renewal that have developed since the break of 1956, and largely since the intellectual leftism of the late 1960s. The themes posed in Thompson's work over many years – determination and agency, base and superstructure, culture, consciousness and class – will certainly be central to any re-thinking of Marxism in this context. His response to more recent attempts to grapple with these problems, often in different idioms, has however been a growing sense of isolation. In the *Poverty of Theory* an attack on the supposedly baneful influence of Althusser provides a peg on which to hang these responses.

If 1956 was crucial, on Thompson's own account, for his political and intellectual project, '1968' was crucial for the Marxisms against which he is reacting. The two moments are arguably of equal importance for the longer-run trajectory of Marxist politics and theory in Britain. New political protagonists emerged in the late 1960s, and the politics of protest was carried from global issues (especially the Vietnam war) to demands for cultural and institutional transformation. In several countries there was growing industrial militancy with tensions between workplace struggles and established forms of labour representation: in Britain this centred on incomes policies and attempts by the Wilson government to impose legal regulation of industrial activity. This crisis of social democracy could be read, no doubt naively, as the beginning of a new kind of revolutionary politics, based on the convergence of varied forms of social protest. These developments were certainly marked by a degree of naive subjectivism, vanguardist arrogance and plain silliness – a veritable 'infiltration' of voluntarism into the vocabulary of Marxism. Thompson's sense of distance from all this may indeed owe something to the classical – and often valid – Communist critique of 'ultra-leftism'. (The preoccupation of the French Communist Party leadership in 1968 with provocation and the dangers of military repression was, for instance, not without justification, though this does not make the actual stance adopted beyond criticism.) But underneath their excesses, the movements of *c*.1968 represented a significant cultural change. The repercussions extended well beyond the organized left (however that somewhat elastic term is to be defined), but for the left they posed new agendas which have, if anything, increased in importance. Any renewal of the left, in the face of the continuing political and cultural offensive of the right, will depend on the incorporation of these agendas into feasible political alternatives. This poses large, and so far intractable problems of organization, representation and the construction of alliances. The politics of social movements has certainly displayed more resilience in the face of right-wing governments than 'official' opposition parties; but parties, the traditional form of popular political organization, nevertheless retain an indispensable role in the construction of any cohesive alternative. And most parties of the left, whether social democratic or communist, have encountered considerable difficulties in transforming themselves to rebuild their social constituencies – or even, in many cases, perceiving that such a transformation might be needed. Problems of representation, social forces and forms of political organization are at the centre of the crisis of Marxist politics and theory.

A dislocation of Marxism from traditional social constituencies and agencies within organized labour movements (often as a militant minority, but nevertheless part of the movement) was one element in the growing sense of crisis. This aspect is sharply registered in Thompson's critique of Althusser and 'Althusserianism'. This reflects a sense of dislocation and blockage in the late 1970s, 'a particular "conjuncture" which has broken the circuits between intellectuality and practical experience'.[21] The intellectual leftism deriving from the 1960s found its moment of greatest expansion, just as the left and the labour movement entered a phase of political paralysis and recession: a phase marked by the degeneration of social democratic management into crude pragmatism and of industrial militancy into narrow corporatism, in the period of the Wilson–Callaghan governments of 1974–9. If the leftism of the 1960s meshed in with wider cultural changes, the 1970s saw less favourable trends, and the cultural initiative passed, unregarded until afterwards, to the right. What Thompson had long pointed out as the problem of 'agency' was thus coming to the surface in new ways. One response, though not the only response, to this was indeed a retreat into theoreticism and a displacement of political struggle onto intellectual life.

A number of features of post-1960s Marxism, which help to explain this impasse, have already been touched on. The new Marxisms took their political bearings from a politics of movements, and of generalized cultural disaffection. Within this, a number of groups, sects and currents of thought competed, but also cooperated, while the traditional parties associated with the labour movement – the Labour Party and to some extent the Communist Party – were not major poles of attraction. The challenge to 'consensus politics', in which organized labour – or at least its leaders – were seen as implicated, was a characteristic theme. Some hopes were invested in the 1964 Labour government, whose political appeal did have resonances in the cultural radicalism of the period, but a credibility gap quickly opened and became a yawning chasm during the Vietnam war.

This alienation from the official political system found its reference-points in various international sources of inspiration: Cuba, the black and campus revolts in the USA, Vietnam, France in 1968, to some extent the Cultural Revolution in China, as well as the earlier heritage of revolutionary politics. It is easy enough to caricature all this; enthusiasm was not always combined with information or critical perception. But, as at some analogous historical moments, obsessive interest in international movements and events could reflect a deeper questioning of the resources of our own culture, including, on the left, a questioning of the institutions and traditions of the British labour movement. This could take the form of too easy dismissal, as in Anderson's 'Origins of the Present Crisis'.[22] Thompson's brilliantly argued riposte continues to inspire important historical work.[23] But if Anderson's analysis was over-schematic, impressionistic and often downright wrong, it was still of significance as an attempt to think the political movement of the mid-1960s – the diminished credibility of what it became fashionable to call the 'Establishment', and the advent of a Labour government with a rhetoric of modernization – in relation to its deeper historical determinations. Anderson also produced some more thoughtful and disciplined arguments about socialist organization and strategy in the developed civil societies of advanced capitalism, attempting to address 'the enduring political supremacy of one class, under conditions of universal suffrage', and the need to 'move beyond the traditional preoccupations of the labour movement, towards a political programme which conceives men [*sic*] in their entirety, and tries to liberate them in their whole social life.'[24] Thompson also hinted at these strategic concerns,[25] but the attempt to ground political analysis in a historical critique was not taken up in the wider debates on the left.

If the attempt at a critique of English culture could too easily slide into facile dismissals, expressed in the tones of the 'public school *enragé*', it is still important to register the cultural disenchantment that produced that tone, and the wider social and cultural mutation it represented. The culture came to feel parochial and narrow, blocking access to significant kinds of knowledge. Thompson is probably right to detect a shift in the concerns of *New Left Review*, towards greater theoretical abstraction, and especially the introduction of recent – or recently recovered – European Marxist thought to English readers. This was in important ways liberating, not least in convincing part of a generation that 'orthodox' economistic readings of Marx were not the only possible ones; but it was at the expense of a shift away from more concrete and historical concerns with the British social formation, a shift largely coinciding with rapid disillusionment with the Wilson government.

One motif in this renewal and diversification of Marxism was the attempt to re-read Marx, in the belief that there was a 'real Marx' – and perhaps also a 'real Lenin' et al. – behind successive layers of tendentious interpretation, and that the discovery of the real Marx would somehow illuminate the way forward. Hence the emphasis on Marx's early writings, the humanist critique of alienation and the dialogue with existentialism seemed to offer a reading of Marx pertinent to the felt oppressions and contradictions of advanced capitalism – as well as of the Stalinist state socialism often originally addressed in such ideas. In this context, the British reception of Althusser – initially in the shape of a translation of 'Contradiction and over-determination' (*NLR*, 147, 1967) – marked an important theoretical moment. Althusser's work, and his emphasis on critical textual readings, intensified the search for the real

Marx, pointed it in new directions – and, in the end, exploded the whole enterprise from within. For Althusser suggested – and this may be his permanent contribution – that the real Marx produced texts that were uneven, inconsistent, groping to express new thoughts in borrowed (Hegelian, etc.) languages. This demanded a 'symptomatic reading', attending to silences and incoherences, rather than assuming the essential unity of Karl Marx as an originating subject. Althusser's importance lay in the questions he asked; despite a dogmatic tone, the challenge to the assumption that there was an essential Marx whose ideas would spring forth, fully armed, from the text, was an encouragement to think for ourselves. Althusser's answers – his divide between 'science' and 'ideology', his deployment of 'symptomatic' reading not to explicate texts but to annihilate them, his rigid periodizations of Marx' work, and so on – were always debatable, and could indeed lead his followers into moments of theoreticist mania. The structuralist schemes of *Reading Capital* do seem to invite us into an 'orrery', and Thompson scores some palpable hits against this. A decade or so after 'Contradiction and Over-determination', at the moment of the *Poverty of Theory*, the theoreticist excesses seemed to be reproducing themselves endlessly, in internecine strife and fission, while the broader political and cultural climate was shifting to the detriment of the left.

Althusser's work also indicated approaches, under the general rubric of 'relative autonomy', to problems which were becoming central to any credible Marxism: the emergence of new political protagonists, and the difficult project of an alliance with the traditional labour movement. While it is true that 'relative autonomy' is a theoretical slogan rather than a developed concept, marking the site of a problem rather than offering any real solution, it was at least a more *helpful* slogan than some of those on offer. It appeared to offer a way of thinking about the diverse social struggles which were exploding in the late 1960s and were to become permanent features of the social landscape, without collapsing them into 'the "beautiful" contradiction between Capital and Labour'.[26] This may in the end, as Thompson suggests, simply have proposed 'to sophisticate the clockwork',[27] and formulations about relative autonomy could function to paper over the cracks in an incipient crisis of Marxism. Some of the cracks had, however, been prised open by Althusser himself, above all in the re-thinking he encouraged around the materiality of ideology; this re-thinking then rendered the base–superstructure model deeply problematical. And if 'theoretical practice' could provide a 'Marxist' cover for a self-regarding academicism, it was also important to assert the value of intellectual work. Even the flirtations with structuralism, or with intellectual fashions in general, were perhaps a risk attached to an engagement with contemporary intellectual life.

The moment of Althusserian theoreticism came at a point of curious dislocation, an uneven development in which 'academic' Marxism reached its maximum expansion – with monetarist policies only just beginning to cut back on the growth of higher education and the graduate schools – while the historic agencies of socialist politics entered a recession which threatened, and still threatens, to become a secular decline. There were also healthier responses to this conjuncture, and the 1970s saw a notable shift in the direction of Marxist work, away from the search for the real Marx, and towards concrete studies of problems of British capitalism, cultural and political change, the nature of the State, the recomposition of classes.[28] Althusser had some influence on this, but only as one among several influences, critically handled and, increasingly, put to work in concrete analysis. If there has been an overarching influence, it has surely been that of Gramsci, whose anglophone reception largely coincided with that of Althusser, and has proved of deeper significance to the re-thinking of Marxism.[29]

As so often in the history of Marxism, the political setbacks of the 1980s have encouraged theoretical renewal. This has taken a number of directions, and one permanent gain of the diversity of the 1960s is that notions of a unitary 'orthodox' Marxism, needing only to be restored, have gone for ever; there are, to be sure, people who still think in this way, but they say too many different things for the proposition to be plausible. The conception of Marxism as a self-sufficient world-view, or even an omnibus 'science of society' has also become questionable. Feminist critiques have been especially important here, and cannot simply be assimilated, as a regional sub-theory in a reconstructed Marxism; patriarchy can be argued to be as fundamental as class, or 'production' in the conventional sense, to the organization of human societies. There are important issues about the identity and status of Marxism, behind its apparent intellectual vitality. Many of these questions are touched on in Thompson's *Poverty of Theory*, as well as in his work over the preceding years.

II

The *Poverty of Theory*, appearing in the midst of the controversy around Richard Johnson's interesting attempt to map the lines of development in Marxist historiography, aroused a good deal of sound and fury, including several long reviews and (from Perry Anderson) a whole book.[30] Yet the excitement died down fairly quickly, and, in retrospect, the discussion seems oddly dated, misplaced – and at some moments distasteful. It has to be said that, if there was indeed a kind of *lumpen* theoreticism among those contemptuous of empirical work, there was also a deeply philistine strand in some of the enthusiasm for Thompson's critique, and the 'absolutist' tendencies in the presentation of the issues marked a further deterioration in the tone of debate on the left.[31] How far Thompson himself bears responsibility for this is, of course, another matter. It is certainly true that the undiscriminating character of many of his arguments was not helpful. People one encountered bore little relation to his picture of the 'Althusserian'; all the traits he criticized were, and still are, around but rarely all together in the nauseous mixture Thompson concocts. The alleged 'spell' of Althusser, in so far as it ever existed, had already been broken.[32] The 'Althusserian school', on both sides of the channel, quickly dispersed. Many figures associated with it have had new and interesting things to say about Stalinism, the impasse of the western labour movements, democracy and the state and the 'crisis of Marxism'.[33] Poulantzas' untimely death silenced a voice that was challenging us to re-think many of the categories of Marxism, while Althusser himself has also been silenced under terrible circumstances. As for the British influence of Althusser, it has dispersed in a number of directions within and in some cases beyond Marxism. At the theoretical level, there seems to be a convergence around the need to transcend the false dichotomy of 'structuralist' against 'culturalist' approaches,[34] combined with a general turn to more concrete and empirical work of contemporary relevance. In this process, Althusser's ideas have been selectively and critically assimilated and put to work; they are no longer the basis for any distinguishable school of thought.

The *Poverty of Theory* is of interest because it registers a sense of crisis. The issues it raises, quite apart from any local argument with Althusser, are issues about Marxism itself. In his 'Open Letter to Leszek Kolakowski' of 1973, Thompson, while rejecting Marxism as doctrine and Marxism as method, declared continued adherence to Marxism as tradition: 'In choosing the term tradition I choose it with a sense of the meanings established for it within English literary criticism.'[35] In *The Poverty of Theory* he concludes by seeing the tradition as definitively ruptured: 'Politically, it has long been impossible for the Stalinist and anti-Stalinist positions to cohabit with each other. It is clear to me now, from my examination of Althusserianism – and my implicit critique of other related Marxisms – that we can no longer attach any theoretical meaning to the notion of a common tradition.'[36]

The notion of Marxism as tradition is an attractive one, but it is not free of difficulties, either in its literary derivation or its application to Marxism. Thompson's objections to Marxism as doctrine – the Marxism of churches and sects – and to Marxism as method – the Marxism of scholastics – are certainly well taken. But tradition does not necessarily provide an adequate alternative. If for doctrine we substitute 'determinate propositions about the social world' and if for method we substitute 'procedures for investigating the social world', then any identifiable Marxist tradition would seem to entail both these things. Unless the Marxist approach can be expressed as a set of (provisional and debatable) propositions of this kind, it will remain in some sense beyond knowledge and beyond rational debate. That the propositions should be seen as debatable, modifiable, to the point where their development presses on the boundaries of Marxism as commonly understood, should require no further emphasis. But the notion of tradition is not altogether helpful in this respect. Marxism as tradition would seem to be open to some of the same deformations as Marxism as doctrine. As the literary analogy should suggest, a tradition may be constructed by inclusions and evictions quite as brutal as anything in the history of Marxism. Indeed, Williams' account of tradition as 'a deliberately selective and connecting process which offers a historical and cultural ratification of a contemporary order'[37] would seem, if anything, to best fit the official Marxisms of Eastern Europe.

The concept of tradition may be deployed in varied, more or less general or historically specific senses. To follow the analogy with literary tradition, this may in one sense be seen as stretching from *Beowulf*, Homer or whoever, together constituting 'important' literature; or one may define more specific traditions – of the romantic lyric, the realist novel, modernism, etc. – with moments of transition and rupture between them. The history of Marxism has also been a history of breaks – within the work of particular theorists, as well as between them – related in complex ways to political exigencies. Any reconstruction of Marxism from its present crisis must read all these Marxisms in relation to the situations they addressed, as well as to their filiation from particular sources within and beyond a Marxist tradition, and then try to define what they contain of continuing use. (The answer to this may, of course, be 'nothing': that is a tenable opinion, but not one I share.) Marx's own work, needless to say, is not exempt from this critical, contextualized reading, and Thompson, among others, has offered helpful comments on, for example, the degree to which Marx's texts are affected by the ('bourgeois') intellectual climate of the mid- and late nineteenth century.[38] While Thompson certainly recognizes the need for this kind of critical reading, and has indeed contributed to it, the ambiguities of 'tradition' can exert a conservative pressure. Tradition generally implies judgements of value, emanating from an undisclosed moral centre; and this may actually work to inhibit critical engagement, except around local issues.

The conservative pressure affects Thompson's views both of Marxism and history. One hint of this is the recurrent use of the metaphor of apprenticeship to evoke the transmission of tradition. This metaphor, like that of tradition, is appealing; we are reminded of Marc Bloch's *Historian's Craft*.[39] But the metaphor presents some problems on closer examination. Feminists might criticize its allusion to particular, masculine forms of 'skill'. Thompson's use of apprenticeship slides between two senses: the historian's way of working with sources (about which he has much of value to say); and a theoretical formation in historical materialism. The notion of apprenticeship renders the whole process of transmission rather opaque. Knowledges transmitted by apprenticeship tend to change in piecemeal, molecular, unregarded ways.

There is thus a certain tension in Thompson's argument, between a view of Marxism as requiring critique and reconstruction, and a view of Marxism (or 'historical materialism') as established ground, rendering further theoretical elaboration not only gratuitous but positively harmful. The former position is reflected in a running critique, not just of Althusser et al., but of Marx himself, raising many important questions about base and superstructure, determination and agency, and the status of political economy in Marx's work. The latter position, however, negates this, pressing us back into the complacent assumption that all that is worth saying at the theoretical level was said long ago, and that the further development of Marxism is simply an ongoing confrontation of these propositions with empirical evidence, including that of political experience. The impatience with theoreticism and the desire to vindicate the empirical tradition of Marxist historiography is certainly justified. But vindication slips into an unhelpful defensiveness, as damaging to the possibilities of real dialogue as the arrogance of some theoreticist young Turks.

This defensiveness is most strongly expressed in some of Thompson's arguments about history as a discipline. Historical materialism is elided with the discipline of history, with a consequent hostility or indifference to other disciplines – such as sociology or linguistics, though literary criticism and aspects of anthropology are, it seems, to be admitted to civilized conversation – which might contribute to a critical Marxism.[40] It is not entirely clear to what extent Thompson is referring to historical materialism, an ideal discipline of history which *should* exist, or the activity conducted under the rubric of history in various institutions of teaching and research. These things cannot readily be equated. Sociologists and others have as many – or as few – claims as historians in the narrower sense to inscribe themselves as practitioners of historical materialism, the intellectual enterprise of Marx. And any history, Marxist or otherwise, which ignores their contributions will be impoverished. While one may share Thompson's sense of the substantial achievement of British Marxist historians, it is more doubtful whether that achievement can be regarded as self-sufficient in the way he sometimes suggests.

Thompson stresses the definition of history as a 'humanity'. More than this: '"History" must be put back upon her throne as the Queen of the humanities.'[41] Claims to a scientific status for history (or Marxism) are to be rejected, since historical knowledge is 'selective', 'provisional' and 'limited'. 'Her knowledge will never be, in however many thousand years, anything more than proximate. If she makes claims to be a precise science these are wholly spurious.'[42] And Thompson offers important arguments about the indeterminacy of historical eventuation, and the appropriateness of notions of 'logic of process', rather than anything at all like the 'laws' of natural science as commonly understood. The political implication, 'that the project of Socialism is guaranteed BY NOTHING ... but can find its own guarantees only by reason and an open choice of values',[43] still, unfortunately, needs underlining. However, to insist so stridently on the identity of history as a humanity may itself be to concede too much to a dominant scientism. The point is not necessarily to claim the status of 'science' for history, Marxism or the social sciences – this is a difficult argument, however it is to be concluded, which I leave aside – but to contest the conventional divide between 'science' and the 'humanities'. Divides between 'thinking' and 'feeling', 'facts' and 'values', 'rational' and 'intuitive', 'objective' and 'subjective' are all condensed in this sort of distinction; and, for historical reasons, this has been a particularly marked tendency in British intellectual life. Thompson's own historical work, and the cultural criticism of Raymond Williams have consistently challenged just these dichotomies; but the ordinary academic discourse of the 'humanities' or 'sciences' presses us back, on one side or the other. This was less marked when Marx was writing *Capital* – if 'Marx . . . knew, also, that History was a Muse',[44] then Darwin for instance knew that biology was a muse – though divisions rigidified towards the end of the century, when Marxism itself was read, with some warrant in the texts of Marx and Engels, in terms of the prevailing positivism and evolutionism. We perhaps now need to argue less about the placing of this or that activity in terms of such definitions, and more about the critical placing of the definitions themselves.

If the term 'science' has become encumbered with positivist ideological baggage, this should not lead back to an uncritical recourse to conventional notions of the humanities, which may be equally loaded. The argument about the potential scientific knowledge of historical materialism remains a significant one, though not one that can be embraced in its simpler forms. Historical materialism could be said to construct coherent explanatory frameworks, subject to empirical controls and capable of orienting further empirical investigations; this is no less

than might be said for any of the disciplines commonly accepted as
sciences. Moreover, the attempt to think 'scientifically' about society, and
to found political action on this analysis has been an important and
valuable part of the Marxist tradition, albeit one which is apt to
degenerate into empty rhetoric. The contingent and indeterminate
character of social and historical explanation, and the reflexive action of
human agents as makers of their own history do not necessarily
undermine this enterprise.

> Indeed one might say that only to the extent to which the objective
> aspect of prediction is linked to a programme does it acquire its
> objectivity: 1. because strong passions are necessary to sharpen the
> intellect and help make intuition more penetrating; 2. because reality
> is a product of the application of human will to the society of
> things . . .[45]

In these terms there may, despite the positivist accretions of the Second
International and official 'Marxism-Leninism', be something worth
retaining in Engels' original claim to construct a scientific socialism.

The privileged place Thompson assigns to history, 'the queen of the
humanities', seems, despite disclaimers, to involve imperial pretensions
couched in a rhetoric of territoriality and boundaries. In the sense that all
the objects of study of the humanities (and/or the social sciences) exist
within the medium of human history this is valid. A critical historical
materialism can, and to some extent does, function to draw connections
between discrete disciplines; there is an 'avowed kinship' between the
concepts employed by Marxist scholars in diverse fields.[46] But the
ambiguities of Thompson's definition of history, the constant slippage
between the discipline as practised and the project of historical
materialism, leave some dissatisfaction here. Marxism, given its concerns
with total social formations and their transformation, has developed
complex relations with a range of disciplines, marked by differently
constructed objects of study and procedures. None of these disciplines
can be equated with the project of historical materialism *tout court*.
Thompson refers to 'academic procedures of isolation which are abjectly
disintegrative of the enterprise of historical materialism', and rightly
suspects that some of Althusser's formulations about levels, regional
concepts and relative autonomy may simply provide a 'Marxist' licence
for such academicism.[47] But, as Thompson seems to recognize, the
problem does not end there; there are in existence 'discrete disciplines
informed by unitary concepts',[48] and attempts to synthesize these within
some higher proclaimedly Marxist totality do not always provide happy
precedents. Thompson sometimes seems to assign to history, 'the Queen

of the Humanities', this kind of integrative function. But this glosses over the issue of how far history as generally practised, even by Marxists, is adequate to the aspirations of historical materialism, and how far the concepts and practices of other disciplines may expose and remedy its inadequacies.

The justifiable concern to vindicate Marxist historiography thus slips into an unhelpful defensiveness about history as a discipline. Thompson says little about how the necessary 'exchanges' at the borders of disciplines are to be achieved, or about the way they might challenge or displace the ordinary practice of historians. At times, there is a lapse into metaphors of territory and invasion that are actively disruptive of any dialogue: 'certain structuralisms . . . which periodically attempt to over-run the historical discipline.'[49] Lying behind this there seems to be a devaluing of the necessary theoretical moment in any historiography, especially any historiography of Marxist inspiration, and of the potential contribution of other disciplines and traditions, with their emphasis on formal model-building, to its development. Thus Thompson argues that the borrowing of certain historical concepts by other disciplines is 'the misfortune of Marxist historians'.[50] But it could equally be argued that, because of the pressure of empiricist traditions in mainstream history, the theoretical moment in Marx's enterprise came to be detached and separately developed by sociologists, economists and others. The concept of class can scarcely be regarded as the original property of historians, many of whom have devoted much time and energy to denying its existence or pertinence to large stretches of history. It is only relatively recently, and partly under the critical pressure of sociology, that class, and with it the work of Marxist scholars, has gained recognition within academic history. There was, for example, in my recollection, a far quicker and more generous response to *The Making* from sociologists than historians. It is odd to find Thompson, who more than most historians addresses issues that cut across conventional disciplines, adopting a defensive rhetoric normally encounted in the more retrograde corners of the historical profession.

In this respect, Thompson's suggestion that there is a 'court of history' to which the validity of Marxist, or any other concepts must be referred, needs qualification. It is, of course, quite justifiable, and perhaps needed saying, to assert that theories have to seek empirical verification. But the significant arguments about Marxism – or about conceptualization in general – are rarely purely empirical. What are to count as pertinent 'facts' or 'evidence' is often at issue. Marxist and feminist historians have had to extend the range of historical knowledge to embrace such topics as the consciousness of the labouring poor; the growth of capitalism and the events of the seventeenth century; the reality of class struggles whose agents lack a vocabulary of class; the hidden labour of women within the household. These investigations have again and again entailed challenging the prevailing rules of evidence, sometimes so stridently as to risk being sent down for contempt. And this has often been a matter, not just of ideological suspicion of Marxism – in which all uses of class, even those of anti-Marxist derivation tend to get caught up – but also a certain disinclination to arduous conceptual engagements of any sort. These features of academic history have become less marked in recent years, and the opening up of a dialogue with sociology and cognate disciplines has played some part in this.

Given some of the ambiguities of the notion of history, Thompson's privileging of historical materialism as the 'common ground for all Marxist practices',[51] needs more elaboration; especially as regards the theoretical moment, the levels of necessary abstraction, which Marx certainly saw as inherent to his project. This theoretical element can scarcely be equated unproblematically with history, or any other existing discipline; it has rather to be seen as a space for continuing theoretical debate which might inform work in a range of disciplines, but also needs to be constantly criticized and reformulated in the light of specific work, including work of non- or even anti-Marxist inspiration. In this conception, in the spirit of the diversification and renewal of Marxism after the Cold War, there can be no imperial pretensions, no privileging of particular traditions, disciplines or practices, any more than of particular states or parties. A fruitful dialogue cannot develop through blanket condemnations such as Thompson's anathemas on structuralism (which are quite as arbitrary and dogmatic, in their way, as any pronouncement of Zhadanov). Moreover, if there is an organizing centre to Marxism, it has surely to be sought in political practice, the collective project of building a new form of society, and the critical engagement with the whole field of human knowledge and culture that must flow from that. Neither Thompson's equation of historical materialism with empirical history, nor Althusser's 'theoretical practice' can be regarded as the privileged moment within Marxist theory and practice.

As a polemical response, a 'bending of the stick', Thompson's defensive attitude to history may have some justifications. But it could induce a dangerous intellectual complacency, discourage historians who lack Thompson's own theoretical culture from acquiring it, and close off dialogues with those forms of study which appear difficult, abstruse and non-historical. The very lively development of social history since *The Making of the English Working Class* will atrophy if historians retire into splendid isolation, and refuse to meet the challenge of the contemporary intellectual terrain. Equally, the failure to define a space for the theoretical moment in historical materialism – a moment always present in Thompson's own substantive work – dissipates the force of some important critical points about Marxist theory itself. These points, relating to the 'Thompsonian' themes of class and culture, agency and determinism, and the critique of economism are germane to wider difficulties of Marxism and the political left.

III

Thompson's arguments about class are his best-known contribution both to history and Marxist theory, and are discussed elsewhere in this volume. It is, however, necessary to make some comments in the present context. The main direction of Thompson's work is, of course, to establish class as an historically defined relationship, rather than a static category, and to insist that 'classes do not exist as separate entities, look around, find an enemy class, and then start to struggle'.[52] This is well put, and 'Eighteenth-century English Society' stands as a major theoretical statement, clarifying and in some respects going beyond the protocols set out in *The Making of the English Working Class*. Thompson's work has placed class firmly on the agendas of historical research, and extended our understandings of class struggle. It is in the medium of culture, understood in its broadest sense, that classes define their identities in relation to each other, and this requires the kind of sensitive decoding of popular behaviours exemplified in Thompson's work.

There are, however, some problems in the handling of class, and they relate to Thompson's general aversion to explicit theorizing. If class is 'something which in fact happened',[53] which can only be defined in an empirical historiography, this still leaves the issue of what *sort* of happening it is and how we are to recognize it. As Anderson has noted, a liberal historian might well accept much of Thompson's account of eighteenth-century society, but still ask, why not talk simply of 'social conflict' rather than of 'class struggle'?[54] There is, as Thompson is certainly aware, a theoretical hinterland to the use of class terminology, which would refer us to productive relations and to antagonisms arising from the unequal distribution of power and resources. Thompson tends to take economic dimensions as given, and to move to 'the way in which these experiences are handled in cultural terms'.[55] The validity of this is not at issue, but it is doubtful if the 'economic' history of industrialization can simply be taken as read, still less can that of commercial and agrarian capitalism in the eighteenth century. Indeed, Thompson's own emphasis on the artisans and weavers has helped to stimulate an interest in relationships between factory and other labour processes and their transformations, with a consequent revision of our notations of 'industrial revolution'.[56]

One effect of treating the economic level as established ground is, oddly in view of Thompson's reiterated critique of mechanistic Marxisms and sociologies, to actually *reinforce* the separation of the cultural from the economic: 'If the experience appears as determined, class-consciousness does not'.[57] Recent studies of work relations and labour processes have emphasized elements of struggle and negotiation, in which culture – often in the shape of patriarchal values – plays a large role, rather than the inherent necessities of technology.[58] In the light of this, it may be questionable how far the experience does 'appear as determined'. This direction is certainly indicated, and partly inspired by Thompson's own work, especially his recent concerns with broadened anthropological definitions of culture, and of production itself. But Thompson is in one sense not culturalist *enough*: in his eagerness to move on from the (determined) realm of economic relations to the realm of cultural self-making, he leaves intact many received notions of economic change.

The merit of Thompson's approach is that it brings us back to a conception of class in terms of relationship, antagonism and change, and forces us out of culture-bound assumptions about the possible forms such conflicts might take – assumptions which anyhow have a diminishing purchase on the political problems of western societies. Marxists certainly need to be alert to the fact that 'class . . . does not occur only in ways prescribed as theoretically proper',[59] and not only with reference to the eighteenth century. But this approach seems less effective in probing further questions about different modes of class activity, accommodation as well as resistance, and forms of popular expression which cut across incipient class identities. Thompson is certainly too good a historian to ignore such realities – thus he refers to 'the extraordinarily deep sociological roots of reformism' in the mid-nineteenth century, and to the reciprocal relations which held crowd and gentry in a common 'field of force' in the eighteenth.[60] But his work presses us towards culture-as-resistance, the integrity of popular tradition below the surface of incorporative pressures. Thompson perhaps evades some hard questions about these traditions, which might be raised, for example, in the light of black and feminist politics. The central figure of the 'freeborn Englishman' is limited by gender, race and – by the implied contrast to the Catholic despotisms of other countries – by religion.[61]

The continuing critique of mechanistic Marxism has come to centre on concepts of culture and experience. These emphases are important, but they perhaps mark the site of a problem, rather than point to any satisfactory solutions. Thompson argues, against the base–superstructure model, for the materiality of culture:

Values are neither 'thought' nor 'hailed'; they are lived, and they arise within the same nexus of material life and material relations as do our ideas. They are the necessary norms, rules, expectations, etc., learned (and 'learned' within feeling) within the '*habitus*' of living; and learned, in the first place, within the family, at work, and within the immediate community. Without this learning social life could not be sustained, and all production would cease.[62]

This oddly parallels one of Althusser's major themes, his emphasis on the materiality of ideology – a term Thompson, however, prefers to avoid, or reserve for its derogatory and reductive uses. Culture – or ideology, in the less reductive uses of that term – is not epiphenomenal, but constitutive of social relations themselves. This calls into question the metaphor of base and superstructure, with its reification of distinct levels, an undialectical separation rather than the 'dialectical intercourse between social being and social consciousness' which was Marx's original insight.[63]

The criticisms of base and superstructure are well taken. It may, however, be important to retain the 'rational kernel', the original insight that Marx was struggling to express. His original formulation – one of several, although it is the one which, perhaps by virtue of a treacherous simplicity, has been seized on – was attempting to understand social formations as complex wholes, with determinate and determining relations between different elements (although there are then further difficulties with the concept of 'determination'). In these terms, it may still be possible to give a qualified defence of the use of base and superstructure.[64] It is essential to add, however, first, that the distinctions have to be understood as analytical and not substantive – *all* the elements are co-present and effective in all social life and all history, and Marx is not embarking on the byzantine game of assigning this or that institution or activity to this or that level. Second, that social structures are only reproduced by active and conscious practice, and this is historically struggled over rather than guaranteed; determination works as the setting of limits, a 'repertoire' of possible outcomes to any situation. Third, that the value, if any, of the formulation is in analysing contradiction, rather than in assuming mystical homologies; situations of more or less radical disjuncture between the levels are more characteristic, and certainly more interesting than securely established correspondences. Marxism, in a word, is not a functionalism. It was in this direction that Gramsci, who kept alluding to Marx's famous preface and whose work may perhaps be seen as the 'limit case' of the base and superstructure model, developed the notion. It may well be, however, that the formula cannot survive this critical development and is best abandoned, as Thompson among others has suggested.

But if base and superstructure are to be abandoned, we still may require some analogous set of analytical distinctions. Alternative formulations about the 'dialectic of social being and social consciousness' are rather too generic to meet the needs of concrete analysis. Capitalist societies are marked by a separation of 'economic' and 'political' spheres, with a cluster of related, but not identical distinctions between public and private, coercive and consensual/voluntary relations, etc. The problem is to find a conceptual vocabulary that enables us to draw such distinctions without reifying them. In this respect it is not just base and superstructure that are at issue but such distinctions as those between state and society, private and public, and so on – a problem registered in Gramsci's shifting formulations about state and society.[65] These divisions are, on the one hand, real, in lived experience as well as at the analytical level; but, on the other hand, never fully formed and fixed. Thus 'the market' itself is politically and culturally constructed and may, even within capitalism, be constructed in different ways distributing advantages differently. On the other hand, markets do have a real existence, resist attempts to mould them in certain directions and even have a disconcerting habit of re-emerging in spheres where they are supposed to have been abolished. The task for a critical social theory is to grasp these realities – for example, the way that economies *appear* to behave autonomously, and to confront states and governments, even 'capitalist' governments, as awkward and intractable givens – while avoiding their reification. It is probably true, as Thompson argues, that such difficulties are unlikely to be resolved by 're-arranging and elaborating our vocabulary'.[66] But, as the tangled debate on base and superstructure should warn us, the vocabulary used does have substantive consequences, and there may be more merit than Thompson allows in a continuing theoretical scrutiny of the terms and concepts of Marxist analysis.

The problem of determination, which lies behind much of the base and superstructure debate, is linked to another of Thompson's abiding concerns, with agency and moral choice. Indeed, Thompson's emphasis on culture seems to conceive it as a privileged space for the formation of moral agents. Such concerns are certainly present in Marx – and not only the young Marx, despite all Althusser's anathemas on humanism and historicism – and subsequently notably in Gramsci. However, Thompson's construction of culture as the moment of moral choice and conscious human agency leads to an oddly selective reading of the cultural. Culture is made to carry all the weight of active practice, as against determining pressures. Hence Thompson's repeated allusions to romanticism as the carrier of an immanent moral critique. The struggle over values during the Industrial Revolution is sometimes presented as an epochal confrontation between acquisitive entrepreneurial utilitarian values and a popular moral economy with romantic resonances: 'a resistance movement, in which both the Romantics and the Radical craftsmen opposed the annunciation of Acquisitive Man'.[67] This points to real problems of cultural change, but it rather oversimplifies the lines of demarcation. Neither Utilitarianism nor Romanticism were unitary phenomena, and both were, as Thompson indicates elsewhere, differently appropriated in different contexts. Nor can the ideology of the new capitalists be reduced to 'the annunciation of Acquisitive Man'; it also contained strong organicist and paternalist impulses, often of religious inspiration, and drawing, precisely, on the language of romanticism.[68]

The Making of the English Working Class is, of course, a rich and complex work, and I am not offering a total critique. I would, however, draw attention to a tendency to treat culture and values as constitutive of polarized world-views, linked to opposing classes. This is in some ways reminiscent of vulgar Marxism – if the 'working class did not rise like the sun',[69] it nevertheless rose – even if Thompson gives a far richer account of mediating processes of cultural self-making. Similar problems affect, on both sides, the debate about the 'peculiarities of the English'. Thompson's essay is a brilliant and compelling argument, distinguished by a compressed presentation of complex theoretical issues, as well as sensitivity to historical and cultural nuances; the argument certainly carries more conviction, twenty years on, than Anderson and Nairn. But there are difficulties common to both sides, which relate to an expressive model of the links between culture and class. Thompson rightly notes the pluralism and internal divisions of the British state, and the complex make-up of the dominant class, so that 'the aristocratic ethos still had a life of its own', but counter-balanced (and perhaps ultimately controlled) by 'bourgeois' institutions and influences.[70] But the relative emphasis on 'aristocratic' and 'bourgeois' elements can then become a matter of assertion and counter-assertion. Moreover, the assignment of particular institutions or cultural forms to one or the other can be debatable. There could be considerable mobility, and interpenetration of cultural elements, and this has to be understood as a process of active appropriation across a cultural 'repertoire', rather than as an expressive totality.[71]

The view of culture as the privileged site of conscious agency and moral choice tends to establish a polarity of culture and 'non-culture', and to locate all the determining pressures at the non-cultural pole. But these pressures can themselves be cultural in form, indeed they will necessarily take this form in lived experience. 'Men make their own history . . . but under the given and inherited circumstances with which they are directly confronted'; Marx then goes on to define these determining pressures in terms of 'the tradition of all the dead generations'.[72] Here the problem of determination is not posed simply in terms of base and superstructure;

elements of the 'superstructure' are themselves seen as determining. This is not, however, to argue that people are inexorably trapped within given cultural forms, as some structuralists (including Althusser in his more structuralist moments) might suggest. As elsewhere in Marx, the determinism proposed is a *critical* one; to see oneself as determined is already to begin to hold the determinations at a critical distance, even as, necessarily, one continues to live them. Feminists, in opening spaces of struggle around patriarchy and sexual politics, have had much to say about this problem of determination and conscious agency, as well as about the ways that precisely 'the cultural' can appear as determining and constraining.

Thompson is certainly right to resist structuralisms (including aspects of Althusser) that appear to consign historical agents to passivity. But his proposed alternatives contain their own difficulties. He offers the term 'experience' as the key to understanding how men and women live their own history, the dynamic of struggle and change. Some notion of experience and its mediations is, in one sense, a necessary part of any adequately dialectical history, part of the working models of the historian. Arguments in social history – and not only those of Marxist historians – generally take the form of constructing the 'typical' experience of this or that group, and examining responses to that experience. Thompson also makes larger claims for the notion of experience, offering it as the missing 'genetics' of Marx' account of social change.[73] In the sense that people make their own history under given conditions, and as a corrective to reified theoretical schemes that lose sight entirely of actual human agents, this has some force. But the recourse to experience cannot quite be taken at face-value. For experience is a construct, in at least two senses. It is, in the first instance, constructed by historical agents through the culture and language available to them, as Thompson's account of the 'freeborn Englishman' amply demonstrates. This is not to say that the cultural construction of experience is without difficulties and contradictions. 'Experience walks in without knocking at the door.'[74] But the conclusions to be drawn from experience, however traumatic, are rarely unambiguous: the bitterness of men from the trenches (one of Thompson's examples of a transformative experience) could, after all, be articulated by left or right in the 1920s, and to suggest that survivors of famine will necessarily 'think in new ways about the market' implies a somewhat optimistic view of popular consciousness.[75] There thus remain problems about the ways in which particular experiences disrupt and rearticulate the elements of culture, and the point at which this rearticulation constitutes a fundamental transformation, such as that marked by the consciousness of class; and structuralist protocols of interpretation may in fact give us some purchase on this problem.

Secondly, the experience of which historians tell us is, as it were, a second- or third-order construct. As such, it is based on real processes, and real evidence of those processes, but it is not a simple reflection of them. Social historians habitually talk about 'the experience of the artisan', or of slavery, or modern war, or middle-class women. Their accounts are not based on any *particular* artisan, slave, etc., nor always on everything that is known about the category in question, but rather on some ordering of information, involving degrees of generalization, abstraction, judgements about typicality and wider significance. Theoretical elements – for example, concepts of intensifying exploitation as it might affect particular categories – will necessarily enter into this kind of construct. This is not, of course, to suggest that the theoretical element is self-sufficient and self-validating; the discipline of the sources, and the possibility of challenge and refutation from a reading of sources is a central feature of history as a discipline, Marxist or otherwise.

If, then, experience is necessarily constructed – and the metaphor of construction, despite its post-structuralist provenance, has the merit of suggesting an active process of appropriation – we need to examine the ways in which this construction takes place, the cultural resources employed, the determining pressures at work. A materialist understanding of language is, for example, central to these issues; without language, people could not speak to themselves about their experience, much less leave traces for the historian.[76] The recourse to experience itself raises large theoretical issues, and cannot simply be adopted as an empirically-based corrective to theoreticism.

IV

Thompson is surely right to oppose Marxisms and structuralisms which offer static formal categories as models of dynamic social processes, and to insist on a flexible, historically contextualized and relational under-standing of such key concepts as class. Whether he is right to identify the tendencies he opposes with Althusser and 'Althusserianism' is a separate issue, and one which, in Thompson's presentation of the matter, muddies the waters. It is anyway an argument that belongs in its own historical moment: I have preferred to leave it there and have tried to focus on the wider substantive issues – issues about Marxism itself, and not just about Althusser.

The questions that Thompson raises have figured, in varying formulations, in much recent Marxist debate – including, paradoxically, some aspects of Althusser. More than most Marxist historians, Thompson's history writing is integrated with a running critique and attempted reconstruction of Marxist theory. Yet, and this is another paradox, Thompson presents himself, especially in the *Poverty of Theory*, as a plain-minded empirical practitioner of historical materialism, abandoning his garden to administer correction to recent aberrations which have provoked him beyond endurance. This is a peculiarly English literary figure, whose roots may perhaps be traced back to the independent Radical-leaning gentry of the late eighteenth and early nineteenth centuries, a reconstruction and transformation of the Tory humanist tradition, 'the only one to emerge with much honour from the first half of the [eighteenth] century'.[77] As a way of conducting theoretical debates it has the advantage, which Thompson would claim, of a healthy scepticism about the pretensions of Grand Theory (of whatever kind), and an insistence on confronting it with actual lived experience – including those large-scale historical experiences of our own century that Marxists have still adequately to face. But it also has limitations. As a rhetorical mode, it generally involves argument from supposedly established ground, an implied moral centre, which is characteristically alluded to rather than defined. This sets up a conservative and defensive pressure within the argument. Both Marxist theory, or whatever it contains worth retaining, and the practice of empirical history are both taken as common ground, traditions passed on by 'apprenticeship'. Both are seen as needing defence against the barbarian hordes of Althusserian '*lumpen*-intellectuals'. And the theoretical element in Marxist history is then dissolved in a rather undiscriminating assault on theoreticism. This is unfortunate, not least because it can obscure the innovative direction of much of Thompson's own work, both as historian and Marxist. Furthermore, the effect of the rhetoric may be to close off further theoretical debate and inhibit a necessary engagement with Marxist theory, and indeed other relevant theoretical traditions (including structuralist explorations of the materiality of language and ideology). Thompson himself has certainly engaged with much of this work, whatever one thinks of his judgements about it, but his mode of argument will scarcely encourage others to follow.

It would, however, be unfortunate if these limitations were to obscure the major things Thompson has had to say about Marxism and the practice of history. The issues he raises about class, culture, determinism and agency remain at the centre of Marxist debate; though Thompson has far less to say about the crucial dialogue between Marxism and feminism. These are also, in a way that has become harder to evade in the 1980s, pressing political issues. If Thompson does not resolve them, this may be because we continue to live them. And, if it is no longer possible to believe that a real Marx, to be disclosed by peering at this or that text, will solve our problems, this may mean that Marxism, faced with severe political set-backs and unthinkable dangers, is at last coming of age. We may still find an indispensable starting-point, politically and theoretically, in the central insight of Marx – that history is to be understood in terms of the way human societies produce and reproduce themselves, and that any emancipatory politics has to address itself to deep transformations at that level. But to take this on board is also to take on board the multiple difficulties of Marxism.

Notes

1 See, e.g., *Making Histories*, ed. R. Johnson et al. (London: Hutchinson 1982); R. J. Holton, *The Transition from Feudalism to Capitalism* (Basingstoke: Macmillan, 1985); H. J. Kaye, *The British Marxist Historians* (Cambridge: Polity Press, 1984); F. Poirier, 'L'école historique anglaise', in *Les Aventures du marxisme*, ed. R. Galissot et al. (Paris: Syros, 1984).

2 See, in addition to E. P. Thompson's work and especially his *The Poverty of Theory and Other Essays* (London: Merlin, 1978), E. J. Hobsbawm, 'Karl Marx's Contribution to Historiography', in *Ideology in Social Science*, ed. R. Blackburn (London: Fontana, 1972); idem., 'Marx and history', *New Left Review*, 134 (1984).

3 'The Poverty of Theory', in Thompson, *Poverty of Theory*, hereafter *PT*: further citations from this volume refer to the title essay unless otherwise indicated; subsequent impressions print the essays in a different order, all references are to the original (1978) impression. Key responses include P. Anderson, *Arguments Within English Marxism* (London: Verso, 1980); G. McLennan, in *Literature and History*, 5 (1979); idem., 'E. P. Thompson and the discipline of historical context', in *Making Histories*; K. Nield and J. Seed, in *Economy and Society*, 8 (1979); P. Q. Hirst, ibid.; and the debate at the History Workshop reprinted in *People's History and Socialist Theory*, ed. R. Samuel (London: Routledge & Kegan Paul, 1981). My own piece in *Marxism Today* (June 1979) was an immediate response related to its particular political and theoretical context; the present essay is an attempt to explore some wider issues.

4 *PT*, pp. 287–8.

5 R. Williams, *Marxism and Literature* (Oxford: Oxford University Press, 1977), p. 4.

6 'Socialist Humanism', *New Reasoner*, No. 1 (1957).

7 E. P. Thompson, *The Making of the English Working Class* (Harmondsworth: Pelican edn, 1968), preface and afterword.

8 E. P. Thompson, 'The Peculiarities of the English', reprinted in *PT* (first published 1965); idem., 'Eighteenth-century English Society: class struggle without class?', *Social History*, 3 (1978).

9 See, e.g., R. Aronson, 'Historical Materialism', *New Left Review*, 152 (1985); E. Balibar, 'Marx, the Joker in the Pack', *Economy and Society*, 14 (1985); 'The Poverty of Theory' in some respects moves in similar directions.

10 B. Schwarz, '"The People" in History: the Communist Party Historians' Group, 1945–56', in *Making Histories*; I am heavily indebted to this essay.

11 See E. P. Thompson, 'Caudwell', *The Socialist Register 1977*, ed. R. Miliband and J. Saville (London: Merlin Press, 1977).

12 See R. Williams, *Culture and Society, 1780–1950* (Harmondsworth: Pelican edn, 1963); E. P. Thompson, *William Morris: Romantic to Revolutionary* (London: Lawrence & Wishart, 1955; revised edn, London: Merlin Press, 1977) explores the relations between romanticism and revolutionary socialism.

13 These ambiguities are explored in A. Agosti, 'Réformes, révolution et transition dans la conception de la IIIème Internationale', in *Les Aventures du marxisme*; and D. Sassoon, *The Strategy of the Italian Communist Party* (London: Frances Pinter, 1981), ch. 1.

14 This is the project of the various contributions of the Birmingham Centre for Contemporary Cultural Studies: see esp. R. Johnson, 'Edward Thompson, Eugene Genovese and Socialist Humanist History', *History Workshop Journal*, 6 (1978); and *Making Histories*: while their interpretations may be open to debate, the enterprise itself seems entirely valid.

15 See especially 'Open Letter to Leszek Kolakowski', in *PT*, pp. 303–42.

16 Ibid., p. 333; see also E. J. Hobsbawm, 'The Historians' Group of the Communist Party', in *Rebels and their Causes: essays in honour of A. L. Morton*, ed. M. Cornforth (London: Lawrence & Wishart, 1978).

17 'Open Letter', *PT*, p. 339.

18 N. Branson, *History of the Communist Party of Great Britain, 1927–41* (London: Lawrence & Wishart, 1985) covers the popular front period and the early war years.

19 *PT*, p. 264.

20 See L. Marcou, 'Le marxisme de guerre froide', in *Les Aventures du marxisme*, for a characterization of Stalinism in this period.

21 *PT*, p. 195; and cf. Aronson, 'Historical Materialism'.

22 P. Anderson, 'The Origins of the Present Crisis', *New Left Review*, 24 (1963).

23 'Peculiarities of the English', in *PT*; see also P. Corrigan and D. Sayer, *The Great Arch* (Oxford: Basil Blackwell, 1985).

24 *Towards Socialism*, ed. P. Anderson and R. Blackburn (London: Fontana, 1965) introduction; and see also Anderson's essays 'Problems of socialist strategy', ibid., and 'The Limits and Possibilities of Trade Union Action', in *The Incompatibles: trade union militancy and the consensus*, ed. R. Blackburn and A. Cockburn (Harmondsworth: Penguin, 1967).

25 'Peculiarities', *PT*, p. 71.

26 L. Althusser, *For Marx*, trans. B. Brewster (Harmondsworth: Penguin 1969), p. 104.

27 *PT*, p. 275.

28 See, e.g., S. Hall et al., *Policing the Crisis* (London: Macmillan, 1978); *The Politics of Thatcherism*, ed. S. Hall and M. Jacques (London: Lawrence & Wishart, 1983); B. Jessop, 'The Transformation of the British State', in *The State in Western Europe*, ed. R. Scase (London: Croom Helm, 1981); R. Rowthorn, *Capitalism, Conflict and Inflation* (London: Lawrence & Wishart, 1980).

29 Cf. T. Bennett, 'Introduction: the Turn to Gramsci', in *Popular Culture and Social Relations*, ed. T. Bennett et al. (Milton Keynes and Philadelphia: Open University Press, 1986).

30 Johnson, 'Edward Thompson, Eugene Genovese . . .'; for the reception of 'The Poverty of Theory', see note 3.

31 R. Johnson, 'Against Absolutism', in *People's History and Socialist Theory*.

32 S. Hall, 'In Defence of Theory', ibid.

33 L. Althusser, 'The Crisis of Marxism', *Marxism Today* (July 1978); Balibar, 'Marx: the Joker in the Pack'; N. Poulantzas, *State, Power, Socialism* (London: New Left Books, 1978); and cf. B. Jessop, *Nicos Poulantzas* (Basingstoke: Macmillan, 1985).

34 See Bennett, 'Introduction: the Turn to Gramsci'.

35 'Open Letter', *PT*, p. 116.

36 *PT*, p. 380.

37 Williams, *Marxism and Literature*, p. 116.

38 *PT*, pp. 247–62; Balibar, 'Marx: the Joker in the Pack'; Williams, *Marxism and Literature*, part ii, ch. 3.

39 M. Bloch, *The Historian's Craft* (Manchester: Manchester University Press, 1954).

40 Thompson's view of sociology is perhaps over-influenced by his criticisms of Smelser, and is admittedly tempered by his regard for Wright Mills; while these judgements may be justifiable, they constitute a somewhat dated view of the sociological scene.

41 *PT*, p. 262.

42 Ibid.

43 Ibid., p. 363.

44 Ibid., p. 231.

45 A. Gramsci, *Selections from the Prison Notebooks*, trans. and ed. Q. Hoare and G. Nowell Smith (London: Lawrence & Wishart, 1971), p. 171.

46 *PT*, p. 236.

47 Ibid., p. 286.

48 Ibid., p. 236.

49 Ibid., p. 237.

50 Ibid., p. 238.

51 Ibid., p. 236.

52 Thompson, 'Eighteenth-century Society', p. 149.

53 Thompson, *Making of the English Working Class*, p. 9.

54 Anderson, *Arguments*, p. 42.

55 Thompson, *Making*, p. 10.

56 See, e.g. M. Berg, *The Age of Manufactures, 1700–1820* (London: Fontana, 1985); P. Hudson, *The Genesis of Industrial Capital: a study of the West Riding wool textile industry, c.1750–1850* (Cambridge: Cambridge University Press, 1986); R. Samuel, 'The Workshop of the World: steam power and hand technology in mid-Victorian Britain', *History Workshop Journal*, 3 (1977).

57 Thompson, *Making*, p. 10.

58 See esp. M. Burawoy, *The Politics of Production* (London: Verso, 1985).

59 Thompson, 'Eighteenth-century Society', p. 150.

60 Thompson, 'Peculiarities', in *PT*, p. 70; 'Eighteenth-century Society', pp. 155ff.

61 Cf. Schwarz, '"The People" in History', pp. 87–9.

62 *PT*, p. 367; and cf. Williams, *Marxism and Literature*, pp. 59–60.

63 'Peculiarities', in *PT*, p. 79.

64 Cf. S. Hall, 'Rethinking the "Base-and Superstructure" Metaphor', in *Class, Hegemony and Party*, ed. J. Bloomfield (London: Lawrence & Wishart, 1977); Hobsbawm, 'Karl Marx's Contribution to Historiography'.

65 Gramsci, *Selections from the Prison Notebooks*; and cf. A. S. Sassoon, *Gramsci's Politics* (London: Croom Helm, 1980), esp. pp. 109–19.

66 *PT*, p. 286.

67 Thompson, *Making*, p. 915.

68 See S. Denith, 'Political Economy, Fiction and the Language of Practical Ideology', *Social History*, 8 (1983); A. Howe, *The Cotton Masters, 1830–60* (Oxford: Oxford University Press, 1984), esp. ch. 8; P. Joyce, *Work, Society and Politics* (Brighton: Harvester Press, 1980); J. Seed, 'Unitarianism, Political Economy and the Antinomies of Liberal Culture in Manchester, 1830–50', *Social History*, 7 (1982).

69 Thompson, *Making*, p. 9.

70 'Peculiarities', in *PT*, pp. 52–6.

71 Cf. R. Johnson, 'Barrington Moore, Perry Anderson and English Social Development', *Working Papers in Cultural Studies*, 9 (Centre for Contemporary Cultural Studies, University of Birmingham, 1979), especially pp. 24–6; J. W. Oakley, 'The Boundaries of Hegemony: Lytton', in *1848: the sociology of literature*, eds. F. Barker et al. (Colchester: University of Essex, 1978).

72 *The Eighteenth Brumaire of Louis Bonaparte*, in *Surveys from Exile: the Pelican Marx Library* (Harmondsworth: Pelican, 1973), p. 146.

73 *PT*, pp. 355–6.

74 Ibid., p. 201.

75 Ibid.

76 Cf. G. Stedman Jones, *Languages of Class* (Cambridge: Cambridge University Press, 1983); I offer some criticisms in 'The Deconstructing of the English Working Class', *Social History*, 11, no. 3 (1986).

77 Thompson, 'Eighteenth-century Society', pp. 143–4; cf. Anderson, *Arguments*, p. 88.

7

E. P. Thompson and 'the Significance of Literature'

John Goode

I

In the 1976 MARHO (Middle Atlantic Radical Historians' Organization) interview, Thompson denies taking a decision to become an historian:

> I was teaching as much literature as history. I thought, how do I, first of all, raise with an adult class, many of them in the labour movement – discuss with them the significance of literature. And I started reading Morris . . . Morris took the decision that I would have to present him. In the course of doing this I became much more serious about being a historian.[1]

In order to explain 'the significance of literature', he becomes an historian, but being an historian to begin with means writing a literary biography. Thompson's centrality in English intellectual life is, like Raymond Williams', partly due to his transgression of the academic boundaries. Moreover, it is a politically motivated transgression – its purpose is to serve those who are marginalized by the institutions that determine those boundaries. The transgression is thus an intervention. It is therefore necessary to see his work in the moment to which it is a response, but it also makes it impossible – and improper – to see it dispassionately or as anything other than a narrative of impact.

This narrative must begin with *The Making of the English Working Class* because the book on William Morris did not, as both Thompson himself and Anderson have noted,[2] find its way to the centre of the debates on the left in the late 1950s. This was partly because it was locked into an historical moment walled off by Hungary and Suez, but, as importantly from the point of view of literary studies, it was ahead of its time, both because of its subject and because of the framework of literary and cultural history in which it was placed. In 'Components of the National Culture', Anderson identified the strange anomaly of radical critical discourse finding its place with the highly conservative idealism of 'English', which meant that the most influential book of the period was not *William Morris: Romantic to Revolutionary* but *Culture and Society*.[3] Williams transformed a predominantly Conservative tradition criticizing 'the bourgeois idea of society' and transformed it into an agenda of socialist renewal.

In spite of its clear centrality of theme, and notwithstanding its eventual power to generate new analyses of literature such as *Modern Tragedy* and *The Country and the City*, Williams' argument had a decisive negativity. An analysis which began with Radicals as unreliable as Owen and Cobbett and analysed them in terms set by Burke and Southey and which focused on the word used by Arnold to cover his enmity for the working class seemed to offer many hostages to reactionary ideology. The move from continuity to solidarity was very difficult to make: even after the publication of *The Long Revolution* one felt locked in a marginal protest. My own attempt to seek out a conjuncture between the values of this tradition and the incipient working-class organization of the 1880s confirmed this negativity. Interestingly, the only text that productively measured its values in the light of popular politics was a novel set in the 1820s and 1840s, *The Revolution in Tanners Lane*.

Two books, published in 1962 and 1963 respectively, loosened this knot. First, there was a translation of Lukács' *The Historical Novel*, followed by *The Making of the English Working Class*.[4] Thinking back, it is clear that Lukács prepared the way for a sympathetic reading of Thompson. First, he made revolutionary change rather than continuity the determinant perspective of literary history. Moreover, it is the period from the French Revolution to the *Communist Manifesto* which creates the positive terms of this change. Williams began with Romantics but only in so far as they could be seen preparing a discourse elaborated coherently from Arnold to Eliot and Leavis.

But conversely, though Lukács' perspective is international it also leaves a clearly defined vacuum. The French Revolution is seen in conjunction with a German philosopher to condition a literary form founded by a Scottish novelist and transmitted through an American, Cooper, to Balzac and Stendhal, and through them again to Tolstoy. But although the historical novel has its origins in English, no major English writer figures in his portrayal and there was no clear way in which English writing could be accommodated within it. *The Making of the English Working Class* demonstrated that there was an English Jacobin movement and that the enclosure of England from the world movement that emerges, say, from Halévy's emphasis on the quiescent influence of Methodism needed much revision. This also meant that the literature of the period – not, of course, the realism privileged by Lukács, but the romantic positions on which realism is in fact based – gained a context in which connections between those positions could be made with the course of history.

Anderson complains that *The Making of the English Working Class* does not give sufficient attention to the impact of industrialism or the American and French revolutions. It is precisely the new emphasis that comes out of this which has made the literature of the period more legible. The whole concept of the 'Industrial Revolution', with its absurd implication that somehow the development of industrial capitalism is an equivalent to 1776 or 1789, has been very disabling for the study of literature which has tended to see the response to 'industrialism' as the basis of coherent cultural values. Moreover, one certainly did not register the lack of reference to the impact of the American and French revolutions which are taken as given – there is also an English movement, however suppressed by government violence or written out by ideological historiography. Thus, for example, Wordsworth's comment in *The Prelude* that the French Revolution seemed like something natural to him, or Shelley's analogy between the overthrow of tyranny and the dance of matter in Act Five of *Prometheus Unbound*, could not be seen as the ideas of a man with his head in the clouds and an ineffectual angel beating his wings in the void. The influence of the book on the literary historiography of the Romantic period has been pervasive.[5] It is no longer common to assume that Burke and Jane Austen are the only writers to see life steadily and to see it whole. Austen, indeed, has increasingly been seen as the purveyor of a middle-class myth, and the other voice, Wollstonecraft and the Jacobin novel for example, are no longer marginalized as historical curiosities. *Whigs and Hunters* extends the perspective back – in the light of its argument finer discriminations have to be made in the dominant ideology, which helps to account for what would otherwise be a mysteriously more complex social vision in Pope than the Whig interpretation permits.

The impact of Thompson's work on literary studies is based on two of the three claims made in *The Making of the English Working Class* and identified and criticized by Anderson – the affirmation of agency and the portrayal of the embryonic working class through the concept of class consciousness. The argument that 'the working class made itself as much as it was made'[6] is crucial to the understanding of the politics of Romantic literature and obviously cannot be dealt with as a reflection of its own time because it affords so much emphasis on the imagination. In fact,

Arnold's Victorian perspective on the Romantics was precisely that the Romantics were premature and effectively the creator of beautiful fictions. Even the revival of Blake in the nineteenth century was based on the assumption that his visionary symbolism took him out of the world of the historical actuality. These images of the major Romantics as beautiful and harmless were certainly not unchallenged in twentieth-century criticism but, with the notable exception of Erdman's study of Blake, *Prophet against Empire*, such rectifications did little to validate any kind of specific historical genesis. Thus, for example, Leavis's discriminations within Wordsworth and of Keats as against Shelley privilege their capacity to renew a tradition of morally-centred and concretely-focused poetry which is effectively continuous with the line of wit. Defences of the Wordsworth that Arnold did not like, such as Bateson's or Danby's *The Simple Wordsworth*, restored a general sense of social concern without a specifically radical and political significance.

The Making of the English Working Class, however, provides a detailed context in which, for example, the writing of *The Lyrical Ballads* is bound up with the revolutionary activities of Thelwall and so is a text politically motivated by the repressive and resistant tensions of the era. The artisanal contexts of Blake underwrite Erdman's political interpretation. It is not simply a matter of providing a context but of seeing the writer's work, however conditioned by its bourgeois origins, as part of an active struggle to establish a power-base not at the behest of the Hanoverian state and the dominant capitalist ideology. The poet works with language that is, of course, highly structural and determining, but he uses it as well. He deforms as well as reflects reality, but history is seen in *The Making of the English Working Class* as partly the story of people trying by actions and even more by words to deform reality.

The ambiguity of the word 'agent' to which Anderson draws attention (*Arguments Within English Marxism*, p. 18) is no problem here – it is, in fact, essential to the perception of the interaction of literary history. No Romantic poet would have any difficulty in seeing himself as at once a maker of truth and the medium through which it is made manifest. The aeolian harp which makes music as the winds of change blow through it is indeed the central image of the poet, who thus becomes a double agent. This links the question of agency to that of consciousness. If class is only to be defined in terms of function as Anderson at one point (ibid., p. 40) argues, this double agency is made instantly illegible. The literary text becomes merely the transparent screen of the writer's class and ideological formation and, in fact, some recent 'Marxist' literary criticism substitutes that kind of passivity for the reflectionist vulgarity of earlier Marxist criticism. 'Consciousness' is indeed a very problematic term and I shall have to return to it. But Williams and Lukács are again relevant here, as is another dominant theorist of the 1960s who provides a relevant context for *The Making of the English Working Class*, Lucien Goldmann.[7] All of these critics were highly aware of the problematic relationship between a text's meaning and its authorship and had to develop a flexible and, in the end, makeshift term to denote the consequent complexity of the relationship between a text and its historical moment. 'Structure of feeling', 'consciousness', 'possible consciousness' – these are terms that defer the question of the precise relationship between text and history in the interest of avoiding either its eradication or its over simplification.

This may explain why, even when I re-read *The Making of the English Working Class* for this essay, I must have failed to take the assertion that 'class happens when some men, as a result of common experiences . . . feel and articulate the identity of their interests as between themselves' (p. 9), as Anderson (*Arguments*, p. 40) puts it, 'literally'. Surely Thompson does not take it 'literally', as the central section of the book dealing with the deformed relationship between experience and consciousness (the transforming power of the cross), and the brutally direct relationship between experience and material reality (standards and experiences) shows. The gain of the concept of class-consciousness over mere function is that it shows class formation to be a complex historical process, not a non-relational structure or, more specifically, an element of a wholly articulated structure. It may be true that a class can exist without consciousness, but it can clearly have no agency as a class without consciousness as the history of the bourgeoisie clearly shows and as the closing sentence of *The Communist Manifesto* memorably acknowledges.

The significance of literature can only be elaborated in the non-functional double agency of the writer. It is clear that the formative consciousness of a subordinate class cannot be defined exclusively from within since crucial to its subordination is the denial of its access to the most powerful agencies of its expression. The struggle to establish the vernacular is an obvious precedent – it was not carried on by the bourgeoisie, nor in the interests of capitalism, but it is highly relevant to the political formation of its culture. Thompson's history does not make it possible to raise the concept of class above its firm relationship to production, but it does clarify the ways in which, through the struggles and egoisms of those who turned themselves into its organic intellectuals, the subordinate working class gains a potential and actual voice. The literary text expressing and exposing by what it says and what it suppresses, is a factor in and product of this history whose documents have to be read with the double vision literary texts demand. Tony Harrison's *School of Eloquence*, which is a major tribute to Thompson in itself (the title is taken from one of the 'covers' of the LCS), sharply focuses this process in the closing lines of a poem, 'On Not Being Milton'

which brings the official paternalistic literature of the mid-eighteenth
century (Gray's *Elegy*) shatteringly into collision with the new world
defined in *The Making of the English Working Class*:

> Three cheers for mute ingloriousness!
> Articulation is the tongue tied's fighting.
> In the silence round all poetry we quote
> Tidd the Cato Street conspirator who wrote:
> Sir I Ham a very Bad Hand at Righting.[8]

The angry triumph of the ambiguous 'Righting' celebrates a complex
relationship between Milton, Gray, Tidd, Thompson and Harrison in
which the violent oppression of the new new world of the 1790s is neither
unmarked by its subjects nor discarded as the wrath of God, nor
patronizingly buried in obscurity. It is true that this way of vindicating
both agency and consciousness through the significance of literature
supports the third of Anderson's constatations against the claim that, by
the end of *The Making of the English Working Class*, the class is made.
This seems to be empirically unarguable (and has a direct bearing, of
course, on *William Morris*) but more decisively and problematically, to be
theoretically impossible since both agency and consciousness are not
simply there – they have to be discovered and revealed, narrated,
composed by Thompson the Historian. *The Making of the English
Working Class* is clearly part of its making, which to judge from the rapid
demise of the left in the 1980s is far from completion. Of course,
Thompson will dismiss this kind of point in *The Poverty of Theory*. But I
do not think that it denies that history has actually happened to say that it
goes on happening as it is spoken for.

· 'Consciousness' is a term used by Thompson most specifically for the
1820s and 1830s and in this respect is very precise since it relates centrally
to the popular press and its address to the working class. It also permits at
this level a discussion of the complex relationship between the traditional
and the organic intellectual either with a writer such as Blake or between
writers such as the analysis of Hazlitt's writing about Cobbett. The
question of experience, the psychological impact of historical complexity,
grants even more relevance to the privileged ambiguity of literary effect,
since consciousness is at its most revealing fractured. The way to see the
importance of Cobbett is through the eyes of the 'bruised' Jacobin. As the
breaking of a saucer in *The Sykaos Papers* shows, it is in the close
proximity of breakdown and resolution that the highest level of historical
consciousness takes place. The two essays that follow *The Making of the
English Working Class* with specific interventions in literary history make
this clear, as they make clear also the limits to which the historian is
prepared to go.

'Disenchantment or Default: a lay sermon' (1969) argues that in Wordsworth and Coleridge in different ways and on a different scale, the creative energies of Romanticism emerge from a break with abstract Godwinism not to a 'rejection of republican ardor', but rather to a 'Jacobinism in recoil', or a 'Jacobinism of doubt', which leads to a second creative conflict between human aspiration and communal pressure.[9] The creativity only ends when this conflict subsides into apostasy: 'it is not the apostate point of rest that is worth our attention, but the conflict along the way out of which great art sprang.' This echoes Yeats' inflection of Blake's celebration of contraries and reminds us that Yeats is a deeply formative influence, both good and bad, on Thompson's understanding of the influence of literature from *William Morris* to *The Sykaos Papers*. Here it directs him to the detailed interplay of enabling and foreclosing possibilities in the writing of Wordsworth and Coleridge from the 1790s and beyond. It also reveals that creativity does not simply begin at the point at which the radical formation is abandoned.

The value of this kind of historical contextualizing is that it forces us to break away from simple-minded explanations without launching us into an anarchic play of differences. This emerges firmly from the essay on Blake's 'London'.[10] 'Mind forg'd manacles' is shown not to lift the poem out of the specific political arena into a psychologistic and metaphysical realm of the inevitable, but rather into that of a Radicalism in specific conflict, a conflict that, for example, Paineites would recognize but be unable to express.

But this essay also identifies a problem. This may be formulaically stated as the difference between the significance of Thompson to literature and the significance of literature to Thompson. It emerges first of all in the problematic relationship between language and consciousness. In order to recapture the very strong effect of Thompson's approach to history on our understanding of literature, I have consciously elided the difference between the concept of fractured consciousness and the ambiguity of language. And yet, of course, it was not Tidd who spotted the triumphant ambiguity of 'Righting'. Language, as Anderson rightly argues, is deeply embroiled in the structure which is why any agency with regard to language use is manifestly double. The precedent for this ellision is Volosinov's remarkable embrace of those German Philologists who see language as a manifestation of consciousness as against Saussure whose theorization of the sign is theoretically closer to Volosinov but who merely, he decides, deals with the dead husk of language.[11] I think that for all its theoretical difficulties, Thompson's concept of consciousness as historical agent teaches us more about the actual behaviour of literary texts in history than most of the analyses of the behaviour of signifiers.

Nevertheless, 'Blake's London' has a strange duality of argument. Most of the essay is preoccupied with the historical complexity of the meaning of certain keywords in the poem – 'chartered', 'marks', 'mind forg'd manacles', 'appalls'. Nevertheless, the opening paragraph denies that an understanding of this complexity is necessary for a grasp of the poem; indeed, it goes further and denies that an analysis of the poem can do more than 'confirm . . . what a responsive reader had already experienced' (Phillips, *Interpreting Blake*, p. 5). What follows is consigned to history, not the poem (which is 'product') but 'the process of its creation'. This suggests that the literary text has a certain stable meaning, though there may be a history of its arrival at that meaning. It seems to me to be very difficult to make this case about Blake's poem. Surely 'a responsive reader' will experience not clarity of meaning but precisely puzzlement, especially over words such as 'chartered' and 'appalls' and awareness of the special significance of 'marks'. 'Close reading' is not an exercise undertaken gratuitously; it is a necessary task undertaken because the use of language is not clear.

This is a trivial criticism of this essay since what we gain from the historian is an enrichment of the text, confirming, indeed, the simultaneous levels at which the poem may be perceived but helping to ensure that they do not short-circuit one another. But it has far-reaching implications for the later work. As far as *The Making of the English Working Class, Whigs and Hunters* and the essays on the Romantics is concerned, 'literature' is less an object than a process of understanding. History, like poetry, needs to be *read*, transitively, like a dialogue. Its marks, its signs, like the signs motivated in literary texts are veiled by the obscurity not merely of time but of domination and assimilation. Here in the Blake essay, there is a trace of something less fluid, the idea that concrete and self-sufficient images within a text are unproblematically available to the 'responsive reader' experiencing it. Literature itself will become less a process than a value; the significance of literature becomes the significance of Literature. Nobody willingly contradicts himself – the value of literature is that embodying contradiction it places creativity, its own special meaning, 'beyond' will and ultimately beyond the rational. The key figures in this transformation are the two William Morris's – the ungainly figure of 1955, and the slimmer version of 1977.[12]

II

I said that *William Morris: Romantic to Revolutionary* was not simply anachronized by 1956 but was equally ahead of its time. This is obviously true of its subject. Morris could well seem marginal to Williams in

Culture and Society, in which he is treated, out of sequence, as the tail-end of a tradition dominated by Carlyle and Ruskin and left out of the 1880s and 1890s which prepares the way for the central concerns of Lawrence, Eliot, Leavis et al. In fact, Morris's polemical writing is contemporary with Mallock, Gissing and the other interregnal commentators of the modern era, and in historical terms is more in touch with the actual and decisive history of the working class than any other writer of the period. The reason for this marginalization is not, of course, his Radicalism, but rather his hedonism and optimism, which runs counter to the cultural tradition Williams is trying to rescue from conservative ideology. Equally, of course, there is an anarchic motif, the hatred of 'civilization', incompatible with the organicism which is the major positive value of the cultural tradition.

By 1970, clearly, these values – hedonism, optimism, anarchism – are not so marginal to a culture that has been opened up to Marcuse, as well as Laing, the early Marx and the later Freud. But not only Morris himself but Thompson's approach to Morris, which traced a development from within the contradictions of Romanticism through the entrenched post-Keatsian aesthetics of the Pre-Raphaelites to revolutionary socialism and which thus posed a view of literary history completely opposed to the parameters defined by Eliot and *Scrutiny*, was no longer so foreign to the agenda of literary studies – partly, of course, because of the impact of *The Making of the English Working Class*. The time was right for a fresh look at Morris, but anyone who worked on him at that time was profoundly aware that he had to work on Morris in the light of Thompson's 1955 study, but for an audience to whom most study was largely inaccessible. In fact, I worked on Morris myself at that time because John Lucas had asked me to invite Thompson to write a concluding essay for his *Literature and Politics in the Nineteenth Century* and Thompson had declined with a characteristically friendly but decisive growl. I did not hope to add more than a confirmatory evaluation of Thompson as against Williams' marginalization. Most of the points I made had been made in 1955: I merely showed that they could be related to a positive and articulate literary strategy. This involved a certain negativity (which I overstressed) since, if literary strategy was not seen to be marginal, it must be on the basis that Morris's conversion to Marxism did not in its complex vision of history provide all the answers because literary strategies are only necessary if there are questions that cannot be answered or gaps that need to be covered up. This was on the assumption, proved by Thompson in 1955, that Morris was unquestionably Marxist after his conversion to socialism, but that Marxism was not a closed or completed 'system' and so he was still required to make a contribution to its development. I was surprised to find myself enlisted with Abensour in the formation of an a-Marxist Morris in the postscript of 1976. I have totally failed to obtain Abensour's book and, in any case, the arguments about Morris's 'Marxism' are fully rehearsed by Thompson and Anderson and I doubt whether they can be resolved. How you read Morris in relation to Marxism depends on how you read Marxism and this depends in turn on how you read history. What I think I can rehearse is the question of how you read Morris in relation to the significance of literature.

Morris was, as Thompson puts it, 'the first creative artist of major stature in the history of the world to take his stand, consciously and without the shadow of a compromise with the revolutionary working class' (1955, p. 841; 1977, p. 727). Prolific, tentative, experimental, its ideas subject to change and contradiction, Morris's writing from 1883 to his death is inevitably an endless source of debate. This is not a limitation, but its major virtue. To read Morris is to engage with the fascinating and challenging process of a highly developed traditional imagination taking full in the face in its unfinished, barely elaborated state, the most important body of ideas of our era. We need a very open approach which, at first glance, the 1977 revisions seem to ensure, letting Morris out of the straitjacket of the British road to socialism, making him more central to a general Radical culture, and, of course, this later text is in many ways a great improvement, shorter, less dogmatic, less strident, less given to covering its own doubts with colourful metaphor and rhetorical demolitions of easy targets. It is also, of course, much truer to Thompson's present position. Paradoxically, however, I think it is a narrower reading of Morris than 1955.

Specifically, Thompson privileges one term of the dialectic of necessity and desire, which entitles his analytic final chapter. Morris, and *News from Nowhere* especially, is now concerned with the 'education of desire', and desire itself is strongly activated against necessity. Thus Morris's writing is about what 'Marxism' fails to be, what lies beyond its power of rational explanation. Thompson argues in the postscript that the book should be seen as a contribution to the analysis of Romanticism and its trajectory in Morris's life. This gives it continuity, of course, with *The Making of the English Working Class* and later texts, but alters the emphasis in the original title which clearly implies '*from* romantic to revolutionary', to one which stresses the persistence of values, and specifically the place of literature within this culture.

Its place, in the new edition, is a re-ordering within Marxism, but in the history of literary studies it is a more familiar theme. Quoting Morris's statement that socialism aims at 'the full development of human life set free from artificial regulations in favour of a class', Thompson comments that the underlying metaphor, 'drawing upon the old Romantic critique of Utilitarianism, is the "organic" one: the natural growth of "life" will be set free from the artificial (or "mechanical") constraints of "civilisation"' (1977, pp. 802–3). This interpretation is not justified by the vocabulary. 'Artificial' cannot be replaced by 'mechanical' – it is a word as familiar to rationalist critiques of tradition as to Romanticism, and the implicit naturalism of 'development' has, if anything, overtones of evolutionary theory. As a whole, this statement belongs much more to John Stuart Mill and the libertarian 'new life' discourse of Ellis and Carpenter than with anything that could be linked with post-Romantic organicism, which, after all, had been commandeered by the Arnold of whom Morris, as Thompson himself indicates, disapproved. It is a statement nearer anarchy than culture, but above all it is a very straightforward and lucid remark which Thompson obfuscates by trying to produce an underlying metaphor from an entrenched tradition in which to accommodate it. But this suggests that not only has the implication that Morris arrives at a revolutionary position 'from' Romanticism been diluted, but that Romanticism itself is interpreted more narrowly in the light of the tradition it leads to. The revisions of the book itself show this to be the case.

Morris is seen in both editions as a writer who moves to socialism in the wake of a despair that follows on from Keatsian subjectivism. But the context of the latter has changed in 1977. Chapter 1 in 1955 ends with the third section, 'Mr Gradgrind', and on the point that, since two writers as different as Hopkins and Morris could both look to Medievalism in the light of the triumph of the realism of Fact, 'therefore we must use sympathy to break free from our preconceptions and to understand this climate of the past' (1955, p. 23). Chapter 2 begins with a later deleted section called 'The Great Romantics' which has a strong focus on Shelley. Shelley is cast as a revolutionary poet who in the end, under the stress of 'a triumphant evil unbearable to his consciousness', takes refuge in the contradiction between poetic aspiration and inadequate reality, which is to be the ideological starting point of Keats and some Victorians. Keats in 1955 is not simply the Romantic forerunner of anti-Gradgrindism but also the residuum of a defeated Romantic revolutionary aspiration. The anti-Utilitarian tradition, which certainly borrows from Keats, is thus shown to be an entrenched reaction rather than a possible alternative ideology – and it precisely does need to be treated with 'sympathy'. In the earlier edition, it is a position Morris has to abandon more than he has to transform. The disappearance of Shelley from the book is remarkable. Of course, Thompson could argue that Keats is more relevant to Morris than Shelley, and probably regard 'The Great Romantics' as over-hasty and schematic. But the fact that Morris explicitly owes more to Keats, does not make Shelley less important (he has *his* line, of course as well, through

Browning and Swinburne, and Morris would certainly have been aware of this). Moreover, the recognition of Shelley in 1955 was one of the ways in which the book was ahead of its time. The suppression and emasculation of Shelley is and remains a scandal of literary history relieved only by radical interventions from Eleanor Marx to Paul Foot. It is one of the ways, however, that Thompson boxes Morris into a specific anti-Utilitarian tradition. Of course, Morris was anti-Utilitarian as his admiration for Dickens and Ruskin confirms, but he was not only that, and not tied to that. Just as there is a Jacobin presence in English politics, there is also a Radical literary line in English writing which does not fear rationality and progress but sees that the bourgeois version of these terms is, as Morris puts it, tied to a class. The Pre-Raphaelite Brotherhood itself, not merely in fact but more importantly in the version of it offered by Morris's retrospect in 1891, is as aggressive as it is retrenching, a movement *of* 1848. The 1977 Morris conforms much more to a line defined by *Culture and Society* which ironically in 1976 Williams himself was turning on its head with the radical critique of Literature as an ideological value in *Marxism and Literature*.

1955 Morris is ungainly because its subject is not to be contained within that literary tradition which gains its identity, indeed its institutional legitimacy in opposition to the dominant ideology of Empiricism, Utilitarianism and Positivism. Morris does not belong to this official opposition because what he encounters is the negative of this domination ('imagination') only to find it a source of despair. The despair is resolved because he discovers a superior rationality, a dominant beyond the dominance, 'scientific socialism'. The changes to 'Necessity and Desire', the concluding chapter, play down this difference. The section originally entitled 'Political Theory' is drastically cut and finally merged into 'The Vision of the Future' as though it were undesirable to suggest that Morris had a political theory. Of course, Morris's writings are unsystematic and changeable, but this is because of the strict unity of theory and practice necessitated by his conversion, as well undoubtedly as the alien habits of thought he brought to Marxism. It would certainly be inaccurate to extract a political theory like a blueprint from the mass of material. But this is very different from suggesting that theory is not important to him, and certainly not to be absorbed into a mere 'vision'. One of the omitted sentences comes in a paragraph beginning to answer the question, 'what was the source of the greatness of Morris'. After the acknowledged limitations of his aesthetic achievement, political organization and theories of the arts, 1955 says this about his 'political theory': 'important as it is in the English tradition, it appears as bold crayon work beside the firm and fine drawn analysis of Marx and Engels'. There are objections which could be made to this, not least to its metaphoric afflatus which perhaps disguises a refusal to meet the challenge Morris posed to orthodox Communist Party strategy as it was in 1955 (see Anderson, *Arguments Within English Marxism*, p. 186). But it does acknowledge that a critical account of Morris's theoretical positions is a matter of importance in the English tradition. 'Scientific' is another word that is under attack. In 1955, Morris actively resents the suggestion that the perception of the artist is irrelevant to Scientific Socialism (1955, p. 839). In 1977 this has become 'Scientific Socialism' leaving open an ironic view of the Marxism Morris encountered. Not surprisingly, but none the less disconcertingly, 'the socialist future' is another phrase that is silenced. These and other emendations make Morris less different from the tradition he transforms.

Again, as with the section on Shelley, this is most importantly evident in the contextualization. The section, 'Desire and Necessity' begins with a comment about the relationship of morality and socialism. In 1955, Morris's commitment to 'the appeal to man's conscience [the moral consciousness, 1977] as a vital agency of social change' (1955, p. 831; 1977, p. 721) is contextualized by a discussion of morality in Marx and Engels which is omitted in 1977. This is open to the charge of marginal relevance once more, especially as the connections between Morris and his putative mentors are not specific. But it has the tendency to polarize Morris the socialist Romantic, from Marxism the closed economistic ideology. Thus Morris is no longer in 1977, well equipped to lay bare the moral truths of his society 'as a true creative artist' (1955, p. 834). The emphasis of 1955 on Morris's 'moral realism' which 'Flowed directly from his understanding of social development, his Marxism' is excised.

Explicitly, in 1955, Morris's confrontation with 'scientific understanding' marks him off from the literary tradition: 'without this understanding his intuitions must have been haphazard, utopian or nostalgic: like Carlyle and Ruskin and contemporary "railers against progress", his indignation had been impotent to guide and inspire to action.' In 1977, Romantic revolt tends to become Romantic critique and it becomes less clear how Morris actually changes as opposed to inherits this critique. In 1955, Morris 'mastered and gave a qualitatively new revolutionary content to the current of profound social criticism of industrial capitalism' (1955, p. 841). Instead, in 1977, he 'draws deeply on the strengths of a more local tradition' (1977, p. 728). In general, Carlyle and Ruskin assume more importance and as though to stress the continuity, Thompson adds without obvious need in 1977, 'the society of the future he saw not as the rupture of all continuities but as a revolution of past contradictions: it must *grow* out of the other positives in human labour, art and sociability' (1977, p. 929). This is certainly a less abrasive and disruptive Morris than the revolutionary of 1955, and one that I find difficult to reconcile with what I have read of Morris who again and again welcomes the imminent destruction of civilization and the catastrophic end towards which industrial capitalism is tending. But it is much more like Ruskin and Carlyle for whom organicism is as often as it is anything else a cover for submission. Actually, I think, Morris flagrantly travestied Ruskin's ideas, though he found the rhetoric useful, by harnessing them to a hedonistic and materialist morality. There is nothing natural about the way Nowhere develops historically, and once nature is allowed to prevail it is far from the Protestant search for leadership and redemption that Carlyle and Ruskin privilege. It is Lawrence they lead to, not Morris, at least on the level of moral discourse.

However, I am very aware that Thompson's new Morris is the very opposite of submissive. What is important is that Literature, the literary tradition, has become something that can withstand Utilitarianism and the Utilitarian elements of Marxism, whereas in 1955 it was clearly the product of the Utilitarianism it could not defeat. Another deletion from the 1955 text is a comment on the end of 'A Dream of John Ball' on 'this unity, in the fight of Socialism, of necessity and desire'. It is this understanding that the action by which man takes hold of his own history is also the consummation of past history, and is 'central to the thought of Marx and Engels' (1955, p. 837). The postscript of 1977 makes it clear, however, that this unity is to be denied by the literary tradition which manifests itself in Morris as the 'education of desire', which is not beyond the criticism of sense and of feeling, although the procedures of criticism must be closer to those of creative literature than those of political theory (1977, p. 793). The paralysing bourgeois opposition of utility and culture is restated as an opposition of disciplines. 'It should now be clear', he writes in a sentence which distressingly demolishes the difficult, necessary, transgressive project of 1955, 'that there is a sense in which Morris as a "utopian and moralist", can never be assimilated to Marxism, not because of a contradiction of purposes but because one may not assimilate desire to knowledge.' 'Creative literature' has become the 'utopian' other, a kind of feminine which the masculine Marxism cannot absorb and had better not demolish. It is a theme which will reach its fullest statement in *The Sykaos Papers* in which, in the zone of Eden, love will undermine the masculinist dystopia of ultimate reason. However, in the first place, the creative literary tradition does not lead there – Carlyle, Ruskin, Lawrence, Yeats all yearn for aristocratic, phallocentric structures. More importantly, it is precisely because he does not fall into that ideological opposition, or rather because he has fallen in so deeply, that he can only survive by annihilating it that Morris is, like Shelley, a writer who cannot be let in to the institution of literature.

This is bound up with the question of Utopianism which Thompson makes central to the postscript. It is in his view Morris's Utopianism which makes him a-Marxist, and more closely linked to the Romantic critique of industrialism. In the first place, this needs to be questioned. In so far as he is utopian, Morris makes himself radically different from the dominant literary tradition, which is pastoral. Pastoral, and its various manifestations in myths of the golden age or rural retreat, is essentially looking backwards. It locates ideals in what has been lost not in what can be constructed by the human mind; it is, as Bakhtin argues, tensed against the future.[13] Among the great Romantics only Shelley resisted this historical inversion. Keats, in particular, uses myth as the narrative of loss which, of course, is also anti-rational. Morris wrote texts of this kind before he became a socialist. *Sigurd the Volsung* in particular is a remarkable manifestation of it. But once he became a socialist, he conceives of the ideal community as something to be striven for in the course of history. *A Dream of John Ball* is a rehearsal, rejection and refocusing of the literary tradition's comforting myth that, however bad industrial capitalism is, time is on its side and we can do little to stop its flow except cultivate our inner resources.

But I need to go further and question how utopian Morris really is. Thompson criticizes me for being evasive about Morris's Utopianism, and I accept this – it produces a reading of *News from Nowhere* which is ineptly pessimistic as though importing the 'scientific' through the failure of the utopian dream. Nevertheless, the 'scare' some of us have had about Utopianism comes not from the *Anti-Dühring*, but from the end of the *Communist Manifesto* whose English edition was published in 1888. *News from Nowhere*, as Thompson tells us, was a provoked text, a text in response primarily to Bellamy's *Looking Backward* which, as it were, put Utopianism on the agenda. Morris thought that utopias were chiefly an expression of a man's temperament. It is as though Bellamy's complacent dream, which is finally offered as an objective vision, challenged Morris to identify his own conception of the future which is *not* finally offered as anything more than it is, a dream, in spite of the careful historical causality by which it is produced. This seems less to me like a utopian vision than the opportunist seizure of the utopian genre in order to clarify the difference between evolutionary social democracy and revolutionary communism. *News from Nowhere* is, as its title implies, a self-conscious exercise in a genre. You do not exploit what you really believe in. Moreover, as Bernard Sharratt has shown (without in my view understanding the complexity of Morris's position), *News from Nowhere* has a larger target than the utopian model, and that is the realist novel against which it is polemically deployed.[14] That is why 'How the Change Came' is not a strangely honest admission of failure as I once thought it,

but an attempt to lay out the conditions upon which Communism would
be possible and which therefore instantly prepares us for Guest's eventual
personal alienation since he is not part of its history. The education of
desire includes the embrace of necessity, and one way in which this is
manifest is that Guest has to learn that however like his image of the past,
the fourteenth century, Nowhere looks at first, it belongs to the future
which is yet to be made. Unlike his major predecessor, Keats, or his
major disciple, Yeats, Morris absolutely refuses the polarization of
knowledge and dream as he equally refuses to deploy an idealized past as
an institutional opposition to the present.

This is too negative an account of a book which will remain the most
important work on the only great socialist writer in the language. I
mainly want to stress that the debate about literature which is manifest in
Thompson's work can be sharply focused in the comparison of its two
editions. 1955 Morris seems to me to be raising the question of Morris
whereas 1977 seems to be laying it to rest in a larger perspective. The end
of the postscript certainly demurs from this kind of assimilation, but
Morris is merely left hanging while the transformation of Romanticism
proceeds. It is certainly the case, of course, that Morris should be seen in a
literary history which includes Keats and Yeats, but the early edition
made it clear that he did not fit in to this history. The history has become
something else, of course. In the MARHO interview, Thompson refers to
his continuing work on Blake and Wordsworth which forms 'a total
critique of bourgeois utilitarianism' (Phillips *Interpreting Blake*, p. 22) to
be linked with the sense in the early Marx that 'the injury is in defining
man as "economic" at all'. Easing Morris into this critique condemns him
to significance as Literature, and this can come to mean the representation
of a tradition of values beyond the actual political situation, whereas
Morris does not retreat to this posture.

It is only a posture, of course, since no literary text however thickly it
disguises itself in tradition is unformed by its historical identity.
Thompson wants, however, to constitute creative literature as a thing
apart to be brought polemically in to contest the dominant. This is
ironically most clear in 'The Heavy Dancers', an essay about the
importance of trespassing which praises 'the remarkable contribution
made to our nation's political discourse' by the major poets. They are not
'interior decorators', 'not part of what life was about, they asked where
society was going'.[15] This is exactly what we should expect the author of
William Morris: Romantic to Revolutionary to affirm, but the concrete
example offered makes us wonder how accurate we can expect their
questions to be. Yeats' *Second Coming*, he argues, is one of the most full-
throated and necessary political statements of this century, 'Yet I couldn't
begin to translate it into party political terms . . . but it questions the

values from which any adult politics should start.' A failure to 'respond' to this poem should warn us off any politician.

In fact, Yeats' poem has very precise political composition, part of which is the disdain of party politics not for humane reasons as, say, in Swift, but as part of post-Romantic disdain of practice. But it is also composed of highly conservative, aristocratic values, 'ceremonies of innocence', Falcons and Falconers, and Yeats' own occult variation of Spenglerian pessimism which embraces as it deplores the onset of violent apocalypse. It sits on the ideological margin between Yeats' homage to Lady Gregory and reactionary nationalism and his flirtation with Fascism. It is very much a specific historical event and the product of an entirely despicable *parti-pris*. I am not sure how questioning the values on which an adult politics must be based is a praiseworthy activity, but adult is the last word I would use about Yeats. If it is a great poem (and it is certainly a very fine one) it is because of the high level at which it articulates the politics which shape it and the distance from its values that a critical reading of it enables us to take. God help us all if any politician responds to its full-throated prophesy. Yeats would have loved the bomb.

The issue here is between what I call critical reading and response. For Thompson literature has become something that lies beyond rational scrutiny or embodies values which lie beyond it. The obverse of this is the hierarchy of discourses which emerges from *The Poverty of Theory*. Althusser's procedures are dismissed because they produce knowledge 'which is critical rather than substantive'.

> To confuse these procedures (appropriate within their own limits) with all procedures of knowledge production is the kind of elementary error which (one would suppose) could be committed only by students early in their careers, habituated to attending seminars in textual criticism of this kind and apprentices rather than practitioners of their discipline. They have not yet arrived at those other (and equally difficult) procedures of research, experiment, and *of the intellectual appropriation of the real world*, without which the second (but important) critical procedures would have neither meaning nor existence.[16]

This is not about 'literature', but it is about the critical reading which the study of literary texts as opposed to the response to literature demands. Texts are evidently not part of the real world. It comes as no surprise, though it is still a disappointment, to be told that '"History" must be put back upon her throne as the Queen of the humanities' (*PT* p. 79) – disappointment because it militates against the whole project of Thompson's work from *William Morris* to *Whigs and Hunters*, a project in which history and literature were part of a socialist republic without boundaries.

This may seem to have arrived at the end of debate, to an assertion that the significance of Thompson to literature is incompatible with the significance of literature to Thompson, but it is difficult to measure the tone of *The Poverty of Theory*. Is it angry or exasperated? Is it an attack on Althusser merely, or is it the self-dramatization of the attack and its consequences? I ask these questions because, as far as literature is concerned, the temptation has been to say that, for Thompson, literature becomes, eventually, a kind of Other, a feminine which quarrels with the masculine foreclosure of utilitarian Marxism, or ultimately the feminine consorting the transvestite Queen of the humanities (with its appropriation of the real world). This is partly true and, in so far as it is true, distressing. What is equally the case, however, is that Thompson is capable of seeing the incongruity and humour of that position, and it is this that has produced the latest major disciplinary transgression, *The Sykaos Papers*.

III

It would be wrong to be too heavy-handed with *The Sykaos Papers*,[17] which is a capacious joke allowing Thompson to vent his wrath at everything from deconstruction to deterrence and an intensely felt warning about the real threat of apocalypse. In any case, it is forbidden to the Club of Critics 'as any part of it would throw that company into deformities of judgment' (though this is an Oitarian – rational rule, and I suppose the reader is still thought to be sykotic). The contrasts between the 'Magnetic lusts' (p. 14) of earth, however, and the 'structuralist paradise' (p. 239) of Oitar is only eventually dialectically as polemical as that abstract antithesis suggests. In the meantime, the Oitarian visitor has as much to teach as to learn. But what he takes apart is the human frailty constructed from the self-aggrandisement of language. Thus half the fun is Oipas' insisting on meaningful connections by resembling signifiers. Oitarian, the novel's linguist argues shortly before falling into a catatonic state of marriage, is a 'grammar cured of choice' – not, above all, 'out of nature' in Yeats' sense of therefore available to art, but available only to rule. There is a strongly political point being made here. Oitarians are bound heavily to rule, but 'on aesthetic matters there is a large space for freewheel'. The poets Oipas responds to are not Donne and Yeats but Milton, Thomson and even Martin Tupper – poets presumably bent on justifying the ways of God to man. However unreasonable, self-destructive and egocentric mortals are, the intrinsic plurality of the aesthetic is bonded to their very nature. Right at the beginning Oipas the poet responds to earthly nature as a disorderly order 'like a hidden code'. But he cannot come to terms with the hidden code of metaphor, and 'the mortal language' is offered as a priority for arrest by the Mission of Adjusters, because of its metaphoric ambiguity (lies) and this is closely allied to the second sykotic aporia, the incongruous noise, laughter. It may seem that the novel which is itself endlessly parodic, code-centred, deconstructed, is engaging with rather than transcending structure in that sense. For what is grammar except rule? And what is bending the rules if not taking revenge on the grammar which binds us to its demands?

But this is only a phase of the novel. As Oipas moves to his fall, laughter seems to become more marginal (though finally he does laugh at his own son). But from the beginning there has been a silent, unlaughing woman who looks after him and marries the linguist and effectively demolishes his linguistic activity. And what survives is sex, then love, then procreation (if anything – this novel does not end sentimentally), and if the woman of beauty and wisdom (Helena Sage) takes 'my Blake' to the moon, it is to find in the end that the languages of earth are no problem for Oitarians and the computerized rule (which is Urizenic, of course) – 'however, they can't crack earth concepts' (p. 437). Human positivity is a transcendent signified.

On a single reading it is difficult to know whether this book *engages* with the language it so fully mocks and deploys or whether Thompson merely shows that he can do that as well as anybody and still end up with a transcendent signified. Certainly it seems to flaunt *News from Nowhere* which Guest cannot personally enter. In Thompson's 'Zone of Eden' (but he calls it that so he is covered!) there is miscegenation. *More* – in the penultimate phase, the phase in which the affirmations are worked out and the dialogue between reason and nature takes place or rather gives birth, we effectively have that most natural of texts, a country house novel – precisely the kind of novel which intramurally allows human nature to be itself, that is to be a play of unsupported individualities.

One startling omission from this powerful 1988 history of the future is that the two-thirds of hungry humanity play no more role than the army of redressers in a Jane Austen novel. I am sure this is all conscious. But the base which allocates resources in a structured oppression endlessly silences its ruling with language. *Concepts* cost money. The revolt of humanity against its rulers ought to be aware of that. The debate between Thompson and Anderson has a common ground in seeing the welfare state merely as a means to perpetuate capitalism. I am sure that this is intellectually correct but without it, as the majority of British people are about to be, will they ever come to know that? *The Sykaos Papers* is a post-post-modernist text, mockingly self-conscious of its own self-consciousness but as it turns in on itself it turns out as well to be a dire and genuinely terrified warning. The Zone of Eden in its protected state can modify the rule of reason, but it is not protected unconditionally and nothing prevents the apocalyptic end.

But this returns us to the debate. For the end of *The Sykaos Papers* is, in my response to it, deeply pessimistic. I take it that the resolution of this is the agency of the text itself – it is surely a joke that turns into a warning. Thompson is carefully and consciously working on his reading public. And it is the effectiveness of that, not the self-destructing opposition of values it reflects that makes it politically still a radical text. It is precisely not the concepts but the articulation of them in the play of words and the play of forms that save us from its misanthropic humanism.

Notes

1 Interview with E. P. Thompson in H. Abelove et al. (eds), *Visions of History* (New York: Pantheon, 1983), p. 13.

2 E. P. Thompson, *William Morris: Romantic to Revolutionary* (New York: Pantheon, 1977), p. ix; P. Anderson, *Arguments Within English Marxism* (London: Verso, 1980), p. 157. Subsequent references to Anderson's book are in parenthesis.

3 P. Anderson, 'Components of the National Culture', *New Left Review*, 50 (May–June 1968); reprinted in A. Cockburn and R. Blackburn (eds), *Student Power* (Harmondsworth: Penguin, 1969), pp. 214–84.

4 G. Lukács, *The Historical Novel* (London: Merlin Press, 1962) (trans. from German by Hannah and Stanley Mitchell). Lukács' original text was published in 1937. An earlier volume, *Studies in European Realism*, appeared in 1950, but other than a couple of casual references in Arnold Kettle's *An Introduction to the English Novel* (London: Lawrence & Wishart, 1951) I do not recall Lukács having any influence on literary criticism in England before 1962.

5 Among recent general books on the literature of this period which have certainly been influenced by, though they do not always agree with Thompson, see M. Butler, *Romantics, Rebels and Reactionaries* (Oxford: Oxford University Press, 1981); S. Prickett (ed.), *The Romantics* (New York: Holmes and Meier, 1981); R. Sales, *Pastoral and Politics* (London: Macmillan, 1983). See also L. James (ed.), *Print and the People 1819–1851* (New York: Columbia University Press, 1976).

6 E. P. Thompson, *The Making of the English Working Class* (Harmondsworth: Penguin, 1980, repr. 1986), p. 213. All references are to this edition.

7 See R. Williams, *Problems in Materialism and Culture* (London: Verso, 1980), pp. 19–27.

8 T. Harrison, *Continuous: Fifty Sonnets from The School of Eloquence* (Newcastle, 1981), Cf. Thompson, *The Making of the English Working Class*, p. 787.

9 C. O'Brien and W. Vanech, *Power and Consciousness* (London: University of London Press, 1969), pp. 149–81.

10 M. Phillips (ed.), *Interpreting Blake* (Cambridge: Cambridge University Press, 1978), pp. 5–31.

11 V. Volosinov, *Marxism and the Philosophy of Language* (Cambridge, Mass.: Harvard University Press, 1973), p. 71.

12 E. P. Thompson, *William Morris: Romantic to Revolutionary* (London: Lawrence & Wishart, 1955, rev. edn 1977) (see note 2 above). Further references are to '1955' and '1977' respectively, followed by page number.

13 M. Bakhtin, *The Dialogic Imagination*, ed. Michael Holquist (Austin: University of Texas Press, 1981), p. 155.

14 I. Gregor (ed.), *Reading the Victorian Novel: Detail into Form* (London: Macmillan, 1980), pp. 288–305.

15 E. P. Thompson, *The Heavy Dancers* (London: Merlin Press, 1985), p. 4.

16 E. P. Thompson, *The Poverty of Theory and Other Essays* (London: Merlin Press, 1981), p. 11. The parenthetic concessions confirm even as they appear to modify the hierarchization. The essay on Caudwell in *The Socialist Register, 1977* (London: Merlin Press, 1977), confirms Thompson's relative indifference to critical analysis. Remarking correctly that the posthumous appearance of *Romance and Realism* shows that Caudwell was, in fact, a literary critic of formidable analytic ability, he does not allow this to modify the main argument that Caudwell is not primarily valuable as a literary critic.

17 E. P. Thompson, *The Sykaos Papers* (London: Bloomsbury, 1988). Subsequent page references appear in parenthesis.

8

Socialist Humanism

Kate Soper

The term 'socialist humanism' has an ambiguous history, as Edward Thompson himself has said.[1] Many and various are the parties that have laid claim to it.[2] But for Thompson it has throughout meant one thing only – the movement of communist libertarian opposition to Stalinism which first took root in Europe in the late 1950s.

The core themes of the 'socialist humanism' defended by Thompson at that time were the rejection of the antithetical 'philistinisms' of social democracy and Stalinist Communism; the insistence that the sole route to genuine socialist emancipation lay on a course between the two; and the affirmation of our moral autonomy and powers of historical agency. Together, these have provided the unbroken thematic thread of all Thompson's writings. The early study of William Morris and the critique of Stalinism in the 1950s, the wrestlings with labour movement reformism in the 1960s, the polemic against Althusser, the assaults upon the erosion of civil liberties and the manufacture of consensus in the late 1970s, and – perhaps most pressingly of all – the denunciation of Cold War stasis and the 'exterminist' logic of the arms race in the 1980s, have been part of a singular project: to rescue the 'moral imagination' from 'philistinism' (the disposition to accept and defend any existing reality as immutable necessity), and thus to check the mindless drift towards the obliteration of all human culture.

In charting Thompson's 'socialist humanism' we are therefore charting both a moment in his political thinking (one which also belonged to a larger moment of European history) and the conceptual framework within which that thinking has always been cast. But while this framework has proved a constant, Thompson has not shown himself disposed to cling to the early formulas of his 'socialist humanism' as if their ritualistic repetition could ward off all diabolisms, whether of left or right. On the contrary, they have been continually modified and reformulated as new circumstances have come into being, requiring different emphases, struggles and polemic. Sulk in his tent as he has at times, Thompson has also always emerged again to renew the dialogue, to take issue again with history and to put veteran arguments to work for new campaigns. In this sense, his socialist humanism has a history of development within its relative fixity of outlook.

Out of Stalinism

Thompson has always maintained that the crucial inaugural date for socialist humanism was 1956. In reaction to the revelations made at the Twentieth Congress of the CPSU and the Soviet invasion of Hungary, the term, he tells us,

> arose simultaneously in a hundred places, and on ten thousand lips. It was voiced by poets in Poland, Russia, Hungary, Czechoslovakia; by factory delegates in Budapest; by Communist militants at the eighth plenum of the Polish Party; by a Communist premier (Imre Nagy), who was murdered for his pains. It was on the lips of women and men coming out of gaol and of the relatives and friends of those who never came out.[3]

In fact, the movement of anti-Stalinist rebellion had arisen somewhat earlier, if we count as its first manifestation the uprising in East Germany which took place almost immediately upon Stalin's death in 1953 – an uprising that was crushed, we might add, in a way premonitory of later events in Hungary.[4] But Thompson is certainly right to suggest that what happened in 1956 proved more catalytic for the emergence of a distinctive 'socialist humanist' formation. In Britain the key factors in its making were the massive resignation from the Communist Party (one third of its membership) occasioned by the suppression of the Hungarian revolt, and the subsequent regrouping of former Communist dissidents and others into the 'New Left'. The twin journals of this new movement – *The New Reasoner*, co-edited by Thompson and the main organ of his political writings in the late 1950s, and the more universities-oriented and less politically heavyweight *Universities and Left Review*[5] – were both explicitly committed to the promotion of 'socialist humanism'.

Disillusionment with Soviet Communism was not, it should be said, the sole motive behind these developments – which were inspired also by fears of a wholesale rejection of socialist argument. In a cautionary anecdote related in the first issue of the *The New Reasoner*, we are told of the *Daily Worker* subscriber who, in the wake of the Hungarian massacre, opened the door to her usual deliverer of the paper with stony refusal rather than her accustomed welcome. No explanation was forthcoming until finally a voice from within shouted, 'Go away – we don't trust you.' By defending the 'socialist humanist' impulse of the Hungarian rebellion, the New Left hoped also thereby to retain a foot in the door of the former *Daily Worker* reader. For if left to itself, demoralization might well lead to a slamming of doors on any form of socialism. Abhorrence at what 'Marxism' had come to encompass, anxiety lest disenchantment lead to its complete abandonment: these were the impulses of the New Left in general and of Thompson's argument in particular.

In line with this, the New Left conceived its task in actively political terms: the aim was to build a nation-wide campaigning base for socialist renewal (hence the importance attached to the formation of the network of New Left clubs). Its critique of Stalinism and the British Communist Party was also immediately political. As Thompson himself describes it, it was concerned with the structure and organization of the Party, the control of the membership by the full-time apparatus, the Moscow orientation (and training) of that apparatus, and the self-perpetuating modes of control ('democratic centralism' the 'panel' system, the outlawing of 'factions', etc.).[6] The larger themes of the 'return to man', cultural creativity, a respect for individuality and so on, that were so central to 'socialist humanism' in continental Europe were by no means absent; but the more concrete conception of its political mission does seem to mark out the British New Left.

Rather in contrast to this emphasis, the socialist humanist revolt on the continent was much more directly associated with a flowering of Marxist philosophy based on a reappraisal of Marx's debt to Hegel and an awakened interest in his early texts. New readings of Hegel[7] were of critical importance in this process, as was the influence of the 'humanist-Hegelian' Marxism first developed in the inter-war years by Gramsci, Korsch and, above all, Lukács. As a philosophical critique, in fact, we can think of socialist humanism as comprising rather more than Thompson mentions – as including, for instance, the existentialist Marxism of Sartre, Merleau-Ponty and de Beauvoir, a good part of Frankfurt School argument, the *Praxis* group in Yugoslavia, the Christianized Marxism of writers such as Calvez, Bigo and Rubel, as well as the somewhat disparate arguments to be found in Erich Fromm's large volume of socialist humanist writings.[8]

The broader the church, however, the more rudimentary tends to be the creed uniting the communicants. This is certainly true of socialist humanism in this larger definition. For Marxist humanists have occupied a range of epistemological positions and diverged widely on such crucial issues as the nature of the dialectic or interpretation of the theory of alienation. On the other hand, where they have found agreement is in their critique of positivistic metaphysics and their rejection of deterministic interpretations of historical materialism. Hence the stress placed on praxis as purposeful human action, and its role in the creation of social processes and institutions.

Though the general claim of these humanists was that they were doing no more than reassert the authentic Marxist dialectic of human beings as both 'made' by historical circumstances and active in their making, it was inevitable, given the mechanistic orthodoxy to which they were reacting, that they placed the stress on the active and creative component. At times this brought them close to a denial of economic or ideological determination altogether, a denial associated in the existentialist argument with a tendency to re-cast relations of production as interpersonal relations, and thus to put in question the whole idea of 'unwilled' social forces possessed of their own dynamic and exigency. At the same time, and incompatibly in some ways, there was an emphasis on *alienation*, a process associated with the failure of individuals to perceive the social source of the value of commodities (fetishism) or to understand the true nature of social relations and institutions.

The tension between these emphases is reflected in a certain polarization of Marxist humanist argument. On the one hand, a more Hegelian–Lukácsian school of thinking points to the importance of generalized processes of reification and alienation as the 'theft' of our humanity, but encounters difficulties in consequence when it comes to specifying the means of escape from these. (Thus Lukács was led to posit a hyper-organic collectivity – the proletariat in its 'ascribed' consciousness – as the universal 'subject' of history, and to view its project in directly Hegelian terms as the realization of an immanent historical reason.) The existentialist tendency, on the other hand, has emphasized the irreducibility of conscious, or 'lived' experience, and insisted upon the intelligibility of history as aggregated human praxes. This is an argument that rightly regards history as made by real men and women rather than by hypostatizations, but has difficulties in reconciling these themes with the recognition by historical materialism of 'alien' or 'unwilled' social forces possessed of their own intrinsic order.

Turning back to Thompson, where upon this spectrum should we place his socialist humanist argument? Nearer to the existentialistic pole than to the Hegelian–Lukácsian in the stress it places on conscious experience, it should none the less be distinguished from both, not only on account of its sharper political focus and moral passion, but also by what might be described – though not without ambiguity – as its resistance to 'philosophical anthropology'. The first point is the easier to state: Thompson, as most would agree, has brought an urgency and clarity to the socialist humanist argument missing from more abstract, and often rather pious, effusions penned in its name. As Thompson himself wrote in 'Outside the Whale', at a certain point in the post-war declension towards Natopolitan quietism the 'blaring moral loudspeakers ("progress", "humanism", "history" and the rest) were simply switched off with a tired gesture. . .'[9] Among the many who turned them on again in 1957, Thompson was one of the relatively few who managed to make them sound both interesting and morally compelling.[10] These features of his writing have their bearing on the other and more complicated factor differentiating his position from that of his European counterparts. As an historian by training and inclination, rather than a philosopher, his encounter with Marxism was mediated not primarily through Hegel, Husserl and Heidegger, but through the very English figure of William Morris: as we shall see, this has had a definite impact on the tenor of his humanism. At the same time – and herein lies the ambiguity of suggesting any anti-philosophical bent – his analysis of agency and of the nature of historical process is without doubt 'philosophical', and invites direct comparison with the argument of continental theorists, and most notably Sartre.

In what was to prove a seminal article in the first issue of *The New Reasoner*,[11] Thompson wrote of 'socialist humanism' that

> it is *humanist* because it places once again real men and women at the centre of socialist theory and aspiration, instead of the resounding abstractions – the Party, Marxism-Leninism-Stalinism, the Two Camps, the Vanguard of the Working-Class – so dear to Stalinism. It is *socialist* because it reaffirms the revolutionary perspectives of Communism, faith in the revolutionary potentialities not only of the Human Race or of the Dictatorship of the Proletariat but of real men and women.

And he proceeded to defend it as the truth of Marxism, which Stalinist 'ideology'[12] had systematically distorted and betrayed.

The rejection of the Trotskyist critique of Stalinism implicit in this position was made explicit in Thompson's curt and dismissive references to Trotsky ('the anti-Pope to the Stalinist Pope').[13] What was also implied – and again made explicit in the 'Epistle' – was the exoneration of Marxism of any blame for the Stalinist deformation.[14] However, this position was swiftly revised in the light of Charles Taylor's insistence that there were roots for the distortion in Marx's conception of the proletariat as the 'class that suppresses all classes'.[15] Expressing a good measure of agreement with Taylor, Thompson wrote in reply that he now saw more clearly that 'if Stalinism is a mutation of Marx's ideas, the very fact that they are capable of undergoing such mutation while remaining in a direct line of relationship indicates an original weakness which goes beyond mere ambiguity.'[16] The weakness in question here was the implicit determinism of the 'base–superstructure' model – its invitation to view economic activity as a separate 'level' causing a certain set of automatic effects at another 'level' ('superstructure'). Thompson rejected this suggestion on two main grounds. First, he argued that it misrepresents the essential imbrication of economic, legal, political and cultural relations in any actual society;[17] second, it denies human agency, treating consciousness and affectivity as the unmediated reflex of, seemingly quite autonomous, social structures. However, what has not been made clear in Thompson's discussions of this 'determinism' is how far he regarded the base–superstructure metaphor as itself to blame for it, as opposed to those economic functionalists from Stalin through to Althusser who interpret it substantively. In this sense, the question of classical Marxism's responsibility for its Stalinist 'ideology' has been given no unambiguous answer in his work.

However, it can be said that Thompson's criticism of Marx has become sharper over time. Thus *The New Reasoner* articles read into Marx's commentary on the relations between 'being' and 'consciousness' an account of the mediating role of experience, which in reality was almost entirely his own;[18] but in *The Poverty of Theory* he finds Marx himself guilty of encouraging Althusserian rationalism by his silence on the crucial category of experience. The same goes for the Althusserian reduction of the moral and affective component of experience to the status of ideology: for that, if for little else in the 'orrery', says Thompson, there is indeed a valid licence on offer from Marx.[19]

But these are essentially changes of emphasis, and in the end what Thompson has wanted to maintain is the fertile because ambiguous nature of the pronouncements of Marx and Engels on the relations between 'being' and 'consciousness'. These pronouncements were 'socialist' in their recognition of the socially conditioned nature of 'consciousness' and 'humanist' in their refusal to treat the latter as wholly predetermined. In defending this account of the relations of structure and agency Thompson places himself firmly within the camp of Marx's humanist interpreters, all of whom regard a dialectical approach of this kind to be indispensable to any coherent conception of socialism. As they have justly argued, the treatment of individuals as passive 'supports' or 'effects' of social relations renders any socialist project both impossible and pointless. The anti-humanists, in short, are trapped in a dilemma. Either we are no more than 'supports' or 'effects', in which case no political theory, their own included, can have any bearing on what we do; or else we are the kind of creatures for whom anti-humanist argument could have political relevance, but in that case we are not really the 'supports' or 'effects' figuring in the theory.

Yet the humanist alternative *is* an ambiguous dialectic with its own difficulties. There is the theoretical problem of how an ambiguity of this kind can be registered other than through a fluctuation of stress, falling now on the conditioned, now on the creative dimensions of experience. There is also the related difficulty of juxtaposing 'humanism' and 'socialism' as if these were two clearly complementary impulses of a single *political* strategy.

To take the second point first. No sooner had Thompson formulated the argument for 'socialist humanism' than the charge of idealism – and thus evasion – was laid against it from both sides of the political fence. The more liberal critics suggested that 'socialist humanism' was all very fine as an aspiration, but Stalinism had made clear the impossibility of any such route to Communism, and therefore commitment to the latter had to be rethought anew. The more 'Stalinist' argument was that it was simply unrealistic to suppose that a movement committed to the interests of a particular class could hope to proceed to its goals without offending against a 'humanist' regard for all individuals 'as such'. In short, a class-based morality was incompatible with any humanist ethic, and the linking of the two purely verbal: 'socialist humanism' offered no guide at all on the crucial issue of the means that Communists could justifiably use in pursuit of their ends. As one of the 'liberal' critics, Charles Taylor, put it:

> the ideal conjuncture of events, whereby humanity as a whole will accept spontaneously the end of class society is not likely ever to be realised. The question remains: What value has a man, even unregenerate and obstinately resisting the most elementary social justice? This question is a crucial one for humanism.[20]

Thompson's general line of reply to all this (though never as fully articulated as it might have been) was that so abstract and stark a posing of the 'question' was itself an evasion of the socialist humanist response – which was precisely to the effect that no general guidance on the application of its principles could be given. The particular constraints of each situation had always to be taken into account in assessing the justice or morality of acts. As Thompson put it, humanist attitudes should find expression 'whenever and to the degree that contingencies allow'. As he later admitted, it was a clumsy formulation but an unavoidable one: 'what else can one say? That they must always find expression irrespective of contingencies?'[21]

The implication here was that the charge of 'contradiction' laid against the socialist humanist argument was inappropriate, since the appeal was not to a seamless theoretical unity but to a certain sensibility or instinct: we know very well what we are talking about when we call for a more democratic and humanist socialism, and we also have a pretty good idea what sort of practices conform to it; but to attempt any rigid specification of those principles and practices would be to betray the very spirit of flexibility which they oppose to Communist dogma.

That said, it cannot be denied that a 'socialist' recognition of the class-conditioned nature of experience and affectivity is in uneasy tension with Thompson's 'humanist' appeals to a more universal and apparently 'natural' moral sense. The problem can be formulated thus: if this morality is genuinely universal (i.e. to be human is to be possessed of it) then how do we explain evil except as a form of corruption accountable to social conditioning? But to explain it in that way would appear to deny the essential element of moral autonomy central to the 'humanist' case. If, on the other hand, we take the view that individuals are morally autonomous, and thus good or bad 'in themselves', it is not clear why 'humanists' should be so concerned to defend the principles of the moral equality of persons. Nor can we allow, it would seem, for the possibility of moral error. There are passages of Thompson's writing in the 1950s which bring this problem very forcefully to mind: arguing against Arnold Kettle, John Gollan and their ilk, he wrote that 'wrong theories do not frame up, slander and kill old comrades, but wrong men, with wrong attitudes to their fellow-men'.[22] And he went on to insist that no amount of speculation upon intention (Stalin, Rakosi, Beria, etc. 'believed' they were defending the interests of the working class) could mitigate the horror of trials such as that of Kostov (the Bulgarian Party Secretary shot in 1949):

> Those moral values which the people have created in their history, which the writers have encompassed in their poems and plays, come into judgment on the proceedings. As we watch the counsel for the defence spin out his hypocrisies the gorge rises, and those archetypes of treachery, in literature and popular myth, from Judas to Iago, pass before our eyes. The fourteenth century ballad singer would have known this thing was wrong. The student of Shakespeare knows it is wrong. The Bulgarian peasant, who recalls that Kostov and Chervenkov had eaten together the bread and salt of comradeship, knows it is wrong. Only the 'Marxist-Leninist-Stalinist' thinks it was – a mistake.[23]

I am inclined to agree. But it should also be remembered that it was one of Stalinism's more malevolent moves to dismiss any plea of 'intention' or 'belief' when it suited *its* purposes: hence its identification of moral turpitude with what was objectively 'counter-revolutionary'. Thus the case of Bukharin: persuaded that speculation on his intentions could not 'excuse' the outcome of his acts, he came to 'confess' to charges that were obviously false.[24] In other words, the construction that people put upon their acts is surely of relevance to our assessment of them. Inversely, it must be allowed that wrong acts can be committed by those convinced of their rightness and acting with the best intention. An inherent moral sense of the kind invoked here by Thompson may be the only guide in the end as to what is right and wrong. However, it can never be a guarantee against our acting badly; at least not if we accept, as Thompson appears to do, that the consequences of our acts, and not merely our beliefs about them, have to enter into consideration of their ethical status.

But if we acknowledge that individuals can make moral 'mistakes' of this kind, then moral consciousness must be open in some sense to forces it cannot grasp and to which its response is 'irrational'. In fact, some recognition of this was implicit in Thompson's claims regarding the 'ideological' status of Stalinism. For to treat it as an 'ideology' was to imply that it was not so much a deformed moral character but the grip of false ideas that drove the Stalinists to their crimes. Thompson was critical of the view (attributed to the Trotskyites) that Stalinism was a 'hypocrisy' rather than an 'ideology' on the grounds that this underestimated its strength, inner logic and consistency, and so reduced it to a matter of 'personality'.[25] But in the passage cited above it is significant that he spoke of 'hypocrisies': the logic of his argument implies that a much more central role should be accorded the moral 'personality'.[26]

This may be compared with the argument of *The Poverty of Theory*, where Thompson is well aware of the potential conflict between his insistence upon the irreducibility of 'lived experience'[27] and the acceptance of certain Marxist categories (e.g. alienation, 'fetishism', 'ideology') by many Marxist humanists on the continent. For instance, he writes:

> It is not true that Marx passed over in innocence the need to provide his theory with some 'genetics'. He attempted such a provision, first, in his writings on alienation, commodity fetishism and reification; and, second, in his notion of man, in his history, continuously making over his own nature . . . Of the first set of concepts I wish only to say this: they propose to supply a 'genetics' – to explain how history is determined in ways which conflict with the conscious intentions of subjects – in terms of mystified *rationality*. Men imprison themselves within structures of their own creation because they are *self-mystified*. While historians may find these notions suggestive in certain areas (as in the study of ideologies), they would

argue – I certainly will argue – that, in more general application, they are the product of an overly-rational mind; they offer an explanation in terms of mystified rationality for *non*-rational or *ir*rational behaviour and belief, whose sources may not be educed from reason. As to the second set of concepts (man making over his own nature), while they are important and point the right way, they remain so undeveloped that, in effect, they do little more than restate the prior question in new terms: we are still left to *find out* 'How'.[28]

The possibility of systematic misunderstanding of social relations along lines argued for by Marx is here more or less ruled out. Experience is itself a form of truth, and if we 'handle' it irrationally, that is not due to misconceptions about its causes or consequences but to our own intrinsic (affective, moral) being. Women and men, that is to say, are not only, or even primarily, ignorant or ideologically determined, but good or evil; they do not simply act in error, they act well or badly. Here again, then, as in the 1950s articles, the individual's 'moral character' is presented as a kind of base-line grounding the assertion of human agency which lies at the heart of the socialist humanist critique of Stalinism.

Part of the reason, one supposes, for Thompson's resistance to the idea of 'self-mystification' is that it appears to rely on the idea that consciousness can be moulded by forces that it cannot know. This was very much Sartre's objection to the Freudian Unconscious, and it is curious that Thompson appears so little inclined to recognize any intellectual kinship here. For Sartre is not of the party of the anti-humanists, as Thompson is wont to imply,[29] but is at one with Thompson in rejecting the idea of 'unconscious' forces which are excluded from experience while determining its content. For Sartre 'lived experience' is all there is; consciousness is translucent and the individual capable in principle of total self-understanding. Yet 'lived experience' is also a 'mystery in broad daylight'[30] since it has no means to express what it 'sees'. It *comprehends* totally, but lacks the conceptual means and reflexivity to articulate that comprehension in the form of *knowledge* or *intellection*. Through this concept of 'lived experience' and the associated epistemological distinction between 'comprehension' (an understanding of human action in terms of the intention of its agents) and 'intellection' (an understanding of human action without necessary reference to intention), Sartre has attempted to account for the opacity of experience to itself in a manner that avoids recourse to the notion of ulterior and radically unknowable forces controlling it. In other words, he has attempted to preserve the possibility of human emancipation based on rational understanding. Indeed Sartre suggested that what was wrong with the existentialism of *Being and Nothingness* was that it could not account *rationally* for those processes 'which are "below" consciousness and which are also rational, but lived as irrational'. The concept of 'lived experience' represents, by contrast,

> an effort to preserve that presence to itself which seems to me indispensable for the existence of any psychic fact, while at the same time this presence is so opaque and blind before itself, that it is also an absence from itself. Lived experience is always simultaneously present to itself and absent from itself.[31]

How far Thompson would want to go along with this more complex conception of 'lived experience' is not clear, given his warnings against seeking explanations of 'irrational' behaviour. On the other hand, it is surely something much more like the Sartrean conceptual framework that is needed to do justice to that favourite of Thompson's quotes from Morris – that men and women are the 'ever-baffled and ever-resurgent agents of an unmastered history'. Indeed, one might almost claim that the *Critique of Dialectical Reason* is an extended gloss on that remark; in other words, that it is a sustained attempt to theorize (through the concepts of 'lived experience', 'the group', 'seriality', 'the practico-inert', 'alienation', 'alterity', etc.) the Vico–Marx–Engels–Morris–Thompson conception of history as a humanly created but largely unauthored (in the sense of unintended) process.

What is more, Sartre insisted that this is a process in which action is both conditioned and free (by which he means that it is able to transcend or 'totalize' existing experience). 'Subjectivity', as he wrote, 'is neither everything nor nothing; it represents a moment in the objective process (that in which externality is interiorised), and the moment is perpetually eliminated only to be reborn.'[32] Out of the dead ashes of the 'practico-inert', the phoenix of human freedom continually re-arises – or so Sartre would have us believe. Is this so very different from Thompson's faith in the ever possible resurrection of the 'moral imagination' from the deadening processes of bureaucratization, state encroachment, the arms race and media manipulation?

Out of neo-Stalinism

It was, of course, precisely because he felt a need – two decades on from 1956 – to reaffirm this 'moral imagination' and to rescue it from the deadening effects of Althusser's structuralist Marxism, that Thompson wrote *The Poverty of Theory*. For younger readers of the book are not, he tells us, the 'post-Stalinist' generation they fondly imagine themselves to be. On the contrary, Stalinism as *theory* and attitude still 'weighs like an alp' on the brain of the living; the agenda of 1956 is still to be completed; the 'post-Stalinist' generation yet to be born.[33] Thompson proceeds to call for 'relentless war' upon the Althusserians, for they are the latest representatives of that current of Marxism against whose inhumanity and irrationalism the agenda of 1956 was originally drawn up. The book ends, in effect, with a call to all Marxist intellectuals to come out of their academic ivory tower to renew, in 1978, the programme of the (old) New Left sketched in the original 'Epistle' of 1957.[34]

In *The Poverty of Theory* all the main themes of the socialist humanist polemic against Stalinism are re-enacted but in the form of an attack upon its theoretical legitimation rather than directly upon its practice. As might be expected, the argument converges in an assault on Althusser's anti-humanist denial of agency. But directly associated with that, and equally repugnant to Thompson, is the downgrading of ethical protest to the status of ideology. This is, indeed, an important move to contest, for it is by means of it that Althusser is able to assimilate the humanist defence of morality to 'moralism'. That is, Althusser invites us to suppose that those who offer moral protests are assuming that moral argument is sufficient to bring about political transformation. And by highly selective quotation of a passage from *The German Ideology* he would persuade us that this was Marx's own position.[35] My own view is that, when read in full, the passage in question tends otherwise: the burden of Marx's attack was not upon the making of value-judgements as such but upon the idealism of supposing that it is *values themselves* which determine the degree to which they are realized in actuality. Whether or not I am right to impute this distinction to Marx, it is an important one for humanists to defend.[36]

The distinction is also very relevant to the reproaches levelled by Perry Anderson against socialist humanism. Adopting a somewhat biblio-centric viewpoint, he has argued that no special significance attaches to 1956 since the protest movement it generated issued in no substantial studies of the USSR in the Kruschev years, an analytical dearth which he attributes to the 'merely moral' nature of the socialist humanist critique.[37] The fault of Thompson and of the old New Left in general, was a substitution of 'moralism' for historical materialism. This, suggests Anderson, is the central point from which radiate all the oppositions of outlook dividing the 'old' New Left from the grouping, led by himself, which took over the editorial direction of *New Left Review* in 1962. As one reads through Anderson's punctilious charting of their disagreements on historiography, Marxism, philosophy, internationalism and political strategy, a series of antinomies and equations impresses itself upon one: moralism versus historical materialism equals empiricism versus rationalism equals humanism versus anti-humanism equals reform versus revolution equals the parliamentary road versus (probably violent) class struggle equals the Labour Party versus international Communism. In short, the issue of 'moralism' appears to carry a heavy load.

But whatever the strains and stresses of the socialist humanist argument, it is simply not true that Thompson and the old New Left were guilty of 'moralism' in the sense of supposing political action to be exhausted in moral protest. In the discussion of '1956', one cannot help feeling that Anderson has uncritically adopted the same reductive attitude to moral criticism that Thompson justly objects to in Althusser. And yet, elsewhere in *Arguments Within English Marxism* Anderson states explicitly that he does not think Thompson's engagement with communist morality can be reduced to a mere 'moralism', or that we can dispense with moral critique.[38] Thus he writes that

> the dominant emphases in the writing of the 'old' and 'new' levies of the New Left should be complementary rather than conflictual ones. Strategy without morality is a Machiavellian calculus, of no interest or use to a real socialist movement. Stalinism did indeed reduce Marxism to that, power without value, in its time: men like Rakosi or Zachariadis are the malignant mementoes of it. Morality without strategy, a humane socialism equipped with only an ethic against a hostile world, is doomed to needless tragedy: a nobility without force leads to disaster, as the names of Dubcek and Allende remind us. Thompson's formula for William Morris furnishes the fitting synthesis: what revolutionary socialism above all needs today is *moral realism* – with *equal* stress on each of the terms. For that kind of synthesis to start to emerge, here or anywhere, initial divisions of labour on the Left must connect into eventual forms of active cooperation.[39]

This is certainly a more even-handed appraisal of the contribution of the 'old' New Left. One can note too that some new and different dialogues have been taking place, whether or not they properly represent the synthesis Anderson calls for. One index of this was the publication of *Exterminism and Cold War* in 1982: among those paying tribute to Thompson's 'key' essay was the allegedly arch 'neo-Stalinist', Etienne Balibar.[40]

Has it all, then, been a matter of emphases, and the furore around Althusser a storm in a tea-cup – one, moreover, largely whipped up by Thompson himself? Yes and no. For Althusser was not calling for 'equal stress' on both the terms of 'moral realism' but ejecting the moral component itself. Nor was the bias of *The Poverty of Theory* misplaced given the relentless war that was waged at the time by the Althusserians against the merest intrusion of anthropology. No doubt we are talking about a handful of Marxist intellectuals, but Thompson's diatribe has been of critical importance in restoring some balance to their outlook. On the other hand, *The Poverty of Theory* is a very uneven work, at times intemperate and frequently unfair in the impression it promotes of Althusser's arguments and intentions. Anderson has rightly wanted to defend Althusser against the wilder charges of Thompson. He has also homed in unerringly on some of the weaker links in *The Poverty of Theory*'s own chain of reasoning.[41] To Anderson, too, must go credit for placing Althusser's attack on socialist humanism in its correct context – the Sino-Soviet dispute of 1960–4.[42] As he points out, in 1960 the USSR revised its position: the 'class humanism' which it had been defending in the 1950s against Marx's 'revisionist' detractors ceded to a 'personal humanism' based on the slogan 'Everything for Man!'. This signalled four years of contumely on the part of the Chinese against what they regarded as the opting by the USSR for 'revisionism' and 'bourgeois humanism'.[43] Since he does not take any account of this, Thompson fails to appreciate that Althusser is writing as a Maoist sympathizer and thus remains 'deaf' (as Anderson puts it) to the irony of his commentary on the Soviet Union. But while it is true that Thompson misjudged the real target of Althusser's polemic, it is not clear why Anderson should suppose that in revealing Althusser's Maoist leanings he has vindicated him of the charges laid against him by Thompson. Moreover, Anderson is surely mistaken in suggesting that we should interpret the irony of Althusser's remarks as a veiled rebuke of the USSR for its failure to practise the principles of socialist humanism that it was preaching in the official 'ideology'. If that were the case then Althusser would have subscribed in secret to the very critique of Stalinism that he dismisses as 'bourgeois' moralism, as the 'obsession' with ethics,[44] of those western 'humanist' intellectuals of whom Thompson was certainly one in 1956.

Out of Apathy

In 1960, Thompson looked back upon the 1950s as a decade of apathy in which only the alarm call of CND had seriously disturbed public complacency. Capitalism had been left to rot on the bough and Britain was over-ripe for socialism. Yet never had the orthodox labour movement shown itself less concerned to foster the immanent growth.[45]

Along with this gloomy retrospection went a distinct change of emphasis. The call was not for Communist renewal but for a socialist 'revolution' in Britain, and it was directed primarily at members and fellow travellers of the Labour Party rather than to disaffected Communists.

It is as if accounts had been settled with Stalinism, at least for the time being. The immediate task was to correct the flight from humanism of 'Natopolitanism', not Communism.

This really amounted to an admission of defeat for the original socialist humanist project: the pattern of the 1930s *had* been followed in that disenchantment had indeed only served to 'fatten the whale' of capitalism. What is more, responsibility for this retreat from the left (which Thompson acknowledged had become a rout during the 1950s) was now laid directly at the door of the Russian revolution, which had made the concept of *any* transition to socialism 'appear synonymous with bloodshed, civil censorship, purges and the rest'.[46]

In a climate that Thompson himself had defined as one of apathy, the call for 'revolution' was a bold (even a presumptuous?) move. For who was to be its agent? The question can be put, of course, to Thompson's argument more generally, for his tendency has always been to assume a 'moral community for socialism',[47] while remaining rather vague about its specific political form. In the writings of the early 1960s, this vagueness was exemplified in the terms in which he re-defined the political struggle: the battle was less between 'workers' and 'ruling class' than between 'the people' and 'monopolies', between the 'common interest' and the 'business oligarchs'.[48] At the same time, the more orthodox Marxist categories were still providing the basic framework of his argument. For while he agreed that it would be foolish to dispute the evidence of working-class adaptation to capitalism, he yet argued that changes brought about by automation (displacement of primary workers into secondary occupations, etc.) would shatter not the 'working class' but traditional notions of the working class as a fixed, unchanging category with a definite consciousness and immutable forms of expression. Clearly, Thompson still intended the abolition of capitalism to be the aim of a new consciousness, less cloth-cap and class-bound; and while he rejected the Trotskyite reliance on the traditional 'working class' as the agent of change, he also rejected Wright Mills' alternative of the 'intellectuals' with its Fabian overtones. Yet there is more than a hint here that the task of socialists was less to foment revolutionary desires than to adjust to the new 'common interest' of 'the people' at each stage in the development of affluence. At the same time, and not entirely consistently with the more pragmatic conception of the task of socialism, he was arguing that

> we can *fix* this new working-class consciousness and give it goals. More than that, I am saying that it is the constant business of socialists to endeavour to fix this consciousness, since – if we do not do it – the capitalist media will 'fix' it for us. Political consciousness

is not a spontaneous generation, it is the product of political action and skill.[49]

The argument is not necessarily in conflict with the earlier defence of agency: as a socialist rather than liberal humanist, Thompson had always recognized that ideas do not arise spontaneously. But there is a change of emphasis here – from consciousness as an active 'handler' of experience to consciousness as 'passively' moulded by cultural forces. And where in *The New Reasoner* Thompson remained vague as to where ideas did come from, here he gave a more definite answer, and one more in line with his comment in 'Outside the Whale' that 'the shape of cultural history is determined by minorities'.[50]

Here then, in the articles of the early 1960s, we encounter the same tensions in the socialist humanist argument, the same difficulties in sustaining its 'ambiguous' dialectic, but now viewed, as it were, from the opposite pole: where the former stress on the irreducibility of moral feeling and consciousness had the cost of not making proper sense of the notion of cultural conditioning, the later stress on the openness of consciousness to manipulation put in question the assertion of our moral autonomy. But a certain vacillation between these poles is, as I have suggested, inevitable. It should be noted too that these theoretical difficulties were due, in part, to a preparedness to question the traditional Marxist wisdoms in the face of new historical developments. In that sense, they were the problems of any socialist analysis sensitive to the problems posed by the transformation and break-up of the traditional working class under conditions of relative material comfort. The New Left was not alone with its dilemmas, nor was Thompson the only Marxist at the time to be accused of abandoning faith because he questioned the continuing validity of some of its categories. At around the same time, in the United States, Herbert Marcuse (of whom Thompson has been markedly critical), was writing:

> *One-Dimensional Man* will vacillate throughout between two contradictory hypotheses: (1) that advanced industrial society is capable of containing qualitative change for the foreseeable future; (2) that forces and tendencies exist which may break this containment and explode this society. I do not think that a clear answer can be given. Both tendencies are there, side by side – and even the one in the other.[51]

Both these 'tendencies' were registered turn by turn in Thompson's writings of the period. On the one hand, 'revolution' is said to be in prospect and the continued possibility of socialist transformation justified by reference to 'the long tenacious revolutionary tradition of the British commoner'.[52] On the other hand, we are reminded of how easily the revolutionary impulse is contained and defused by the 'fixing' of popular consciousness and the systematic manipulation of opinion. At the same time, and over-arching any such sociological accounting, we are offered an argument of an altogether different and more deeply pessimistic temper, one that invites us to think in terms of the failure of the socialist project as such:

> it is not Stalin, nor Khruschev, nor even Gomulka who must be seen to have failed, so much as the entire historic struggle to attain a classless society with which the particular, and more or less ephemeral, systems of Communist Party organisation and doctrine have been associated. What must be seen to have 'failed' is the aspiration itself: the revolutionary potential – not within Russian society alone – but within *any* society, within man himself.[53]

Here, revolution is no longer presented as an issue of rulers and ruled nor even of 'oligarchs' and 'people'. It is rather that human nature in some more collective, trans-class, trans-individual, even trans-historical sense has 'betrayed' itself, and we are all – exploited and exploiters, manipulated and manipulators – to blame.

The note of pessimism continued to sound throughout the 1960s[54] and into the writings of the 1970s, where a deep and sometimes even despairing concern with the encroachment of State power, the erosion of civil liberties and above all with the sclerotic effects of the Cold War, came to take precedence over the defence of Marxism or the advocacy of revolution. Maybe even, Thompson suggested at one point, we have been passing through a counter-revolution.[55] Together with pessimism went a relative retreat from political action and, it has been said, a lessening of interest in the affairs of the communist nations. Anderson claims, pointing in particular to Thompson's low profile during the Vietnam Solidarity Campaign, that 'when the challenge of '56–'58 faded, his interest correspondingly waned'.[56] But to suppose, as Anderson implies, that this represented a falling-off of socialist commitment is disingenuous. For the issue had never been purely one of strategy alone, but concerned the extent to which the existing 'socialist' nations could still be conceived as providing any sort of model for socialism. As a 'socialist humanist' Thompson has always opposed US imperialism and favoured the overthrow of capitalism; but he has also, as part of that same identity, persisted in his criticism of the Soviet Union and been wary of all political organizations and strategies that would bring him into alignment with it. This, one feels, is the real significance of 1956: that it marked the beginning of Thompson's long and unswerving pursuit of a non-aligned programme for socialist renewal. 'Socialist humanism' thus understood does not simply amount to a Eurocommunist endorsement of the parliamentary road to socialism; it is also distinguished by its hostility to the methods and ideologies of both the superpowers, and by its demand for the transcendence of the bloc system as such.

Out of Cold War

In the early 1980s, as the peace movement burgeoned again in response to the agreement on INF deployment, this demand for an end to the Cold War and the dissolution of the blocs assumed central political importance. It became the major theme of all Thompson's political writings and the core of the political agenda to which he has devoted unremitting energy for the better part of a decade.

But sounded as it was with a new urgency and with a definition that obviously reflected the specific historical moment, the 'out of Cold War' politics of the 1980s must also be seen as a continuation of a central motif of the 1950s 'socialist humanism'. From the beginning, in fact, Thompson's major fear was that the Cold War would pre-empt all moves towards an authentically democratic socialism in Eastern Europe: a fear that issued in numerous warnings of the repercussions this would have on socialist projects in the West, and reminders of the common interest of the opposed Soviet and US elites in repressing popular initiatives.[57] It is true that nothing in the earlier argument matched the bitterness and irony with which he was in his later 'exterminist' writings to illustrate this 'mirroring' of Soviet attitudes in Western postures.[58] But the call of these writings – for European Nuclear Disarmament, for a movement 'beyond the blocs', for active British neutrality and the uncoupling of Europe from superpower domination, for solidarity with independent peace initiatives in Eastern Europe, and for resistance to pro-Sovietism in the Western movements – this is of the same logic that lay behind the initial demand for a 'socialist humanism' as a mid-course between the opposing but complementary philistinisms of Soviet socialism and complacent anti-communism.

In more marked contrast, perhaps, was the quality of the response to the rallying-call of the early 1980s. Anyone involved in the early days of the peace movement renaissance is likely to have felt the historical significance of Thompson's opening of the classic disarmament argument to the European dimension and the politics of the Cold War and in particular, perhaps, of the 'moment' of *Protest and Survive*,[59] with its insistence on the importance of consolidated pan-European opposition to the warmongers, its visionary sense of the alternative to their 'degenerative logic', and its signalling of the emergence of the 'All-European Appeal for END'. Individuals do not make history, but some more than others help it on its way, and to Thompson must go some of the credit for pushing it minimally towards the END end rather than the other end.[60]

That there has been some swing of the needle away from the pole of 'exterminism' is undeniable, even if it would be rash to speak at this time of any definitive dissolution of Cold War. Movement there has been, but into a transition period in which we must pit the 'positives' of the advent of *glasnost* and *perestroika*, of the signing of the INF treaty, of the current (albeit very tentative) moves towards strategic weapons agreement, and of the developing East–West economic and cultural détente against a number of negatives: the more globally confrontational and self-regarding US policy which may follow from the breakdown of Atlanticism and redeployment of US forces from Western Europe to more volatile areas; the parallel commitment of the West European NATO powers to the economic strengthening and nuclear consolidation of Europe; and the instability of the Gorbachevian programme given the extent of Western resistance to further demilitarization and the growing ferment of ethnic and national self-determination in the USSR itself and other Warsaw Pact countries. That said, it would be absurd to deny that there has been an overall improvement in East–West relations since the beginning of the decade.

Paradoxically, however, it is precisely this degree of movement beyond the stasis of Cold War which has led some to call into question the adequacy of the 'exterminist' thesis with its emphasis on the role played by social movements and citizens' initiatives – and hence, by implication, to cast doubt on the contribution of the peace movement itself (especially in its END formation) in bringing about these changes in international relations. The 'exterminist' vision, it has been suggested, with its portrayal of the blocs as locked into reciprocal antagonism, formulated the dynamic of arms accumulation and of peace movement opposition to it in terms that excluded the possibility of state-led initiatives to break the impasse. Since this perception has been self-evidently wrong-footed by the INF agreement, it must be seen to have offered no more than a superficially plausible account of the politics of the Cold War.[61]

This argument seems to imply, however, that in stressing the role of social movement (rather than class) struggle and of a 'citizens' détente' rather than state initiatives, END politics was operating some sort of historical veto on these other forms of intervention: had these alternative distraints on the arms race been obviously forthcoming at the beginning of the 1980s, no one would have been more pleased than Thompson and his fellow campaigners (who would probably have cast doubt themselves, in the light of it, on the appropriateness of the 'exterminist' image). Secondly, it mistakenly suggests that END politics was exhausted in unofficial inter- or trans-bloc citizens' dialogues when in fact a great deal of energy went into pressurizing East European officialdom and influencing western governmental and opposition parties precisely with a view to bringing about some state led defence and foreign policy initiatives. Thirdly, it tends to a hypostatization of the 'State' as an 'agent' constantly out-manoeuvring peace movements and other naive forms of citizen protest in the pursuit of an overarching and always perfectly coherent historical rationality. In reality, states muddle along much as do peace movements (who also, incidentally, have played no small part in more recent governmental confusions). But finally, all these other mistaken tendencies derive from the fundamental error of interpreting Thompson's arguments about 'exterminism', the mirroring of the blocs and the self-sustaining dynamic of the arms race in too literal a fashion. The 'exterminist' account was surely never offered as a finished conceptual analysis, but rather as a heuristic formula, and above all as a parable to capture the political imagination at a moment when the maximum mobilization of opposition to the deployment of INF was clearly called for.[62]

That the first measure of nuclear disarmament has come about through state negotiation is therefore by no means an embarrassment to the 'exterminist' thesis, or its falsification. Or it is not unless it is assumed that either the thesis was a profession of nihilism (when, in fact, as everyone knows it was a summons to humanist resistance), or else that it implied that the 'people' themselves would physically dismantle the weapons systems without the mediation of any governmental or institutional forces at all, which is plainly absurd.

It is true that there can be no certain pronouncement on the respective role played by peace movement pressure (as opposed, for example, to that of economic reformist pressure within the USSR) in bringing about the sequence of moves which led to the INF agreement, but this is a rather separate issue from that of the plausibility of the 'exterminist' argument and strategy. (Even if the peace movement had had minimal impact on the change of direction issuing in the INF Treaty – which of course cannot be established – it would not invalidate END politics unless it were known for sure – which it cannot be – that some other politics would have had at least the same or greater impact.) Of one thing, however, we may be fairly confident and that is that the new directions of Soviet defence and foreign policy were assisted rather than disabled by the non-aligned policies pressed for by Thompson and his END supporters – and this has been acknowledged of late even in Soviet official circles.[63]

What, then, of the other more directly 'socialist humanist' aspect of

Thompson's END politics? The suggestion, that is, that democratic socialist developments in both halves of Europe are blocked by Cold War and advanced by its erosion. Can it be argued that this too makes unwarranted assumptions which the history of the last few years has tended to confound?

So *in media re* are we still that it would be falsely knowing to speak on these matters with any confidence. If it is accepted, however, that even on the most optimistic accounting we are only on the brink of emerging from our Cold War epoch, then the absence of any significant advance hitherto in socialist democratic programmes can hardly be counted against the Thompsonian thesis.

This is not to deny that neo-rightist policies have continued to retain the command established in the earlier part of the decade, especially in Britain and the USA. Nor is it to deny that the 'new realist' turn of the Labour Party has brought a very noticeable acceleration of the general drift away from any serious socialist commitment which has characterized its policy in the post-war period. If we think, that is, of the values for which Thompson and the New Left stood in the 1950s – anti-nuclear,[64] anti-nationalistic, anti-capitalist and anti-consumerist – then we must acknowledge that the record of the Labour Party has been generally countervailing for some thirty years now, and has probably never shown fewer signs of reversing this tendency than at the point where some minimal progress has been made on disarmament and the democratization of socialism in Eastern Europe. Indeed, the leadership of the Labour Party has celebrated the INF agreement by signalling its desire to ditch the one commitment it had made which brought it more into line with New Left demands – that of unilateral disarmament. Finally, it must be admitted that despite present attempts to reaffirm socialist policies and to develop an international opposition to counter the prevailing tendencies of West European policies, much of the former radical anti-capitalist sentiment has gone into a 'consumer communist' style very much at odds with that of the original New Left.

In Eastern Europe, on the other hand, while it is much too early to predict what new political formations may come out of the re-thinking and criticism set in motion by *glasnost* and the accompanying expansion of 'civil society', it is clear that in a general sense de-Stalinization has gone together with a lessening of East–West tension and bellicosity.

It will be said, of course, that the Gorbachevian liberalization can in no way be regarded as a *response* to an alleviation of western hostility, but has rather to be seen as accommodation to its sheer intransigence. But even if this too crude analysis is allowed, it does not invalidate the logic of the mutually reinforcing nature of disarmament and democratization, which precisely pointed the finger at the impasse of Cold War politics so long as both of its superpower parties were incapable of seeing the wisdom of a more conciliatory approach. Mr Gorbachev may well have launched the USSR on the path of *glasnost* and *perestroika* for primarily domestic reasons. But he knew, too, that the disarmament and improved international climate essential to the success of his reforms could not be brought into being through the continued pursuit of Brezhnevian Cold War foreign policy – and he therefore took the appropriate measures to side-step its implacable logic.

Of course, it must be recognized that de-Stalinization is proceeding very unevenly in Eastern Europe, and in some places, like Romania, not at all. It must also be recognized that it is limited, reversible and meeting with significant opposition. Above all, it must be recognized that it goes together with an economic restructuring whose long-term effects may be to hand over the East European economies to the inherently undemocratic and unsocialist control of market forces.

But against all this must be set the element of uncertainty which is introduced with any extension of the space for more pluralistic politics: an uncertainty which has been seeded now in the USSR and may eventually take it in directions which transcend at least some of the philistinisms of either capitalism or Stalinist Communism. Equally, in the established pluralist society of the West, this same element of uncertainty – which arises ultimately from the failure of people ever quite to comply in their moral outlook and political choice with the deterministic conceptions of an anti-humanist theory – makes it impossible to say finally that no form of democratic socialism will ever flourish on its soil.

Indeed, just as one is about to yield to pessimism on this score, one is given cause to reflect again in the sudden flurry of concern for Third World suffering and exploitation manifest in the response to Live Aid and Band Aid; in the emergence of all sorts of half-articulated conflicts about needs and life-styles; in new laments for the loss of old communities; in the unease about the New Right celebration of greed; and above all, perhaps, in the growing alarm about the environment and ecological sustainability.

Reflecting himself on this disquietude in 1985, Thompson spoke of the need for the 'whys' of the people to be reasserted against the 'hows' of the television experts, who

> go on and on, in these frames, to the point of tedium, with the *how* questions only. How do we get inflation down? How should we cut up the defence budget between Trident and the fleet? A national 'consensus' is assumed – but in fact is manufactured daily within these frames – as to questions of *why* and *where* .... But across the world people are asking questions of *why* and *where*? Do we have

the right to pollute this spinning planet any more? To consume and lay waste resources needed by future generations? Might not nil growth be better, if we could divide up the product more wisely and fairly?[65]

Without pretending that the alternative values embodied in these 'whys' and 'wheres' have any very effective support at the present time, it has to be said that they are implicitly being espoused in any expression of 'green' concern – and that this concern has moved sharply up the political agenda since Thompson penned those words.

Indeed the ecological crisis is so alarming, the 'green' response to it so obviously rational, and capitalism so clearly unhelpful in countering environmental degradation and resource attrition, that in the coming years a renewal of a much stronger, greened socialist movement in West Europe remains a distinct possibility. Should it emerge, it will have the advantage of the parallel ecological concern of increasing numbers of citizens in Eastern Europe, and their complementary recognition that neither the orthodox communist or capitalist models will be adequate to the solution of the dilemmas posed by the shared East–West commitment to current forms of growth and industrialization.

Rather than speculate further on these issues, however, let me conclude simply by pointing to the way in which any such 'greening' of the socialist outlook would be a realization of Thompson's earliest political aspirations, in so far as these were based around a union of the wisdoms of Marx and William Morris. In other words, the same Marx/Morris argument which has been 'working inside' Thompson for some thirty years now – and it was, he has said, upon Morris's modes of perception that he fell back in 1956[66] – would now seem, in updated form, to be 'working inside' a good part of the left also. With what outcome we cannot as yet say. But in this longstanding commitment to the Marx/Morris nexus, Thompson must surely be allowed to have had a certain prescience about the outlook and preoccupations of any movement laying claim to be both 'socialist' and 'humanist' as we approach the end of the century.[67]

Notes

1 E. P. Thompson, *The Poverty of Theory and Other Essays* (London: Merlin Press, 1978), p. 326.

2 Cf. Louis Althusser, *For Marx* (Harmondsworth: Penguin, 1969), pp. 221–2; 236–41; and see below, p. 206 f.

3 Thompson, *Poverty of Theory*, p. 322.

4 The rebellion erupted in June 1953 and was put down with the aid of Soviet troops.

5 Cf. Raymond Williams' account of the character of these journals in *Politics and Letters* (London: New Left Books, 1979), pp. 361–2. Both journals were founded in 1957. They merged in 1960 to form *New Left Review*, edited by Stuart Hall with a large editorial team drawn from both previous journals. Shortly after Hall's resignation as editor in 1961, editorial direction passed into the hands of a small group led by Perry Anderson. Copies of *The New Reasoner* and *Universities and Left Review* are extremely difficult to come by these days. I should like to express my gratitude here to Robin Blackburn and *New Left Review* for allowing me to remove their 'not to be removed' copies from the *Review* office.

6 *Poverty of Theory*, p. 326.

7 Those of the Frankfurt Institute theorists before the war and the very influential lectures given by Alexandre Kojève in France in the 1930s deserve particular mention.

8 Erich Fromm (ed.), *Socialist Humanism* (London: Allen Lane, 1965).

9 *Poverty of Theory*, p. 10. The essay was first published in E. P. Thompson (ed.), *Out of Apathy* (London: New Left Books, 1960).

10 He was one of the few to do so, but by no means the only one, as is evidenced by the poets and authors already cited. Among the philosophers, special mention should be made of Leszek Kolakowski, to whose voice in the 1950s Thompson pays such well-deserved tribute. (See 'An Open Letter to Leszek Kolakowski', in *Poverty of Theory*.) Kolakowski's remarkable polemic, 'Responsibility and History' (first published in *Nowa Kultura*, 1957) is included among other of his essays of 1956–8 in *Marxism and Beyond*, introduced by Leopold Labedz (London: Pall Mall Press, 1969).

11 'Socialist Humanism, an Epistle to the Philistines' (henceforth referred to as 'Epistle'), *The New Reasoner*, 1 (Summer 1957), pp. 103–43.

12 'Epistle', pp. 109ff. By 'ideology' Thompson meant 'a constellation of partisan attitudes and false, or partially false, ideas with its own inner consistency and quasi-religious institutional forms'. See 'Agency and Choice', *The New Reasoner*, 5 (1958), p. 95.

13 'Epistle', pp. 139–40; cf. pp. 107–8. Perry Anderson has suggested that Thompson's war experiences, and their formative influence on his Communism, may have contributed to his hostility to Trotsky, who condemned the war as an 'inter-imperialist struggle'. (See *Arguments Within English Marxism* (London: Verso, 1980, p. 154.) This may certainly have shaped Thompson's original attitude to Trotskyism, but the persistence of his antagonism has more to do with what he regarded as the sectarianism and dogmatism of the Trotskyists.

Anderson goes on to charge Thompson with a 'repression' of Trotsky's writings, (ibid., pp. 154ff.), suggesting that this is all the more surprising since not only did Trotsky provide the most durable Marxist theory of Stalinism – the prime object of Thompson's concern after leaving the British Communist Party – but was also the first great Marxist historian. Certainly, Thompson offers no systematic review of Trotsky's work, expressing such criticisms as he has in a vague, off-hand kind of way. But we should recall that Trotskyism was a fairly marginal phenomenon in Western Europe until the late 1960s and that Trotsky's writings were largely outside the effectively available stock of political theory until then. (Anderson admits as much in his *Considerations on Western Marxism* (London: New Left Books, 1976, p. 101.) In any case, 'repression' is too strong. Thus in the 'Epistle' (p. 108) Thompson writes: 'In understanding the central position of the Russian bureaucracy, first in developing and now in perpetuating, this ideology, i.e. Stalinism, we have a great deal to learn from the analyses of Trotsky and even more from the flexible and undogmatic approaches of Isaac Deutscher and others.' Deutscher is saluted again in *The Poverty of Theory* along with Victor Serge, and so too are the 'old comrades' of *Socialisme ou barbarie*. (See *Poverty of Theory*, pp. 329, 360.)

14 'Epistle', pp. 111–12.
15 Charles Taylor, 'Marxism and Humanism', *The New Reasoner*, 2 (1957). Taylor was the most cogent, and at the same time the most sympathetic of Thompson's critics during this period. In the same issue Harry Hanson charged him with 'romanticism' and 'utopian socialism'. These responses to the 'Epistle' were followed by contributions from Tim Enright, John St John and Jack Lindsay in *The New Reasoner*, 3 (1957–8). Thompson's 'Agency and Choice' was offered in reply to these critics.
16 'Agency and choice', p. 96.
17 On this, see Ellen Meiksins Wood in this volume.
18 'Epistle', p. 132f. Cf. *Poverty of Theory*, p. 357f.
19 *Poverty of Theory*, pp. 364–5, but see also the whole of section XV.
20 Charles Taylor, 'Marxism and Humanism', p. 96.
21 'Epistle', p. 128; 'Agency and Choice', p. 103.
22 'Epistle', p. 119; Kettle was a literary critic and leading Communist Party intellectual, Gollan a full-time Party official.
23 'Epistle', p. 119.
24 Cf. Merleau-Ponty's comments in his 'Bukharin and the Ambiguity of History': 'the true nature of the tragedy appears once *the same man* has understood both that he cannot disavow the objective pattern of his actions, and that the motive of his actions constitutes a man's worth as he himself experiences it.' *Humanism and Terror*, trans. J. O. Neill (Evanston, Ill.: Beacon, 1964), p. 62.
25 'Epistle', p. 107.
26 Stalinism, however it is finally understood, was not the coherent and seamless fabric that the term 'ideology' implied. On the contrary, it was as inconsistent in its 'anti-moralist' stance as it was in its economism (from which, of course, Stalin's own ideas were exempted) and in its actual political strategies. Charles Taylor made the point in his reply to Thompson that Stalinism combined unbridled voluntarism with economic determinism. Isaac Deutscher conveys a very powerful sense of the role played by the sheer *inconsistency* of Stalin's policies in creating the disaster of 'Stalinism' in his 'Tragedy of the Polish Communist Party', in *The Socialist Register 1982*, ed. R. Miliband and J. Saville (London: Merlin Press, 1982).

27 Interestingly enough, Thompson refers us to Merleau-Ponty when he invokes this term in *The Poverty of Theory* (p. 366), yet he employs it not so much as a technical term in phenomenology, but as more or less equivalent to the ordinary concept of 'experience', which in the 1950s articles and elsewhere in *The Poverty of Theory* he seems to find quite adequate.

28 *Poverty of Theory*, p. 357.

29 In his 'Open Letter to Leszek Kolakowski' Thompson associated Sartre with Althusser as part of the same Parisian culture with which he cannot hope to compete (*Poverty of Theory*, p. 104) and the same lumping together of 'western Marxists' as denying human agency and creativity recurs in his review of Perry Anderson's *Considerations on Western Marxism* (*The Guardian*, 16 September 1976). Sartre, however, wrote as a fellow 'socialist humanist' in *The New Reasoner*, 1 (1957), pp. 87–98.

30 See David Archard's *Consciousness and the Unconscious* (London: Hutchinson, 1984), pp. 50–2.

31 Jean-Paul Sartre, *Between Marxism and Existentialism*, trans. John Matthews (London: New Left Books, 1974), p. 42.

32 Jean-Paul Sartre, *The Problem of Method*, trans. Hazel E. Barnes (London: Methuen, 1963), p. 33n.

33 *Poverty of Theory*, pp. 331–3.

34 Ibid., p. 383.

35 *For Marx*, pp. 236–7.

36 What is under attack in the passage from *The German Ideology*, in Marx and Engels, *Collected Works* (London, Lawrence & Wishart, 1975–), 5, pp. 431–2 is Stirner's reduction of 'the world historical struggles' between classes to a clash of concepts, not the ideological status of the concepts themselves. There are, of course, passages where Marx does appear to disown morality and to argue for its ideological status (cf. *The German Ideology*, pp. 184, 247, 254, 285) and it is no doubt on the basis of these remarks that Thompson has seen fit to concur with Althusser's assessment of Marx on this issue. But against his professions of moral relativism must be set Marx's recognition of 'desires which exist under all relations, and only change their form and direction under different social relations' (p. 256), and the fact that he clearly regarded hitherto existing societies as 'inhuman' because they were based on the oppression of one class by another, and thus on the exclusion – be it under capitalism, feudalism or slavery – of one class from development.

37 'The mainstream of '56 proved in the end surprisingly thin, and left rather little trace.' *Arguments Within English Marxism*, p. 120; cf. pp. 116–20.

38 In fact, Anderson has apologized for his suggestion in 1966, in 'Socialism and Pseudo-Empiricism', *New Left Review*, 35 (1966) that 'Thompson's most distinctive political concerns could be reduced to the category of "moralism"'. He associates this misconstruction with his failure to appreciate the real force of Thompson's engagement with communist morality in his study of William Morris. (See *Arguments Within English Marxism*, p. 157.)

39 *Arguments Within English Marxism*, p. 206.

40 Etienne Balibar, 'The Long March for Peace', in *Exterminism and Cold War*, ed. *New Left Review* (London: Verso, 1982). In the introduction to this work,

the editors wrote of Thompson's intellectual role in the revival of the peace movement following the NATO decision to deploy Cruise and Pershing missiles in Europe as 'an act of public service with few comparisons in the recent history of any country' (p. ix). Thompson's article, 'Notes on Exterminism, the Last Stage of Civilization' appeared originally in *New Left Review*, 121 (1980).

41 For example, the equivocation as to whether we are indeed free agents or must only think ourselves to be so; the multivalent notion of 'experience': see *Arguments Within English Marxism*, pp. 16–58.

42 *Arguments Within English Marxism*, pp. 105–7.

43 Some flavour of this is provided by a speech given by Chou Yang in 1963:

> The modern revisionists and some bourgeois scholars try to describe Marxism as humanism and call Marx a humanist . . . . In particular they make use of certain views on 'alienation' expressed by Marx in his early *Economic and Philosophical Manuscripts, 1844* to depict him as an exponent of the bourgeois theory of human nature. They do their best to preach so-called Humanism using the concept of alienation. This, of course, is futile.
> (Cited in Raya Dunayevskaya, *Philosophy and Revolution* (New York: Delacorte, 1973), pp. 181–2.)

It should be said that there were some definite political motives for this 'philosophical' dispute, since the Chinese were hoping to establish an alliance with the Indonesians as a 'third force' to which all those genuinely opposed to American imperialism might turn for leadership.

44 *For Marx*, p. 239.

45 *Out of Apathy*, pp. 9–10.

46 Ibid., p. 11.

47 I owe this phrase to Keith McClelland. One might argue that this trust in the existence of such a 'community' reflects at the social level Thompson's faith in the essential 'humanity' of the individual.

48 'Revolution Again! Or shut your ears and run', *New Left Review*, 3 (1960), pp. 19–31. Cf. 'Commitment in Politics', *Universities and Left Review*, 6 (1959).

49 'Revolution Again!', p. 28.

50 *Poverty of Theory*, p. 21.

51 Herbert Marcuse, *One-Dimensional Man* (London: Routledge & Kegan Paul, 1964), p. xv. Thompson's differences with Marcuse were stated in 'An Open Letter to Leszek Kolakowski': see *Poverty of Theory*, pp. 141–2, 174.

52 *Out of Apathy*, p. 308.

53 'Outside the Whale', *Poverty of Theory*, p. 11.

54 Thompson did, however, continue to press for a gradual and non-violent 'revolutionary' transition to socialism in his 'The Peculiarities of the English' (1965; now included in *The Poverty of Theory*). He was also a contributor to the New Left 'May Day Manifesto' which urged a similar policy in 1968. (See Raymond Williams (ed.), *May Day Manifesto 1968* (Harmondsworth:

Penguin, 1968.) For the French 'events' of May 1968 Thompson did not express any great enthusiasm, either at the time or later.

55 'The State of the Nation', in *Writing by Candlelight* (London: Merlin Press, 1980), p. 252. (The series of articles comprising 'The State of the Nation' were first published in *New Society* between 8 November and 13 December 1979.)

56 *Arguments Within English Marxism*, p. 151. Thompson still resists any 'canonization' of the VSC and, he has written, dissents 'sharply from the analysis of Anderson and others which tends to demote CND (pacifist, neutralist, middle-class "failed")': *Exterminism and Cold War*, p. 33, n. 48.

57 The role of the Cold War in crushing socialist initiatives both East and West is one of the major themes of Thompson's article on 'The New Left', in *The New Reasoner* 9 (1959), and was repeated in 'Outside the Whale' the following year. Cf. also 'Agency and Choice', p. 94; *Universities and Left Review*, 4 (1958) and 'The Doomsday Consensus', in *Writing by Candlelight*, p. 273, where Thompson himself remarks on the persistency of his warnings since 1958.

58 Though cf. 'An Open Letter to Leszek Kolakowski' (1973): 'the failure of "1956" was in part a failure imposed by "the West". The West as anti-communist aggression; and the West as inadequate socialist response. Suez consolidated Soviet reaction; Kennedy's dance of death during the Cuban missile crisis precipitated the pragmatic Khruschev's fall; the bombs falling in Vietnam were a background to the occupation of Prague' (*Poverty of Theory*, p. 168). This was echoed in his call for European nuclear disarmament in 1980: 'The hawkism of the West directly generated the hawkism of the East . . . . On the Cold War billiard table, NATO played the cruise missile ball, which struck the Afghan black, which rolled nicely into a Russian pocket' (*Writing by Candlelight*, p. 278).

59 This was first issued as a pamphlet in 1980 by CND and the Bertrand Russell Peace Foundation, and later included along with writings by other authors in the Penguin of the same name (Harmondsworth, 1980). Nothing here should be taken to imply that Thompson was the sole initiator of the END idea or unaided architect of its organization. For an account of the origins of the 'European campaign', see James Hinton's book, *Protests and Visions* (London: Hutchinson/Radius, 1989), and for a sense of the currency of 'END' ideas in left political parties at the time and of the role of the Bertrand Russell Peace Foundation, see Ken Coates (ed.), *Détente and Socialist Democracy* (Nottingham: Spokesman Books, 1975) and *Listening for Peace* (Nottingham: Spokesman Books, 1987).

60 Cf. the closing words of *Protest and Survive*: 'The acronym of European Nuclear Disarmament is END. I have explained why I think that the arguments of Professor Howard are hastening us towards a different end. I have outlined the deep structure of deterrence, and diagnosed its outcome as terminal. I can see no way of preventing this outcome but by immediate actions throughout Europe, which generate a counter-logic of nuclear disarmament.

Which end is it to be?'

61 For an elaboration of some of these themes, see Simon Bromley and Justin Rosenberg, 'After Exterminism', *New Left Review*, 168 (1988).

62 Bromley and Rosenberg seem partially to admit this at one point (p. 78), but only at the cost, one feels, of undermining a good part of their earlier analytic critique.

63 Cf. the interview with Tair Tairov of the Soviet Peace Committee, in *END Journal*, 36 (Autumn 1988).

64 It should be noted, however, that the attitude to nuclear *power* was generally favourable. While much of the writing in *The New Reasoner* remains depressingly relevant today (for instance, Claude Bourdet's 'The Way to European Independence', in no. 5 (1958), might almost have been written yesterday), one reads now with shock and a sense of datedness remarks such as that Marx 'pointed to the kind of unitary consciousness which is alone adequate to grasp and handle the secrets of material transformation such as nuclear fission, and to express the human unity of world-brotherhood' (Jack Lindsay, 'Socialism and Humanism', *The New Reasoner*, 3 (1957–8), p. 96). One cannot but feel that Thompson might have preferred to do without this kind of thing.

65 *The Heavy Dancers* (London: Merlin Press, 1985), p. 3. (The title essay from which this quotation comes was first delivered as a television talk in 1982.)

66 'Postscript' to *William Morris. Romantic to Revolutionary* (2nd edn, London: Merlin Press, 1977), p. 810.

67 For some more contemporary comments, see his introduction to Rudolf Bahro, *Socialism and Survival* (London: Heretic, 1982), pp. 7–8, and his tribute to Lucio Magri's definition of the possible relationship between the European peace movement and the Third World in 'Europe, the Weak Link in the Cold War', in *Exterminism and Cold War*, p. 347. Magri's very fine essay, 'The Peace Movement and Europe', is included in that volume, pp. 117–34. Cf. also Thompson's resistance to any dismissive attitude to green-type sentiments and his support for those who would affirm 'life values' against 'rationalized career values'. (See 'An Open Letter to Leszek Kolakowski', *Poverty of Theory*, p. 176; cf. p. 170.)

9

From Total War to Democratic Peace: Exterminism and Historical Pacifism

Martin Shaw

Edward Thompson has written of the point at which he took up the cause of European nuclear disarmament as one at which he set aside his historical work, and so it may seem to readers who are mainly interested in his writings about the past. But history is the interrelationship of past, present and future, and in directing all his energies into the new peace movement, Thompson was confronting – in ideas and action, if not in scholarship – the largest historical problems. As he has developed his ideas, in essays and articles over the last decade, it has become clear that the issues of war and peace are where all the big questions of Thompson's work come to rest. History and theory, biography and politics, culture and ideology: war, Cold War and nuclear weapons cast each in a different light. Much of what was written about Edward Thompson before 1980 was one-sided in that it neglected influences that were always important, if submerged, in his thinking.

The peace movement has called forth Edward Thompson in all his brilliance as polemicist, agitator and pamphleteer. The most obvious way to write an appreciation of his role might simply be to chronicle its unfolding, from the first warnings in 1979 through the early days of the END appeal, to the sudden upsurge of a mass movement with 'Professor E. P. Thompson' at its head, through all the strivings, urgings and occasional moments of despair to which his writings give vent, meshed with the public and private histories of actions, movements and committees. Some day, a biographer may tackle this task, daunting as it would be since he has done, written and said so much for peace in what must surely be the most hectic phase of an active life.

In this essay I shall try to do a very different job: to discuss the intellectual issues that are involved in Thompson's writings about war and peace, and the questions which these raise both for an understanding

of his ideas as a whole, and for *our* ideas. It is the argument of this paper
that Thompson has helped to open up crucial matters which have been
very weakly dealt with both in social knowledge in general and in socialist
theory in particular. But so inadequate has been the discussion that it is
hardly surprising that Thompson's contributions, written for particular
purposes in the thick of a political movement, are much better at raising
questions than solving them. This paper can help towards a resolution, if
only by setting out more clearly what the issues seem to be.

The History and Politics of Total War

Thompson's best-known writing about war concerns the nuclear arms
race: in advancing the concept of 'exterminism' he deliberately challenged
established socialist categories. By contrast with earlier polemics in which
he assailed abstract and speculative theorizing, in this case he saw an
urgent need, from experience and practice, for new categories to express
radical problems. The 'immobilism' of the Marxist left was to be seen in
the way it clung to ideas such as 'imperialism' as watchwords for all its
discussions of international politics and militarism.

Later in this paper I shall discuss in some detail how Thompson has
explained nuclear war preparation, and look at some of the reactions to
his work. First, however, in order to underline some weaknesses which
are common to Thompson and his Marxist critics, and the scope of the
issues which are neglected, it is necessary to reach back into the history of
war. For if it is true that 'imperialism'-based analyses of war are
anachronistic, it is also the case that such concepts were never fully
adequate to understand the problem of modern war. Their use by
Marxists reflected an original inability of Marx's theory, in common with
most major strands of nineteenth-century social thought, to come to
terms with warfare. The problems that Thompson seeks to meet with his
category of 'exterminism' are not simply new: the threat of the nuclear
age is the culmination of a long process of historical development, whose
earlier stages have been equally badly understood, even if the consequences
of failure have not been as potentially disastrous. Thompson himself has
commented on earlier phases of warfare in modern society, especially on
World War II which was formative for his ideas (in ways which we shall
explore). But I shall argue that while his comments are suggestive, they
have only touched on the problems.

The main issue is whether war is given any major importance as a
distinct form of social process in its own right, and one which has a
determining influence on society in general. Most social science, theory
and history, has seen war either as a consequence of more fundamental

social realities or, when it obviously has an influence on society, as an intrusion which if not accidental is nevertheless abnormal – a temporary interruption of the usual pattern of economic development, class struggle, etc. Even where these intrusions and interruptions produce obviously interesting results, the study of these does not always give rise to reflection on warfare. This can be illustrated by two examples, prompted by a recent, rather frustrating attempt to study Marxist attitudes to war and peace in Britain from the existing historical literature.[1] One is E. P. Thompson's seminal *The Making of the English Working Class* itself, written at a time when he was active in the first phase of CND, and covering a period which includes the Revolutionary and Napoleonic Wars.[2] This is full of references to the effects of the wars in particular, but generates no discussion of the significance of the wars (let alone of 'war' in general) for the development of class-consciousness. Secondly, we may take the work of James Hinton, like Thompson himself an historian active in CND Mark II: his otherwise excellent study of *The First Shop Stewards Movement* deals mainly with the response of the working class to the economic effects of World War I, but concerns itself neither with the response to the war as such, nor with the role of the war in generating new forms of working-class organization.[3] This book was published, admittedly, long before its author became involved in CND, but its defects are reproduced in his more recent general history of the labour movement.[4]

The point of this criticism is not to attack either Thompson or Hinton, but to suggest that even historians who are manifestly alert to the danger of war in the present have shared in a general inability to theorize war historically. Even when discussing the working class in a war situation, socialist historians remain within a problematic which marginalizes war. Of course, the working class themselves have often been more concerned with wages, conditions and rights than with 'the war': but this surely needs to be explained, not assumed.

By no means is this weakness peculiar to historians. On the contrary, it has been transmitted from sociology and, particularly, from Marxism. Social theory has been formed one-sidedly in periods of 'peace': Comtean sociology with its absurd notion of 'pacific' industrialism, and Marxism with its conceptual apparatus of the capitalist mode of production in which the state was abstracted out and warfare nowhere to be seen. (Engels was well aware, of course, of changing military technology, but this seemed an effect of developing industrial capitalism, not a potentially determining feature.) Late twentieth-century sociology has echoed Comte, not so much by denying militarism as by ignoring it, and a new Marxism has grown up more alert to the class struggle in the base of society than to the nuclear arms race overarching it. Again, the period is

the key: this theoretical renaissance coincided with détente, when war
was seen as a normal feature of revolutionary struggle in Vietnam, not as a
threat to the very foundations of human society.

To argue against these conceptions, which have influenced social
science of all kinds, it is necessary to turn to the work of a small and
disparate band of historians of war, who have stressed the inexorable
growth of new forms of warfare out of new forms of society. The French
Revolution has been seen as a primitive model of total war, as well as of
political revolution.[5] The way in which the revolutionary energies of the
people were expressed and channelled into military expansionism is thus
as significant as the example of their struggle for freedom. The experience
inspired, after all, Clausewitz's concept of 'absolute war' as well as Marx's
idea of proletarian revolution, and the Revolutionary Wars are as much a
forerunner of 1914–18 as the Revolution itself is of 1917. If Thompson
had been writing about France rather than about England, he might well
have been more concerned with such issues.

To the economic and political mobilization of Revolutionary and
Napoleonic France, the later nineteenth century added the application of
industrialized technology to war. The industrialization of warfare, as
McNeill argues, proceeded apace from about 1840:[6] Engels picked up its
early intimations, and lived to see the naval arms race with its massive
battleships which he naively believed were 'so outrageously costly as to
be unusable in war'.[7] By the turn of the century, major sectors were
growing within the capitalist economy which were dependent on
government, not the market. The outcome of all this was the first fully-
fledged 'total' war of 1914–18: total in the sociological sense of mass
mobilization, and also alarmingly becoming total in the Clausewitzian
sense of absolute destructiveness.

The issue is really how to understand these processes, because they are
crucially relevant to the later history of war and society up to the present
day. Marxists theorized them, belatedly and incompletely – for the most
part during 1914–18 itself – as products of imperialist rivalries for
markets. Lenin's concepts of capital and State were however archaic
reconstructions of Marx and Engels; and even Bukharin, who in some
respects *over*-generalized the militarization of State and economy, saw
this affecting only the relations of production.[8] No one recognized the
military capture of the forces of production, with the long-term threat of
technological improvements up to the full realization of Clausewitz's
destructive ideal.

Thompson's 'Notes on Exterminism' pursue a forceful and ironic
analogy with imperialism, but they do not really question its original
adequacy as an explanation of emerging military capitalism. My point is
that Thompson's contemporary position, that a concept like 'exterminism' is

needed which will largely if not wholly displace 'imperialism', can be extended backwards historically. 'Imperialism' was always an 'external' concept of the motives of states and capitals, while the potential for war had become 'internal' to the society in the technology and social organization of militarism. Only this can explain the nature of total war in 1914–18.

To follow Thompson's polemical example, we could argue that industrial capitalism was, almost from its origins, 'exterminist' in potential. Once the machine-gun was invented, was not the H-bomb inevitable? But such a technological determinism would obstruct a more fruitful line of argument: for the development of warfare was determined not by technology alone, but by the interaction of technology with strategy, politics and socio-economic organization. What we are searching for is not a primitive 'exterminism' but concepts that emphasize the mutual interaction of social system and (to use Mary Kaldor's concept) mode of warfare.[9] What was emerging before 1914 were the social, economic and political-ideological as well as the technical conditions for what is best still described as 'total war'. The Revolutionary-Napoleonic Wars and (even more) the American civil war can be regarded as forerunners of this new form of warfare; the other wars of the mid- and late nineteenth century provide less complete examples. Twentieth-century industrial societies have been in actuality what their nineteenth-century forerunners were chiefly in potential, 'total war' societies. The interaction of mode of production, society and mode of warfare has defined both periods of war and periods of 'peace'. This relationship has had its own profound dynamics, which have produced a succession of radically different phases.

One transition in this process, from World War II militarism to the nuclear age, is manifestly of central importance to E. P. Thompson's ideas, defining not only his theoretical model of 'exterminism' but also his political approach to problems of peace. World War II is, by implication, a very special moment in the history of modern militarism, different from what went before as well as what followed: 'I can only see the dead of the First World War as victims, futile losses in the ledgers of rival imperialisms. But I hold the now-unfashionable view that the last war was, for the Allied armies and the Resistance, an anti-Fascist war, not only in rhetoric but in the intentions of the dead.'[10]

This position – with which, basically, I agree – nevertheless raises difficult conceptual and political problems which neither Thompson nor any other of its many supporters have ever really resolved. Why, if the same sort of imperialist interests existed in both world wars, should it be possible to support the Allies in the Second, while condemning them as equal imperialists in the First? If the answer lies in politics, why should politics be the criterion in this case, while economics are apparently dominant in Marxist considerations of the First? And if we can make a political judgement as to whom to support in 1939–45, why cannot we make the same judgements in the Cold War? If the answer to this lies, as Thompson says, in technology, why do we keep shifting our ground, first from economics to politics, and now from politics to technology?

It seems clear that while one or other of these problems might appear to be soluble with the aid of some sort of Marxist economic or political theory (or preferably both), these cannot answer the full range of questions which arise, and that need to be tackled as a whole. What we need in order to do this is something that Marxism has never developed and that Thompson gives us only a suggestive tail-end for in his theory of 'exterminism': a theory of modern total war as a whole, in its changing relationships with the underlying social systems. This would involve seeing total war as a process in which one phase leads to the next, bringing new elements to the fore, and in this way changing the criteria of political choice.

This is a case in which historical schemata are desperately needed to make sense of hopelessly under-theorized realities. The dual social and military 'totalization' of war needs to be explored, and the stages in the relationship. I have suggested that political and economic totalization can be traced back at least to the French Revolution; the later nineteenth century adds industrial technology; World War I completes a first phase of labour-intensive militarism, in which the distinction between the mass army in the trenches and the mass labour force producing the munitions is (more or less) intact. Politics (nationalism), essential to motivate mass armies and workforces, is nevertheless subordinate to the interests of states and ruling classes. World War I itself changed that, both structurally by giving states enormously greater potential for dominating society, and more particularly by generating the particular revolutionary and counter-revolutionary movements which led to Stalinism and Nazism. Their emergence ensured in turn that World War II would be a conflict of state systems, ideologies and classes as well as of particular states. The other main development from World War I to II was that, once civilians had become essential to the supply side of war, they inevitably came to be seen as potential targets too. This strategic requirement quickly called forth appropriate technology: the development of aerial warfare meant that whole populations were at risk. During most of World War II, such bombing only reinforced 'morale': technological change intensified the political polarization of the war. In the final stages, however, with area bombing like that of Dresden and then with the atom bomb, this strategic-technical development showed a clear capacity to negate the strongest political meanings of the war in almost indiscriminate killing. The moment of technology succeeded the moment of politics: the development of what Thompson sees as a key feature of the nuclear age emerges as a conclusion to the entire historical process of total war.

Some such account of the dynamics of total war really needs to be supplied in order to make sense of major links in Edward Thompson's thought. He has recently insisted, for example, on the connections between the military struggle for a democratic Europe in 1939–45 and the anti-military struggle of the peace movement in the 1980s.[11] To some, it might seem much more obvious to link the present movement with war-resistance in 1914–18.[12] Thompson, however, wishes to claim the legacy of his generation's struggle against fascism for the peace movement: in so doing, he wishes to deny historical validity to the absolute pacifism of many nuclear disarmers, without at the same time re-legitimizing contemporary varieties of 'conventional' warfare.[13] In making such claims and judgements, Thompson clearly resorts to an implicit theory of the historical phases of modern warfare which needs to be more sophisticated than a simple dichotomy between nuclear and non-nuclear arms. This is the sort of theory that I have tried to indicate, and we shall need to return to these issues when we discuss Thompson's prescriptions for the peace movement. But the point has arrived when we must look at the overriding problem of the contemporary situation and in Thompson's thought: the nuclear arms race.

Nuclear Arms Race and 'Militarized Society'

Edward Thompson's popular writings in 1979–80 had a tremendous impact because of the virtual absence of information, ideas and protest about nuclear weapons even among politically aware people in Britain and other western societies. His more theoretical intervention, in the 'Notes on Exterminism, the Last Stage of Civilisation', similarly stirred the intellectual circles of the left, whose ignorance, complacency and anachronistic modes of thinking about the bomb he challenged. Some years later, although *Protest and Survive* has been superseded by a vast anti-nuclear literature from many hands, the attempts of the more orthodox left to surround the 'exterminism' thesis with more comforting political ideas still leaves its sharp edge exposed. The questions it raises will not go away, even if Thompson's original formulation has to be qualified and extended. I shall argue that the issues which now need to be addressed are not, on the whole, those of his Marxist critics, but the internal difficulties of Thompson's argument which arise largely from their abstraction from a more thoroughgoing historical analysis of modern war.

Thompson's case is obviously well known, and will be only briefly restated here. Essentially, it is that whatever the political *origins* of the nuclear arms race in the interests and ideologies of the superpowers, it has become a self-sustaining process which has enveloped the societies which originally produced it. By a direct analogy with Marx's analysis of the value-secrets of the commodity as the basis of capitalism, Thompson gives us the bomb, not as an isolated 'thing' but as a component in a 'weapon-*system*': and 'producing, manning and supporting that system is a corresponding social system'. The point is most dramatically made in an extension of this analogy which has caused Thompson a good deal of trouble with his critics:

> There is an internal dynamic and reciprocal logic here which requires a new category for its analysis. If 'the hand-mill gives you society with feudal lord; the steam-mill, society with the industrial capitalist', what are we given by those Satanic mills which are now at work, grinding out the means of human extermination? I have reached this point more than once before, but have turned my head away in despair. Now, when I look at it directly, I know that the category which we need is that of 'exterminism'.[14]

It is not difficult to see a number of problems here. First of all, as Raymond Williams was quick to point out, there is the technological determinism – which Marx himself never seriously pursued, and which is 'especially disabling' in the case of nuclear weapons since ironically it promotes 'a sense of helplessness beneath a vast, impersonal and uncontrollable force'.[15] Thompson has, naturally, disavowed any such intentions and has more or less repented of his original analogy.[16]

Secondly, if there are nuclear military–industrial sectors in East and West with 'an internal dynamic and reciprocal logic' these are not, obviously modes of production in the same sense as those to which Marx referred. Of course, Thompson is well aware of this, and used the analogy precisely to point up the extent to which, in Kaldor's terminology, mode of production has become subordinate to mode of warfare. But what is useful as a polemical device can be confusing analytically, and thus blunt the effect of the polemic. Those who have devoted great theoretical energy to deploying the categories of the capitalist mode of production are unlikely to be sympathetic to their instant abolition.[17] Nor, indeed, as Thompson has recognized, are categories like 'capitalism' and 'imperialism' utterly outmoded by his argument: he is arguing, rather, the limits to their validity, the point at which they need to be displaced by categories of the 'exterminist' mode of warfare. The difficulty is compounded because this point of displacement is not at all precisely indicated.

Thirdly, there is the point of agency: who are the forces for change in an 'exterminist' process, and what happens to the agencies indicated by traditional Marxist analyses? Critics have, not surprisingly, in reasserting the importance of capitalism and imperialism to the explanation of the arms race, tried to restore either the working class or the oppressed nations of the Third World as major forces for defeating western militarism.[18] Against this, Thompson's advocacy of a cross-class European peace movement whose strategy is loosely defined by comparison with orthodox socialist models, has not always impressed – although in the short term it has been vindicated by the extraordinary momentum of the forces campaigning for peace.

Thompson's proposal that we should see an inner logic to the East–West arms race, which may be leading to a climax which is neither intended by, nor in the rational interests of, either superpower, should be neither new nor surprising to Marxists. The specific idea was elaborated more than twenty-five years ago by C. Wright Mills, to whose *The Causes of World War III* Thompson has acknowledged a consistent debt.[19] The general concept is quite in line with Marxist analyses of capitalism as a society in which rational organization of the parts produces anarchy in the whole. This idea, which goes back to Marx and Engels themselves, was the nub of Lukács's critique of Max Weber's concept of bureaucratic rationalization, and specifically elaborated, with nuclear weapons in mind, by Herbert Marcuse.[20] Why it cannot be recognized in the nuclear arms race is a real puzzle of contemporary Marxism: it seems to have a great deal to do with a difficulty in accepting the full complicity of the USSR in the preparation of nuclear extermination. Thus for Ralph Miliband, the world is basically polarized between western imperialism and revolutionary forces: granted that the USSR is far from being unambiguously part of the latter, it cannot be assimilated to the former either.[21] Similarly, for Fred Halliday the decisive conflict is ultimately imperialism's in the Third World, and the USSR's role in the East–West arms race, while not denied, is seen as decidedly subordinate to the USA's.[22] Thompson, of course, does not deny that the USA has, for the most part, led the arms race, but to acknowledge this does not in any way undermine his argument that there is reciprocal competition. Yet this idea, it seems, is unacceptable to many contemporary Marxists because it implies a concept of a world system in which the roles of the USA and USSR are fundamentally similar in kind, if different in degree or in secondary respects.

A deeper set of reasons for the resistance to Thompson's concept of a 'reciprocal inner logic' to the arms race relates to the difficulties many Marxists, like other social scientists, have in accepting the *reality* of war. Their responses frequently vindicate Thompson's original accusation of complacency. Ernest Mandel, for example, first acknowledges the very point we have made, that nuclear war 'is a classical example of the combination of partial rationality and global irrationality . . . . The immediate goal is perfectly "rational"; the overall result is totally irrational.' But he immediately negates this by adding, 'But the process remains under the control of the imperialist ruling class, and remains therefore subordinated to its overall class goals and motivation. The weapons systems are ruled by the Pentagon which is ruled by Washington which is ruled by Wall Street and not the other way round.'[23] These comments show that the initial recognition of the irrationality of nuclear war is a purely theoretical one, for rhetorical use against capitalism: Mandel simply does not believe – indeed his system will not allow him to believe – that a nuclear war can take place. Yet the notion that, in an international crisis, Washington will wait to be 'ruled' by Wall Street, let alone be able to make every decision in the light of a rational assessment of capitalist interests, is so fanciful as to be worth no further comment.

What these remarks show, in addition to the dangerous influence of a class-essentialist rationalism, is an ignorance of the nuclear arms race itself. Under the influence of a general resistance to technological explanations, it is dogmatically asserted that there must be class-economic and political causes for war preparation. Thompson's specific analysis of the arms race, which is neither narrowly technologist in particular nor the product of any general technologism, is then dismissed. What he is trying to show, however, is precisely what is happening within the mode of warfare and its potential effects on society. It is a matter of fact, not of theoretical prejudice, that Pershing II missiles will – if they work – fly from West Germany to the Soviet Union in well under ten minutes, inviting a 'launch-on-warning' automated response. The disabling prejudice lies with those who cannot see the novel significance of such facts: that war preparations have developed to a stage where – if it is wrong to say 'the technology *takes* over' – nevertheless it is true to say that, given certain military assumptions, the technology *has to be allowed* to take over. This is a *military-technical* logic at work, and while it must certainly be seen in relationship to other logics – economic, political, ideological – it is naive to think it is always and inevitably subordinate to these.

Another who has difficulty with the arms race is Miliband. While recognizing its irrationality and its role as a 'contributory cause' of World War III, he sees it as decidedly subordinate to the conflict between revolutionary forces and the status quo in the Third World. He argues that, with the freezing of the division of Europe, revolutionary strivings in the Third World have become the main cause of antagonism between the superpowers. He sees successful revolutions as inviting Soviet involvement and hence producing US responses which lead to localised conflicts, which in turn may escalate to world war.[24]

It is certainly true that the most dramatic changes in the world order since 1945 have come, and are likely to continue to come, in the 'Third World'. It is also true – and Thompson would not disagree with this – that any major East–West war is very likely, in the foreseeable future, to *originate* in the Third World. But in other respects the analysis is less impressive. The 'Third World' was always a broad and loose concept, and has become more so. The changes which are going on within it are by no means all part of a broad revolutionary movement: they primarily involve the consolidation of nation states seeking to play independent military as well as political and economic roles. Moreover, changes within the East and West, within the 'blocs', while not always so dramatic, have nevertheless had as fundamental effects on the superpowers as changes in the Third World. The eastern states seek greater autonomy, urged on by repeated popular uprisings; the lesser western states, notably in Europe, are challenging the US politically as well as economically. All these changes affect relations between the superpowers, even if changes within blocs are more subject to some sort of control than those outside.

Miliband argues that there are no real direct issues – such as border disputes – between the superpowers, and therefore concludes that indirect (Third World) issues must be the prime causes of any war. But his analysis inverts the real situation: it is the Third World conflicts which may act as catalysts for war, but it is the stalemated European situation and the arms race itself which will determine whether a *world* war breaks out. Third World conflicts, in themselves, can be controlled, or fought as limited wars, often through clients or surrogates, as they have been without world war since 1945. World nuclear war will only occur when European tensions are activated or when the arms race itself becomes so unstable as to invite pre-emptive strikes; or through some combination of these and Third World factors.

Miliband's commentary does at least have the merit of drawing our attention to the problem of the relationship of 'arms race' and 'Cold War'. Quite obviously, even if the arms race does have 'internal and reciprocal logic', this interacts with economic, political and ideological forces within the societies. The important questions here are how, in what directions, on what terms this interaction takes place. Thompson invites us to consider the possibility that, since the origins of the Cold War in the conflicts at the end of World War II, it has simply become a consequence of the military competition which it set in motion: 'the Cold War is now about itself. It is an ongoing, self-reproducing condition, to which both adversaries are addicted. The military establishments of the adversaries are in a reciprocal relationship of mutual nurture: each fosters the growth of the other. Both adversaries need to maintain a hostile ideological posture, as a means of internal boding or discipline.'[25]

This is a view very much opposed to Halliday's and Miliband's, that the Cold War reflects the conflict between western imperialism and the Third World revolution, but paradoxically in line with the latter's contention that there are no fundamental *direct* issues between the USA and USSR. The truth of the matter may be that there are major issues, which do not arise directly *from* the Cold War, but which nevertheless feed into it. These issues arise in all sectors of the world: in the Middle East and Latin America, but equally in Eastern and Western Europe. But Thompson may be right that these are not what the Cold War is about: the Cold War is the political and ideological conflict sustaining the military competition of the rival superpowers. Indeed, some of the conflicts which sustain and reproduce the Cold War, such as those in Eastern Europe, can be seen (as Thompson suggests) as very much the consequences of it. Without the Cold War's disciplinary function, the Soviet Union's rationale for tight control over, say, Poland would be greatly reduced, and the Polish upheaval, which in turn fed the Cold War, might not have occurred.

Thompson seems to be suggesting that in the 1980s, the Cold War/ arms race has been simultaneously intensified and weakened. The conflict of the superpowers over both weaponry and geopolitical issues has sharpened; the support of the people for their rivalry, especially in Europe, has declined. Indeed, the divergence of these two processes, the 'elite' and the popular, can be seen as a longer trend, linked in the case of Europe to a geopolitical split. It is partly because of a falling away from the Cold War that the superpowers intensified it; the intensification has in turn further alienated support. Cruise missiles are the key instance of this process: introduced because of a perceived political need to bond together the USA and Western European NATO, they have contributed more than any other single factor to dividing West European peoples from American power.

This argument is absolutely crucial to Thompson's political hopes for the peace movement, but it is one of the most poorly elaborated parts of his analysis. It relates to the point made above that Thompson relies on an implicit socio-historical theorization of modern warfare, but this remains undeveloped. In this case the point at issue is the integration of societies into the Cold War system. In his 'Notes on Exterminism', Thompson seems to rely on an ill-defined concept of the 'militarization' of society. 'Science-intensive weapons systems civilianize the military', he writes, 'but in the same moment more and more and more civilians are militarized.' In explaining this view, he refers once again to 'a science-intensive war economy', but the main emphasis lies with the ideological life of societies: 'At a certain point, the ruling groups come to *need* perpetual war crisis, to legitimate their rule, their privileges and their priorities; to silence dissent; to exercise social discipline; and to divert attention from the manifest irrationality of the operation. They have become so habituated to this mode that they know no other way to govern.' Britain in the 1980s 'offers itself as a caricature of an exterminist formation'.[26]

There is a sense in which Thompson's analysis catches fundamental realities. International conflict is the defining context for the ideologies of state elites, East and West; and with the revival of the Cold War, if not so much before that, these ideologies have performed a mobilizing function (although this has varied greatly not only between East and West but between states within the blocs). Similarly, the continuing ability of the war sectors to command economic resources at the expense of others has been clearly demonstrated: to this extent it is right to write of 'war economies'. But the main trend, as Thompson vaguely suggests that he is aware, but does not at all clearly recognize, is actually towards a demilitarization of society. Thompson's emphasis on the ideological actually reflects the fact that in other, harder, practical and institutional senses, the great bulk of society is not involved in the war machines. The highly technological character of militarism means that the military sector, although consuming vast resources, employs relatively few people. The 'science-intensiveness' of the military economy is indeed crucial, but while it makes sense to say that this 'civilizes the military', it is hard to see how (except in residual ideological terms) 'more and more civilians are militarized'.

Here Thompson's lack of a historical perspective on warfare weakens his case. For the striking thing about the last forty years is the decline of military participation from its peak in World War II (a phenomenon which has engaged sociologists of war).[27] The first two phases of total war required that the people should be involved, not just ideologically, but practically: in conscript mass armies and in labour-intensive war industries. This high level of practical involvement meant too that the ideologies of total war were highly charged, full of direct meaning to those they affected. 'Democracy' in 1939–45 was not just a loose codeword, but a matter of survival against fascism and the promise of crucial social reforms. The first phase of the Cold War, in which nuclear weapons had not fully displaced 'conventional' at the core, maintained something of this sort of militarism. But the supremacy of nuclear weapons meant that the people were dispensable: not just in the future war itself, but increasingly in its preparation too. Far from being an active ideological factor, nuclear war-preparation became almost invisible in most western societies between the early 1960s and the end of the 1970s.

States were not seeking to mobilize their societies against external threats; they, and the people, were engrossed in economic and social problems in this period. And what has changed since 1979? Although Conservative politicians in the USA, Britain and West Germany have used military politics to some effect, and have in any case been forced to respond to the peace movements, there is no serious re-militarization of society – not even a real attempt at it.

Historical Pacifism and Social Change

This argument is important because it has major implications for the prospects, strategy and proposals of the peace movement. The original Cold War, like the war that preceded it, was a period of great political and social discipline in most western as well as eastern countries. The loosening of the Cold War system, coinciding with the economic boom, released diverse cultural and political energies. Social movements developed for nearly twenty years, after the brief anti-nuclear movement of the late 1950s and early 1960s, without directly engaging with the Cold War system or the arms race. Then, suddenly, at the turn of the 1980s, we had a massive peace movement, the social reasons for which (apart from the international and military developments) I suspect no one quite understands.

Where previously people had been engaging, in trade unions and political parties, churches and student movements, and in music, literature and film, with problems closer to 'home', they were now grappling with the largest, most overriding problems of their societies. It was a rapid discovery, or rediscovery, which involved recognizing both specific, horrifying realities *and* a general truth of the times. There has been a consequent tension in the peace movements between the focus on particular nuclear systems and opposition to the wider range of social and political supports for the Cold War.

Edward Thompson's analysis of the arms race did leave a problem of agency which his more orthodox socialist critics took up. Certainly the 'internal dynamic and reciprocal logic' of nuclear weaponry creates few forces for change within its own structures, narrowly defined. The science-intensive military establishments and arms industries supply a steady trickle of impressive individual critics to the peace movements: but there is no social force. This is very much in contrast to the earlier phases of total war, in which mass armies and civilian political mobilization created the conditions for social movements.

Where the potential for change arises is in the vast majority of society whose lives are ultimately conditioned by the nuclear arms race, and whose social existence here and now is affected by the economic and political priority for things nuclear. But there is a problem: the fact that this majority is only 'mobilized' for nuclear war preparations in relatively indirect ways means that there is no obvious dialectic of military participation and social movement as there was in the two world wars. Nuclear war is so vast and so remote that while realization of its awful nature can create intense awareness and activism, it can also make it difficult to sustain detailed campaigning and mass involvement in peace movements, and especially difficult to mobilize a social majority for peace.

Thompson's answer to this problem is to see the clear need for the peace movements to respond to the fundamental issues which are bound up with the Cold War. 'Peace' must be re-linked to 'freedom' (he develops a brilliant critique of the way in which these two concepts have been misappropriated by the two sides in the Cold War).[28] The peace movements must not be afraid to tackle the political consequences of the Cold War division of Europe, including the issues of human rights and democracy. They must 'draw on every affirmative response in our culture'. 'What is needed', he suggests, from and for all of us, 'Is a space free of Cold War crisis in which we can move.'[29]

The analysis here would suggest that this already exists. The bifurcation of society in nuclear-war preparation – between the 'deterrence-science militarism' of the elite and the 'spectator-sport militarism' of the mass, as Mann has put it[30] – means that most of society is largely demilitarized. People may enjoy (if that is the word) a vicarious, media-based ideological participation in distant local wars. There is a vicious 'sediment' of nationalism and militarism which wars like the Falklands may stir, 'clouding our political and cultural life', as Thompson put it.[31] But this is marginal to most people's daily lives – as Thompson says, 'The young are *bored* with the Cold War'[32] – and there are much more important, positive responses on which the movement against the nuclear arms race can draw.'

What this suggests is that peace movements must see themselves, if anything even more than Thompson's early 1980s writings suggest, as part of a broader social movement for change in Europe and beyond. Peace movements are not going to disappear as CND did in the mid-1960s: partly because of the developments in the arms race itself, partly because the movements exist on a wide international plane and have implanted themselves in institutions such as parties and churches which keep the issues at the centre of national debate in many countries. But the demonstration movement has clearly waned at the time of writing, and peace energies need a broadened focus to continue their impact.

Thompson's own concept of a strategic goal for the peace movement in Europe is that of a 'democratic peace', the hopes of which, thwarted after

1945, he sees as revived in the last few years. However vague and redolent of long-gone popular frontism this may seem, it is not such a bad banner under which to march. It links together the struggle against the nuclear-armed states with the struggle for human rights and democracy, in the West as well as the East. In the way it is proposed, it is clearly a programme for resolving, initially from below, the forty-year-old division of our continent. It stresses that this should be on the basis of democratic involvement of the peoples, and it does not foreclose – although some socialists might think it should, this might be to march ahead of our situation – the question of whether this will have an explicitly socialist form. Thompson judges, rightly in my view, that the logic of the failure of existing models of socialism is that a new socialist project will have to develop out of the democratic initiatives of the people.

Thompson's perspective offers both a way forward for the wider radical and democratic movements in both halves of Europe, and a perspective for the peace movements. To the former it says that they must bring their various issues and concerns together and challenge the Cold War division and nuclear threat to the peoples. To the latter it argues the breadth and depth of the movement which needs to be aroused. It also has implications for the way the peace movements define their goals and policies. This is a point of growing importance on which Thompson could, however, lay himself open to misinterpretation.

Put at its simplest, the problem is that if we affirm the military struggle for a democratic peace in 1939–45, but deny the nuclear arms race, we could seem to be advocating a conventional military defence as a solution to today's problems. The issue is complicated because peace movements are called upon to participate in the 'defence debates' of their countries. In such debates the assumption of the need for military defence is implicit and if you reject nuclear weapons you are asked to put something in their place. Political parties that reject nuclear weapons are quick to emphasize their commitment to military alliances and 'strong conventional defence'. The problem, as a recent advocate of 'alternative defence policies' has acknowledged, is that

> any superpower conflict in Europe would sooner or later become a nuclear war, even if there were no nuclear weapons in the continent. Even the Second World War went nuclear in the end. You *cannot* disinvent nuclear weapons. Therefore you have to disinvent war. The non-nuclear defence debate is not about rehabilitating war-fighting at lower levels of destruction. It is about developing defence postures and foreign policies which minimise the risk of war breaking out.[33]

The problem for the peace movement is, therefore, to put forward defence policies as 'stages along the road of disarmament' while being clear that no such defence policies can ever be applied in practice. In essence, it is to participate in the politics of deterrence while refusing the politics of war: trying to square the same circle as that of the nuclear armers, but with radically different ends in mind. Any version of an 'alternative defence policy' which puts forward a conventional weapons strategy as one which might actually be used in war is historically anachronistic in quite a dangerous way.[34]

Edward Thompson's own view on this issue has been defined in different ways. In some contexts he has defined himself narrowly as a 'nuclear pacifist';[35] in others he has elaborated further, concluding from the horrors of conventional weaponry that, 'It follows that it is no longer sufficient to clamour for nuclear disarmament. If European nations should go to war then the distinction between the nuclear and the conventional will soon be lost. We must therefore enlarge our objectives. We must work to disallow any kind of recourse to war.'[36]

This view might better be called 'historical pacifism' than nuclear pacifism: historical in the sense that it is based on the argument that we have reached a stage in the development of warfare and society where the recourse to war is increasingly unviable. However much earlier stages of total war offered meaningful political choices, no form of warfare in the advanced world can do that today; indeed nuclear proliferation combines with the alignment of regional and global conflicts to reduce the circumstances in which war is still justifiable anywhere to very much a residual category. E. P. Thompson's, and my, sort of pacifist is one who recognizes the role of war in the past, and is ready to support, even today, the right of the Nicaraguans to defend themselves against the CIA-funded 'Contras'. But we must see this as an increasingly exceptional and, in the context of the East–West conflict, risky policy, which we must work to avoid wherever we can.

The peace movements must, then, be seen as genuinely movements for peace, for a society without war or preparations for war: not for an alternative form of military 'collective security', even if we will accept that as a step along the way. While particular weapons systems remain focuses of attention, we must also define our political aims. If we accept a democratic peace as our goal, we must work to give this real meaning by building both within and between societies the kinds of freer, more equal and sharing relationships which will no longer permit of war.

Notes

This chapter was written in 1985. At that point the peace movement of the early 1980s, which Edward Thompson did so much to develop, had begun to subside – indeed it appeared (with the successful introduction of cruise missiles into Western Europe) to have been defeated. However, as William Morris once noted, it is often the case in human affairs that the things which people fight for, and appear to lose, are then achieved by different means and under another name. When I wrote, neither *perestroika* nor *glasnost* was in our common vocabulary, but the politics which they signify in the Soviet Union have succeeded in opening up scope for 'democratic peace' which is beyond anything we could have hoped for at the start of the decade. I write on the day after the Berlin Wall has been opened; a dramatic moment which shows how far 'beyond the Cold War' we have moved in a very short space of time. Edward's vision – and that of European Nuclear Disarmament as a whole – has been triumphantly vindicated, however many obstacles remain to our hopes of a united, democratic and peaceful Europe, and however real are still the dangers of war on a global scale. The argument of this chapter is, I believe, fully sustained by the deconstruction of 'socialist militarism' in Eastern Europe, a remarkably rapid extension of the process of 'demilitarization' which I have outlined. But if I were writing it today I would wish to stress even more the historic importance of the European peace movement in calling forth the end of the Cold War and the re-unification of Europe – and Edward Thompson's unique contribution to this. (November 1989)

1 Martin Shaw, 'War, Peace and British Marxism, 1895–1945', in Richard Taylor and Nigel Young (eds), *Campaigns for Peace* (Manchester: Manchester University Press, 1986).

2 E. P. Thompson, *The Making of the English Working Class* (London: Victor Gollancz, 1963).

3 James Hinton, *The First Shop Stewards Movement* (London: Allen & Unwin, 1973).

4 James Hinton, *Labour and Socialism* (Brighton: Wheatsheaf Books, 1983).

5 For example, Geoffrey Best, *War and Society in Revolutionary Europe, 1770–1870* (London: Fontana, 1982), chapters 1 and 2.

6 W. H. McNeill, *The Pursuit of Power* (Oxford: Basil Blackwell, 1983), chapters 7 and 8.

7 Friedrich Engels, 'The Force Theory', in Bernard Semmel (ed.), *Marxism and the Science of War* (Oxford: Oxford University Press, 1981), p. 57.

8 Martin Shaw, 'War, Imperialism and the State System: a Critique of Orthodox Marxism for the 1980s', in Shaw (ed.), *War, State and Society* (London: Macmillan, 1984), pp. 52–9.

9 Mary Kaldor, 'Warfare and Capitalism', in Thompson et al., *Exterminism and Cold War* (London: Verso, 1982), pp. 268–70.

10 E. P. Thompson, 'The Liberation of Perugia', in *The Heavy Dancers* (London: Merlin, 1985), p. 200.

11 Ibid., pp. 199–201, and 'VE Day', *Sanity* (May 1985), pp. 18–24.

12 Martin Shaw, *Socialism and Militarism* (Nottingham: Spokesman, 1981).

13 Thompson, 'The Liberation of Perugia', pp. 190–4.
14 E. P. Thompson, 'Notes on Exterminism, the Last Stage of Civilisation', in Thompson et al., *Exterminism and Cold War*, pp. 4–5.
15 Raymond Williams, 'The Politics of Nuclear Disarmament' in ibid., pp. 67–70.
16 Thompson, 'Europe, the Weak Link in the Cold War', in ibid., p. 330.
17 See Mike Davis, 'Nuclear Imperialism and Extended Deterrence', in ibid., pp. 35–64; Ernest Mandel, 'The Threat of Nuclear War and the Struggle for Socialism', *New Left Review*, 141, (Sept.–Oct. 1983).
18 For the working class, Mandel, 'The Threat of Nuclear War'; for Third World revolution, Davis, 'Nuclear Imperialism', Fred Halliday, 'The Sources of the New Cold War', in Thompson et al., *Exterminism and Cold War*.
19 C. Wright Mills, *The Causes of World War III* (London: Secker & Warburg, 1958).
20 Georg Lukács, *History and Class Consciousness* (London: Merlin, 1973); Herbert Marcuse, 'Industrialisation and Capitalism', *New Left Review*, 30 (March–April 1965).
21 Ralph Miliband, 'The Politics of Peace and War', in Shaw (ed.), *War, State and Society*, pp. 119–36.
22 Fred Halliday, *The Making of the Second Cold War* (London: Verso, 1983).
23 Mandel, 'The Threat of Nuclear War', p. 29.
24 Miliband, 'The Politics of Peace and War', pp. 122–3.
25 E. P. Thompson, *Beyond the Cold War* (London: Merlin, 1982), p. 23.
26 Thompson, 'Notes on Exterminism', pp. 22–3.
27 Shaw, 'The Rise and Fall of the Military-Democratic State: Britain 1940–85', in Colin Creighton and Martin Shaw (eds), *The Sociology of War and Peace* (London: Macmillan, 1986); for the analyses of the 'wartime participation' effect, see particularly the work of Arthur Marwick, *Britain in the Century of Total War* (London: Bodley Head, 1968) and *War and Social Change in the Twentieth Century* (London: Macmillan, 1977).
28 Thompson, *Beyond the Cold War*.
29 Ibid., p. 33.
30 Michael Mann, 'The Roots and Contradictions of Modern Militarism', *New Left Review*, 162 (March–April 1987).
31 E. P. Thompson, 'The War of Thatcher's Face', in *Zero Option* (London: Merlin, 1983), p. 195.
32 Thompson, *Beyond the Cold War*, p. 32.
33 James Hinton, 'The Case for the Defence', *Marxism Today* (April 1985), p. 17.
34 A book which, in my view, succumbs to this danger, by trying to reinstate a 1939–45 model of 'home defence' which is now anachronistic, is Peter Tatchell's *Democratic Defence* (London: GMP/Heretic, 1985).
35 Thompson, 'VE Day', p. 18; interestingly, Miliband also opts for 'nuclear pacifism', 'The Politics of Peace and War', p. 131.
36 Thompson, 'The Liberation of Perugia'.

10

E. P. Thompson, the British Marxist Historical Tradition and the Contemporary Crisis

Harvey J. Kaye

In this final chapter I would like to present a set of reflections on the continuing relevance of the British Marxist historical tradition in the face of the contemporary mutual crises of history and socialism, in which the great 'governing narratives' by which we comprehend past, present and possible futures are being revised or rejected.[1] Thus, after reviewing the principal contributions of the British Marxist historians to history and social thought as a collective or tradition, I shall consider those contributions in terms of what they offer to historical and political practice today, focusing in the latter half of the essay on their work, especially that of E. P. Thompson, as 'historical critics'. I begin, however, with an autobiographical note.

When I was a child, my grandfather would come to our house almost every weekend and on those occasions he introduced me to 'the past' – or at least what I took to be the past. Most often he would read to me from a collection of Old Testament Bible stories. On other occasions, he would tell me about coming to America as a Russian-Jewish immigrant and about growing up on the lower East Side of New York. My grandfather was a courtroom lawyer (a barrister) and he had a fantastic way of telling stories. Equally important, I later learned, was that he had been a young socialist before and during his years in law school. It is quite likely that his particular – perhaps 'political' – renderings of the Old Testament shaped my sense of the stories. What I heard from my grandfather was a history of exploitation and oppression but, also, a history of dissent and struggle *and* exodus, redemption, liberation and revolution. I was captivated and inspired by the narrative he offered and in spite of the mediocre and unchallenging history I was taught at school, I was determined to read it at university.

Indeed, I eventually did receive a first degree in History, but I switched to the social sciences at the graduate level, assuming that I could work in what was coming to be known as historical sociology. For several reasons I was committed at the time to Latin American Studies and specifically I wanted to write my doctoral dissertation as an historical sociology of landlord–peasant relations in Spanish America.[2] What I had found in writings on the subject was that, although attention had been given to the landlords' domination of the peasantry and, increasingly, peasant resistance and rebellion, there was still little sense that the movement, the historical development, of those polities and social orders were shaped by peasant and worker struggles. The crucial conflicts were adjudged, historically, to be those between landed and mercantile elites. Of course, there were historical models available in North America for the kind of work I wanted to pursue. There was Barrington Moore, Jr's *Social Origins of Dictatorship and Democracy*, which effectively licensed the historical-sociological enterprise for many of us; and also there were the studies of southern slavery by Eugene Genovese.[3] It was in Genovese's writings in particular that I found a theoretical perspective and it was through him that I discovered the British Marxist historians, for the path from Genovese led to Maurice Dobb and the 'transition question', then to Rodney Hilton and landlord–peasant conflicts, and onwards to Christopher Hill, George Rudé, Eric Hobsbawm and E. P. Thompson. Essentially, in the British Marxist historical tradition I not only came upon a range of ideas and insights for my dissertation; I rediscovered the kind of history to which my grandfather had introduced me twenty years earlier. It recounted both the experience of exploitation and oppression *and* the episodes of dissent and struggle; it was committed and passionate; and it was connected to a larger problematic. (Little did I know that its authors were in several cases themselves raised in Old Testament traditions!)[4]

The British Marxist historical tradition is hardly singular. Consider the variety in the following. The 'debate on the transition to capitalism' initiated by Maurice Dobb's *Studies in the Development of Capitalism*: originating in the deliberations of the Communist Party Historians' Group and pursued on an international scale in the pages of the American journal, *Science & Society*, the debate established the framework for most of the historians' later works.[5] 'People's History': imbued in the Historians' Group by A. L. Morton's pioneering synthesis, *A People's History of England*, and the efforts of Dona Torr, exemplified by *Tom Mann and His Times*, this practice connects the senior historians with the History Workshop movement of socialist and feminist historians among the principal instigators of which has been Raphael Samuel, a schoolboy member of the original Historians' Group.[6] 'Labour history': fomented by the Society for the Study of Labour History which includes among its founders Eric Hobsbawm, John Saville and Dorothy Thompson, this field now encompasses both the chronicles of the 'Labour Movement' and the broader history of the working class.[7] 'Cultural Studies': originating in the writings of Richard Hoggart, Raymond Williams and Stuart Hall and pursued most energetically by the students and graduates of the Birmingham Centre for Contemporary Cultural Studies, this enterprise was also clearly inspired by E. P. Thompson's *The Making of the English Working Class*.[8] And yet another strand of the 'tradition' (to which I shall return), represented by the work of Victor Kiernan, Ralph Miliband, John Saville and Perry Anderson, and more recently Philip Corrigan and Derek Sayer, has attended to ruling classes, power and the State.

Nevertheless, if we treat the 'core' of the tradition – which in our respective ways is what Bill Schwarz did in his article on the 'Historians' Group, 1946–56'[9] and I did in *The British Marxist Historians* – then it would have to be said that beyond the outstanding accomplishments of the historians in their particular fields of study there have been four paramount contributions which they have made as a 'collective'. First has been the development of 'class-struggle analysis'. Derived from *The Communist Manifesto*, the central working hypothesis of the British Marxist historians has been that 'The history of all hitherto existing society is the history of class struggle'. Thus, the medieval world was not harmoniously organized into three estates but was an order of struggle between lords and peasants; the conflicts of the seventeenth century were not a mere civil war but a 'bourgeois revolution' driven by struggles of the lower orders as well; the eighteenth century was not conflict-free but shot through with antagonisms between 'patricians and plebians' which, moreover, were expressions of 'class-struggle without class', and the Industrial Revolution entailed not only economic and social changes but, in the course of the conflicts between 'Capital and Labour', a dramatic process of class formation determined in great part by the agency of workers themselves. Revisions have been made to these stories but the centrality of class struggle persists. Moreover, such struggle has not been limited to moments of outright rebellion or revolution. The British Marxist historians have enlarged the scope of what is to be understood as 'struggle' and, thus, in addition to rebellion and revolution we now have 'resistance' as part of our historical vocabulary.

The second contribution has been the pursuit and development of 'history from the bottom up'. Perhaps the finest statement of the imperative behind this perspective was offered by the German-Jewish critic, Walter Benjamin, when he wrote: 'Only that historian will have the gift of fanning the spark of hope in the past who is firmly convinced that *even the dead* will not be safe from the enemy (the ruling class) if he wins. And the enemy has not ceased to be victorious'.[10] The British Marxist historians have sought to redeem, or *reappropriate*, the experience and the agency of the lower orders – peasants, plebians, artisans and workers. In fact, history from the bottom up has come to be equated with the 'history of the common people' and I expect we are all familiar with the words, quoted before in this volume, which have become something of an 'oath' for young social historians: 'I am seeking to rescue the poor stockinger, the Luddite cropper, the "obsolete" handloom weavers, the utopian artisan and even the deluded follower of Joanna Southcott, from the enormous condescension of posterity . . .'[11] Granted that the *Annales* historians can be seen as having initiated 'history from below', they did not, however, pursue it with an interest in class struggle and 'agency' as have the British historians. Actually, it might be said that whereas the British Marxists have been pursuing a 'revolutionary' English past, the *Annales* historians seem to have been running from the demands of 1789, 1830 and 1848. Again, history from the bottom up was originally conceived to be a 'perspective'. As I tell my students, let's get our prepositions straight: it is not merely history *of* the bottom, but *from* the bottom *up*. Through the history of the common people we have gained much, but perhaps some revision is in order.

The third contribution of the historians has been the recovery and assemblage of a 'radical democratic tradition' in which have been asserted what might be called 'counter-hegemonic' conceptions of liberty, equality and community. In Gramscian – as opposed to Leninist – fashion, the historians have revealed not a history of political ideas originating inside the heads of intellectuals, but a history of popular ideology standing in dialogical relationship to the history of politics and ideas. Alongside Magna Carta we are offered the English Rising of 1381; outside of Parliament in the seventeenth century we encounter Levellers, Diggers and (dare one say it?) Ranters; in the eighteenth century, we not only hear Wilkes but also the crowds of London asserting the 'rights of the freeborn Englishman'; and in the Age of Revolution, we are reminded that within the 'exceptionalism' of English political life there were Jacobins, Luddites, Captain Swing and Chartists (the last representing the first working-class political party seeking, at the least, political democracy). At the same time, it must be noted that the British Marxists do have their 'intellectuals': John Ball and his fellow priests; Milton and Winstanley; Wilkes, Paine and Wollstonecraft; Wordsworth and Blake; and Cobbett, Owen, Jones, Marx and Morris.

Finally, another contribution of primary importance is that by way of class-struggle analysis, history from the bottom up and the recovery of the radical-democratic tradition, the British Marxist historians have effectively helped to undermine the great 'Grand Narratives' of both the right and the left. Their labours directly challenged the Whig version of history in which the development of English life and freedoms is comprehended as a continuous evolutionary and progressive process. And they also helped to clear away the (supposedly) Marxist presentation of history in which historical development is conceived of in unilinear, mechanical and techno-economistic terms.[12] This may not have been their intention back in the early days of the Historians' Group, but surely their persistent stress on the *historical* in historical materialism led them to it. I hope we are all in agreement that this fourth contribution has been a liberating process though necessarily one which entails its own challenges of both a historiographical and a political nature.

It is tempting to claim that the British Marxist historical tradition has actually become an Anglo-American tradition, for the influence of the British historians on American historical writings has been remarkably extensive. Their work has shaped both American labour studies – from writings on colonial and republican artisans to those on immigrant workers and industrial proletarians – and agrarian studies – from writings on the Antebellum and Reconstruction South to those on farmers' movements in the Midwest.[13] Additionally, American historians and social scientists have taken the British Marxist tradition to such places as highland South America, Southeast Asia, Europe and even back to Britain itself. In fact, considering the aggressive and enthusiastic efforts of Robert Brenner and Immanuel Wallerstein, has not the debate on the transition to capitalism now migrated to America?[14] Moreover, British Marxism has influenced women studies and feminist scholarship, educational, cultural and literary studies, and the exploration of contemporary social and political questions including 'critical legal studies'.[15] In turn, one might register the influence of the work of American Marxist historians like Eugene Genovese and David Montgomery, on that of the British.[16]

Noteworthy in this vein is that the attacks on socialist, especially Marxist, historians initiated by Thatcher and her allies[17] have been echoed most loudly in America by Professor Gertrude Himmelfarb, a leading historian of nineteenth-century British political culture and ideas and *the* leading voice of neo-conservative historiography in the United States. Himmelfarb's critiques of recent historiographical developments are well known. She decries the rise of the 'new' social history for its neglect of politics and its rejection of a narrative style of presentation (criticisms for which I must admit to having a certain sympathy). However, as one might imagine, since the British Marxist historians' scholarly efforts are essentially 'political' history framed by a specific narrative scheme, Himmelfarb's hostility to their work is of a different order. In her review article of *The British Marxist Historians* and the MARHO interviews, *Visions of History*, in the American magazine, *The New Republic*, she pursued a decidedly 'Cold War' attack on their scholarship.[18] That is, she did not challenge their studies as history – at least not directly – but, rather, she conjured up a shadowy image of 'Stalinism' standing behind their careers. We should not be too surprised to see that, in the past few years, Himmelfarb has fervently taken up Thatcher's celebration of a particular rendition of Victorian Britain and that she is proffering it on both side of the Atlantic.[19] Once again we are reminded that history *is* politics.

This brings us to the present juncture. After almost a decade of the Thatcher government[20] with its class warfare from above against the unions, local democracy, freedom of expression, and the welfare state, and its concomitant service to Capital and centralization of State powers, it has been presumed that the Conservatives have undermined the post-war 'social democratic' consensus. Excuse the sociologist in me for resorting to them, but the polls I have read indicate that although Britons in the majority do see the country after ten years of 'Thatcherism' as 'richer' they also see it as 'sadder' – which is not exactly the basis for a new 'consensus'. In fact, other surveys seem to indicate that the social-democratic consensus may not have actually collapsed for, apparently, working people still believe in the justice of a 'downwards' redistribution of wealth to be carried out by the State.[21] That seems to run directly counter to the Conservatives' hegemonic ambitions. We ought not to be optimistic, however, for here's the rub: the very same surveys indicate a widespread cynicism about the ability of the 'common people' to do anything to bring about such a project. In other words, what we find is 'resignation' not consensus. Of course, no historiography should subordinate itself to the politics of the moment, but surely the problem of resignation and accommodation in the face of an aggressive anti-democratic politics should make us reflect a bit, especially since the British Marxist historical tradition has been a historiography of 'agency'. At the same time, it must be acknowledged that the British Marxists' narrative has been essentially a long chronicle of 'tragedy' or, to play with the title of a recent work by Christopher Hill, 'the experience of defeat'.[22] We might put a somewhat more 'progressive' spin on it by recalling William Morris's words in *The Dream of John Ball*: 'I pondered how men fight and lose the battle, and the thing they fought for comes about in spite of their defeat, and when it comes turns out to be not what they meant, and other men have to fight for what they meant under another name.' We can probably do no better than to read the past in exactly such a manner, but at present we need to put it more starkly: 'The enemy has not ceased to be victorious.'

In that light I would like to offer a few thoughts on the practices fostered by the British Marxist historians considering in particular their recovery of the radical democratic tradition and what it represents for the regeneration of a left 'public discourse' and, possibly, the making of a new grand narrative. First, regarding class-struggle analysis, it should be evident that we need to explore ever more deliberately the intimate relations between and among the experiences of class and gender and race and ethnicity. A fuller understanding and appreciation of, for example, the formation of classes and their identities – above and below – and, thus, their modes of inclusion and exclusion depends on it. Obviously, British Marxist historians have begun to take up the question of gender and class (one immediately thinks of Sheila Rowbotham, Barbara Taylor and Catherine Hall, among others),[23] but such work has just started, relatively speaking. As Hall states in conclusion to her contribution to the present volume: 'The complexities of the relation between class and culture have received much attention. It is time for gender and culture to be subjected to more critical scrutiny.'

Even less often explored is the articulation of class, race, ethnicity and national identity. Very much on the political agenda and in 'the news', this question must join the Marxist historical agenda. Perhaps on this question British historians might want to have a look at the work of American social historians of the Left, not because of the media 'line' that Britain is now suffering what the United States has long had, a 'race problem', or because after all the benefits Americans have derived from British historians, we owe you something; but, rather, because American studies in this area indicate both the ways in which ethnicity and race presented obstacles to effective class formation *and* how such seemingly insurmountable barriers have on certain occasions been transcended.[24] I am suggesting no more than what I did for my dissertation: read the American works not for formulas but for questions and ideas. Britain has had its own *long* history of race and ethnicity intersecting with class conflicts and, most significantly, nation-state formation. In such terms consider again the notion of being 'British' as opposed to Welsh, Scottish or English (not to mention Irish). Furthermore, as Victor Kiernan recounts in 'Britons Old and New', the Norman Conquest was hardly the last arrival of Europeans alone to settle on the island and greatly upset the locals.[25] Marxist historians might even wish to take the lead in deliberations on how to incorporate the historical experiences of black people into British historical education; imagine the innovations which might be effected in the tradition of the 'free-born Briton' past and present in this generation and the next by way of the black and Asian presence in Britain. In this light, as a counterpart to 'imperial history', Marxist historians should consider the international and multi-racial 'British' history proposed by Robin Blackburn's recent book, *The Overthrow of Colonial Slavery*, in its exploration of the connections between political and class struggles for 'freedom' in Britain and the Caribbean.[26]

The second observation, or suggestion, I would make relates to history from the bottom up. Whereas some would call for a break with this approach, I would say that what is really needed is a return to a fuller idea of history from the bottom up as a 'perspective', or as Barrington Moore Jr put it: 'a [critical] sympathy with the victims . . . and a skepticism about the claims of the victors'.[27] And from that vantage point we do need to be more concerned with what Perry Anderson has called the 'intricate machinery of class domination'. That is, more investigation should be undertaken of: ruling-class formation, deformation and reformation; ruling-class values, aspirations and expectations; the State in all its complexity; modes of exploitation and appropriation; and processes of hegemony within and without the State apparatus. We just do not know enough about these things; yet they are what makes the perspective of history from the bottom up necessary, and how are we to comprehend class *relations* without them? As F. Stirton Weaver has observed: 'Class societies are not a product of nature. It takes great human effort and struggle to create and maintain a system in which some people do the work from which others derive the benefits'; and as Victor Kiernan has remarked: 'In general, as in Britain today, the upper classes have been in the driving seat because they are more united, more class conscious, better equipped, and politically more intelligent.'[28]

Perhaps American social history and social science have something to offer here as well. I am thinking in particular of such writers as C. Wright Mills, Paul Sweezy, Paul Baran, Harry Braverman, William Appleman Williams, James Weinstein, Gabriel Kolko, William Domhoff and Christopher Lasch whose respective works and theoretical perspectives are quite varied, but might all be encompassed by the term 'power structure studies'.[29] The goal of such research and writings has been to uncover the power, wealth and degree of cohesion of the elites, or ruling classes, and to reveal the modes of appropriation, manipulation and political and ideological domination which they have exercised or others have exercised on their behalf. This practice is the scholarly counterpart to the radical American political tradition of decrying the concentration of wealth and power (and, thus, the emergence of an 'aristocracy') as a corruption of the American democratic ideal – which, I tell my students, is derived in part from the Levellers. In one respect, British socialist writers would do very well to attend to such a model for those American scholars of the Left have not hesitated to explore twentieth-century and contemporary history – a pursuit which has been significantly absent from the British Marxist historical tradition. Otherwise, however, we should all be careful with such studies for they have characteristically denied working-class and popular agency. What is actually required is not merely power-structure studies, but class *structuration* studies focusing on the ruling classes; and class structuration has been, as I have argued before, a central concern of the British Marxist historians.

Therefore, after considering the American studies one might return to the British tradition for, as I noted earlier, there is a strand which has concerned itself with ruling classes, power and the State. It is best represented by the writings of Victor Kiernan such as *The Lords of Human Kind*, *State and Society in Europe, 1550–1650*, and *The Duel in European History: Honour and the Reign of the Aristocracy*.[30] Also, one must note the volumes on European State formation by Perry Anderson, *Passages from Antiquity to Feudalism* and *Lineages of the Absolutist State*; that on English State formation, *The Great Arch*, by Philip Corrigan and Derek Sayer; and a recent work, *1848: The British State and Chartism*, by John Saville.[31] The last is an excellent study of a dramatic moment in the making of the Victorian State and ruling-class hegemony which, it should be added, makes us think again about English 'exceptionalism' and reminds us that at least in the nineteenth century the propertied realized that the struggle for democracy and socialism were co-equal. Arguably, all of this has also been present, at least to some extent, at the 'core' of the tradition; especially if one thinks about Hill's early writings on the Church, English State and Puritanism, Hilton's book *A Medieval Society*, Thompson's *Whigs and Hunters*,[32] and Eric Hobsbawm's magnificent trilogy on the long nineteenth century.[33]

Remember, there is always the danger that such history can have the effect of merely inspiring even greater cynicism about the worth of popular agency – unless Walter Benjamin was right when he said that working-class political struggle is 'nourished more by the image of enslaved ancestors than liberated grandchildren'.[34] Nevertheless, it is essential that Marxist historical study continue to work towards the recognition of the ways that the agency of the lower orders have actually *structured* power, a recognition of the fact that it has made a difference. Such agency includes revolution, rebellion and resistance in all their variety possibly including even accommodation which may well signify an intense will to survive, to bear witness, and perhaps, to fight another day. A possible starting point for what I have in mind was proposed by the English literary critic, Terry Eagleton, at an American conference on 'The Literary Imagination and the Sense of the Past' when he said: 'What is meant by reading history from the standpoint of the oppressed is not that the oppressed are the concealed, forgotten, inarticulate, abandoned "subject" of history; it means, rather, grasping history as constructed from within the constraints that the oppressed, by their very existence impose.'[35] In essence, we need to reveal the faces of power and to de-reify their expressions by showing their *social* origins and indicating how they have also been determined by the dominated themselves.[36]

Lastly, then, what about the further recovery of the 'radical democratic tradition' and the possibility of a new synthesis or grand narrative of British history developed from a Marxian perspective? My call for increased study of ruling classes past and present is not at all intended to discourage the effort of mobilizing and further articulating a radical democratic and socialist heritage. Indeed, such labours are crucial to my final suggestion which is that at the same time that socialist historians (on both sides of the Atlantic!) continue to work within the historical discipline they should seek the reinvigoration of the practice of historical and social *criticism*. Admittedly, this ambition arises most immediately from the growing recognition within the American Left that it has been marginalized – or, as some have argued, marginalized itself – from the realm of *public* discourse. While the right continues to rail on (to truly myth-making proportions) about the strength and significance of the left's presence in American academic life, left scholars and writers are themselves ever more conscious of the fact that they have failed to confront adequately the rise of the New Right and its commanding presence in public intellectual and political debates.[37] Yet my proposal also emerges from ongoing discussions in Britain and Europe regarding the future of socialism as a movement and historical project. However sceptical I remain of the arguments of 'post-Marxist' and 'post-modern' socialists who believe that contemporary history has transcended 'class struggles', leaving the imperative of working-class agency in its wake, they have reawakened the left to the legacy of liberal and democratic thought and rhetoric and, at the same time, compelled a reconsideration of the political and moral role of intellectuals.[38] Furthermore, common to the deliberations of both the American and British lefts, it seems, are the beginnings of a renewed appreciation of the necessity of history in 'breaking the tyranny of the present'. For example, John Keane has recently reiterated the importance of a 'democratic remembrance of things past': 'An active democratic memory recognizes that the development of fresh and stimulating perspectives on the present depends upon criticisms that break up habitual ways of thinking, in part through types of criticism which remember what is in danger of being forgotten.'[39]

At the outset, the further recovery of the radical democratic tradition is for our own edification because it will provide an essential reminder that the most effectively democratic criticism is advanced, as Michael Walzer contends in his book, *Interpretation and Social Criticism*, not by alienated or detached intellectuals equipped with new and better theories discovered on a distant mountain-top or invented in the solitude of a philosopher's study but by 'connected critics' engaged in the interpretation and 'original' elaboration of existing or historically recovered and grounded values and aspirations. This does not, it should be made clear, represent a commitment to the status quo. Indeed, more than others, Marxists should be sensitive to the fact that it is in the very nature of class-structured societies that there is an incoherence between ideal and reality and that the differential experience of that reality by rulers and ruled affords an opening for political engagement: 'Morality is always potentially subversive of class and power.' Furthermore, as Antonio Gramsci realized, in the course of the struggle to secure its hegemony, a ruling class must necessarily take into account the interests and expectations of the ruled and, too, make sacrifices. Thus, even in a seemingly 'coherent' social order there is a ground, a space, an opening, for criticism. As Gramsci contends in *The Prison Notebooks*, socialist critics must initiate 'a process of differentiation and change in the relative weight that the elements of the old ideologies used to possess. What was previously secondary and subordinate, or even incidental, is now taken to be primary and becomes the nucleus of a new ideological and theoretical complex.'[40]

On reflection, is this not what has been best in the 'Radical-democratic tradition', according to the British Marxist historians? Against those who had portrayed the English Rising of 1381 as 'fanatical *prophetae* mixed with disoriented and desperate masses on the very margin of society', Hilton has shown that the Rising was a uniquely class-conscious movement of peasants and artisans; and, moreover, that the importance of John Ball and his fellow village clerics was that they 'seem to have reinforced the peasant demands for freedom of status and tenure by a broader articulation of contemporary feelings'. Indeed, he continues:

> What is remarkable is the way that their vision of a society of free and equal men and women fused with the ancient peasant demand for freedom of status and tenure, in the formulation of a programme which, though entirely capable of realisation, given the historical forces at work in the late middle ages, did challenge root and branch the ideas of the ruling class.[41]

Then there are Hill's studies of the religious and secular dimensions of the ideological origins of the English Revolution in which he highlights the respective roles of Puritan preachers and lecturers and of 'intellectuals' such as Bacon, Raleigh and Coke in inspiring 'confidence' in 'the middle sort of people' by articulating and giving voice to their ideals and aspirations. And it was this 'class' which made the Civil War into a revolution. Similarly, there are Hill's portraits of the radical religious figures, like Winstanley, whose 'original' renditions of the ideas of the middle sort began to capture the imagination of the lower orders threatening a '"democratic" revolution-in-the revolution'.[42]

Thompson's classic, *The Making of the English Working Class*, also reveals such a political praxis. The book magnificently illustrates how the *formation* of the working class in the Industrial Revolution entailed a broadening and deepening of the tradition of 'the free-born Englishman' and, too, as Terry Eagleton denotes, the making of a '*counter*-public sphere' to that of the 'bourgeois' public sphere: 'In the Corresponding Societies, the radical press, Owenism, Cobbett's *Political Register* and Paine's *Rights of Man*, feminism and the dissenting churches, a whole oppositional network of journals, clubs, pamphlets, debates and institutions invades the dominant consensus, threatening to fragment it from within'.[43] In the late eighteenth century it was Tom Paine who contributed most as an 'intellectual' to advancing the tradition of the free-born Englishman; although, as Thompson argues, the significance of the ideas he set forth in *The Rights of Man* was not so much in their originality, which was limited, but in their connecting with and re-articulating existing sentiments, assumptions and aspirations. Paine provided 'a new rhetoric of Radical egalitarianism which touched the deepest responses of the "free-born Englishman" and which penetrated the sub-political attitudes of the urban working people'. The arguments of the *Rights of Man* broke through the categories and conventions of constitutionalism which had structured the moral consensus and set forth far wider democratic claims that were so crucial to the emergence of the labour movement.[44] A few years earlier Thompson had written 'Homage to Tom Maguire' in which he appreciatively revealed a political practice that embodied in real historical terms Gramsci's 'organic intellectual'. Maguire, the worker, poet and socialist organizer who was so instrumental in the establishment of the ILP in the West Riding of Yorkshire 'had been the point of junction between the theoretical understanding of the national leaders, the moral teachings of Morris and Carpenter, and the needs and aspirations of his own people'.[45]

Indeed, I would propose that in their very efforts to recover the radical democratic tradition, the British Marxist historians have themselves been working not simply as historical scholars but, at the same time, as historical critics, most especially (though not alone) Edward Thompson. Indeed, Thompson is greatly admired for this in the United States and in the aforementioned American discussions on the need to reinvigorate the 'public voice' on the intellectual Left his work is regularly cited as a model of historically-informed political and social criticism. For example, writing in review of Perry Anderson's critique of Thompson's history, theory and politics, *Arguments Within English Marxism*, Marcus Rediker poses the question: 'How can historians produce politically useful knowledge?' Acknowledging the theoretical rigour of Anderson's criticism, Rediker nevertheless endorses Thompson's practice over that of Anderson not only because he is more sympathetic towards Thompson's view of the purpose of Marxist historical study but, also, because of the 'democratic' aspirations and commitments which characterize Thompson's thought and are expressed in his writings. In particular, Rediker recommends Thompson to us for the manner in which he seeks to engage his audience: 'Thompson writes with continual human reference, affirming certain values over and against others, and he tries to make his readers active valuing agents as they think about history and politics.' Moreover, in contrast to Anderson, whose primary audience is 'the Left, in both its academic and institutional forms', Thompson addresses himself not merely to the Left and to fellow historians, but as well, to a popular *and* working-class audience.[46]

To refer once again to *The Making of the English Working Class*, it should be recalled that it was written by a politically engaged socialist both as a critique of Old *and* New Left assumptions about working-class consciousness and agency and as a challenge to historians' and social scientists' renditions and assessments of working-class experience and struggles in the Industrial Revolution and their contributions to the making of modern British political and cultural life. Moreover, as an adult education tutor during the years in which he was preparing the book, Thompson says he wrote it not for academics but with working people and the Labour Movement in mind. In the preface to a collection of essays by the American radical historian, Staughton Lynd, whom he refers to as a fellow 'Objector', Thompson explains that 'as we argue about the past so also are we arguing about – and seeking to clarify – the mind of the present which is recovering that past. Nor is this an unimportant part of the mind of the present. For some of the largest arguments about human rationality, destiny and agency, must always be grounded there: in the historical record.'[47] In just this spirit, Fred Inglis, the English education critic, has described *The Making of the English Working Class* along with Thompson's other historical studies, as providing the working class with 'a new past to live from; it changes the social memory so that, differently understanding how the present came about, the agent thinks forward to a new set of possibilities.'[48]

The historical imagination and intentions which have determined his study of the past have also shaped Thompson's specifically political writings. As I have observed before, Thompson's political interventions recall those of Tom Paine and William Cobbett. Indeed, I recently came upon G. D. H. Cole's portrait of Cobbett from which it is worth quoting at length, for Cole's description of the Radical Cobbett might well have been provided as an introduction to Thompson:

There are certain Englishmen who, being memorable for much besides, make me think, whenever they come into one's mind, of

England . . . Cobbett was an Englishman in this very special sense . . . .
Bluff, egotistical, shrewd, capable of meanness as well as of
greatness, positive in all things and desperately wrong in some – but
also devastatingly right in many more – no theorist till he could see
with his own eyes the human stuff of which problems are made,
quick to anger and indignation but also infinitely friendly; didactical
and often overbearing and yet full of sympathy; very well satisfied
with himself and ever ready to hold his own experience up as an
example to others; and therewith possessed of a singular power of
identifying himself with the country he loved and the people for
whom he fought – there you have the portrait of this tall, gawky,
florid exuberant farmer who looked like a farmer . . . . Above all else,
I think of Cobbett as the man who, at a wretched time in the history
of the English people, put hope into their hearts, not by telling lies or
painting fancy pictures, either of this world or the next, but by good
solid cursing that never degenerated into a whine or a mere
vapouring of despair, but bade men gird up their loins and struggle
for the right . . . . He was angry, exceedingly angry; but there was
always love as well as anger in his words. He loved the people on
whose behalf he made crusade; and, equally with the people, he
loved the land they lived in – the villages and churches, the great
houses with their parks of orderly trees, the birds and beasts, the
downs and valleys and rivers and streams, the crops that grew out of
the earth and, last but not least, the earth itself. The smell and feel of
the countryside were his tonic.

For Cobbett was one of those evangelists who see the future by
looking to the past. Maybe the past they think they see is not quite
what really was; for they are as ready to pick out from it the things
they love and value as to pick out what is bad in the present . . .[49]

Thompson's own anger is well known. Over the past decade it has been
directed against a range of targets. In the early 1950s he spoke out against
the 'threat' posed by the importation of US capitalism and commercial
values; then, in 1956, against the Soviet invasion of Hungary and the
British Communist Party which had refused to denounce the action and,
in the process, democratize itself; and, thereafter, against the politics of
both the so-called 'revolutionary' left and the Labour Party leadership.[50]
During the 1960s he turned to confront the new editorial leadership of the
New Left Review, in particular Perry Anderson and Tom Nairn, who
had taken over the journal from Thompson and his fellow co-founders
and were proceeding to offer what they called a 'global critique' of British
history and society *and* the Labour Movement from the vantage point of
historical and theoretical models derived from continental European

Marxisms.[51] In the 1970s Thompson continued to question the 'importation' of Western European Marxisms by a younger generation of theorists; most aggressively and spectacularly he challenged the ascendance of the 'structuralist Marxism' developed by the French Communist philosopher, Louis Althusser. But also in these years he directed broadsides against the powers-that-be of the British Establishment who, in the face of a series of political and economic crises, had proceeded to trample on civil rights and liberties and threaten the social and economic gains secured in the past.[52] Finally, in the 1980s Thompson joined in the reinvigoration of the Campaign for Nuclear Disarmament (CND) and, as a co-founder of European Nuclear Disarmament (END), energetically called for the tearing down of the Cold War blocs and opposed Thatcher's championing of Reagan's missile deployment and the military adventurism of both.[53]

It is not merely that Thompson has regularly been moved to anger and indignation, but that in venting them he has persistently sought to position himself *within* and to speak *from* English experience and traditions and, from that site, to articulate an interpretation of English history which both the Left *and* 'the people' might recognize and appreciate as belonging to them and to which they have to answer. For example, in conclusion to *Out of Apathy* (1960), the collection of essays he edited as the first 'New Left Book', Thompson rejects the prevailing 'extremist' visions of socialist transition, both the Fabian model of 'piecemeal reform' and the Leninist model of 'cataclysmic revolution', and proposes instead a 'democratic strategy' of socialist 'revolution' which calls for both extra-parliamentary 'direct action' and, ultimately, parliamentary politics. The strategy he wishes to advance, he declares, emanates from a 'democratic socialist tradition' which of all the western nations is 'strongest' in Britain. Even then he was sensitive to the likelihood of being accused of 'utopianism' which was, of course, to recur in later criticisms of his political thought; yet, he expectantly counters, it is 'foolish also to underestimate the long and tenacious revolutionary tradition of the British commoner':

> It is a dogged, good-humoured responsible tradition: yet a revolutionary tradition all the same. From the Leveller corporals ridden down by Cromwell's men at Burford to the weavers massed behind their banners at Peterloo, the struggle for democratic and social rights has long been intertwined. From the Chartist camp meeting to the dockers' picket line it has expressed itself most naturally in the language of moral revolt. Its weaknesses, its carelessness of theory, we know too well; its strengths, its resilience and steady humanity, we too easily forget. It is a tradition which could leaven the socialist world.[54]

In 'The Peculiarities of the English' (1965), his extended reply to Anderson and Nairn, Thompson takes umbrage at their readings and assessments of English history. Their 'ideal type' of revolution, drawn from (supposed) French experience, and 'critical theory', derived from continental Marxism (which, Thompson notes, has failed to engage the English 'empirical' idiom), have led them, he argues, to misconstrue the social character of the seventeenth- and eighteenth-century landed aristocracy, 'ignore the importance of the Protestant and bourgeois-democratic inheritance', and 'overlook the importance of capitalist political economy as "authentic, articulated ideology"'.[55] His answer to their portrait of the British Labour Movement had already been offered, in great part, in *The Making of the English Working Class*. Later, in 'An Open Letter to Leszek Kolakowski' (1973) Thompson refers to the literary and theoretical company he prefers to keep – in contrast to the 'greats' of European philosophy:

> Take Marx and Vico and a few European novelists away, and my most intimate pantheon would be a provincial tea-party: a gathering of the English and the Anglo-Irish. Talk of free-will and determinism and I first think of Milton. Talk of man's inhumanity, I think of Swift. Talk of morality and revolution, and my mind is off with Wordsworth's Solitary. Talk of the problems of self-activity and creative labour in socialist society, and I am in an instant back with William Morris . . .

Further along in the 'Letter' he identifies the figures of the British Marxist historical tradition as his immediate intellectual comrades – those who 'sustain him' – and, once again, he defends the richness of working-class culture and values against the supposed cultural superiority of intellectuals.[56] Then, of course, there is the famous (or infamous, depending on your view) counter-attack on Althusserian structuralism, 'The Poverty of Theory', in which he defends the *historical* in historical materialism against a scientifically discovered and theoretically elaborated version of Marxism proffered by philosophers. In the foreword to the volume in which it is published, Thompson responds to the criticism that he is merely an 'English nationalist' who has failed to appreciate properly the theoretical contributions of Western European Marxists: 'The "adoption" of other traditions – that is adoption which has not been fully worked through, interrogated, and translated into the terms of our own traditions – can very often mean no more than the evacuation of the real places of conflict within our own intellectual culture, as well as the loss of real political relations with our own people.'[57]

Admittedly, Thompson is capable of a certain self-indulgence and, even, vanity in his writing style (as I have implied by way of Cole's picture of Cobbett), but as well there is humour and a wonderfully evocative imagery to be found there reflecting his eagerness to root himself in a specifically English historical and cultural landscape. Consider his description of himself in the 'Letter to Kolakowski' as a 'bustard' in comparison to the high-flying 'eagles' of European philosophy; or, in the conclusion to *Whigs and Hunters*, his expression of scepticism about the orthodox Marxist assertion that 'the law' – being merely a 'superstructural' feature of capitalist production relations – will be dispensable in a socialism structured by 'new forms of working-class power' advising us to 'watch this new power for a century or two before you cut your hedges down'. Or, again, in the closing lines of 'The Poverty of Theory', his announcement that 'My dues to "1956" have now been paid in full. I may now, with a better conscience, return to my proper work and to my own garden. I will watch how things grow.'[58] (It is arguable that in his recent novel, *The Sykaos Papers*,[59] Thompson departs from this 'rooting' in English experience for he resorts to the arrival on earth – to England in fact – of an 'alien' in order to provide himself with a new vantage-point for social criticism. However, as Walzer notes regarding the very same device having been used in the eighteenth century by another 'connected critic': 'If it suits their purposes, they can play at detachment, pretend to see their own society through the eyes of a stranger – like Montesquieu, the well-connected Frenchman, through the eyes of Usbek. But it is Montesquieu, the well-connected Frenchman, not Usbek, who is the social critic. Persian naivete is a mask for French sophistication.' We might merely insert Thompson and Oi Pas the Oitarian for Montesquieu and Usbek the Persian.[60])

These episodes portray Thompson as a critic of the Left, which he certainly has been, but it must be reiterated that however antagonistic his words have been they are those of a *connected* critic arguing with his comrades on the Left from *within* their own history. Furthermore, his voice has just as angrily – and for just as long – been directed against the Right and the inner circles of the British Establishment, most expressively perhaps in the 1970s and 80s on the subjects of civil liberties and nuclear disarmament. Here too, however, Thompson has actually been concerned with articulating an interpretation of English history and the radical democratic tradition which would serve to recall the Left and especially, in these instances, 'the people' to their political and cultural 'inheritance' ever aware that the Conservatives have themselves regularly sought to lay a prior claim to 'the past' and, in the process, to champion a different version of it. Speaking to a broad liberal and left audience in the pages of *New Society* in the midst of the political turmoil of the early 1970s – heightened by the miners' strike (1972) then underway – Thompson acknowledges that 'One tends to think of history as a reserve of the conservative and "traditional"'. Nevertheless, he insists, 'there is still today an enormous reserve of radicalism stored within our culture'.[61] With this in mind he warns in 1977 that along with the increasing powers of 'the secret state' one of the most worrying of contemporary developments is the apparent historical amnesia of the British people. For the past twenty years, Thompson writes, there has been 'a dulling of the nerve of resistance and outrage'. He states this even more directly in his 1982 television address, 'The Heavy Dancers' (on Channel 4), when, attending once again to the hidden wielders of power in the British State, he decries that 'These non-elected and self-vetted persons arrogate to themselves powers which would astonish our ancestors . . . . We've forgotten what any "freeborn Englishman" knew 200 years ago – and what Americans still know [I hope – H. J. K.] – that the State exists to serve us: we don't exist by permission of the State. Why have we forgotten? Why do we let these people get away with murder?' Confronting this historical amnesia, Thompson reminds his fellow citizens of both the tradition of English poets who regularly 'asked where society was going' and the 'tradition of popular "dissent" . . . the alternative nation, with its own vibrant but unofficial culture – the true dissent of John Bunyan, but also the political dissent of Cobbett, the Chartists, women's suffrage pioneers . . . [who] brought their influence to bear on the segregated world of Britain's rulers – campaign for the vote – for the rights of press and opinion – and the rights of labour and women.'[62]

Perhaps reflecting as well on his own practice, Thompson writes in 'Homage to Thomas McGrath': 'Yet anger demands an alternative. If the alternative be only the elegiac recollection of the past, then anger's alternative may only be nostalgia'.[63] However, even if we might argue about the priorities he establishes it should be clear that Thompson does not seek a return to a previous age and experience but to inform *present* struggles and intellects with the experiences and aspirations of the past. It may well be true, as Perry Anderson claims, that, grounded in the 'radical libertarian tradition', Thompson's political thought has failed to formulate a specifically *socialist* project. Yet it must be registered that however much he seeks to articulate the radical democratic and socialist traditions as one, Thompson does not equate liberal, or 'bourgeois', with socialist democracy. Rather, what his historical and political writings do propose is that if socialist democracy is to be made in Britain (or, I would add, America) it is crucial – for the sake of both an effective democratic mobilization of popular and working-class political participation in the present and to help secure the formation of an increasingly libertarian and democratic polity in the future – that it be developed out of and remain connected to the radical democratic tradition even as it seeks to broaden, deepen and recompose it. Again, whatever their inadequacies, Thompson's writings, along with those of his fellow historians, compel the recognition that the radical-democratic *and* socialist traditions have been central to English and British political development – which is all the more essential today when a Conservative government is striving once again to advance a narrative of British history in which socialism appears an 'alien' thing (a process already well effected in America).

Beyond our own political education, then, the recovery of the radical democratic and socialist tradition, along with the history of exploitation and oppression and the conflicts to which they have given rise, is to bear witness to the creativity of popular struggles and the values and aspirations they have asserted and to secure the 'dangerous memories' which might yet engage critical thought and action. Thus, it is to advance the *historical* 'education of desire' and to continue the practice Victor Kiernan had in mind when he dubbed socialism 'the prophetic memory'.[64] At the same time, we should not fail to consider the subversions and corruptions of popular ideology and aspirations and, yes, the tragedies which have characterized past and present. To repeat my concluding argument of *The British Marxist Historians*, the objective of Marxist history must be to contribute to the formation of the kind of historical consciousness which Gramsci envisaged as the goal of a critical education: 'which understands movement and change, which appreciates the sum of effort and sacrifice which the present has cost the past and which the future is costing the present, and which conceives the contemporary world as a synthesis of the past, of all past generations, which projects itself into the future.'[65]

As to the development of a new grand narrative to replace the old ones: well, that awaits both politics *and* the skills of historians and historical critics who can assimilate the past and imaginatively articulate the political and moral aspirations of the present.[66] Yet for those of us who are radical democrats and socialists the real question surely is: 'How *original* will that new grand narrative be?'; the answer to which, I would insist, depends in fair measure on the consequences of the historical consciousness that we help to fashion. Though we will have to find our own voices, I still maintain that we can find no better guides than E. P. Thompson and the British Marxist historians.

Notes

1 This essay first took shape in the form of an invited talk presented to the conference, 'Back to the Future', held in London in July 1988. For their critical instigation and conversations with me leading up to that presentation

and since, I thank Henry Giroux, Richard Gott, Ellen Wood, David Lowenthal, Bill Schwarz, Carl Chinn, Victor Kiernan, Tony Galt, Craig Lockard, Dave Jowett, Michael Bess and Lorna Stewart Kaye.

2 The dissertation was titled 'The Political Economy of Seigneurialism' (Louisiana State University, 1976).

3 Barrington Moore Jr, *Social Origins of Dictatorship and Democracy* (Boston: Beacon Press, 1966); and the writings of Eugene Genovese are: *The Political Economy of Slavery* (New York: Vintage Books, 1967), *The World the Slaveholders Made* (New York: Vintage Books, 1971), *In Red and Black* (New York: Vintage Books, 1972) and *Roll, Jordan, Roll: The World the Slaves Made* (New York: Pantheon, 1974).

4 See Raphael Samuel, 'British Marxist Historians, 1880–1980', *New Left Review*, 120 (March–April 1980), pp. 42–55; and Harvey J. Kaye, *The British Marxist Historians* (Oxford: Polity Press, 1984), p. 103.

5 Maurice Dobb, *Studies in the Development of Capitalism* (London: Routledge, 1946); and R. H. Hilton (ed.), *The Transition from Feudalism to Capitalism* (London: New Left Books, 1976).

6 A. L. Morton, *A People's History of England* (London: Lawrence & Wishart, 1979, rev. edn); and Dona Torr, *Tom Mann and His Times* (London: Lawrence & Wishart, 1954).

7 See the *Bulletin of the Society for the Study of Labour History*.

8 E. P. Thompson, *The Making of the English Working Class* (Harmondsworth: Penguin, 1968, rev. edn). See Stuart Hall, 'Cultural Studies and the Centre', in S. Hall et al. (eds), *Culture, Media and Language* (London: Hutchinson, 1980), pp. 15–47.

9 Bill Schwarz, 'The People in History: The Communist Party Historians' Group, 1946–56', in R. Johnson et al. (eds), *Making Histories* (London: Hutchinson, 1982), pp. 44–95.

10 W. Benjamin, 'Theses in the Philosophy of History', in his *Illuminations* (New York: Harcourt Brace, 1969), p. 255.

11 Thompson, *The Making of the English Working Class*, p. 12.

12 Ellen Wood, 'Marxism and the Course of History', *New Left Review*, 147 (September–October 1984), pp. 95–108.

13 For examples, see Alan Dawley, *Class and Community: The Industrial Revolution in Lynn* (Cambridge, Mass.: Harvard University Press, 1976); Sean Wilentz, *Chants Democratic: New York City and the Rise of the American Working Class* (New York: Oxford University Press, 1984); Herbert Gutman, *Work, Culture and Society in Industrializing America* (New York: Vintage Books, 1977); the works of Genovese cited above in note 3; and Scott G. McNall, *The Road to Rebellion: Class Formation and Populism, 1865–1900* (Chicago: University of Chicago Press, 1988).

14 For examples, see Steven Stern, *Peru's Indian Peoples and the Challenge of Spanish Conquest* (Madison: University of Wisconsin Press, 1982); James Scott, *Weapons of the Weak* (New Haven, Conn.: Yale University Press, 1986); T. H. Aston and C. H. E. Philpin (eds), *The Brenner Debate* (Cambridge: Cambridge University Press, 1985); and Immanuel Wallerstein, *The Modern World-System* (New York: Academic Press, 1974).

15 In literary studies see Michael Fischer, 'The Literary Importance of E. P. Thompson's Marxism', *ELH*, 50 (4) (Winter 1983), pp. 811–29; and on 'critical legal studies', see Mark Kelman, *A Guide to Critical Legal Studies* (Cambridge, Mass.: Harvard University Press, 1987).

16 This is especially true regarding the writings of E. P. Thompson; for example, on Genevese's influence, see 'Eighteenth-century English Society: Class struggle without class?', *Social History*, 3 (2) (May 1978), pp. 133–65.

17 See Harvey J. Kaye, 'The Use and Abuse of the Past: The New Right and the Crisis of History', in R. Miliband, L. Panitch and J. Saville (eds), *Socialist Register 1987* (London: Merlin Press, 1987), pp. 338–9, 343.

18 Himmelfarb's article is reprinted in her collection of essays titled *The New History and the Old* (Cambridge, Mass.: Harvard University Press, 1987). The MARHO interviews are published as H. Abelove et al. (eds), *Visions of History* (New York: Pantheon, 1984).

19 In the UK, see G. Himmelfarb, *Victorian Values and 20th-Century Condescension* (London: Centre for Policy Studies, 1987), and in the USA, see her 'Manners into Morals: What the Victorians Knew', *The American Scholar*, 57 (2) (Spring 1988), pp. 223–32.

20 As I write, there is at least some reason for hope in the upcoming American presidential elections. (Post-election note: I was being optimistic!)

21 I refer the reader to *The Observer* (22 May 1988), p. 1; G. Marshall et al. (eds), *Social Class in Modern Britain* (London: Hutchinson, 1988); and *The Guardian* (17 September 1988), p. 4.

22 Christopher Hill, *The Experience of Defeat* (New York: Viking-Penguin, 1984). Also, see V. G. Kiernan, 'Problems of Marxist History', *New Left Review*, 161 (January–February 1987), pp. 105–18.

23 For example, Shiela Rowbotham, *Hidden From History* (London: Pluto Press, 1973); Barbara Taylor, *Eve and the New Jerusalem* (London: Virago, 1983); and L. Davidoff and C. Hall, *Family Fortunes: Men and Women of the English Middle Class, 1750–1850* (Chicago: University of Chicago Press, 1987).

24 For example, see the essays collected in Herbert Gutman, *Power and Culture* (New York: Pantheon Books, 1987) and chapters of David Mongomery, *The Fall of the House of Labor* (Cambridge: Cambridge University Press, 1987).

25 V. G. Kiernan, 'Britons Old and New', in Colin Holmes (ed.), *Immigrants and Minorities in British Society* (London: Allen & Unwin, 1978), pp. 23–59.

26 Robin Blackburn, *The Overthrow of Colonial Slavery, 1776–1848* (London: Verso, 1988).

27 Barrington Moore Jr, *Social Origins of Dictatorship and Democracy*, pp. 522–3.

28 F. Stirton Weaver is the author of *Class, State and Industrial Structure* (Westport, Conn.: Greenwood Publishers, 1980). The remark by Victor Kiernan was made in a letter to the author in June 1988.

29 For examples, see C. Wright Mills, *The Power Elite* (New York: Oxford University Press, 1956); Paul Baran and Paul Sweezy, *Monopoly Capital* (New York: Monthly Review Press, 1966); Harry Braverman, *Labor and Monopoly Capital* (New York: Monthly Review Press, 1974); William Appleman Williams, *The Tragedy of American Diplomacy* (New York: Dell Publishing, 1962, rev. edn); James Weinstein, *The Corporate Ideal in the Liberal State*

(Boston: Beacon Press, 1968); Gabriel Kolko, *The Roots of American Foreign Policy* (Boston: Beacon Press, 1969); G. William Domhoff, *Who Rules America?* (Englewood Cliffs, NJ: Prentice-Hall, 1967); and Christopher Lasch, *Haven in a Heartless World* (New York: Basic Books, 1977).

30 V. G. Kiernan, *The Lords of Human Kind* (London: Radius repr. edn, 1988); *State and Society in Europe, 1550–1650* (Oxford: Basil Blackwell, 1980); and *The Duel in European History* (London: Oxford University Press, 1988). Also see the first volume of his Collected Essays, Harvey J. Kaye (ed.), *History, Classes and Nation-States: Selected Writings of V. G. Kiernan* (Oxford: Polity Press, 1988).

31 Perry Anderson, *Passages from Antiquity to Feudalism* and *Lineages of the Absolutist State* (both books: London: Verso, 1974); P. Corrigan and D. Sayer, *The Great Arch* (Oxford: Basil Blackwell, 1985); and John Saville, *1848: The British State and Chartism* (Cambridge: Cambridge University Press, 1987).

32 Christopher Hill, *Economic Problems of the Church* (Oxford: Oxford University Press, 1956); Rodney Hilton, *A Medieval Society* (Cambridge: Cambridge University Press, 1983); and E. P. Thompson, *Whigs and Hunters* (Harmondsworth: Penguin rev. edn, 1977).

33 E. J. Hobsbawm, *The Age of Revolution, 1789–1848; The Age of Capital, 1848–1875;* and *The Age of Empire, 1875–1914* (London: Weidenfeld & Nicolson, 1960, 1975 and 1987).

34 W. Benjamin, 'Theses in the Philosophy of History', p. 262.

35 Terry Eagleton, 'Marxism and the Past', *Salmagundi*, 68–9 (Fall 1985–Winter 1986), pp. 291–311.

36 Here I must call attention to two outstanding works in the historical demystification of industrial development by American historian David Noble: whereas the first, *America by Design* (New York: Alfred A. Knopf, 1977), is a power-structure study of the rise of the engineering profession in the Second Industrial Revolution, the second, *Forces of Production* (New York: Alfred A. Knopf, 1985), is a study of the class structuration of technology in the machine tools industry. Also, for excellent examples of studies of a ruling class and the structuration of power by the oppressed see James Oakes, *The Ruling Class* (New York: Vintage, 1982) and his article 'The Political Significance of Slave Resistance', *History Workshop*, 22 (Autumn 1986), pp. 89–107.

37 See, for example, the discussions in Russell Jacoby, *The Last Intellectuals* (New York: Basic Books, 1987); and Norman Birnbaum, *The Radical Renewal* (New York: Pantheon, 1988).

38 See, for example, E. Laclau and C. Mouffe, *Hegemony and Socialist Strategy* (London: Verso, 1985). For a critical Marxist rebuttal (with which I sympathize) to the 'post-Marxists', see Ellen Wood, *The Retreat from Class* (London: Verso, 1985).

39 John Keane, *Democracy and Civil Society* (London: Verso, 1988), p. 33.

40 Michael Walzer, *Interpretation and Social Criticism* (Cambridge, Mass.: Harvard University Press, 1987); and Antonio Gramsci, *Selections from the Prison Notebooks*, ed. and trans. Q. Hoare and G. Nowell-Smith (New York:

International Publishers, 1971), p. 155; quoted in Walzer, *Interpretation and Social Criticism*, p. 42. Also, see Walzer's *The Company of Critics* (New York: Basic Books, 1988).

41 R. H. Hilton, 'Wat Tyler, John Ball and the English Rising of 1381', *Marxism Today* (June 1981), p. 19; and 'The English Rising of 1381', *New Society* (30 April 1981), p. 173.

42 See Christopher Hill's books: *Society and Puritanism in Pre-Revolutionary England* (London: Secker & Warburg, 1964); *Intellectual Origins of The English Revolution* (Oxford: Oxford University Press, 1965); and *The World Turned Upside Down* (Harmondsworth: Penguin, rev. edn, 1972).

43 Terry Eagleton, *The Function of Criticism* (London: Verso, 1984), p. 36.

44 Thompson, *The Making of the English Working Class*, pp. 84–110. Also, see the discussion in Harvey J. Kaye, 'Political Theory and History: Antonio Gramsci and the British Marxist Historians', *Italian Quarterly*, 97–8 (Summer–Fall 1984), pp. 145–66.

45 E. P. Thompson, 'Homage to Tom Maguire', in A. Briggs and J. Saville (eds), *Essays in Labour History* (London: Macmillan, 1960), p. 314.

46 Marcus Rediker, 'Getting Out of the Graveyard: Perry Anderson, Edward Thompson, and the Arguments of English Marxism', a review of Perry Anderson's *Arguments Within English Marxism* (London: Verso, 1980) in *Radical History Review*, 26 (1982), pp. 120–31. Also see, for a most appreciative reference to Thompson, Jim Merod, *The Political Responsibility of the Critic* (Ithaca, NY: Cornell University Press, 1987), pp. 5 and 201–2.

47 E. P. Thompson, Preface to S. Lynd, *Class Conflict, Slavery and the United States Constitution* (Indianapolis: Bobbs-Merrill, 1967), p. xii.

48 E. P. Thompson, 'Interview' in H. Abelove, et al. (eds), *Visions of History*, p. 7; and F. Inglis, *Radical Earnestness* (Oxford: Basil Blackwell, 1982), p. 199. I am very much in agreement with Inglis's presentation of Thompson (pp. 193–204). Also, see Renato Rosaldo's contribution to the present volume.

49 G. D. H. Cole, 'William Cobbett (1762–1835)', in his *Persons and Periods* (Harmondsworth: Penguin, 1945), pp. 116–18.

50 See E. P. Thompson's 'William Morris and the Moral Issues To-day', *Arena*, 2 (8) (June/July 1951), pp. 25–30; his contributions to *The New Reasoner*, the dissident Communist journal which he organized with John Saville; and his edited volume, *Out of Apathy* (London: New Left Books, 1960).

51 See 'The Peculiarities of the English' (1965), reprinted in E. P. Thompson, *The Poverty of Theory and Other Essays* (London: Merlin Press, 1978). On the Anderson–Thompson exchange, see Keith Nield, 'A Symptomatic Dispute? Notes on the Relation between Marxian Theory and Historical Practice in Britain', *Social Research*, 47 (3) (Autumn 1980), pp. 479–506.

52 See E. P. Thompson's *Warwick University Limited* (Harmondsworth: Penguin, 1970); *Writing by Candlelight* (London: Merlin Press, 1980); 'The Poverty of Theory' (1978), in Thompson, *The Poverty of Theory and Other Essays*, pp. 1–210; and *The Heavy Dancers* (London: Merlin Press, 1985).

53 See E. P. Thompson's *Protest and Survive* (Harmondsworth: Penguin, 1980), co-edited with Dan Smith; *Beyond the Cold War* (New York: Pantheon, 1982); *Exterminism and Cold War* (London: Verso, 1982); *Star Wars*

(Harmondsworth: Penguin, 1985); *Mad Dogs* (London: Pluto Press, 1986); and, again with Dan Smith, *Prospectus for a Habitable Planet* (Harmondsworth: Penguin, 1987). For an admittedly more comprehensive and critical examination of Thompson's 'politics', see Perry Anderson's *Arguments Within English Marxism*, esp. pp. 100–207. Anderson discusses Thompson's practice in comparison with Althusser's and, also, that of the *New Left Review* which he headed.

54 E. P. Thompson, 'Revolution', in *Out of Apathy*, p. 308.

55 Thompson, 'Peculiarities of the English', pp. 274, 267.

56 E. P. Thompson, 'An Open Letter to Leszek Kolakowski' (1973), in *The Poverty of Theory and Other Essays*, pp. 319, 333, 385.

57 E. P. Thompson, Foreword to *The Poverty of Theory and Other Essays*, p. iv.

58 E. P. Thompson, 'An Open Letter', p. 319; *Whigs and Hunters*, p. 266; and 'The Poverty of Theory', p. 192.

59 E. P. Thompson, *The Sykaos Papers* (London: Bloomsbury, 1988).

60 M. Walzer, *Interpretation and Social Criticism*, p. 39. Of course, Thompson also writes social criticism for *The Nation*, an American weekly somewhat similar to the British *New Statesman*. Here he speaks as a cultural cousin and comrade of the American left; but also he reminds us that his mother's side of the family was American. Thus, even in the United States he attempts a degree of 'connectedness'. In this regard I recommend 'Remembering C. Wright Mills' and 'Homage to Thomas McGrath', in *The Heavy Dancers*, pp. 261–74 and 279–337; 'The Passing of the Old Order', *The Nation*, March 22, 1986, pp. 377–81; and 'The Reasons of the Yahoo', *The Yale Review*, 75 (4) (Summer 1986), pp. 481–502. I should add that however much I am stressing Thompson's attempts to ground his criticism in an 'English idiom' I would not for a moment deny his commitment to 'socialist internationalism'.

61 E. P. Thompson, 'A Special Case', in *Writing by Candlelight*, p. 75.

62 E. P. Thompson, 'The Secret State' (1977), in *Writing by Candlelight*, p. 163, and *The Heavy Dancers*, pp. 6, 4–5.

63 E. P. Thompson, 'Homage to Thomas McGrath', p. 284. McGrath, an American friend, is Thompson's favourite contemporary poet.

64 V. G. Kiernan, 'Socialism, The Prophetic Memory', in H. J. Kaye (ed.), *Poets, Politics and the People: Selected Essays of V. G. Kiernan* (London: Verso, 1989). I also recommend Walter L. Adamson, *Marx and the Disillusionment of Marxism* (Berkeley, Cal.: University of California Press, 1985), esp. pp. 228–43; and Henry Giroux, *Schooling and the Struggle for Public Life* (Minneapolis: University of Minnesota Press, 1988).

65 Antonio Gramsci, *Selections from the Prison Notebooks*, pp. 34–5.

66 I have elsewhere proposed (as a modest act of social criticism) in the wake of a third Thatcher election victory that a new grand narrative of British history be built around the theme of 'lost rights' and the radical-democratic tradition. See Harvey J. Kaye, 'Our Island Story Retold', *The Guardian* (3 August 1987), p. 7.

E. P. Thompson: A Select Bibliography

Books and collected essays

William Morris: Romantic to Revolutionary, London, Lawrence & Wishart, 1955; rev. edn, New York, Pantheon, 1977.

The Making of the English Working Class, London, Victor Gollancz, 1963; 2nd edn with a new postscript, Harmondsworth, Penguin, 1968; 3rd edn with a new preface, 1980.

Whigs and Hunters: The Origins of the Black Act, London, Allen Lane, 1975; reprinted with a new postscript, Harmondsworth, Penguin, 1977.

The Poverty of Theory and Other Essays, London, Merlin and New York, Monthly Review Press, 1978.

Writing by Candlelight, London, Merlin, 1980.

Zero Option, London, Merlin, 1982; in USA: *Beyond the Cold War*, New York, Pantheon, 1982.

Double Exposure, London, Merlin, 1985.

The Heavy Dancers, London, Merlin, 1985; in USA: *The Heavy Dancers*, New York, Pantheon, 1985. This edition incorporates *Double Exposure* but excludes selected essays of the British edition.

The Sykaos Papers, London, Bloomsbury and New York, Pantheon, 1988.

Edited Works

There is a Spirit in Europe: A Memoir of Frank Thompson, with T. J. Thompson, London, Victor Gollancz, 1947.

The Railway: An Adventure in Construction, London, The British–Yugoslav Association, 1948.

Out of Apathy, London, Stevens & Sons/New Left Books, 1960.

The May Day Manifesto with Raymond Williams and Stuart Hall, rev. edn, ed. Raymond Williams, Harmondsworth, Penguin, 1968.

Warwick University Ltd, Harmondsworth, Penguin, 1970.

The Unknown Mayhew: Selections from the Morning Chronicle 1849–1850, with Eileen Yeo, London, Merlin, 1971.

Albion's Fatal Tree: Crime and Society in 18th-Century England, with Douglas Hay et al, London, Allen Lane, and New York, Pantheon, 1975.

Family and Inheritance: Rural Society in Western Europe, 1200–1800, with Jack Goody and Joan Thirsk, Cambridge, Cambridge University Press, 1976.

Protest and Survive, with Dan Smith, Harmondsworth, Penguin, 1980, rev. edn in USA, New York, Monthly Review Press, 1981.

Star Wars, Harmondsworth, Penguin, 1985.

Prospectus for a Habitable Planet, with Dan Smith, Harmondsworth, Penguin, 1987.

Pamphlets

The Fascist Threat to Britain, 1947.

The Struggle for a Free Press, London, People's Press Printing Society, 1952.

The Communism of William Morris, a lecture by Edward Thompson given on 4 May 1959 in the Hall of the Art Workers' Guild, London, London, The William Morris Society, 1965.

Education and Experience, Fifth Mansbridge Memorial Lecture, 1968.

Homage to Salvador Allende [a poem], Spokesman Broadsheet, 30 September 1973.

Protest and Survive, CND /Bertrand Russell Peace Foundation, 1980.

Infant and Emperor: Poems for Christmas, London, Merlin, 1983.

Star Wars: Self-Destruct Incorporated, with Ben Thompson, London, Merlin, 1985.

Articles and Essays

Note: All but a few book reviews have been excluded; those included are marked with an *.

Essays reprinted in the following collections have been excluded from this list: *Writing by Candlelight* (London: Merlin, 1980); *The Heavy Dancers* (London: Merlin, 1985).

'Poetry's not so easy', *Our Time*, June 1947.

'Comments on a People's Culture', *Our Time*, October 1947.

'Omladinska Pruga', in E. P. Thompson (ed.), *The Railway*, 1948.

'A New Poet', *Our Time*, June 1949.

'On the liberation of Seoul' [poem], *Arena*, 2 (6), 1951.

'The murder of William Morris', *Arena*, 2 (7), 1951.

'William Morris and the moral issues of today', *Arena* 2 (8), 1951.

'Winter Wheat in Omsk', *World News*, 30 June 1956.

'Reply to George Matthews', *The Reasoner*, 1, July 1956.

'Through the smoke of Budapest', *The Reasoner*, 3, November 1956.

'Socialism and the intellectuals: a reply', *Universities and Left Review*, 2, 1957.

'Socialist Humanism', *The New Reasoner*, 1, 1957.

'God and King and Law',* *The New Reasoner*, 3, 1957–8. [On Peterloo]

'Agency and Choice', *The New Reasoner*, 5, 1958.

'Nato, neutralism and survival', *Universities and Left Review*, 4, 1958.

'Commitment in Politics', *Universities and Left Review*, 6, 1959.

'The New Left', *The New Reasoner*, 9, 1959.

'A Psessay in ephology', *The New Reasoner*, 10, 1959.

'Homage to Tom Maguire', in *Essays in Labour History*, ed. Asa Briggs and John Saville, London, Macmillan, 1960.

'At the point of decay' and 'Revolution', both in *Out of Apathy*, ed. E. P. Thompson (1960). ('Revolution' also appeared in *New Left Review*, 3, 1960.)

'Outside the Whale', in *Out of Apathy*, ed. E. P. Thompson (1960); repr. in E. P. Thompson, *The Poverty of Theory and Other Essays*.

'At the point of production', *New Left Review*, 1, 1960.

'Countermarching to Armageddon', *New Left Review*, 4, 1960.

'Revolution again! Or shut your ears and run', *New Left Review*, 6, 1960.

'The Long Revolution', *New Left Review*, 9–11, 1961.

'The Peculiarities of the English', *Socialist Register 1965*; repr. in E. P. Thompson, *The Poverty of Theory and Other Essays*.

'The book of numbers',* *The Times Literary Supplement*, 9 December 1965. (Anon.: review of Peter Laslett, *The World We Have Lost*.)

Preface to Staughton Lynd, *Class Conflict, Slavery, and the United States Constitution*, 1967.

'Glandular aggression', *New Society*, 19 January 1967.

'Time, work-discipline and industrial capitalism', *Past & Present*, 38, 1967.

'The political education of Henry Mayhew', *Victorian Studies*, 11, 1967.

'Introduction' to Frank Peel, *The Risings of the Luddites, Chartists and Plug-Drawers*, London, Frank Cass, 1968.

'Disenchantment or Default? A Lay Sermon', in Conor Cruise O'Brien and W. D. Vanech (eds), *Power and Consciousness*, New York, New York University Press, 1969, pp. 149–81.

'Mayhew and the *Morning Chronicle*', in E. P. Thompson and E. Yeo (eds), *The Unknown Mayhew* 1971.

'Organizing the left', *The Times Literary Supplement*, 19 February 1971.

'The moral economy of the English crowd in the 18th century', *Past & Present*, 50, 1971.

'Rough Music: *le charivari anglais*', *Annales ESC*, 27, 1972.

'Anthropology and the discipline of historical context',* *Midland History*, 1 (1972). (Review of Keith Thomas, *Religion and the Decline of Magic* and A. Macfarlane, *The Family Life of Ralph Josselin*.)

'An Open Letter to Leszek Kolakowski', *Socialist Register 1973*; repr. in E. P. Thompson, *The Poverty of Theory and Other Essays*.

'Under the same roof-tree', *The Times Literary Supplement*, 4 May 1973. (Anon., review of P. Laslett (ed.), *Household and Family in Past Time*.)

'Alexander Pope and the Windsor Blacks', *The Times Literary Supplement*, 7 September 1973.

'Testing class struggle',* *Times Higher Education Supplement*, 8 March 1974. (Review of John Foster, *Class Struggle and the Industrial Revolution*.)

'In citizens' bad books', *New Society*, 28 March 1974.

'Patrician society, plebeian culture', *Journal of Social History*, 7, 1974.

'A question of manners', *New Society*, 11 July 1974.

'A nice place to visit',* *New York Review of Books*, 6 February 1975. (Review of Raymond Williams, *The Country and the City*.)

'The crime of anonymity', in *Albion's Fatal Tree* (1975).

'Détente and dissent', in *Détente and Socialist Democracy: A discussion with Roy Medvedev*, ed. Ken Coates, Nottingham, Spokesman, 1975.

'The grid of inheritance: a comment', in *Family and Inheritance*, ed. Goody, Thirsk and Thompson, 1976.

'On history, sociology, and historical relevance',* *British Journal of Sociology*, 27 (2), 1976. (Review of Robert Moore, *Pitmen, Preachers and Politics*.)

'Modes de domination et révolutions en Angleterre', *Actes de la Recherche en Sciences Sociales*, 2, 1976.

'Interview with E. P. Thompson', *Radical History Review*, 3, 1976. (Repr. in *Visions of History. Interviews with E. P. Thompson et al.* New York, Pantheon, 1984.

'Romanticism, utopianism and moralism: the case of William Morris', *New Left Review*, 99, 1976.

'Caudwell', in *Socialist Register 1977*, ed. R. Miliband and J. Saville, London, Merlin, 1977.

'Response to Tony Benn', in *The Just Society*, ed. Ken Coates and Fred Singleton, Nottingham, Spokesman, 1977.

'Folklore, anthropology, and social history', *Indian Historical Review*, III (2), 1977. (Repr. in England as 'A studies in labour history pamphlet', John L. Noyce, Brighton, 1979.)

'Happy families',* *New Society*, 8 September 1977. (Review of L. Stone, *The Family, Sex and Marriage in England 1500–1800*.)

'London', in *Interpreting Blake*, ed. M. Phillips, Cambridge, Cambridge University Press, 1978.

'Eighteenth-century English society: Class struggle without class?', *Social History*, 3 (2), 1978.

'The Poverty of Theory or An Orrery of Errors', in E. P. Thompson, *The Poverty of Theory and Other Essays*.

'Sold like a sheep for £1, *New Society*, 14 December 1978. (Review of George Rudé, *Protest and Punishment*.)

'Recovering the libertarian tradition', *The Leveller*, 22, January 1979. (Interview).

'Comment on "Common values? An argument"', *Stand*, 20 (2), 1979.

'The common people and the law', *New Society*, 24 July 1980.

'Danger of being too clever by half', *The Guardian*, 10 August 1980.

'Notes on exterminism, the last stage of civilization', *New Left Review*, 121, 1980. (Repr. in *Exterminism and Cold War*, ed. *New Left Review*, London, Verso, 1982. This volume also contains 'Europe, the weak link in the cold war'.)

'"Rough music" et charivari. Quelques réflexions complémentaires', in *Le Charivari*, ed. J. Le Goff and Jean-Claude Schmitt (Ecole des Hautes Etudes en

Sciences Sociales Centre de Recherches Historiques. Civilisations et Sociétés, 67; Paris, Mouton, 1981).

'A Letter to America', *The Nation*, 24 January 1981.

'European Reborn. An interview with E. P. Thompson', *Peace News*, 15 May 1981.

'European Nuclear Disarmament: an interview with E. P. Thompson' (by Michael Kazin), *The Socialist Review* 58, 1981.

'E. P. Thompson replies to Sabata', *New Statesman*, 4 May 1984.

'East and West Europe belong to the same culture' (a conversation between Thompson and George Konrad), *The Listener*, 13 June 1985.

'Why is Star Wars?' and 'Folly's Comet', in *Star Wars*, ed. E. P. Thompson, 1985.

'Letter to Americans' and 'The view from Oxford Street', in Mary Kaldor and Paul Anderson (eds), *Mad Dogs. The U.S. Raids on Libya*, London, Pluto Press with END, 1986.

E. J. Hobsbawm, Christopher Hill, Perry Anderson and E. P. Thompson, 'Agendas for Radical History', *Radical History Review*, 36, 1986.

'The reasons of the Yahoo', *Yale Review*, Summer 1986.

'The rituals of enmity', in *Prospectus for a Habitable Planet*, ed. E. P. Thompson and Dan Smith, 1987.

'Eighteenth-century Ranters: did they exist?', in *Reviving the English Revolution*, ed. Geoff Eley and William Hunt, London, Verso, 1988.

'Wordsworth's crisis', *London Review of Books*,* 10 (22), 8 December 1988, pp. 3–6. (Review of Nicholas Roe, *Wordsworth and Coleridge: The Radical Years*.)

Index

Althusser, Louis, 8, 59, 62–3, 65, 105, 108, 126, 129–30, 133, 134, 148, 160–6, 168, 173–8, 199–200, 204, 209, 214–17, 266
Anderson, Perry, 7, 8, 12, 48, 67, 114, 129–30, 132, 148, 160–1, 163, 171, 175, 183–4, 186–9, 192, 195, 201, 215–17, 220, 227, 254, 259–60, 263–5, 267, 269
Arnold, Matthew, 184, 186, 193
Asad, Talal, 108
Ashton, T. S., 110
Austen, Jane, 185, 201

Bakhtin, M. M., 197
Balibar, Etienne, 216
Ball, John, 255, 262
Bamford, Jemima, 78–89, 99
Bamford, Samuel, 78–89, 99
Baran, Paul, 259
Behagg, Clive, 23–4
Bellamy, Edward, 197
Benjamin, Walter, 254, 260
Bernstein, Richard, 108
Berreman, Gerald, 108
Blackburn, Robin, 258
Blake, William, 113–14, 118–19, 186, 188–90, 198, 201, 255
Bloch, Marc, 166
Bourdieu, Pierre, 108

Braverman, Harry, 259
Brenner, Robert, 132, 256
Brooks, Peter, 115–16
Bukharin, Nikolai, 212, 236
Bunyan, John, 269
Burke, Edmund, 184–5

Carlyle, Thomas, 191, 195–6
Caudwell, Christopher, 138, 141, 203
Clapham, John, 110
Clausewitz, Karl von, 236
Cobbett, William, 34, 92–4, 112, 118–19, 184, 188, 255, 264–5, 268–9
Cole, G. D. H., 265, 268
Coleridge, Samuel Taylor, 189
Comninel, George, 150
Comte, Auguste, 235
Corrigan, Philip, 254, 260

de Beauvoir, Simone, 206
De Saussure, Ferdinand, 189
Deutscher, Isaac, 228
Dickens, Charles, 115–16, 194
Dobb, Maurice, 253
Domhoff, William, 259

Eagleton, Terry, 260, 263
Eley, Geoff, 5
Eliot, T. S., 191

Engels, Friedrich, 126, 130, 153, 167, 168, 195–6, 209, 235–6
Evans-Pritchard, E. E., 105

Fildes, Mary, 79
Foot, Paul, 194
Foster, John, 33
Foucault, Michel, 22, 108, 120
Freud, Sigmund, 191
Fromm, Erich, 206

Gast, John, 24
Geertz, Clifford, 64, 108, 115, 121
Genovese, Eugene, 253, 256
Giddens, Anthony, 6, 65–6, 108, 114
Ginsburg, Carlo, 75–6
Goldmann, Lucien, 187
Goode, John, 6
Gorbachev, Mikhail, 224–5
Gough, Kathleen, 108
Gramsci, Antonio, 17, 22, 34–5, 39, 108, 163, 174, 206, 262–3, 270
Gray, Robert, 7, 27, 96

Habermas, Jürgen, 13–14, 17, 44
Halévy, Elie, 195
Hall, Catherine, 3, 4, 258
Hall, Stuart, 227, 254
Halliday, Fred, 241, 244
Hammond, Barbara and John, 110–12, 116
Hardy, Thomas, 84, 111–17
Harrison, Tony, 187–8
Hegel, G. W. F., 206–8
Hill, Christopher, 253, 257, 260, 262
Hilton, Rodney, 253, 260, 262
Himmelfarb, Gertrude, 256–7
Hindess, Barry, 129
Hinton, James, 235
Hirst, Paul, 129
Hobsbawm, Eric, 4, 30–1, 37–8, 253, 260
Hoggart, Richard, 254
Hunt, Henry 'Orator', 78–9, 110
Hymes, Dell, 108

Inglis, Fred, 264

James, Henry, 111–12, 115
Jaurès, Jean, 53
John, Angela, 98
Johnson, Richard, 33–4, 67, 163
Jones, Ernest, 255
Jorgenson, Joseph, 108

Kaldor, Mary, 237, 240
Kaye, Harvey J., 7–8
Keane, John, 261
Keats, John, 186, 193, 197, 198
Kettle, Arnold, 211
Kiernan, Victor, 254, 258–60, 270
Kolakowski, Leszek, 164, 227, 267
Kolko, Gabriel, 259
Korsch, Karl, 206
Kuhn, Thomas, 120

Laclau, Ernesto, 151
Lamphere, Louis, 108
Lasch, Christopher, 259
Lawrence, T. E., 196
Leavis, F. R., 184, 186, 191
Lenin, V. I., 161, 236
Linebaugh, Peter, 144
Locke, John, 91, 93
Lukács, Georg, 184–6, 206–7, 241
Lynd, Staughton, 264

McClelland, Keith, 230
McGrath, Thomas, 269
McNeill, William H., 236
Maguire, Tom, 263
Mandel, Ernest, 242
Mann, Michael, 247
Marcuse, Herbert, 191, 219, 241
Marx, Eleanor, 194
Marx, Karl, 51, 56, 61–2, 77, 126, 128, 131–5, 138, 143, 153, 161–2, 166–7, 173–9, 191, 195–8, 206, 209, 212–15, 226, 234, 236, 241, 255, 267
Mayhew, Henry, 58
Merleau-Ponty, Maurice, 206, 228–9
Miliband, Ralph, 241, 243–4, 254
Mill, John Stuart, 193
Mills, C. Wright, 181, 218, 241, 259
Milton, John, 188, 200, 255, 267

Mintz, Sidney, 108
Montgomery, David, 256
Moore, Barrington, Jr, 253, 259
Morris, William, 1, 6, 114, 119, 183, 190–200, 208, 214, 216, 226, 255, 257, 263, 267
Morton, A. L., 155, 253
Mouffe, Chantal, 151

Nader, Laura, 108
Nairn, Tom, 2, 7, 8, 12, 175, 265, 268
Noble, David, 273

Oakes, James, 273
O'Connor, Fergus, 53
Owen, Robert, 30–1, 118, 184, 255

Paine, Tom, 20, 30, 63, 84, 90–1, 255, 263, 264
Pope, Alexander, 185
Poulantzas, Nicos, 130–3, 142, 164
Prothero, Iorwerth, 23–4

Rapp, Rayna, 108
Rediker, Marcus, 263–4
Reid, Alastair, 36, 38
Ricardo, David, 61
Rosaldo, Michelle, 108
Rowbotham, Sheila, 79, 258
Rudé, George, 253
Ruskin, John, 114, 191, 194–6

Said, Edward, 105
Samuel, Raphael, 253
Sartre, Jean Paul, 206, 208, 213–14
Saville, John, 253–4, 260
Sayer, Derek, 254, 260
Schwarz, Bill, 155, 254
Sewell, William H., Jr, 4, 5
Shaw, Martin, 6
Shelley, Percy Bysshe, 185–6, 193–7
Silverman, Sydel, 108
Soper, Kate, 2
Southcott, Joanna, 81
Southey, Robert, 184

Stalin, Joseph, 157, 205, 209, 211, 220, 228
Stedman Jones, Gareth, 4–5, 22–3, 26–7, 29, 72, 146–7
Sweezy, Paul, 259
Swift, Jonathan, 199

Taylor, Barbara, 81–2, 258
Taylor, Charles, 208, 210, 228
Thatcher, Margaret, 256–7, 266
Thelwall, John, 112, 116
Therborn, Goran, 65
Thomas, Keith, 104
Thompson, Dorothy, 35, 45, 46, 253
Torr, Dona, 155, 253
Trotsky, Leon, 208, 227

Vester, Michael, 27–8
Vincent, David, 33, 87, 96
Vincent, John 38
Volosinov, V., 189

Wallerstein, Immanuel, 256
Walzer, Michael, 261, 268
Weaver, F. Stirton, 259
Webb, Beatrice and Sydney, 110–12, 116
Weber, Max, 241
Weinstein, James, 259
Wilentz, Sean, 74
Wilkes, John, 20, 255
Williams, Gwyn, 20
Williams, Raymond, 105, 136, 154, 165, 167, 183–6, 190–1, 194, 240, 254
Williams, William Appleman, 259
Wilson, Harold, 160–1
Winstanley, Gerrard, 255, 262
Wolf, Eric, 108
Wollstonecraft, Mary, 90–2, 185, 255
Wood, Ellen Meiksins, 3, 4
Woolf, Virginia, 58
Wordsworth, William, 112, 116, 119, 185–6, 189, 198, 255, 267

Yeats, W. B., 189, 196, 198–200
Yeo, Eileen, 32

255. role of counter-hegemonic politics

256. get Himmelfarb's attack on political history in
"The New History & the Old

260 need more recognition of [illegible] that
oppressed do structure [illegible]